DAN EMMETT

and the Rise of Early Negro Minstrelsy

Library of Congress Catalog Card Number: 62–10769 √

Copyright 1962 by the University of Oklahoma Press,
Publishing Division of the University.
Manufactured in the U.S.A.
First edition, 1962.
Second printing, 1977.

PREFACE TO THE FIRST PRINTING

IT HAS NOT BEEN MY INTENTION to write a full-scale account of Negro minstrelsy. I have rather confined myself to several of its aspects that intrigued me and only to those of its early, exuberant period. My book—no doubt to the despair of librarians—does not fit into any one literary category. It intermingles biography (a narrative of the activities of Dan Emmett, forgotten composer of "Dixie") with historical discussions; in addition, and emphatically, it is an anthology. For the songs, lyrics, and illustrations presented here must justify the text, or the book will fail in its main purpose—to return an indigenous popular art to American consciousness and tradition.

The first scholars to consider Negro minstrelsy as something more than witless, low-grade entertainment (though it can be that, too) were historians like Constance Rourke, Carl Wittke, and S. Foster Damon, whose publications appeared in the 1930's. Ethno-musicologists and musicologists, however, remained aloof, and understandably so, since the former are concerned with orally transmitted data and the latter with remote periods and in any case with styles more sophisticated than sheet music. When I disregarded these trends, it must have been out of innocence: I was merely cheered by the riches of Harvard's Theatre Collection (which, incidentally, houses most of the playbills referred to in the text) and generally curious about what might be called "American." Once I had located Emmett's manuscripts in an unsuspected chest of drawers in the State Library, Columbus, Ohio, I was of course encouraged to undertake an extensive study of my material.

Several chapters of this book appeared in *Notes, Southern Folklore Quarterly, The Musical Quarterly, Civil War History*, and *The Canadian Music Journal*, and are reprinted here by permission.

Of the many persons from whose advice I have benefited, I am particularly indebted to William van Lennep, former curator of the Theatre Collection, Harvard College Library; to the librarians of the State Library, Columbus, Ohio; to Stephen Somervell, Cambridge, Mass.; to Professor Howard Mumford Jones; to Professor S. Foster Damon; and to William Lichtenwanger and the late Richard Hill, both of the Library of Congress. My profound thanks are extended to Gilbert Chase for having strongly and spontaneously commended my manuscript to the present publisher. I also wish to mention Professor Harlow Shapley, astronomer and musical connoisseur, who was the first to encourage my research in Americana.

While this book was in its initial stages, I was fortunate in receiving a grant-in-aid from the American Philosophical Society. The publication itself was made possible through a generous grant from the Sonneck Memorial Fund at the Library of Congress, administered by Harold Spivacke.

H. N.

January, 1962

PREFACE TO THE SECOND PRINTING

IN ORDER TO make identification of documents easier, since they often appear in abbreviated form, a selective list of sources has been appended to the second printing of this book. Misprints in the text and the musical examples of the first printing have been corrected.

In addition to the sources quoted in the footnotes, bibliographies in the following publications will prove useful: Robert C. Toll, *Blacking Up: The Minstrel Show in Nineteenth-Century America* (Oxford University Press, New York, 1974); Charles Haywood, *A Bibliography of North American Folklore and Folksong* (1951; Dover Publications, New York, 1961, vol. 1); and Frank C. Davidson, *The Rise, Development, Decline and Influence of the American Minstrel Show* (Ph.D. dissertation, New York University, 1952, microfilmed by University Microfilms, Ann Arbor, Michigan, 1953). Early and late Negro characters in plays are listed in James V. Hatch, *Black Image On The American Stage* (DBS Publications, New York, 1970); those appearing in narratives are listed in Sterling Brown, *The Negro In American Fiction* (1937; Argosy-Antiquarian, New York, 1969) and John Herbert Nelson, *The Negro Character In American Literature* (1926; McGrath Publishing Company, New York, 1968). The latter also mentions narratives written by former slaves. Two anthologies contain excellent selections of nineteenth-century articles in English on the music and dances of the slaves as well as bibliographies: Bruce Jackson, ed. *The Negro And His Folklore In Nineteenth-Century Periodicals* (published for the American Folklore Society by the University of Texas Press, Austin and London, 1967); Bernard Katz, ed. *The Social Implications of Early Negro Music In The United States* (Arno Press and *The New York Times*, New York, 1969).

A revision of the text did not seem necessary. A few points, however, have been clarified or else amplified in the subsequent comments.

PREFACE (p. *v*). In a public discussion (transcribed in *Perspectives In Musicology*, edited by Barry S. Brook, Edward O. D. Downes, and Sherman Van Solkema, W. W. Norton, New York, 1972, p. 222) Gilbert Chase made a reference to this book, after which followed this statement by Professor Brook: "Much of the documentation on Emmett had been known to other people before, but no one undertook to explore it systematically—apparently because it was not considered to be a significant field for musicology." There is no quarrel with the latter part of the statement; it confirms what has been said in the Preface. The first part, however, is in error. Of Emmett's work, a few of his songs were probably in the possession of collectors of early American sheet music when this book was being prepared. But beyond this, his music and verse, in print or in manuscript, were virtually unknown, and so were most of his activities.

Preface to the Second Printing

CHAPTER 3 (p. 48, last paragraph, and p. 49). Similar broadsides were distributed in Boston for the same occasion in other years. The Library of Congress has four such broadsides, all in Negro dialect, decorated with crude woodcuts and issued in Boston on July 14 in the following years: 1819, 1821, 1825, and 1832.[1] Antedating these broadsides, Negro dialect appeared in newspapers. In the late eighteenth century it was used in anecdotes, dialogues, letters to the editor, and announcements; among the characters were Sambo, Cato, Scipio, and Cuffee.[2]

CHAPTER 4 (p. 52, first paragraph). A slight change has been suggested in the performance of Rice's "Jim Crow" (in Marshall and Jean Stearns, *Jazz Dance*, The Macmillan Company, New York and London, 1964, 1966, and 1971, p. 41): some sort of hop rather than a jump (but see p. 91 of the present book) and at the end of the tune to the words "[I] jump Jim Crow," not earlier.

CHAPTER 11. It has been shown that Negro minstrelsy was indebted to black as well as white sources. But black elements were often not only conspicuous but genuine. Mere parody would have been sterile; it was theatrically rewarding to imitate the Negro. Thus the statement on p. 153 "... banjo, bones, tambourine, triangle and fiddle ... were a part of the life of the southern slave" remains valid.[3] In this context observations of a French musician and critic, Oscar Comettant, who spent several years in the United States, are of interest. In his book *Trois Ans Aux États-Unis / Étude Des Moeurs Et Coutumes Américaines*, Paris, 1857,[4] he speaks of the minstrel theater as *"un spectacle vraiment national et curieux"* and gives a most vivid and detailed description of a performance (pp. 43–45). Preceding this he writes: "... in order to appreciate this type of entertainment one must have been in the southern part of America and lived in the country, on the plantations, with the Negroes. One must have seen their incredible garments, their impossible hats, studied their physiognomy, so expressively foolish and changeable, become acquainted with their ridiculous fancies,

[1] The Library of Congress, Rare Book Room: portfolio 52, No. 13a; portf. 53, Nos. 11 and 28; portf. 52, No. 13.

[2] A few examples: *Massachusetts Centinel* (Boston), February 1, 1785; January 21, February 15, April 5, 1786; January 13, June 13, 1787.

[3] Dena J. Epstein, skeptical of the relation between minstrel stage and plantation, says in *Notes* XX, 1 (winter 1962/63), p. 53, that this statement "has been disputed." She also finds insufficient evidence for the popularity of the jawbone. Yet in the same review she mentions banjo and fiddle as instruments used by the Negroes and in *Notes* XX, 3 (summer 1963), pp. 382–84 and 390, triangle, tambourine, and jawbone.

[4] Microcards issued by Lost Cause Press, Louisville, Kentucky, 1970; 1858 edition microfilmed by University Microfilms, Ann Arbor, Michigan, 1956 [?]. This book came to my attention through Néstor R. Ortiz Oderigo's *La Musica Afronorteamericana*, Eudeba Editorial Universitaria De Buenos Aires, 1962, where, incidentally, jawbone, bones, and fiddle, among a variety of other Negro instruments, are discussed.

their droll, whimsical mentality, witnessed their inordinate laziness and unequalled cowardliness. Finally, one must know how real and profound is their musical sensitivity and with what dervish-like fury they let themselves go, all night long, in ceaseless, violent exertions of frenetic dancing. Only with all this in mind can one appreciate the originality and raciness of Negro minstrel performances [translated by H.N.]." Perhaps all of these remarks are correct, perhaps only some of them. What counts is that an alert observer in the fifties saw a close relationship between Negro minstrelsy and the southern plantation.

CHAPTER 12. John Lovell, Jr., writes in his *Black Song: The Forge And The Flame* (The Macmillan Company, New York, Collier-Macmillan, Ltd., London, 1972) pp. 460–61: "Hans Nathan in *Dan Emmett and the Rise of [Early] Negro Minstrelsy* says that the influence of Negro hymns on Negro minstrelsy is slight [the reference must be to p. 187, bottom] . . . Nathan's dismissal of the spiritual as an influence upon minstrelsy is far from conclusive. He seems to have avoided a thorough examination of the question for fear of finding an influence . . . . The examples of Foster and Bland show clearly that the spiritual did influence the minstrel, at least in the later years of the nineteenth century . . . .The scope of this influence needs to be worked out by minstrel experts with a passion for, and no fear of, the full truth." Lovell had overlooked that my statement covers only minstrel tunes up to 1845 and thus says nothing about the period between Foster and Bland. This is crystal clear within the chapter, a particularly well-documented one, in which it appears.

CHAPTER 13 (p. 190, end of second paragraph). The practice of tapping the heel to music, in the nineteenth century carried out by a banjoist, was continued into the twentieth century. In Scott Joplin's *Ragtime-Dance* of 1906 (republished in *Classic Piano Rags*, edited by Rudi Blesh, Dover Publications, New York, 1973) the pianist has to produce solo percussive effects by stamping "the heel of one foot heavily upon the floor . . ." and the warning is added "Do not raise the toe from the floor while stamping."

CHAPTER 16 (pp. 269–70). Much of the popularity of "Dixie" was due to extremely successful performances of it, within the play *Pocahontas*, in New Orleans, La., starting April 9, 1860 (see James J. Fuld, *The Book of World-Famous Music*, Crown Publishers, New York, 1971, revised edition, pp. 197–98; here also several early editions of the song and early printings of its text are listed).

H. N.

February, 1977

viii

CONTENTS

Preface to the First Printing   v

Preface to the Second Printing   vi

Chapter 1 Negro Impersonations and Songs in Late
               Eighteenth-Century England   3
         2 The Activities of the English Composer Charles Dibdin   20
         3 Negro Impersonations and Songs in the Early Republic   32
         4 Indigenous Negro Minstrel Types (1820–1840)   50
         5 Negro Minstrel Dances   70
         6 Dan Emmett's Youth   98
         7 Emmett's Career in the Thirties   107
         8 The Virginia Minstrels in New York and Boston   113
         9 The Performance of the Virginia Minstrels   123
        10 The Virginia Minstrels in Great Britain   135
        11 The First Negro Minstrel Band and Its Origins   143
        12 Early Minstrel Tunes   159
        13 Early Banjo Tunes and American Syncopation   189
        14 Emmett's Activities During the Forties and Fifties   214
        15 Emmett on the Stage of the Bryant's
               Minstrels and His Walk-Arounds   227
        16 "Dixie"   243
        17 Emmett's Later Life   276

           Documents   285
           Bibliography of the Works of D. D. Emmett   290
           Anthology   313
           Selective List of Sources   493
           General Index   495
           Index of Song Titles in Anthology   499

ILLUSTRATIONS

1. "The Suffering Negro"   8–9
2. "Yankee Doodle"   11
3. "A Negro Song"   12
4. Charles Dibdin in the character of "Mungo" in the opera
   The Padlock   22
5. An aria of "Mungo"   23
6. "Kickaraboo"   25–27
7. A blackface soldier on the stage of the Theatre Chatham Gardens   38
8. "Massa Georgee Washington and General La Fayette"   39–43
9. "Agamemnon"   45
10. "Jim Crow"   51
11. "Gombo Chaff"   53
12. "Zip Coon"   58
13. A solo banjoist in the circus ring   60
14. John Diamond   61
15. John N. Smith   63
16. The banjoist Whitlock and his partner   64
17. R. W. Pelham and his brother Gilbert in their scene
    "Massa Is a Stingy Man"   66
18. A minstrel love scene   67
19. Juba on the stage of Vauxhall Gardens   74
20. A minstrel dancer   76
21. John Diamond   77
22. John Diamond dancing in high boots   77
23. T. D. Rice   77
24. A characteristic movement of the minstrel dancer   78
25. Another characteristic movement of the minstrel dancer   78
26. The hat figured prominently in the minstrel dance   79
27. The finely balanced weight of the arms and hands
    gave the minstrel dance its fluency   79
28. A minstrel dancer in the restrained posture   80
29. Negro Methodists holding a meeting in Philadelphia   82
30. A dance step reminiscent of the Charleston   89
31. The "long J bow"   90
32. One phase of the "Essence of Old Virginny"   94
33. A Shaker dance on the minstrel stage   95
34. A "challenge dance"   96
35. An early map of Mount Vernon, Ohio   100
36. Dan Emmett's mother   103
37. The Virginia Minstrels in action   124

38. Frank Brower   125
39. Dan Emmett   125
40. Detail from *The Bone Player*   127
41. A "wench performance" of a male actor   132
42. Portion of a playbill of the Virginia Minstrels   137
43. Cover of "Dandy Jim from Caroline"   141
44. The Virginia Serenaders   148
45. The Harmoneons   148
46. The Congo Minstrels   149
47. A Negro minstrel singing to his jawbone on the wall   150
48. The Original Ethiopian Serenaders   152
49. Primitive water color of a southern plantation   157
50. Charley Fox   221
51. Dan Emmett   222
52. The first part of a walk-around   233
53. The concluding dance of a walk-around   234
54. Playbill of a performance of Bryant's Minstrels   246
55. Facsimile of an early manuscript of "Dixie"   249
56. Cover of the first authorized edition of "Dixie"   267
57. Cover of the first edition of "Dixie"   268
58. Emmett's contract with Firth, Pond & Co.   270

Illustrations in Anthology

Songs of the Virginia Minstrels   331
"Jim Crow" on the New York stage   444

MUSICAL EXAMPLES

1. A Jamaican flute melody 13
2. A song from the opera
   Paul and Virginia 17
3. A theme from Clementi's
   "Sonata No. 1" 17
4. A Negro song from the
   opera *Obi* 18
5. A Negro song from the
   opera *Paul et Virginie* 19
6. "The Siege of Plattsburgh" 36
7. "Possum up a Gum Tree" 47
8. "The Lasses of Dublin" 48
9. "Bonja Song" 160
10. "Coal Black Rose" 160
11. "Do I Do I Don't Do
    Nothing" 161
12. "Long Time Ago" 162
13. "Our Guidman Cam Hame
    at E'en" 162
14. "The Bee Gum" 163
15. "The Hon. Miss Rollo" 164
16. "Clare De Kitchen" 164
17. "The Star of the County
    Down" 165
18. "Lady Shaftsbury's Reel" 165
19. "Settin' on a Rail" 165
20. "O! A-Hunting We
    Will Go" 166
21. "The Countess of Percy" 166
22. "Zip Coon" 167
23. "The Glasgow Hornpipe" 168
24. "The Post Office" 168
25. "Sich a Gitting Up Stairs" 169
26. "Getting Upstairs" 169
27. "My Long Tail Blue" 170
28. "Jenny's Babee" 170
29. "Jim Crow" 171
30. "I Wish the Shepherd's
    Pet Were Mine" 171
31. "The Old One Outwitted" 172
32. "Gumbo Chaff" 173
33. "Bow Wow Wow" 173
34. Melodic design of early
    minstrel tunes 174
35. "My Old Aunt Sally" 176
36. "Peggy Perkins" 177
37. "Jim Along Josey" 177
38. "Four and Twenty
    Fiddlers" 177
39. "My Old Dad" 178
40. "A Negro Song" 178
41. "De Ole Jaw Bone" 178
42. "Ole Pee Dee" 179
43. "Old Dan Tucker" 179
44. "De Blue Tail Fly" 180
45. "O Lud Gals" 181
46. "The Spinning Wheel" 183
47. "Dandy Jim from Caroline" 183
48. "The Miller's Maid" 183
49. "Capt. Lockhart of the
    Tartar" 184
50. "Take Her Out and
    Air Her" 184
51. "Dar He Goes! Dat's
    Him!" 184
52. "Duncan Gray" 184
53. "Pompey Ran Away" 187
54. Tuning of the banjo 192
55. "Grape Vine Twist" 192
56. "The Boatman's Dance" 192
57. "The Devil's Dream" 193
58. "De Boatman's Dance" 193
59. "Whoop Jamboree Jig" 194
60. "Clem Titus' Jig" 196
61. "Young Arthur Daly" 196
62. "Hell on the Wabash Jig" 197
63. "The Night We Made
    the Match" 197
64. "Quaker's Jig" 198
65. "The Mourne Mountains" 198

66. "Clem Titus' Jig"   198
67. "Negro Jig"   199
68. "Nigger on de Wood Pile"   199
69. "Gantz's Jig"   199
70. "Joe Sweeney's Jig"   201
71. "Sliding Jenny Jig"   201
72. "Tom Brigg's Jig"   201
73. "Dick Myers' Jig"   201
74. "Pea-Patch Jig"   201
75. "Genuine Negro Jig"   202
76. "Pea-Patch Jig"   202
77. An ornament in banjo
     music   202
78. "Pea-Patch Jig"   202
79. "Dr. Hekok Jig"   203
80. "Genuine Negro Jig"   204
81. "Marty Inglehart Jig"   204
82. "The Reel of Tulloch"   206
83. "Long Dance"   206
84. "Massa Is a Stingy Man"   206
85. "I Saw the Beam in My
     Sister's Eye"   208
86. "Maple Leaf Rag"   210
87. "St. Louis Blues"   210
88. "Hilarity Rag"   210
89. "12th St. Rag"   210
90. "The Cascades"   211
91. "The Memphis Blues"   211
92. "Maple Leaf Rag"   211
93. From a "Buck or Wing
     Dance"   211
94. From a "Buck or Wing
     Dance"   212
95. "12th St. Rag"   212
96. "Jordan Is a Hard Road
     to Travel"   224

97. "O Daniel"   224
98. "Good-Bye"   224
99. "Old K. Y. Ky."   238
100. "O'er the Crossing"   238
101. "The Black Brigade"   238
102. "I'm Gwine to Alabamy"   239
103. "I'm in Trouble"   239
104. "Road to Richmond"   239
105. "I'm Going Home to Dixie"   239
106. "The Lonesome Valley"   240
107. "What O' Dat"   240
108. "Lay This Body Down"   240
109. "Sandy Gibson's"   241
110. "Old Ship Zion"   241
111. The initial rhythmic
      motive of "Dixie"   248
112. A rhythmic jolt in
      "Dixie's Land"   248
113. "Dixie" chorus used in
      "Jonny Roach" and
      "Billy Patterson"   255
114. "Dixie" shows slight
      affinities to the first
      measures of the tune
      "If I Had a Donkey"   258
115. Melodic outline of the
      chorus of "Dixie"   258
116. The opening of "Gumbo
      Chaff"   258
117. The opening of "De Wild
      Goose-Nation"   258
118. Opening patterns of horn-
      pipes and kindred tunes   259
119. Several passages of "Dixie"
      variants of Scottish folk
      tunes   261

DAN EMMETT

and the Rise of Early Negro Minstrelsy

Then read my fancies; they will stick like burs,
And may be, to the helpless, comforters.

—John Bunyan

It is very doubtful whether the reader will like the hero we have selected. That he will not please the ladies one may say with certainty, for ladies insist on a hero's being absolute perfection, and if he has some tiny spiritual or physical blemish then—there's trouble! . . . But all the same I have not taken a virtuous man for my hero. And I may even say why I have not. Because it is high time at last to let the poor virtuous man rest; because the phrase "virtuous man" is too often taken in vain, because they have made a regular hack of the virtuous man and there is not a writer who has not ridden him to death, lashing him on with whip or anything that comes to hand; because they have so overdone the virtuous man that there is not a shadow of virtue left about him, and he is nothing but skin and bone; because it is through hypocrisy they invoke the virtuous man; because the virtuous man is not respected. No, the time has come at last to trot out the rascal! And so let us trot out the rascal!

—Nikolai Gogol

Blow away ye gentle breezes
All among de cimmon treeses,
Dar I sct long wid de muses,
Mendin my old boots and shuses.

—Dan Emmett

Chapter 1

NEGRO IMPERSONATIONS AND SONGS IN LATE EIGHTEENTH-CENTURY ENGLAND

———◈———

ACTORS AND DANCERS blackened or masked their faces long before the practice established itself in the popular American theater. We recall the Greek *phallophoroi* who used soot; the demons, goblins, savages, Indians, Turks, Moors, and Negroes of the lavish entertainments at the courts of the Renaissance and the early Baroque; and Pulcinella and Arlecchino of the *Commedia dell'Arte* who wore their black masks up to the past century. However, none of these phenomena had a direct connection with the blackface performance as it flourished in the early American Republic. Rather this type of theater had its roots, as one would suspect, in the England of the eighteenth century.

When Englishmen spoke of the Negro, they meant the African whom they forcibly imported to sustain the economy of their colonial possessions in the New World. On this matter theirs was the attitude of a mercantile people, and as long as it prevailed, the Negro aroused neither hostile nor amicable feelings. However, as soon as it was realized how arbitrary was the category to which he had been assigned, the Negro became a source of emotional interest and contention.

The first to point out the perversity of the slave trade were writers, poets, and dramatists. From their pens flowed a literature of sympathy and protest which, starting with the second half of the

3

seventeenth century, reached a crescendo towards the end of the eighteenth and the beginning of the nineteenth centuries. It was then that compassion for the black man changed to admiration.[1] And it was particularly at this moment that musicians joined the ranks of the humanitarians in order to give additional emphasis to righteous thought. An early example is Thomas Southerne's *Oroonoko,* a play performed in 1695 on a slave subject in which the black protagonist displayed his nobility of mind and his fellow men sang such idyllic songs as the following one:

A Lass there lives upon the Green,
Cou'd I her Picture draw;
A brighter Nymph was never seen,
That looks, and reigns a little Queen,
And keeps the Swains in awe.[2]

Racial prejudices maintained themselves for some time to come. How deep-rooted they were, especially on the Continent, is revealed by the attitude of one of the greatest minds of the time, the philosopher Immanuel Kant. With conviction he wrote in his book *Beobachtungen über das Gefühl des Schönen und Erhabenen* of 1764, "The Negroes of Africa have, by nature, no feeling which transcends the silly [*das Läppische*]"; at another time, in rejecting the argument of a Negro, Kant allowed himself to remark, "This chap was entirely black from head to toe, a clear proof that what he said was stupid."

In England, however, the humanitarian trends gained momentum and, to judge by the various "fashionable" and "favorite" songs that appeared within a period of a little more than ten years, culminated in a vogue for the oppressed. It was then that the poet William Cowper mentioned in a letter of 1788, "If you hear ballads sung in the streets on the hardships of the Negroes in the islands, they are probably mine."[3] And the composer Muzio Clementi found

[1] See Hoxie N. Fairchild, *The Noble Savage* (New York, 1928), and Eva Beatrice Dykes, *The Negro in English Romantic Thought* (Washington, D. C., 1942).

[2] Act II. Words by Sir Henry Sheeres. Music by Raphael Courteville. Published in Willard Thorpe, *Songs from the Restoration Theatre* (Princeton, 1934).

[3] Dykes, *The Negro,* 17.

4

it appropriate to adorn one of his sonatas of 1795 with variations on an "*Arietta alla negra.*"[4]

The titles alone of such songs, called "pathetic" songs, are indicative of their content. One sang "The Desponding Negro" (words by John Collins, music by William Reeve, 1792), "The Negro's Complaint" (words by William Cowper, music by "a female correspondent—an amateur," 1793), "The Negro Slave" (words by C. J. Pitt, music by V. De Cleve, *c.*1795), "The Dying Negro" (music by James Hook, *c.*1795), "The Negro Mother" (music by John Ross, *c.*1799), "The Negro's Lamentation" (music by William Howard, 1800), "The Negro Girl" (beginning "Sad was de day," words by R. W. J., *c.*1800), "The Suffering Negro," "An African Love Song" (words by "A Lady," music by James Fisin), and others.[5] In them the fate of the African was sometimes presented as if he himself spoke. The stories, weird in themselves but discreetly couched in high-flown language, evoked the reader's sympathy and pity. Firmer tones made themselves heard in statements that nature is alike in all humans regardless of color, as in these lines from Cowper:

> Fleecy locks, and black complexion
> Cannot forfeit nature's claim;
> Skins may differ, but affection
> Dwells in white and black the same.[6]

And direct appeals to the white man's moral conscience took the form of promises of spiritual reward and threats of retribution.

[4] From No. 1 of "Three Sonatas for the Piano-forte with Accompaniments for a Violin and Violoncello," Opus 29 (1795), quoted in De La Laurencie, "America in the French Music of the Seventeenth and Eighteenth Centuries," *The Musical Quarterly* (April, 1921). The full title is "Calemba / Arietta / alla Negra." See Clementi's *Oeuvres Complettes* (Breitkopf Lionel & Härtel, *c.*1815). "Calemba," an African word, is of course nothing but a fancy heading in Clementi. Originally it designated a central African musical instrument, the "kalimba," which according to A. M. Jones in *Studies in African Music* (London, 1959), I, 257, had "a calabash resonator" and "tuned metal prongs . . . plucked by the thumbs."

[5] Only an American edition seems to be known of "An African Love Song" by the English composer James Fisin (G. Gilfert, New York, *c.*1798). "The Suffering Negro" belongs to approximately the same time. See also S. Foster Damon, "The Negro in Early American Songsters," *The Papers of the Bibliographical Society of America* (1934), XXVIII, Part 2, pp. 137–38, 140.

[6] From "The Negro's Complaint."

The Negro had become not only an object of national concern, but, so to speak, a fashionable commodity. Such a collection as *Minuets Cotillons & Country German Dances for the Violin, Mandolin, Flute & Harpsichord. Composed by an African*[7] is less likely to have been an exotic curiosity than evidence of the efforts of a publisher to increase his sales with a designation that was certain to arouse popular interest.

Although the pro-Negro sentiment was basically sound because it finally resulted in the abolition of the slave trade, it was nevertheless also an excuse for sentimentality, a favorite indulgence of the time. A case in point is "The Negro Boy," which began:

> When thirst of gold enslaves the mind
> And selfish views alone bear sway,
> Man turns a savage to his kind,
> And blood and rapine mark his way.
> Alas! for this poor simple toy,
> I sold a blooming Negro boy.[8]

These words, not quite intelligible by themselves, were inspired by a story published about 1792, which must have played on the sensibilities of the English as it did on those of their contemporaries in North America. It tells of an African prince who on his arrival in England was "asked what he gave for his Watch" and who answered, "What I will never give again:—I gave a fine Boy for it."[9] Here was not only a touching line, easy to remember, but the expression of a savage who was noble both by blood and, at least in retrospect, by attitude.

A book that was effective in establishing a new concept of the Negro was *Travels in the Interior Districts of Africa . . . In the Years*

[7] Catalogue of the British Museum (*c*.1790).

[8] Set to music by Edward Miller under the title "The Negro Boy, Who was Sold by an African Prince, for a Metal Watch" (London, *c*.1790). There was also a version by the English composer John Moulds, but it can be found only in *The Musical Repertory* (Boston, 1796).

[9] The story, as quoted by Damon, "Early American Songsters," 140, is taken from an American magazine of 1792; it had been submitted by "a respectable merchant" of Providence, then residing in London.

1795, 1796, and 1797, published by the explorer Mungo Park as an abstract in 1798 and in complete form in 1799.[10] One particular incident in it must have convinced Englishmen that the Negro, like any other human being, was in fact endowed with kindness and pity. Park reports that one day he found himself "weary and dejected" in a village in search of shelter. For many hours none was offered to him, but at the end of the day he was asked into a hut, given food, and provided a place to sleep. While the Negro women in the hut continued spinning cotton, they "lightened their labour by songs one of which was composed extempore, for I was myself the subject of it . . . . The air was sweet and plaintive . . . ." These were its words, "literally translated":

> The Winds roared, and the rain fell.—The poor white man, faint and weary, came and sat under our tree.—He had no mother to bring him milk; no Wife to grind his corn.

> CHORUS. Let us pity the poor white man; no Mother has he, etc.

The words immediately stirred composers and writers into action. The first musical version, based on the original text, was by the French composer F. H. Barthélemon, who was then living in England.[11] Mungo Park appended to his own book a literary paraphrase of the text by Georgiana Cavendish, Duchess of Devonshire, which had been set to music by G. G. Ferrari. Shortly afterward, this same paraphrase was used in a song by Joseph Dale, but S. S. Colman paraphrased the story differently for the composer John Moorehead. Such writers as James Montgomery, W. L. Bowles, and George Crabbe did their best to give Park's story literary significance.[12]

It must be said that practically all English songs on Negro subjects were musically undistinguished. However, "The Suffering Negro" was an exception (see Illustration 1). Its dignified tune is similar

---

[10] The abstract, containing the above quoted story, was published in *Proceedings of the Association for Promoting the Discovery of the Interior Parts of Africa* (London). In the complete book (London, 1799) the story appears in Chapter 15.

[11] "The African's Pity on the White Man" (London, 1798).

[12] The versions of Dale and Moorehead were composed about 1800, according to the Catalogue of the British Museum. See Fairchild, *The Noble Savage,* 490–91.

Illustration 1. An English broadside of the late eighteenth century. Courtesy Boston Public Library.

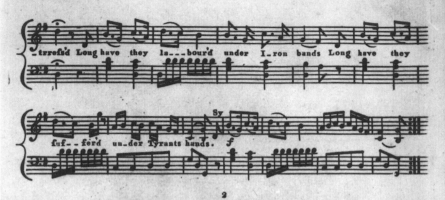

-tress'd Long have they la—bour'd under I—ron bands Long have they
suf—ferd un—der Tyrants hands. *f*

2

Torn from the tenderest ties of friendship hear
From Parents, Wife, and helpless Children dear
Oh cruel Man, that first this spoil did trace
And made a trafic of the human race
Can blessings e'er attend such deeds as these
Or such as seek them ever hope for peace.

3

A gleam of hope, holds out her chearing rays
The wearied yet may look for better days
Britannia's Sons, their native feelings plead
Stretch forth their Arms, to stay the horrid deed
Happy the Men, who helpless sufferers save
A Negro's blessings shall attend their grave.

For the Guittar

to movements in Haydn's string quartets, although it is probably not by the master himself.[13] Nevertheless, the awkward accentuation of the words suggests that they were adapted to a melody which was originally an instrumental one.

While the Negro was usually portrayed as a pitiful or tragic person, he also appeared in less strenuous and thus more realistic attitudes. Characterizations of this kind occurred mainly in operas and in the incidental music of plays. There are, however, two separately published broadside songs which realistically picture the Negro, but even these may have originated in the theater. The words of the two are in some sort of Negro English, which was customary in this genre of song.

The first is entitled "Yankee Doodle or The Negroes Farewell to America" (see Illustration 2).[14] It is uttered by a Negro who is leaving America (the British colonies in the New World) for the mother country where slavery has been abolished:

> Den Hey! for old Englan' where Liberty reigns,
> Where Negroe no beaten or loaded with chains

The first part of the tune is in type a conventional minuet; the style of the lively refrain which follows can be found in English stage songs of the period.

The second broadside song, called "A Negro Song,"[15] the adjective "African" being reserved for more serious subjects, differs from previously mentioned compositions in that it has folkloristic overtones (see Illustration 3). Not only is the jargon of its text close to that of the Negroes in the West Indies, but its tune was perhaps also known to them; a variant of it was found in Jamaica about one hundred years later (see Musical Example 1).[16] However, the original is no doubt

---

[13] See Haydn's Opus 64, No. 1, Movements 1 and 3; and Opus 71, No. 3, Movement 2. According to the Haydn expert Anthony van Hoboken, "The Suffering Negro" is not by Haydn.

[14] Published by Charles and Samuel Thompson with "The Words and Music by T. L." (perhaps Thomas Linley, the Elder).

[15] In the Julian Marshall Collection of English broadsides, Houghton Library of Harvard University.

[16] Walter Jekyll, *Jamaican Song and Story* (London, 1907), 52.

Illustration 2. An English broadside of the late eighteenth century. Courtesy Boston Public Library.

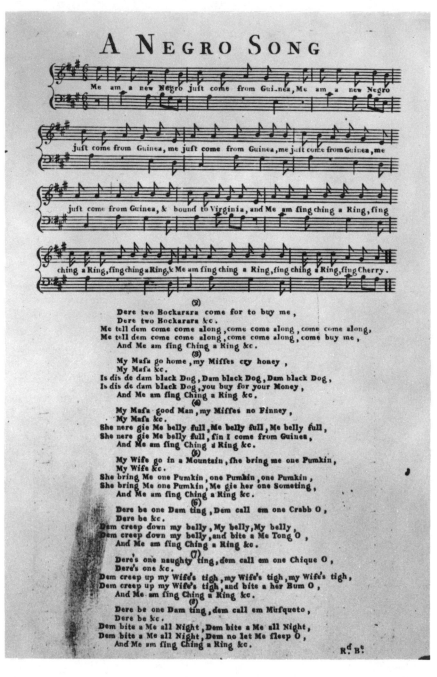

Illustration 3. An English broadside of the late eighteenth century. Courtesy Harvard College Library.

(transposed)

Musical Example 1

A Jamaican flute melody. From Jekyll, *Jamaican Song and Story* (London, 1907).

a white, late eighteenth-century creation, showing some relation to the songs of Charles Dibdin, which was brought to the islands by English travelers. Its down-to-earth story and its language could not help appealing to the Negroes, and the simplicity of its tune, subsequently abbreviated according to their own fashion, was immediately intelligible to them.

In addition to purely literary works, various plays with incidental music, as well as operas, dealt with slave life, or at least used Negro characters; some of the incidental vocal numbers circulated as separately published songs. Among these stage works were *The Padlock* (text by Isaac Bickerstaffe, music by Charles Dibdin, performed in 1768); *The Blackamoor Wash'd White* (text by Henry Bate, performed in 1776); *Inkle and Yarico* (text by George Colman, the Younger, music by Samuel Arnold, performed in 1787); *The Prize or 2, 5, 3, 8* (text by Prince Hoare, music by Stephen Storace, published in 1793); *Blackbeard, or The Captive Princess* ("A serio-comic Ballet of Action," text by J. C. Cross, music by James Saunderson, performed in 1798); *Paul and Virginia* (text by James Cobb, music by William Reeve and Joseph Mazzinghi, performed in 1800); *Obi, or Three-Fingered Jack* (text by John Fawcett, music composed and "adapted to the action . . . with selections from the most eminent Masters" by Samuel Arnold, performed in 1800); *The Africans or War, Love, and Duty* (text by George Colman, the Younger, music

13

by Michael Kelly, performed in 1808); and *The Slave* (text by Thomas Morton, music by Henry R. Bishop, performed in 1816).

These works reveal the two contrasting types of Negroes with which we are already familiar. One is imbued with idealistic sentiments and is of noble bearing; the other is naïve, ignorant, comical, and more or less disreputable. Not infrequently the two types appear together in one play.

An example of the idealistic and noble Negro is Gambia in *The Slave*. He refuses to take part in a slave rebellion, and when asked the reason for his extraordinary action, he is made to say, "Because there is a state worse than slavery—liberty engendered by treachery, nursed by rapine, and invigorated by cruelty." This was a bit of the philosophical jargon of the time rather than a sample of reality. "All his attributes," it was said of the hero, "are preserved—his fierceness, his generosity, his noble nature. Impetuous in his rage—fervent in his affections—his magnanimity and greatness of soul are more powerful than either; and the only revenge he wreaks on a favored rival is to sacrifice his love and liberty in his behalf. This may appear incredible to civilized society; but such instances of friendship and self-control are by no means uncommon in the savage state."[17]

The other Negro character was far less pretentious. And yet when he appears as the faithful servant displaying sympathy for his master, he is still a stereotyped figure. In *The Prize*, for example, there is Juba, a goodhearted chap who plays on his guitar and sings:

> You good to me, dat keepy here,
> No Massa, dat you never fear,
> Long time destroy—
> Me know Death kill, but leave one part,
> He never kill the loving heart
> Of Poor Black Boy.[18]

And in *Blackbeard* (Act I, Scene V) it is a young Negro who, while fanning his mistress, assures her in a song of his devotion:

[17] Act I, Scene III and preface, John Cumberland edition (London, n.d.).
[18] The song begins with "You care for money, ah! care no more!"

Though sunny beams the sky adorn
And glad the laughing Buckra's eye;
I see poor missee weep and mourn
Massa return or missee die.
Sing chink a ching.

But the Negro became livelier as soon as he was cast as the traditional servant of *opera buffa*. In *The Padlock*, encouraged by alcohol, he is delightfully insolent; whereas in *Blackbeard*, while singing a duet with a sailor (Act I, Scene VII), he does not hide the fact that a fight would not appeal to him as much as a drink:

Ah massa, dat hard to my poor way of tinking
To choak de poor troat, dat so doat upon drinking,
But me still drink a little, come ting a ting tang.

This attitude was not the appropriate one at the moment, but it was honest.

The Negro was often shown as ill-mannered and cowardly, but mainly to entertain and not to criticize. There was also his supposed naïveté which was easily exaggerated, as in Act I of *Obi* when Quashee says, "Oh, massa you say what you please, but Obi woman know ebery ting from top of head to bottom of toe; and once she put Obi [the charm] on poor negro man, he no eat, he no drink, he no noting, but pine, pine, pine, pine, pine and die away."

In roles and songs in which the Negro appeared as a plantation hand or as a house servant, an attempt was often made to reproduce the actual speech of the slaves of the West Indies. Thus their habit of distorting the final syllable of English words into *ee*'s and occasionally into *o*'s, as well as their mixing up of pronouns (for example, the substitution of *me* for *I*), were sometimes imitated.[19] Even such

19 *Ee*'s appear in *Blackbeard*, Act I, Scene VII (". . . knees quakee De heart . . . go bump a bump shakee . . . ."), in Dibdin's song "Negro Philosophy" ("You no worky worky"), and in Dibdin's Negro story (see Chapter 2). There are various final *o*'s in "A Negro Song," and Dominique in *Paul and Virginia* several times intersperses his song "When the Moon Shines" with "Ackee-O, Ackee-O." The text of a Negro song transcribed in 1816 appears in Matthew Gregory Lewis, *Journal of a Resi-*

nonsense words as "sing ching a Ring," "sing chink a ching," and "chingaring, chingaring" are indeed related to the Jamaican "ying de ying" and "ting-a ling."[20] But literary realism was seldom carried through consistently.

Nor did a true musical realism exist, although eighteenth-century composers made attempts in that direction. The indigenous music of the West Indies or, for that matter, of Africa, was practically unknown to them. Unable to imitate it, they wrote music which corresponded to what they believed to be the Negro's "*mentality.*" In expressing his childlike mind, they used brief phrases, repeated tones, a narrow range, and simple rhythmic patterns, thus approaching the idiom of nursery rhymes. Examples may be found in Dominique's song in *Paul and Virginia* (see Musical Example 2) and in Dibdin's "Kickaraboo" (see Chapter 2). Clementi's "*Arietta alla negra,*" characteristically called "*Andante innocente,*" sounded similar (see Musical Example 3).[21] Moreover, composers did not hesitate to write in a sort of regional folk song style, be it English, as in *Obi,* or French, as in Rodolphe Kreutzer's opera *Paul et Virginie* of 1791 (see Musical Examples 4 and 5).[22] Of the primitive's physical strength and intensity of introspection—characteristics which to us moderns seem so striking—they had no conception whatever.

The early composers lent Negro dances clearly marked accents

---

dence *Among the Negroes in the West Indies* (London, 1845): "Hey-ho-day! me no care a dammee! / Me acquire a house . . . / Since massa come see we-oh. / Hey-ho-day! neger now quite eerie . . . / For once me see massa—hey-ho-day. / When massa go, me no care a dammee, / For how them usy we—hey-ho-day." Concerning the syllables *ee* and *o* in Jamaican songs, see Jekyll, *Jamaican Song.*

[20] See "A Negro Song"; *Blackbeard,* Act I, Scene V; Dibdin's "Negro Philosophy"; and Jekyll, *Jamaican Song,* 38, 109.

[21] De La Laurencie, "America in the French Music." An additional "Alla Negra. Allegretto Moderato," the sketch of a theme in F Major, was found by William Lichtenwanger among Clementi's manuscripts in the Library of Congress.

[22] De La Laurencie, "America in the French Music." The author also refers to "Negro music" in Jean François Lesueur's opera *Paul et Virginie,* composed in 1794, the libretto of which was fashioned, like Kreutzer's, after Bernadin de Saint-Pierre's book of the same title. In the comedy *Les Nègres* (text by L. E. Billardon de Sauvigny, music by N. Dezède, published in 1782), the setting being in the Isle de Saint-Domingue, we find two "Airs Nègres." One of them contains the folkloristically interesting lines: "Pour danser, vivent nos amans, / Les noirs dansent mieux que les blancs." A duet "Adieu Coeur Moi," called "Negro Air," appears in Domenico Corri, *A Select Collection of the Most Admired Songs . . . .* (Edinburgh, *c.*1779), III.

When the moon shines o'er the Deep Ack-ee - O

Ack - ee - O Whis-ker'd Dons are fast a - sleep.

snor- ing fast a - sleep. From their huts the

Ne - groes run Ack - ee - O Ack - ee - O

Full of fro - lic full of fun ho - li - day to keep.

Musical Example 2

A song of the Negro slave "Dominique" in the opera *Paul and Virginia* (by Mazzinghi and Reeve, performed 1800).

Arietta alla negra
Andante innocente

Musical Example 3

A theme in Muzio Clementi's "Sonata No. 1" (Opus XXIX, 1795).

Musical Example 4

A Negro song in the opera *Obi, or Three-Fingered Jack* (by Samuel Arnold, performed 1800).

Nous por - ter   toi chez tes   pa - rents,

etc.

Sur   le   pe - tit   lit   de   feuil - la - ge

Musical Example 5
A Negro song in the opera *Paul et Virginie* (by Rodolphe Kreutzer,
performed 1791).

and lively tempos, but this degree of animation was tame compared
to the real thing. It could not have been otherwise. When a man like
Rameau composed a vigorous dance in 1725 for an exhibition of
Carib natives in Paris (later to be performed by ballet dancers appearing as "sauvages" in *Les Indes Galantes*), he revealed his customary refinement. Nevertheless, in the opinions of his contemporaries he had already gone too far. One critic blamed his piece for
being "rough and uneven" and warned him to desist from "a road
which one cannot walk without stumbling."[23]

[23] De La Laurencie, "America in the French Music."

Chapter 2

THE ACTIVITIES
OF THE ENGLISH COMPOSER
CHARLES DIBDIN

AN ENGLISHMAN who showed a particular interest in writing "Negro songs" and who, besides, could boast of an aptitude for Negro impersonation was Charles Dibdin, a well-known song writer of his day. In 1768, when he was still in his early twenties, his comic opera *The Padlock*[1] was performed at the Drury Lane Theatre in London, preceded by *Hamlet* with Garrick in the title role.[2] Its success was so considerable that it has been compared with that of *The Beggar's Opera*. The libretto, consisting of spoken parts and a few lyrics for airs and vocal ensembles, was written by Isaac Bickerstaffe after a short story by Cervantes entitled *El Celoso Estremeño (The Jealous Husband)*. Its protagonist was an old miser who kept his young bride-to-be (in Cervantes, his wife) shut up in his house, and, in order to forestall all sinful temptation, placed a padlock on the door. The main comic character of the play was the miser's Negro servant Mungo (called Luys in Cervantes). Knowing that the actor Moody was familiar with the language of the Negroes of the West Indies, Bickerstaffe wrote Mungo's part in dialect.[3] At last, however, it was

---

[1] The libretto of *The Padlock* appears in Thomas Dibdin, ed., *The London Theatre* (London, 1815), XXI.

[2] Arthur Murphy, *The Life of David Garrick* (London, 1801).

[3] Charles Dibdin, *The Professional Life of Mr. Dibdin, written by himself* (London, published by the author, 1803), I, 69.

Dibdin himself who played the part, and guided by suggestive lines, he aroused the enthusiasm of his audience. What histrionic possibilities the part offered can be illustrated by the following scene in which Mungo, in the dead of night, meets his master, Don Diego, who has returned home unexpectedly:

Enter Mungo, from the cellar, with a flask in one hand, and a candle in the other.

Mungo: Tol, lol, lol, lol.

Diego: Hold, didn't I hear a noise?

Mungo: Hola.

Diego: Heaven and earth; what do I see!

Mungo: Where are you, young Massa, and Missy! Here wine for supper.

Diego: I'm thunder-struck!

Mungo: My old Massa little tink we be so merry—hic-hic—What's the matter with me? the room turn round.

Diego: Wretch, do you know me?

Mungo: Know you?—damn you.

Diego: Horrid creature! what makes you here at this time of night? is it with a design to surprise the innocents in their beds, and murder them sleeping?

Mungo: Hush, hush—make no noise—hic-hic—

Diego: The slave is intoxicated.

Mungo: Make no noise, I say; deres young gentleman wid young lady; he play on guitar, and she like him better dan she like you. Fal, lal, lal.

Diego: Monster, I'll make an example of you.

Mungo: What you call me names for, you old dog?

Diego: Does the villain dare to lift his hand against me?

Mungo: Will you fight?

Diego: He's mad.

Mungo: Deres one in de house you little tink. Gad he do you business.

Diego: Go, lye down in your stye, and sleep.

Mungo: Sleep! sleep you self; you drunk—ha! ha! ha! Look, a padlock: you put a padlock on a dore again, will you? Ha! ha! ha![4]

[4] From Act II, Scene VI of *The Padlock: a comic opera: as it is perform'd by His Majesty's servants, at the Theatre-Royal in Drury Lane. A new edition* (London [*c.*1768]).

21

Besides realistic scenes of this kind, there were also others where Mungo, remembering that he was an opera singer, employed the stock gestures of his profession (see Illustration 4).

The music of *The Padlock* clearly reveals the influence of Italian opera. Dibdin indeed was accused of having stolen from an unnamed Italian composer, a charge which he fervently denied in the preface to the printed edition of his work.[5] In any case, Mungo's music was no more Negroid (see Illustration 5) than was Osmin's Turkish in Mozart's *Die Entführung aus dem Serail.*

Mr DIBDEN in the Character of MUNGO
in the Celebrated Opera of the Padlock.
London, Printed for R. Sayer at N? 53 Fleet Street & J. Smith at N? 35 Cheapside

Illustration 4. Courtesy Harvard Theatre Collection.

[5] *The Padlock. A comic opera: as it is performed at the Theatre-Royal in Drury Lane. The words by the author of The Maid of the Mill, &. The music by Mr. Dibdin.* (London, printed for the author and sold by J. Johnston, [1768]).

Illustration 5. An aria of "Mungo" in the comic opera *The Padlock*. From Charles Dibdin, *The Padlock* (performed 1768).

Cervantes, with his deep insight into human behavior, had made Luys a most convincing Negro slave character—extremely droll, literally burning with a love for music, by no means disdainful of a drink, and not too heroic in the face of danger. The scene in which Luys, perspiring with terror, creeps into his bed and hides under his blanket, clasping his guitar to his bosom, was the result of very astute observation. Bickerstaffe's and Dibdin's Mungo, however, is more of a type than of an individual. He is not only fond of music and wine but also of tips, and he is obedient when sober. His alternating servility and humorous impertinence, his shiftlessness, and his cowardice are characteristics of the stage servant in eighteenth-century opera.

Years later Dibdin popularized Negro impersonations in a novel sort of musical entertainment in which he was at once speaker, singer, and accompanist, as well as his own composer, author, and impresario. He presented songs, skillfully linking them with lively narrative and dialogue, and he even performed whole operatic scenes in which he sang all the roles himself. These new "Readings and Music," as he called them first, or "Table Entertainments" were tried out in the provinces during 1787 and 1788, and in 1789 he brought one of them, *The Whim of the Moment, or Nature in Little,* to London. Almost every year thereafter saw anywhere from one to four new shows, usually with fantastic double titles. At first they were performed in rented theaters or chambers, but by 1796 Dibdin was sufficiently well established to build a theater of his own in Leicester Place, calling it by the same name he had given to a previous establishment, Sans Souci. His "Entertainments" lasted until 1805, and after an interval of three years, were revived in 1808 and 1809; however, in these last years they were not quite the same, since he employed other musicians to assist him.

Many of Dibdin's songs glorified the English sailor; most were topical and humorous, and some were even satirical, including burlesques of Irishmen, Italian singers, and Jewish peddlers. Since the pros and cons of the African slave trade were then subjects of heated discussions, Dibdin found it opportune also to present Negro characters. He did not act them out, but sat at a keyboard instrument in the center of the stage, facing his audience.[6] Someone who heard him has left us the following vivid description of his performance:

> His costume was a blue coat, white waistcoat, and black silk breeches and stockings; and he wore his hair, in the fashion of the day, full dressed and profusely powdered. His manner of speaking was easy and colloquial; and his air was more that of a person entertaining a party of friends in a private drawing-room, than of a performer exhibiting to a public audience. He was near-sighted; and when seated at his instrument, he would bend his head close to his book for a few moments, then, laying it down, throw himself back in his chair,

[6] An illustration of "Mr. Dibdin as performing at the SANS SOUCI" appears in Hans Nathan, "Negro Impersonation in Eighteenth Century England," *Notes* (September, 1945).

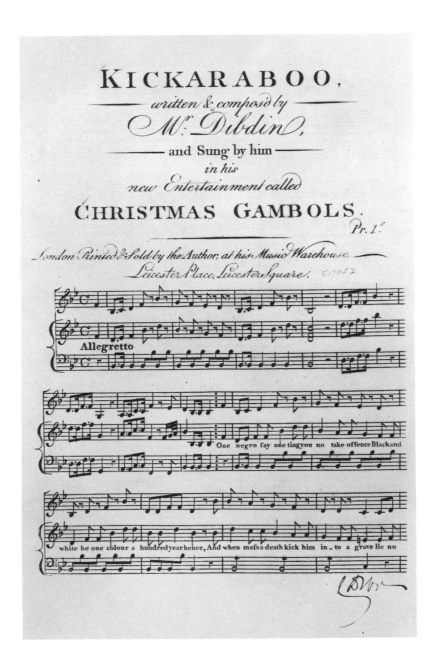

Illustration 6. A Negro song in the entertainment *Christmas Gambols*.
From Charles Dibdin, *Christmas Gambols* (performed 1795).

25

2

One mafsa, one slave, high and low all degrees,
Can be happy, dance, sing, make all pleasure him please;
One slave he one mafsa, he good,honeft brave,
One mafsa bad,wicked,be worse than one slave:

If your heart tell you good,you all happy, all well,
If bad, he plague, vex you worse and a hell;
Let your heart make you merry, then honeft and true,
And you no care no farthing for Kickaraboo.

3

One game me fee mafsa him play him call chefs,
King, queen,bishop, knight, caftle, all in a mefs,
King kill knight, queen bishop, men caftle throw down,
Like card_foldier him fcatter, all lie on a ground

And when the game over, king, bishop, tag, rag,
Queen, knight, all together him go in a bag,
So in life's game at chefs, when no more we can do,
Mafsa death bring one bag, and we Kickaraboo.

4

Then be good, what you am never mind de degree,
Lilly flower good for fomewhat as well as great tree;
You one slave, he no use to be sulky and sly,
Worky, worky, perhaps,you one mafsa by'm by.

Savee good and be poor make you act better part,
Than be rich in a pocket and poor in a heart,
Though ever so low, do your duty for true,
All your friend drop one tear when you Kickaraboo.

and deliver his song without further reference to book or music. His voice was a barytone . . . of no great power or compass, but of a sweet and mellow quality. He sang with simplicity, without any attempt at ambitious ornament . . . and . . . he was particularly attentive to a clear and emphatic utterance of the words . . . . In singing, he accompanied himself with facility and neatness on an instrument of a peculiar kind, combining the properties of the pianoforte and the chamber organ . . . . To this instrument were attached a set of bells, a side drum, a tambourine, and a gong . . . .[7]

One of Dibdin's Negro songs is "Kickaraboo," which was interpolated in his "entertainment" *Christmas Gambols* of 1795 (see Illustration 6). The title seems to be equivalent to the modern colloquialism "kicking the bucket." In the song the death of a Negro is described as something ludicrous, revealing an attitude that was

[7] "Memoir," *The Songs of Charles Dibdin . . . to which is prefixed a memoir of the author by George Hogarth, Esq.* (London, 1842), 20. See also another remark on Dibdin's manner of performance in *Recollections of the Life of John O'Keefe, written by himself* (London, 1826), II, Chap. 6.

perpetuated in American blackface minstrel songs until about the middle of the nineteenth century. There is dialect, but, as was customary in Dibdin's vocal numbers, its use is restricted. Characteristically, some of the elements of the tune are reminiscent of nursery rhymes, qualified by British folk song, while the rest is related to the aria style of Handel.

In Negro anecdotes Dibdin was considerably more realistic than in his lyrics. Aside from his commentary, he availed himself of unadulterated Negro speech, or what passed as such, as in the following example:

> I shall now proceed to shew that the passions of *envy* and *resentment* are as *implacable* and as full of *subtle refinement* in the hearts of the most *uninformed* as the most *polished*. CUDGO was a NEGRO, and QUACO a MULATTO. See how QUACO ridicules CUDGO for being further degenerated only in *one* degree from the European complexion than himself. "Ah damn you," says QUACO, "you a black dog—you a *Jenny Neger*—you don't tan like a me." He then sings:
>
> > Common NEGER go down the road side,
> > UNCLE BEN walk up in the high road,
> > Tan yanda you black *Jenny* rascal,
> > Common NEGER drink out of *wooden bowl,*
> > UNCLE BEN drink out of *china bason.*

Can there be more pointed satire than this? Does it not convey all the conscious force of pride, pre-eminence, place, and precedence, as strongly as words can express? He then goes on upbraiding him with his ignorance. "Ah you black dog, don't you know bout the rum, when you savee put letter under a tone." CUDGO, it seems, was carrying a jug of rum and a letter to a friend of his master, but meeting with another negro on the road, he accosted—"Ah how you do buddy." 'Ah,' replied the other, 'what buddy CUDGO! wat a divle you carry one someting dere.' "Oh dis—he da buckra rum master savee send um to anudder buckra lib in great house yonder." 'Ah buddy—let us all two take a lilly sup.' "Ah dam," says CUDGO, "you no see paper? Paper la talk—he savee tell massa." 'Ah buddy—appose we put paper under a tone—den he no see.' Charmed with this idea, they agreed to hide the letter under a stone. 'Ah buddy, dis be good stuff! savee make a heart jump!' Having drank [*sic*] pretty heartily, they begin to think of the consequence. "Ah dam—jug no full now." 'Buddy, buddy,' says the other, 'come to the ribbor, put lilly wee drop water.' This executed, CUDGO takes the letter and jogs on with the jug to his master's friend, who not finding the rum above proof, exclaims— 'Why what is all this, you scoundrel? You have been drinking the *rum* and filled the jug with *water*.' "Ah, massa," says CUDGO, "don't you vex—indeed I no do nothing." 'Nothing!—what do you think I can't read?' "Ah, massa, if I no tell buddy Tom so—dat dam paper savee talk very wicked for poor neger man."

These and other taunts and reproaches, which have in them all the ridiculous pride and contemptible folly of self-consequence, at length rouses [*sic*] the NEGRO—who falls foul of the MULATTO with equal success, and in such terms, that had JUVENAL been a NEGRO he would have written in the language of CUDGO. "Why now," says CUDGO, "you tink you dam creber fella too I appose—you no NEGER—no BUCKRA—no *any ting*. You dam *yellow copper kin—you no nation*—you a *mule*—I make a sing upon you.

SONG

QUACO BUNGY go about,
Ca'nt tell him nation—
BUCKRA make him foot ball,
JENNY NEGER hate him,
MUSTER won't own him,
So he ca'nt tell him nation.

Now I make a sing upon your sissy.

II

FANNY BUNGY have *pickiny,*
No know him fader
Some say the soldier man,
Some say the sailor man,
Some say the fisherman,
But he no know him daddy.

The MULATTO, who bore with great patience the satire on *himself,*
is roused to the highest pitch of indignation at the lampoon on
his sister. . . . .[8]

At this moment a pure, unspoiled Indian maid, the gentle Ora, is
introduced to save Cudgo from certain death for his slander. The
story, or at least parts of it, was taken straight from life, for quarrels
between Negro and Mulatto are of long standing. They occur even
today, including their forms of derision. Louisiana plantation hands
shortly after the middle of the nineteenth century sang tauntingly:
"Voyez ce mulet là, Musier Bainjo, Comme il est insolent,"[9] and a
Negro, only a few years ago, was overheard to say to a Mulatto: "I
b'longs to a race of people. But you ain't. I didn't never read in de
Bible about whar it speaks of mulattoes as a race of people. You is
mules, dat's whut you is."[10]

In Dibdin's Negro songs "Kickaraboo," "The Negro and His
Banjer,"[11] "Negro Philosophy,"[12] "One Mountain Neger," and the
duet "The Sun Go Down,"[13] the protagonist gives picturesque details
of his life, hard as it was. But these details are amusing rather than
pitiful, because he speaks of himself as something ludicrous, saying
that the whip of the overseer makes him skip like a "pea pon drum
head";[14] yet he is willing to "serve good master till him death."[15]
However, in sly comments on the tricky ways of the white man, he
is allowed to show that he is not quite satisfied.

Indigenous Negro impersonations on the American stage were to
differ fundamentally from those in eighteenth-century England. Note,
for instance, how Dibdin in the opening lines of "Kickaraboo" expressed the idea that death blots out the difference between black

[8] *The Musical Tour of Mr. Dibdin; in which—previous to his embarkation for In-dia—he finished his career as a Public Character* (Sheffield, 1788), 358–60.
[9] William Francis Allen, *et al., Slave Songs of the United States* (1867, repub-lished New York, 1951), 113. For a commentary on "Voyez ce mulet là," see G. W. Cable, "The Dance in Place Congo," *The Century Magazine* (February, 1886).
[10] Dorothy Scarborough, *On the Trail of Negro Folk-Songs* (Cambridge, 1925), 20.
[11] *The Wags, or The Camp of Pleasure,* performed 1790.
[12] *General Election,* performed 1796.
[13] The final two songs appear in the comic opera *The Round Robin,* performed 1811.
[14] "Negro Philosophy."
[15] "One Mountain Neger."

and white. About fifty years later, the Negro minstrel Dan Emmett, who was born in a frontier hamlet of the Ohio wilderness, took up the same thought, but put it this way:

> Old shot gun widout a trigger
> White man jis as good as nigger,
> When dey're dead an' gone to de debble
> Brack an white folks on a lebble.[16]

These are not words befitting a man with powdered wig and a literary education. They are voiced on the stage by an individual whose clothes are ragged, whose manners are crude, and whose reading is nil. In his words there is no condescending giggle—there is the rough laughter of the common people.

[16] Dan Emmett Manuscript Collection (State Library, Columbus, Ohio).

Chapter 3

NEGRO IMPERSONATIONS AND SONGS

IN THE EARLY REPUBLIC

———◆———

Most englishmen had never seen a primitive Negro; all they knew of him came from interpretations of writers and musicians. Americans, on the other hand, had personal contact with him. They were constantly aware of the large unassimilated, black population which contrasted with them so strikingly in appearance, manner, and mentality. No wonder then that Negro impersonations acquired a far greater importance in America than in Europe. They gradually developed into what might be called a national art—the popular theater of the nineteenth century.

The initial and tentative stages of indigenous Negro impersonation and song fell in the years 1815–30. Before this time, many of the English "Negro songs" of the late eighteenth and early nineteenth centuries circulated in America because both countries shared cultural tendencies, even after their political separation.[1] The most popular of those songs were the pathetic "The Negro Boy" and one entitled "Negro and Buckra Man."[2] The text of the latter written by

---

[1] Various of these songs are listed and discussed in Damon, "Early American Songsters."

[2] The text of "Negro and Buckra Man" was published for the first time in America in *The Songster's Repository* (New York, 1811). See Damon, "Early American Songsters," 137. See also *Davidson's Universal Melodist* (London, 1848), II, 217.

Thomas Dibdin and adapted to an English tune, represents the Negro
as someone whose hard luck seemed to cheer rather than depress him
—the comic stereotype of the time. Its opening lines read:

> Great way off at sea,
> When at home I benee,
> Buckra man steal me,
> From the coast of Guinea;
> Christian massee pray,
> Call me hea[t]hen doggee,
> Den I run away,
> Very much he floggee.
> Ri tol lol lol la.

A few American composers—recent European immigrants—contributed their own share to the production of "Negro" music, though
not deviating from established patterns. Both Benjamin Carr and
Francis Mallet made settings based on the versification of Mungo
Park's African song by the Duchess of Devonshire, and Victor Pelissier wrote a Negro dance for the opera *Obi*.[3]

Several of the English plays and operas dealing with Negro subjects were also performed in America, usually shortly after their
premières in Europe—*The Padlock, Inkle and Yarico, The Prize, Obi,*
and *Paul and Virginia*.[4] There existed a few plays in the same vein
by American authors, but their Negro characters were much like their
relatives on the continental stage. Some of these plays contained
music, as in *The Yorker's Stratagem, or Banana's Wedding* by J. Robinson performed in 1792 (Negro characters of the West Indies: Mrs.
Banana, a plantation owner; Banana, her son; and Priscilla); and
The Triumphs of Love; or, Happy Reconciliation by John Murdock,

<hr/>

[3] "A Negro Song," music by Benjamin Carr (Baltimore, J. Carr, [c.1801]); "The
Negroe's Humanity," music by Francis Mallet (Boston, Mallet and Graupner, [c.1801–
1802]); and "Negro Dance" in *Obi, or Three-Fingered Jack* by Victor Pelissier (Philadelphia, G. Willig [after 1800]). All three publications are listed in Harry Dichter
and Elliott Shapiro, *Early American Sheet Music* (New York, 1941).

[4] See Oscar G. Sonneck, *Early Opera in America* (New York, 1915), and George
C. D. Odell, *Annals of the New York Stage* (New York, 1927), II.

performed in 1795 (Negro character: the servant Sambo).⁵ To these may be added a farce by the English general Burgoyne, entitled *Boston Blockade,* performed in Boston about 1776 (Negro character: the female servant Fanfan).⁶

Negro dances within plays and operas were nothing unusual in America, but they were also performed separately, probably as entr'actes. Two of these entr'actes were "A negro dance in character" in 1767 and "A Comic Dance, In Character of a female Negro" in 1796.⁷

The only fact during the late eighteenth and the beginning of the nineteenth centuries which might suggest the potentialities of later Negro impersonation in America is the manner in which Mungo's part in Dibdin's *The Padlock* was acted out. According to someone who saw the performance, it was lent a variety and a realism which surpassed that of the original English interpretation.⁸ With the war between England and America widening the breach between the two countries, it is not by chance that in its wake Negro impersonation in the young Republic took a new turn. The subsequent fifteen years or so represent a period of groping, the results of which are more interesting from a theatrical and literary than from a musical point of view. The few facts known to us can be briefly summarized.

Under the influence of the events of war, the Negro appeared now as a comic figure in uniform. The first song, "The Guinea Boy," presumably written in 1814 but published in 1816, shows him fighting, willy-nilly, for the British.⁹ It is in the customary literary style,

⁵ Copies of the two plays are in the Brown University Library. Plays containing Negro characters but no Negro music are John Leacock, *The Fall of British Tyranny; or, American Liberty Triumphant* (1776), republished in M. J. Moses, *Representative Plays by American Dramatists* (New York, 1918), I; and John Murdock, *The Politicians; or, A State of Things,* performed in 1795 (copy in the Brown University Library). See Arthur Hobson Quinn, *A History of the American Drama From the Beginning to the Civil War* (New York and London, 1923), 124, 131–32, 332–33.

⁶ Damon, "Early American Songsters," 134–35.

⁷ *Ibid.,* 133, and Lillian A. H. [Hall], "Some Early Black-Face Performers and the First Minstrel Troupe," *Harvard Library Notes* (October, 1920).

⁸ Damon, "Early American Songsters," 133. It is frequently stated that Gottlieb Graupner gave a blackface performance in Boston in 1799, but this has been disproved by Hall, "Some Early Black-face Performers," and by H. Earle Johnson, *Musical Interludes in Boston* (New York, 1943), 176–77.

⁹ The text of "The Guinea Boy" (dated 1814) was published for the first time

the Negro English of the West Indies, and it seems unlikely that it was acted out on an American stage. The second song however, called "The Siege of Plattsburgh" and later named "Backside Albany," was performed in Albany in 1815 within the play *The Battle of Lake Champlain*.[10] The comedian was a "Black Sailor" espousing the American cause. Here, for the first time, the Negro spoke no longer as a mouthpiece of the white man. The subsequent popularity of the song could not have been due to the tune—the Irish "Boyne Water"[11]—which had been well known before; it was no doubt in response to the topical character of the scene and to the indigenous flavor of its dialect (see Musical Example 6). Recognizing the humorous possibilities of a contrast between martial appearance and illiterate speech, Micah Hawkins, the author of the text, created a similar figure nine years later—a soldier in full dress and with drawn sword (see Illustration 7).

The song entitled "Massa Georgee Washington and General La Fayette"[12] was presented by the actor James Roberts at Chatham Gardens in New York in 1824 on the occasion of the Frenchman's arrival, no doubt inserted into a play. There was nothing unusual about the music, composed in a fairly nondescript style and slightly related to English stage Negro music of the late eighteenth century,

in the songster *The Star Spangled Banner* (Wilmington, 1816), and in the *Patriotic Songster* (Alexandria, 1816). In the former it was prefaced by this ironical comment: "The following song, composed by one of the 'brave black patriots,' who so nobly 'volunteered' their services, under the redoubtable admiral Cockburn, in the Chesapeake Bay last summer, is intended to be sung in character, with unbounded applause, at the opening of the Theatres Royal, Convent[!] Garden and Drury Lane." The initial lines of the song read: "When me leetle boy, den me cum from Guinea, / Buckra man teal me, bring me to Virgin-a." Its tune was that of "Negro and Buckra Man." See Damon, "Early American Songsters," 144–45.

[10] The text of "The Siege of Plattsburgh" was first published in the songster *Columbian Harmonist* (Albany, 1815). See Damon, "Early American Songsters," 143–44. Sol. Smith in *Theatrical Management in the West and South for Thirty Years* (New York, 1868), 138, called it ". . . the first negro song, I verily believe, ever heard on the American stage . . . ." The sheet music edition with the new title, "Backside Albany," was published by Thomas Birch (New York, 1837).

[11] See the *Columbian Harmonist*. See also P. W. Joyce, *Old Irish Folk Music and Songs* (Dublin, 1909).

[12] "Massa Georgee Washington and General La Fayette as Sung in Character by Mr. Roberts . . . at the Theatre Chatham Gardens. Written & Composed by Micah Hawkins" (New York, E. Riley, 1824). See Odell, *Annals*, III, 135.

Musical Example 6

"The Siege of Plattsburgh." Words from Micah Hawkins, *The Columbian Harmonist* (Albany, 1815); tune from the sheet music edition of "Backside Albany" (New York, Thomas Birch, 1837).

Negro Impersonations in the Early Republic

On 'lebenth day of Sep-tem-ber,
In eighteen hund'ed an fourteen,
Gubbener Probose, and he British soger,
Come to Plat-te-bug a tea party courtin;
An he boat come too
Arter Uncle Sam boat,
Massa 'Donough do look sharp out de winder—
Den Gen'ral M'Comb,
(Ah! he always a home,)
Catch fire too, jis like a tinder.

Bang! bang! bang! den de cannons gin t'roar
In Plat-de-bug, an all 'bout dat quarter;
Gubbener Probose try he hand 'pon de shore,
While he boat take he luck 'pon de water—
But Massa M'Donough
Knock he boat in he head,
Break he hart, broke he shin, 'tove he caffin in.
An Gen'ral M'Comb
Start ole Probose home—
Tot me soul den, I mus die a laffin.

Probose scare so, he lef all behine,
Powder, ball, cannon, tea-pot an kittle—
Some say he cotch a cole—trouble in he mine
Cause he eat so much raw an cole vittle—
Uncle Sam berry sorry,
To be sure, for he pain;
Wish he nuss heself up well an harty—
For Gen'ral M'Comb
An Massa 'Donough home,
When he notion for a nudder tea party.

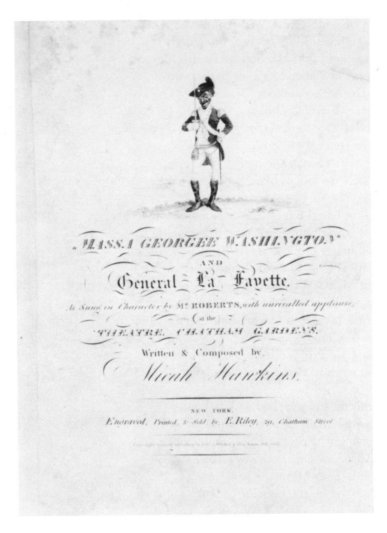

Illustration 7. A blackfaced soldier on the stage of the Theatre Chatham Gardens. From the cover of Micah Hawkins, "Massa Georgee Washington and General La Fayette" (New York, E. Riley, 1824); courtesy Lester S. Levy (Baltimore).

but the act itself went much farther than "The Siege of Plattsburgh"; its protagonist spread himself in a long scene by singing, speaking, laughing, cheering "heartily," dancing, and rattling off a historical

Illustration 8. "Massa Georgee Washington and General La Fayette."
Courtesy Lester S. Levy.

Spoken.

Massa GEORGEE WASHINGTON & General LA FAYETTE . (laughs) dare dey
stan' by an' hear all what Ole John Bull fretten Unkle Sam wid, when
Unkle Sam horn juss pickin' trough de skin. General! LA FAYETTE git
a Ship out he own pocket, an' 'rive from France in Charleton, in Ole
'76 Year, purpose to 'sist Massa GEORGEE WASHINGTON to tell Ole
John Bull—"No—you wont, dough,—nor you shant dough."

Oh! Mas-sa GEOR-GEE WASHINGTON, An' Gene-ral LA FAYETTE!

Mas-sa GEOR-GEE WASHINGTON, An' Gene-ral LA FAYETTE!

Gene-ral LA FAY, Gene-ral LA FAY, Gene-ral LA FAYETTE!

Mas-sa GEORGEE WASHINGTON, An' Gene-ral LA FAYETTE!

41

2d Verse

Unkle Sam, dough young, He fight on —
Stampt act paper He wont write on —
Sides He grow so dainty saucy,
He wont drink Tea — will lick Lassee!

Now de Battle
Make a rattle.
From Lexington
To Great York Town.
How de dust fly!
While de blood dye
Many Jacket.
All is racket —

Unkle Sam — Cool — nebber fret —
He go vent'ring on.

Yet, He some time
Hab a dumb time:
Feel He Heart crack, —
At He weak back.
Howsonebber.
Ebber! ebber!
Stan' an' slap him —
Stan' an' prop him!
Brave Massa GEORGEE WASHINGTON,
An' General LA FAYETTE!

Spoken.

Stan' an' slap him — stan' an' prop him — what! yes, dey did — Jump up, my little Chubby," dey say to Unkle Sam, when Unkle Sam knee knock an' Unkle Sam fall down most . Some time Unkle Sam Horn, bein' in de milk like, get a bruize an' sore; den Massa GEORGEE WASHINGTON an' General LA FAYETTE put Rag on Unkle Sam Horn, an' face Unkle Sam 'gain, When Unkle Sam crowd Ole John Bull, Mazinly!

At de Battle Brandywine, — September '77, General LA FAYETTE git Bullet trough he Leg — What a dat? At Valley Forge, May '78, a dam Quaker try to trap General LA FAYETTE — What a dat? de dam Quaker Perrit dont move quick 'nough for General LA FAYETTE — — Near Jeametown, 1780, dough Lord Cornwallis say, "de Boy General LA FAYETTE can't 'scape me" — an' notwidstandin' dat "de Boy General LA FAYETTE" hab he horse kill fore he own eye, Lord Cornwallis can't speak to "de Boy General LA FAYETTE," by a minute! No not by tree minnie! — (laughs)

42

Dam' ole Lord Cornwallis run arter de Boy General LA FAYETTE till he shake all he Corn off he Cob!

(Sings)

Ob' Massa GEORGEE WASHINGTON,
An' General LA FAYETTE!

3d Verse

Unkle Sam Horn bymeby grow out —
On de tip end — He flag flow 'Bout!
'Independant now's he station
'Mong de whole world Slavy Nation!
　　Since de fight done,
　　An' He right won.
　　What proud Yankey
　　Won't say, "Tanky —
　　"Tanky, Bless Pow'r,
　　"In de stress — Hour
　　"You sen' two men
　　"Who stan' true when
'Liberty He so hard set —
"So Headlong drove on."
　　Den, Bang! Slam! Gun,
　　Unkle Sam Son:
　　Drink! Sing! Waddle　(dancing)
　　Yankydoodle —
　　Ole Furjinnee
　　Nebber Tire! He!! (cheers heartily)
　　For de great Name, —
　　For de great Fame
Of Massa GEORGEE WASHINGTON,
　　An' General LA FAYETTE!

Spoken

As for Massa GEORGEE WASHINGTON — He gone to 'gotiate Unkle Sam business where Trumpet trouble not he ear, nor Cannon more a'sturb he peace; while General LA FAYETTE, — yes, he Laugh-a yet! still stay here to look at Unkle Sam flourishin' Gall an' Boy! (kneeling) An' oh! Long may day hab de Sarrafaxtion to shew deir gratitude — fire deir Futerjoy for General LA FAYETTE, dareby makin' good many Laugh-a yet!

(Sings)　Oh! Massa GEORGEE WASHINTON,
　　An' General LA FAYETTE!

account with many confusing details and in a broken English patterned after the speech of the American Negro (see Illustration 8).

The sentimental as well as the comic literary type of the Negro
had now been superseded by a figure that was rough and ready and
close to life. As soon as the memories of the war had faded, he appeared also as the rustic, plain and simple, without military insignia.
For example, Edwin Forrest lent his great talents to a personification
of Cuffee, a Kentucky Negro, opposite the black Miss Philisy, in the
play *The Tailor in Distress; or, A Yankee Trick*. Performing in Cincinnati in 1823, Forrest probably enlivened his act with singing and
dancing.[13] And one year later in Philadelphia, the English comedian
Charles Mathews presented the runaway slave Agamemnon in one of
his recitations called "All Well at Natchitoches," a parody of Americans and their mode of life.[14] This was a "Lecture," similar in style
to Dibdin's "Table Entertainments." Agamemnon was described as
"a fat unwieldy fellow," who, having been sold, "conceals himself
in the bottom of the well." An engraving shows him as an early "Jim
Crow" type: in ragged costume, with a grin on his face, dancing and
fiddling (see Illustration 9).

How a realistic concept of the Negro was growing in the twenties
is illustrated by Mathews' activities. In 1822 he came to America and
stayed for about one and one-half years. Observing life in the young
Republic with curiosity, mixed in British fashion with scepticism,
he was attracted by the Negroes. Feeling neither condescension nor
pity toward them, he was delighted with their natural humor, and
he incorporated some of his experiences into theatrical acts while
recording others merely in letters. What especially charmed him was
the Negroes' dialect. Enthusiastically he wrote from Philadelphia
in 1823: "I shall be rich in black fun. I have studied their broken
English carefully. It is pronounced the real thing, even by the Yan-
kees. It is a pity that I dare not touch upon a preacher. I know its

[13] An advertisement in the *Cincinnati Independent Press* (July 17, 1823), republished in Laurence Barrett, *Edwin Forrest* (Boston, 1881). An additional, though undocumented, description of the performance is in William R. Alger, *Life of Edwin
Forrest* (London and Philadelphia, 1877), I, 108–109.

[14] *The London Mathews containing an Account of this celebrated Comedian's
Trip to America* . . . . (Philadelphia, 1824).

Illustration 9. The runaway slave "Agamemnon" in the lecture "All Well at Natchitoches." From the account of Charles Mathews in *The London Mathews* (Philadelphia, 1824).

danger, but perhaps the absurdity might give a color to it—a *black* methodist! I have a specimen from life, which is relished highly in private."[15] The following then is a transcription of what Mathews heard in one of the "Black Brimstone Churches"—actually the very first stump speech, preceding others by about twenty years:

> My wordy bredren, it a no use to come to de meetum-house to ear de most hellygunt orashions if a no put a de cent into de plate; de spiritable man cannot get a on widout de temporarilities; twelve 'postles must hab de candle to burn. You dress a self up in de fine blue a cot, and a bandalore breechum, and tink a look like a gemman, but no more like a gemman dan put a finger in a de fire, and take him out again, widout you put a de money in a de plate. He lend a to de poor, lend to de Law (Lord), if you like a de secoority drop a de cents in to de box. My sister in a de gallery too dress em up wid de poke a de bonnet and de furbelow-tippet, and look in de glass and say, "Pretty Miss Phyllis, how bell I look!" But no pretty in de eye of de Law (Lord) widout a drop a cent in de plate. My friend and bredren, in my endeavor to save you, I come across de bay in the stim a boat. I never was more shock dan when I see de race a horse a rubbin down. No fear o' de Law a fore dere eye on de Sabbat a

[15] Mrs. Mathews, *Memoirs of Charles Mathews, Comedian* (London, 1839), III, 390.

day, ben I was tinking of de great enjawment my friend at a Baltimore was to have dis night, dey rub a down de horse for de use of de debbil. Twix you and I, no see what de white folk make so much fun of us, for when dey act so foolish demselve, dey tink dey know ebery ting, and dat we poor brack people know noting at all amose (almost). Den shew dem how much more dollars you can put in de plate dan de white meetum-houses. But, am sorry to say, some of you put three cent in a plate, and take out a quarter a dollar. What de say ven you go to hebben? Dey ask you what you do wid de twenty-two cent you take out of de plate when you put in de tree cent? what you go do den?[16]

Mathews was much impressed by the dark man's love of music, and he eagerly collected "scraps of songs and malaprops."[17] One day he saw, to his amazement, a Negro "driving a stage-coach . . . and urging his horses by different tunes on a fiddle, while he ingeniously fastened the reins round his neck."[18] While in New York, he did not fail to visit the Negroes' own theater and witness a performance of *Hamlet*. His reward was a most unusual rendition of the famous monologue: "To be or not to be, dat is him question, whether him nobler in de mind to suffer or lift up him arms against one sea of hubble bubble and by opossum (oppose'em) end'em."[19] At this point the speaker was interrupted by the audience which, having been reminded of their favorite song, "Opossum up a Gum-tree," clamored for it vociferously. Hamlet complied. Mathews tried later to reconstruct what he had heard. But he did not remember it accurately, because the three transcriptions he made are not identical.[20] He performed the song himself in his lecture "A Trip to America," given in Philadelphia and later in England, where he published it

[16] *Ibid.*, 390–92.

[17] *Ibid.*, 391.

[18] *Ibid.*, 384.

[19] *Sketches of Mr. Mathews' Celebrated Trip to America . . . .* (London, n.d.). A slightly different version is in *The London Mathews*.

[20] The three transcriptions appear in *Sketches*, in *The London Mathews*, and in the sheet music edition of the song. Fragments of the text of the song were used by American minstrels of the thirties and by white backwoodsmen, and are still preserved by the Negroes themselves. See Hans Nathan, "Charles Mathews, Comedian, and the American Negro," *Southern Folklore Quarterly* (September, 1946).

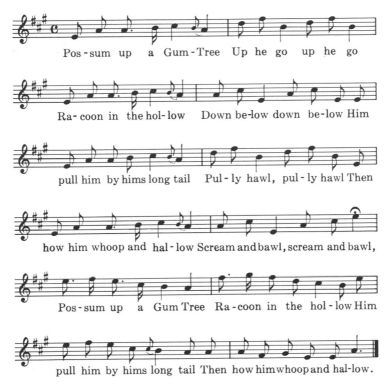

Pos - sum up a Gum - Tree Up he go up he go

Ra - coon in the hol - low Down be - low down be - low Him

pull him by hims long tail Pul - ly hawl, pul - ly hawl Then

how him whoop and hal - low Scream and bawl, scream and bawl,

Pos - sum up a Gum Tree Ra - coon in the hol - low Him

pull him by hims long tail Then how him whoop and hal - low.

Musical Example 7

"Possum up a Gum Tree." From the sheet music edition (London, J. Willis & Co., n. d. [c. 1824]).

with a piano accompaniment (see Musical Example 7).[21] In this edition the melody, in spite of conspicuous relations to British vocal music (see Musical Example 8), is called "A South Carolinian Negro Air." Such a designation did not necessarily mean that the slaves had created the melody, but merely that it was popular among them. We know indeed that about 1817 "The 'possum up the gum-tree,"

21 "A Trip to America" appears in both the Philadelphia and London editions of *The London Mathews*. "Possum up a Gum Tree: A South Carolinian Negro Air as sung by Mr. Mathews in his entertainment 'A Trip to America,' and Arranged Expressly for him by T. Philipps From the Original Negro Melody, of which this is the only correct copy extant" (London, J. Willis & Co., n.d. [c.1824]). There are four stanzas altogether in the sheet music; the second, third, and fourth stanzas, being completely different from the other two versions of the song, are undoubtedly by Mathews himself.

Musical Example 8

"The Lasses of Dublin [transposed]." From *The Edinburgh Musical Miscellany* (Edinburgh, 1793), II.

was in the repertoire of white Southern frontiersmen, who, as was usual, traded or shared it with the plantation.[22] Mathews' version of the tune may be taken as an approximation to an urban Negro variant of it. Thus it seems that he was the first white man to use on the American stage a song which, in a sense, belonged to the Negroes. This was a new realistic development in the history of blackface impersonation and its antecedents.

A broadside which fell into Mathews' hands was "Sold by the Flying Booksellers" on July 15, 1822, in the streets of Boston.[23] On

[22] James Kirke Paulding, *Letters from the South* (New York, 1817), II, as quoted in Floyd C. Watkins, "James Kirke Paulding's Early Ring-Tailed Roarer," *Southern Folklore Quarterly* (September, 1951): "The batteauxman fastened his boat to the stump of a tree . . . and began to sing that famous song of 'The 'possum up the gum-tree.'"

[23] "Grand & Splendid Bobalition of Slavery" (July 15, 1822) is now in the possession of the American Antiquarian Society, Worcester, Massachusetts. For an account of the proposed celebration, see the Boston newspaper *Columbian Centinel* (July 13, 1822). "The Africans and descendents of Africans, in this city and vicinity, will, on Monday next, celebrate the anniversary of the abolition of the Slave Trade. A sermon will be preached by the Rev. Dr. Harris.—Prayers by the Rev. Mr. Paul. A procession will be formed in Belknap Street, at 9 o'clock, A.M. and move through the principal streets to the African Church. After the religious services, the society will dine together."

48

that day the Negro population paraded through the city to celebrate the anniversary of the abolition of the slave trade. The sheet,
written in Negro dialect by the foes of equal rights, was a malicious
parody of the occasion. Though political in purpose, it is nevertheless of literary interest because it too represents an interpretation of
what seemed ludicrous about the Negro's speech and manner. On
the sheet were printed the toasts supposedly to be made by the crowd
at its banquet, with such additional remarks as "40 cheer—4 grin all
round de mout," "3 guess—5 sober look," "2 wink—7 sly look," and "6
laff"; with the titles of the songs, the lines of one quoted in full; and
with a long "Order of de Day" of "Cudjoe Crappo, Sheef Marshal."
The following is a typical passage from it:

> De day is one of dose great nashumnal hepox which will call fort de
> sensumbility and de heraw of good feelum of ebery son and daughter
> of Africa in dis world, and good many udder place beside, which you
> no find tell of in de jography, cause I spose Massa Morse what make
> um, dont know wedder deir any such place or not. De committee of
> derangement hab gib me full power to make de debiltry marshal
> mind what I say—else dey stand chance to get shin kick cause he no
> take de hint and act just like raw soger, who know nothing bout
> milintary dissumpleen.

All these lines, tunes, and theatrical skits are of slight import by
themselves, but they merged into a new and original form of American humor. And in just a few more years, its vitality was proven.[24]

[24] The new development began in the late twenties with the performance of "Coal
Black Rose" and "My Long-Tail Blue" by the comedian George Washington Dixon
(these two songs appear in facsimile in S. Foster Damon, *Series of Old American Songs*
[Providence, 1936]). In them he impersonated the two types of Negro that dominated
the theater for many years to come: the plantation hand and the dandy. Moreover,
when "Coal Black Rose" was presented as a duet between Sambo and Rose in 1830, the
latter was played by a man; see Damon, "Early American Songsters," 148. Thus the
so-called "wench" performances began to establish themselves as well. In England, too,
the interest in Negro satire increased. See, for example, "Life in Philadelphia" (London,
*c.*1827), one of a series of illustrations by Charles Hunt which appears in Marian Hannah Winter, "Juba and American Minstrelsy," *Chronicles of the American Dance,* ed.
Paul Magriel (New York, 1948).

Chapter 4

INDIGENOUS NEGRO MINSTREL

TYPES (1820–1840)

Aᴍᴇʀɪᴄᴀɴ ᴀᴜᴅɪᴇɴᴄᴇs ᴏꜰ ᴛʜᴇ ᴇᴀʀʟʏ ɴɪɴᴇᴛᴇᴇɴᴛʜ ᴄᴇɴᴛᴜʀʏ demanded variety on the stage. They expected to see several plays and several kinds of plays during one evening: tragedies alternating with farces, and vocal and choreographic entr'actes in solo and ensemble style, fitted to the comical or sentimental tunes of the day. The dances were either of the formal ballet type or of such folk types as jigs, highland flings, and hornpipes.[1] It was in the entr'actes on the urban stage as well as in the sawdust ring of the circus that the white comedian with blackened face was able to display his talents.

In the late twenties and early thirties, two main types of Negro impersonation crystallized and thereafter persisted for several decades. One was patterned after the southern plantation hand: uncouth, ragged, and jolly; the other was a ludicrous black replica of the white dandy of Main Street or of New York's Broadway.

Among the plantation types was "Jim Crow," a role created and made famous by the actor Thomas D. Rice. His costume was picturesquely dilapidated, wrinkled all over, and ill-fitting; there were

---

[1] Marian Hannah Winter, "American Theatrical Dancing from 1750 to 1800," *The Musical Quarterly* (January, 1938). Lillian Moore, "John Durang—The First American Dancer," *Chronicles of the American Dance*, ed. Paul Magriel (New York, 1948).

Illustration 10. The Negro minstrel type "Jim Crow." From the cover of the song "Jim Crow" (New York, E. Riley, n.d. [thirties]).

large patches on his breeches and gaping holes in his shoes (see Illustration 10). A broad-brimmed hat perched rakishly on his woolly head; a grin illuminated his face. While singing the first four measures of his song, which are in a narrative melodic style (see Musical Example 29), Rice probably moved cautiously along the footlights. In the refrain, however, to clear-cut accentuations, he began to dance. How strained, sprawling, and distorted his posture was, and yet how nonchalant—how unusually grotesque with its numerous sharp angles, and yet how natural! That it has continued to appeal to the American temperament through the years is proved by the fact that, slightly varied, it has appeared in such fairly recent social dances as the Big Apple and in the performances of blues singers. Rice, according to his own words, wheeled, turned, and jumped. In windmill fashion, he rolled his body lazily from one side to the other, throwing his weight alternately on the heel of one foot and on the toes of the other.[2] Gradually, he must have turned away from his audience, and, on the words "jis so," jumped high up and back into his initial position. While doing all this, he rolled his left hand in a half-seductive, half-waggishly admonishing manner. Imaginative though he was, he was undoubtedly inspired by the real Negro. It is reported that he had borrowed the gestures and steps of his act as well as the tune and the words of its refrain from a colored groom in a stable in a midwestern town where he happened to have been on tour as the member of a theatrical company.[3]

Types like "Jim Crow" and the similar "Gumbo Chaff" (see Illustration 11) were not merely naïve, good-humored farmhands; to judge by their own narratives, they had about them something of the swagger of the real frontiersman and river boatman. Their models indeed were Mike Fink and David Crockett and a host of similar hardfisted fellows of lesser renown. The frontiersmen were colorful and lusty toughs, their Kentucky variety being "styled half man, half

[2] "Negro Minstrelsy—Ancient and Modern," *Putnam's Monthly* (January, 1855), tells of a young lady who, inspired by the song "Jim Crow" and its impersonator, acted out the part by "throwing her weight alternately upon the tendon Achilles of the one, and the toes of the other foot, her left hand resting upon her hip, her right . . . extended aloft, gyrating as the exigencies of the song required, and singing Jim Crow at the top of her voice."

[3] "Origin of Jim Crow," *Boston Transcript* (May 27, 1841). According to Robert P. Nevin, "Stephen C. Foster and Negro Minstrelsy," *The Atlantic Monthly* (November, 1867), Rice was indebted to a "negro-stage-driver, lolling lazily on the box of his vehicle . . . ."

Illustration 11. "Gombo Chaff," better known as "Gumbo Chaff," sailing on his flatboat to New Orleans. From the cover of the song "Gombo Chaff" (Baltimore, John Cole & Son, 1834).

53

horse, and half alligator, by the settlers on the Mississippi, and held accordingly in great respect and abhorrence."[4] As far as the white and black keel- and flatboatmen on the Ohio and Mississippi rivers were concerned, they were no different, and they actually were characterized in similar terms. "Saw for the first time," wrote a traveller on the Ohio River in 1819, "what are termed 'steam-boats,' 'snapping-turtles,' and 'half-horse half-alligators'—a formidable set of fellows, truly."[5] These men had to be endured like fearful events of nature, and the peaceful citizens were informed of their ominous and evil doings by such newspaper items as this one: "The bargemen who bring cotton down the river are a most dissolute set and are known by the significant name of Rowdies. This is their general term; but they are divided into classes, such as —Tuscalusa Roarers, Alabama Screamers, Cahawba Scrougers, and the like gentle names. These fellows, whose meat and drink is to fight, challenge each other by crowing like a cock, or neighing like an ass, from their respective boats; and when these odd sounds are heard loud at night, there is certainly a fair set-to in the morning . . . ."[6]

From men of this mettle sprang the fabulous hero of popular imagination—the "superman" of the early Republic. His adventures and his peculiar jargon went into books, almanacs, and stage characterizations, the "Jim Crows" and "Gumbo Chaffs" as a black variety among them.[7]

[4] Washington Irving, *A History of New York* (1809), Book VI, Chap. 3, as quoted in B. A. Botkin, *A Treasury of American Folklore*, (New York, 1944), 4.

[5] J. F. H. Claiborne, *Life and Correspondence of John A. Quitman* (New York, 1860), I, 42. See also Edmund Flagg, *The Far West* (1838), as republished in Reuben Gold Thwaites (ed.), *Early Western Travels* (Cleveland, 1906), XXVI, 91: "I viewed before me some lingering remnant of that 'horse and alligator race,' now . . . fast fading from the West . . . 'the Mississippi boatman.'"

[6] From a letter from Mobile, Ala., June 8, 1822, in the *Commercial Advertiser* (New York), republished in the *Columbian Centinel* (Boston, July 27, 1822). These early river boatmen had worthy descendants, the lumber raftsmen. According to Mark Twain, *Life on the Mississippi* (1883), Chap. 58, the lumber rafts were "manned with joyous and reckless crews of fiddling, song-singing, whisky-drinking, breakdown-dancing rapscallions."

[7] Many of the expressions in the quotation from minstrel songs that illustrate the "Jim Crow" type appeared literally in American popular adventure stories of the early nineteenth century. See Botkin, *American Folklore*, 2–57.

Indigenous Negro Minstrel Types (1820–40)

Boastful of his untamed force, the minstrel claimed to be of wild, nonhuman origin:

> My mamma was a wolf
> My daddy was a tiger,
> I am what you call
> De Ole Virginny Nigger
> Half fire half smoke
> A little touch of thunder
> I am what you call
> De eighth wonder.[8]

His home was "ole Werginy"[9] or a special region of it—"Tuckyhoe"[10] —or else the "Ohio bluff in de state of Indiana."[11] True to the Negro temperament, he was eager to "play pon de banjo string"[12] or to show himself "a roarer on de fiddle,"[13] but he was proud mainly of his brute strength. To tell of his dangerous exploits was to him a source of deep satisfaction:

> I wip my weight in wildcats
> I eat an Alligater
> And tear up more ground
> Dan kifer 50 load of tater.

> I sit upon a Hornet's nest
> I dance upon my head,
> I tie a Wiper round my neck
> and I goes [to] my bed.[14]

The following is a well-known variation of the above:

[8] "Ole Virginny Break Down" (Boston, 1841).
[9] "James Crow" (Baltimore, Sam. Carusi, 1832).
[10] "Jim Crow" (New York, Firth and Hall, n.d. [late twenties]).
[11] "Gumbo Chaff" (Baltimore, G. Willig, Jr., n.d. [thirties]).
[12] "Ole Virginny Break Down."
[13] "Jim Crow" (Firth and Hall).
[14] *Ibid.*

I wip de lion ob de west
I eat de Allegator;
I put more water in my mouf
Den boil ten load ob tator.

I sets uppon de bulls horn,
I hops uppon dis toe;
I tie de seasarp roun my neck,
An den I dance jis so.[15]

One day he would take off from his plantation and sail down the Mississippi River. Spoiling for a fight, he would have one as soon as he
arrived in New Orleans:

When I got pon de Levey
I let my pashun lose
An John de Arms [gendarme] put me
In de Callyboose.[16]

Once free, he quickly forgot his lesson. Though his manners were
crusty, his heart would soften at the sight of a pretty lady, and as a
rule he was a successful lover. Inspired by David Crockett, who was
a Congressman for a while, he had quite definite opinions on politics,
and he knew better than any one else how things should be run in
Washington:

When Jim Crow is president
Of dis Unitid State
Hed drink mint jewlips
An swing pon a gate.[17]

On occasion he expounded his views on the same or similar themes
in greater detail, as T. D. Rice did on the one hundred and second

15 "Jim Crow" (New York, Atwill's Music Saloon, n.d.), as republished in facsimile in Damon, *Old American Songs.*
16 "James Crow" (Carusi).
17 *Ibid.*

anniversary of George Washington's birthday. He then "discuss[ed] in lyric style [i.e. to the tune of "Jim Crow"] a variety of new subjects, among which: Trip in an Omnibus, Removal of the Deposits, Washington and the Heroes of the Revolution, John Bull and the Yankee Doodles, Trip to Harlem, Carolina in another Scrape."[18]

The other prominent type of early Negro character was the "broadway swell." His name was "Zip Coon" (see Illustration 12)—borrowed from the animal whose meat seemed delicious to the southern Negro—and later "Dandy Jim."[19] He wore ultramodish clothes, tightly fitting pantaloons, a lacy jabot, a silk hat, baubles dangling from his waistband, a *lorgnon* which he held up with an effeminate gesture, and occasionally a walking cane. His craving for luxury was not always quite as extreme as all this, but if there was one thing he could not do without, it was a blue coat with long swishing tails. In a comparatively sober vein he would say:

> Some have de mockazins and some haves none
> But he dat habs a pair of boots he tinks himself a man.
> Wid his big Brass butons and his long tail Blue
> Dem what whe call de dandies of de carolina crew.[20]

And then jubilantly he would exclaim:

> I've come to town to see you all,
> I ask you how d'ye do?
> I'll sing a song not very long,
> About my long tail blue.
> Oh! for the long tail blue.
> Oh! for the long tail blue.
> I'll sing a song not very long
> About my long tail blue.[21]

---

[18] Playbill of the American Theatre (Bowery, New York, February 22, 1834).

[19] "Zip Coon" and "Dandy Jim from Carolina" have been republished in facsimile in Damon, *Old American Songs*.

[20] "The Free Nigger As Sung By R. W. Pelham" (New York, 1841).

[21] "My Long Tail Blue" (New York, n.d. [thirties]), as republished in facsimile in Damon, *Old American Songs*.

Illustration 12. "Zip Coon," the black dandy. From the cover of the song "Zip Coon" (New York, Atwill's Music Saloon, 1834).

He had his locks delicately groomed, and for the one manly attraction that was missing he could at least offer a credible explanation:

> I sometimes wear mustashers
> But I loss em todder day
> For de glue was bad, de wind was high
> And so dey blowed away.[22]

Pretending to be a "larned skolar," he strutted along the footlights
of the stage with precious dignity, donning an affected smile and
singing with pompous deliberation. Completely taken in by himself,
he talked mainly of his elegant appearance and of his narcotic effects
on the ladies. When he touched on topics of the day, he usually did
so in a language similar to that of "Jim Crow."

As was the plantation type, "Zip Coon" and "Dandy Jim" were
close to reality. Merely compare them with the colored dandy in
Boston who was observed "lounging down the street. He was a sable
Count d'Orsay. His toilet was the most elaborately recherché you
can imagine. He seemed intensely and harmlessly happy in his coat
and waistcoat, of the finest possible materials; and the careful care-
lessness of the adjustment of the wool and hat was not readily to be
surpassed."[23]

In the late thirties and early forties, two new types of Negro impersonations developed from the older ones. One was the solo banjoist, the other the solo dancer. Whereas the acts of "Jim Crow" and
"Zip Coon" depended on an orchestral accompaniment (although
T. D. Rice did occasionally dance to the music of a single fiddler),
the banjoist was on his own, both singing his song and playing his
four-stringed instrument (see Illustration 13). It was not possible for
him to dance, and yet he did not remain entirely motionless. In true
Negro fashion he tapped out with one foot the regular beats of his
music. In the circus ring, a raised wooden board on which he stood
gave added resonance to his taps.[24]

[22] "Dandy Broadway Swell," *The Ethiopian Glee Book* (Boston, Elias Howe, 1849).
[23] Lady Emmeline Stuart Wortley, *Travels in the United States . . . During 1849–
1850* (New York, 1855), Chap. 12.
[24] See Chapter 13.

Illustration 13. A solo banjoist in the circus ring. From the cover of the minstrel song "Jenny Get Your Hoe Cake Done" (New York, 1840).

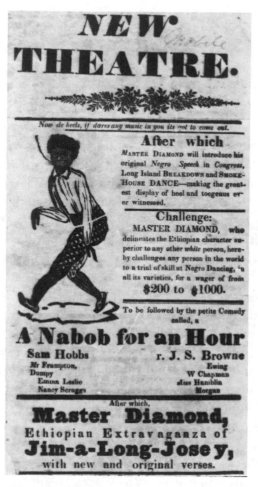

Illustration 14. John Diamond in a characteristic pose. From a playbill of the New Theatre (Mobile, February 24, 1841).

One of the best-known solo dancers was John Diamond (see Illustration 14). He prided himself on his "skill at negro dancing," publicly challenging "any other white person" (thus wisely excluding Juba, a famous colored dancer) for a wager of several hundred dollars to beat him.[25] In such dances of his as "Long Island Break-

[25] All quotations referring to Diamond are from a playbill of the New Theatre (Mobile, February 24, 1841).

61

down and Smoke House Dance" he relied mainly on brilliant foot-work. One of his typical movements was to slink across the stage, looking stiffly sideways, leaning his torso forward with his hands drooping like damp cloths, while treading the ground at once with the heel of one foot and the toe of the other. Thus while his body was relaxed, his feet were highly expressive, showing, in this dance and in others, "the greatest display of heel and toe genus [a favorite minstrel expression for genius] ever witnessed." True to the motto on his playbill: "Now de heels, if dares any music in you, its got to come out," he frequently pointed the back end of his feet sky- or earth-ward, thus burlesquing the protruding heel of the southern plantation Negro. He also danced and sang the Ethiopian extravaganza "Jim-a-Long-Josey with new and original verses" and delivered his "Negro speech in Congress." Of this extravaganza we have the illustration of another dancer, John Smith (see Illustration 15). The free declamatory rhythm of the first part of the song (see Musical Example 37) excluded motion.[26] But in the refrain, enlivened by a clearly phrased melody, Smith no doubt sang and danced at the same time. And while an excited fiddle version of the refrain was heard between the stanzas, he let himself go, lifting his heels high up, keeping his knees wide apart, and raising his hands over his head as a Negro would do in religious ecstasy.

From the beginning of the forties on, blackface comedians banded together. A favorite combination was that of a banjoist and a dancer. A famous duo was heralded thus: "Mr. Whitlock, the King of Banjo players, and the Emperor of Extravaganza Singers. Second night of the engagement of the little 'Wirginny Nigger,' only 12 years old [John Diamond], who can outdance the nation, and come some 'Heel and Toe Breakdowns,' that are a caution to all darkies, and no mistake!"[27] Whitlock played either a straight instrumental piece or else a tune to which he sang simultaneously. There seemed to have been complete co-ordination between him and his partner. Witness the

[26] "Jim Along Josey" (New York, 1840), as republished in facsimile in Damon, *Old American Songs.*

[27] Announcement of Vauxhall Gardens in the *Morning Herald* (New York, July 18, 1840).

Illustration 15. The dancer John N. Smith. From the cover of the minstrel song "Jim Along Josey" (New York, 1840).

Illustration 16. The banjoist Whitlock and his partner—either John or Frank Diamond. From the cover of *Whitlock's Collection of Ethiopian Melodies* (New York, 1846).

droll, froglike leaps of Diamond which are in response to the hard, exciting thumps of the banjoist. In duos of this kind there was a strong element of acrobatics in the display of precise teamwork and physical exertion (see Illustration 16).

Other duos were similar to vocal duets, accompanied either by the orchestra or the banjo. One which in its realism and its combination of an older and a younger performer was similar to the banjo-dance team was entitled "Massa is a Stingy Man." It was often presented by Dick Pelham and his brother Gilbert as Negro servants who enjoyed themselves in the absence of their master. They sang the two brief lines of the text alternately, reporting about massa's stinginess and from there going into nonsense rhymes about Uncle John and his peach cart, a dog in calico trousers, and sister Sal sitting on a tree and flinging corn at a bobtailed rooster.[28] The scene became still livelier in a dance after each stanza. Then to a syncopated fiddle version of the tune (see Musical Example 84), the two Pelhams indulged in hilariously angular steps and strenuous but imaginative twists of their bodies (see Illustration 17).

There existed also duos of parodistic character, their subject being love, with clear emphasis on its ludicrous aspects. In the "negro extravaganzical opera of *The Serenade*," Whitlock as "Sambo Squash," supported by his banjo, tried to gain the affection of his "Dear Fanny," who was played by a specialist in the impersonation of Negro wenches, Dan Gardner.[29] A similar scene, also a duet, was acted out to the song "Tell Me Josey Whar You Bin" (see Illustration 18). It burlesqued the artificiality of classical ballet and grand opera. Josey sang like a professional tenor, his hands yearningly stretched out and his feet firmly planted on the ground (for better tone production!). Before him was Dinah, the object of his passion, in the process of exhibiting her charms: as an amazon with spear and shield, she struck a ballet pose—a traditional arabesque.[30]

Negro extravaganzas *à deux* soon expanded into trios of various combinations: two banjoists and one dancer; one banjoist and two dancers; one fiddler and two dancers; one banjoist, a dancer, and a singer; and other combinations. All of them employed one boy performer.[31]

[28] "Massa Is a Stingy Man" (New York, 1841).
[29] See the program of Vauxhall Gardens in the *New York Herald* (September 21, 1840).
[30] "Tell Me Josey Whar You Bin" (Boston, 1840). A facsimile of another edition (Boston, Henry Prentiss, 1841) appears in Damon, *Old American Songs.*
[31] Announcement of Welch's Olympic Circus at the Park Theatre in the *New York Herald* (February 11, 1843): "Negro Doings By the most neat and active Hoyt, the sweet banjo playing boy Chestnut and the dingy John Diamond"; playbill of the Chatham Theatre (New York, January 27, 1843): "The Ethiopian dancers and the King of the Banjo players, Messrs. Frank Diamond, Pelham, and W. Whitlock in three Original Extravaganzas"; announcement of the Franklin Theatre in the *New York Herald* (November 26, 1842): "Messrs. R. W. Pelham, G. W. Pelham, and Mr. Backus, the great Paganinny, will sustain the Ethiopian Characters"; announcement of the New Arcadian Garden in the *New York Herald* (January 3, 1842): "Grand Ethiopian Trio, Master Diamond, Whitlock, and T. G. Booth."

Illustration 17. R. W. Pelham and his young brother Gilbert in their scene "Massa Is a Stingy Man." From the cover of the song "Massa Is a Stingy Man" (New York, 1841).

At last, barely preceding the minstrel band, it seems that as many as four minstrels performed together. The program of a circus in New York in January 1843 lists "Negro extravaganzas, songs, dances, and locomotive imitations by Whitlock, Diamond, [John] Daniels and Gardner."[32] Unless these minstrels appeared in succession only, we have here a "quartet" consisting of a banjoist and three dancers—a type of combination which might have easily developed from a trio.

In addition to "Ethiopian" scenes based on song, dance, and instrumental accompaniment, there existed also straight ensemble

[32] Announcement of a circus at the Amphitheatre in the *New York Herald* (January 19, 1843). To judge by an announcement of the Circus Welch and Mann in the *New York Herald* (June 20, 1842), there might have been even a team consisting of two dancers (John Smith and T. Coleman), a banjoist (W. Chestnut), and a fiddler (R. Hoffman). However, the simultaneous character of their acts remains uncertain.

Illustration 18. A minstrel love scene burlesquing grand opera and classical ballet, the lady being impersonated by a male actor. From the cover of
the minstrel song "Tell Me Josey Whar You Bin" (Boston, 1840).

dances. A Negro minstrel program of 1842 included an "Alligator
Reel," presented by the two young dancers Nathan and Juba; and
at the very end, three dancers joined in a "Great Trial Dance" (see
Chapter 5), a performance in which the dancers endeavored to
outdo each other.[33]

Extravaganzas—short skits with only a small number of blackface comedians who also sang and danced—were sometimes enlarged
and then called "Ethiopian Operas" or "Black Operas." Two well-
known plays of this kind, popular since the mid-thirties, were by
T. D. Rice: *Bone Squash* and *O Hush! or, The Virginny Cupids.*[34]

[33] A program (August 3, 1842), republished in *The New York Clipper* (June 13,
1874).
[34] Printed versions of *Bone Squash* and *O Hush! or, The Virginny Cupids* (New
York, 1856) were edited by Charles White; the author's name appeared only on early
playbills, but the printed versions probably deviate little from the originals. Of *Bone
Squash* this can be said with certainty: the names of its characters, the content of its
scenes, and the titles of its songs agree almost completely with the details of an extensive synopsis of the play as printed on a playbill of the American Theatre (Bowery,
New York, October 21, 1835). A similar synopsis of *Oh, Hush!* is not available, but the
names of its characters are identical with those mentioned on a playbill of the American
Theatre (Bowery, New York, September 17, 1833). The tunes in *Bone Squash* were
published in *Medley Overture to the Ethiopian Opera Bone Squash Diavolo Or Il Nig-
geretta,* arranged for the piano by Thos. Comer (Boston, Geo. P. Reed, 1842).

Neither play is distinguished in a literary sense, but as samples of a genre they have their place in the history of the popular American theatre. Their scenes are laid in New York: at a street corner, in a saloon, in a barbershop, and so forth. As far as their characters go, much is made of the contrast between the two types frequent in northern cities: the colored dandy and the colored workman, or, to say it in style, between "Nigga Gemmen and Common Niggas."[35]

In *Bone Squash* the colored dandy is represented by a swell called "Spruce Pink" who brandishes such an aristocratic weapon as a sword cane, and in *O Hush!* he becomes "Sambo Johnson," a "consumquencial darkey" who has made money in the lottery and therefore, so he figures, has acquired "edgemcation" (education). The colored workman, on the other hand, is represented by bootblacks, chimney sweeps, and whitewashers who know their station. The protagonist of the first play is the chimney sweep "Bone Squash," who wants to marry "Junietta Ducklegs," a refined soul who keeps a diary and is, of course, in love with another man. After having sold himself to the devil, here called "Sam Switchell, the Yankee devil," and being fitted out with an expensive suit of clothes, "Bone Squash" is ready for matrimony. The evil forces, however, claim him, and he has to make several narrow escapes, one in professional style, through the chimney. Finally he saves himself by ascending in a balloon—a sort of ascension to heaven by means of nineteenth-century technology.[36] *O Hush* is shorter than *Bone Squash*. Its characters as well as its main tune are borrowed from the early minstrel song "Coal Black Rose." Moreover, its plot spins out the story of the same song which tells of "Sambo's" visit to "Rose," "a fascinating wench," and of his angry surprise at detecting there his rival "Cuff."

These two plays are examples of a form which descended from the English ballad opera and thus contained spoken dialogue and a great deal of music to verses, crudely rhymed. The vocal numbers were always Negro minstrel songs or songs popular on the minstrel stage,

[35] These two terms are taken from a circus playbill (August 20, 21, 1840), which announces for the end of the show a "Black Opera . . . entitled *Nigga Gemmen and Common Niggas* or *Virginia Cupids*."

[36] This ending differs slightly from the one as outlined on the playbill (October 21, 1835).

68

performed as solos or divided among several actors and sung as duets, trios, or other ensemble numbers. As a rule, this type of play concluded with a refrain which was usually sung by everyone present on the stage. At times no more than a single tune served to enliven an entire scene. Between the stanzas and sometimes at their conclusion, a dance such as a "breakdown" or a "reel" would be interjected. Instrumental music was not neglected; it introduced a scene, accompanied a dance, or else announced and underlined a sudden and exciting event, such as the appearance of the devil. Climaxes in these plays always crystallized into an action which even the least sophisticated could understand. An example of the concreteness of such a scene is outlined by the following direction in Act II, Scene I of *Bone Squash:* "As Bone is making again for the door, enter all the niggers. The Devil seizes one part of Bone's coat tail; the niggers being divided, one half seizes the Devil's tail, and the other half, the tail of Bone. They struggle violently, when Bone's coat tears up the back. Bone escapes through the door in flat, leaving his coat tail behind. The niggers all tumble—the Devil makes after Bone, the niggers following. All exclaim: Go it, Bone!"[37]

[37] Another popular early play, but without music, was *The Virginia Mummy*, ed. C. White (New York, 1856). The only dark character in its cast, "Ginger Blue," was often impersonated by T. D. Rice.

Chapter 5

NEGRO MINSTREL DANCES

THE NEGRO MINSTREL WAS NEVER more spontaneous and refreshingly direct than in his dances—his characteristic capers, steps, and gestures. With utter disregard for the genteel tradition of the urban stage and to the delight of the populace, he transferred to his art the loud gaiety of a low social stratum.

A rich source for his choreographic imagination was the southern Negro. This source, expressing itself with unmistakable realism, was soon commented upon. For example, a pamphlet based on the authority of the well-known minstrel Charles White stated that what was called "Jig Dancing . . . had its origin among the slaves of the southern plantations . . . . It was original with them and has been copied by those who in the early days of minstrelsy made that a feature of their business . . . ."[1] We know indeed that minstrels like T. D. Rice[2]

---

[1] Ed. James, "The Jig and Clog Dancers of America," *Jig, Clog and Breakdown Dancing Made Easy* (New York, 1873). With the exception of the preface, the pamphlet is an almost literal copy of J. H. Clifford, *The Art of Jig and Clog Dancing Without a Master* (New York, 1864). It also includes portions of Wm. F. Bacon, *Complete Dancing Instructions for Light and Heavy, Genteel and Plantation Songs & Dances* (Boston, 1864). The word "jig" appeared in America, of course, first in connection with dances of the white; for example, in John Vance Cheney (ed.), *Travels of John Davis in the United States of America 1798 to 1802* (Boston, 1910), 150, we read the following in a description of a frontier dance: "Pat Hickory could tire him at a Virginia Jig."

[2] See Chapter 4.

and Bill Whitlock[3] did observe actual Negro dances, and that Juba, a most successful dancer and until about 1858 probably the only colored member of the profession,[4] relied on a native tradition which even extended to the free Negroes of the North. The "Long Island Negroes," in particular, were often mentioned as skilled dancers— and that as early as·the beginning of the nineteenth century.[5]

Some contemporary observers tried to evaluate minstrel dances by comparing them with their folkloristic models. The actress Fanny Kemble, who had lived on a Georgia plantation in the thirties, declared that "all the contortions, and springs, and flings, and kicks, and capers you have been beguiled into accepting as indicative of . . . [the Negro] are spurious, faint, feeble, impotent—in a word, pale Northern reproductions of that ineffable black conception."[6] A London critic in the forties, on the other hand, considered the dances of South Carolina Negroes which he had seen "poor shufflings compared to the pedal inspirations of Juba."[7] Both judgments were based on the mistaken premise that minstrel dances·were nothing but copies of the real thing.

Unlike the improvised, ecstatic dances of the slaves, minstrel dances were consciously worked out, for the stage demanded planned variety and it encouraged showmanship. The dancer was expected to excel in precision, speed, near-acrobatic flexibility, and endurance, and to stress jolliness and clownishness for their own sake.

[3] An article in *The New York Clipper* (April 13, 1878), based on the manuscript autobiography of Whitlock, stated: "Every night during his journey south, when he was not playing, he would quietly steal off to some negro hut to hear the darkeys sing and see them dance, taking with him a jug of whiskey to make them all the merrier . . . ."

[4] Winter, "Juba," 42, says that Juba "had supposedly learned much of his art from 'Uncle' Jim Lowe, a Negro jig and reel dancer of exceptional skill, whose performances were confined to saloons, dance halls, and similar locales outside the regular theatres." A minstrel troupe of four Negroes was referred to as a complete novelty in *The New York Clipper* (November 6, 1858): "A company of real 'cullud pussons' are giving concerts in New Hampshire . . . we do not see why the genuine article should not succeed. Perhaps this is but the starting point for a new era in Ethiopian entertainments. Who knows?"

[5] Washington Irving, *Salmagundi* (1807), Chap. 5.

[6] Frances Anne Kemble, *Journal of a Residence on a Georgian Plantation in 1838–1839* (New York, 1863), 96.

[7] *Winter, "Juba," 50.

71

Organization, virtuosity, and burlesque then were among the non-Negro elements of minstrel dances. Moreover, the white elements inherent in the slave dances themselves were occasionally reinforced on the minstrel stage by influences from the dances of the frontiersmen and river boatmen and from the British folk dance tradition which was alive in the popular American theater.[8] These non-Negro elements merely diversified and formalized the Negro character of minstrel dances. It was only natural that they eventually asserted themselves, leading, in consequence, after the middle of the century to a new, more urbanized style of dancing. It became then imperative to restrict movement to the legs and feet while the body preserved control and "an easy balance" (see Illustration 28).[9] Although more eccentric styles continued to flourish, this was the beginning of one aspect of modern tap dancing.

Various basic steps and gestures of minstrel dancing have been demonstrated in the preceding chapter. References to dances in minstrel songs will immediately yield new information.

> Trike de toe an heel—cut de pigeon wing,
> Scratch gravel, slap de foot—dat's just de ting.[10]

> Old Jo kickin up behind an befoa,
> An de young gall kicken up behind ole Jo.[11]

---

[8] See the passage, undoubtedly based on observation, in the minstrel song "Jumbo Jum" (Boston, 1840): "When the days work is done they take hold of a fiddle / They ballance to their partner and chassy down the middle." To William Howard Russell, *My Diary North and South* (Boston, 1863), Chap. 32, a Negro dance on a Mississippi plantation appeared like "a kind of Irish jig . . . ." D. E. Huger Smith, "A Plantation Boyhood," as quoted in Herbert Ravenel Sass, *A Carolina Rice Plantation of the Fifties* (New York, 1936), 76, equally judged plantation dances in Carolina to be "nought but jigs." Charles Read Baskervill, *The Elizabethan Jig* (Chicago, 1929), 361, wrote: "It is highly probable that these dances [English step-dances of the nineteenth century] kept the characteristic features of the old jig dance and that the same is true of the breakdowns, cakewalks, and other dances current formerly among the American Negroes."

[9] Clifford, *Jig and Clog Dancing*, 3.

[10] "Sich a Gitting Up Stairs" (Baltimore, n.d. [thirties]).

[11] "Old Joe Composed and Sung by . . . F. M. Brower" (Boston, 1844).

Boe your shin, crack your toe
On de head de woolly grow[12]

An tink it is but right dat you should know,
De cut an de spin ob Jim along Joe.

. . . .

He can so cum de toe point heel brush fling
An like a riglar roarin hi win [high wind] sing.[13]

It seems that among the most characteristic movements in early minstrel dances was vigorous leg and foot work, particularly the strike with toe and heel. Sometimes the ground was slapped or brushed; at other times it was kicked hard, no doubt from the hip. In steps of this kind, the hind part of the foot was exhibited as much as possible. John Diamond paraded what he called the music in his heels (see Chapter 4), and the same point was stressed in these lines of a minstrel song:

De ambition that dis nigger feels
Is showing de science of his heels.[14]

Feet and legs moved around and about with astonishing rapidity. "How could he tie his legs into such knots," exclaimed a London observer about Juba's performance at Vauxhall Gardens (see Illustration 19), "and fling them about so recklessly, or make his feet twinkle until you lose sight of them altogether in his energy."[15] A similar description was given by Charles Dickens when in 1842 he visited a dance hall in New York's low-class section, the Five Points, and watched a Negro dancer who was supposed to have been Juba himself: "Single shuffle, double shuffle, cut and cross-cut: snapping his

---

[12] "Juber," *The Ethiopian Serenaders Own Song Book* (New York, n.d. [forties]).
[13] "Jim Along Josey" (London, Duncombe, n.d. [forties or fifties]).
[14] "Jim Along Josey" (New York, 1840).
[15] *The Illustrated London News* (August 5, 1848); an article in the issue of August 12, 1848, stated that the "bones and boots of Pell and Juba are still in full action; it is difficult to say which movements are the most rapid." A writer in *The New York Clipper* (June 13, 1874) said that Juba's style was "novel and his execution distinguished for rapidity and precision of time."

Illustration 19. Juba in rapid motion on the stage of Vauxhall Gardens, London. From *The Illustrated London News* (August 5, 1848).

fingers, rolling his eyes, turning in his knees, presenting the backs of his legs in front, spinning about on his toes and heels like nothing but the man's fingers on the tambourine; dancing with two left legs, two right legs, two wooden legs, two wire legs, two spring legs—all sorts of legs and no legs—what is this to him?"[16]

When the feet came down on the ground, they created sound patterns, which were thus a part of the dance. Juba, for one, aroused admiration for what was called "The manner in which he beats time with his feet . . ."[17] and a minstrel song reads:

[16] Charles Dickens, *American Notes*, (London, 1907), Chap. 6. *The Illustrated London News* (August 5, 1848), in an account of Juba said: "The great Boz immortalized him . . . ."
[17] Winter, "Juba," 50.

Don't you hear de banjo ringin,
An de niggers sweetly singing,
And dat niggers heels a drummin,
Now de fancy step he's comin.[18]

Percussive rhythms were emphasized from the early forties on, when clogs began to be used occasionally.[19] The taps were heard as an accompaniment to the dance, and sometimes appeared as inserts as well. For example, in a minstrel song of the forties, "heel solos" briefly interrupted the music, thus at once varying the motion and furnishing a literal illustration of the question of the text: "Who dar knocking at the door?"[20]

The body of the dancer was always bent and twisted and his legs were wide apart. In the early fifties we find a variant of this gesture: with the pelvis drawn in and the torso leaning forward precariously, the dancer added to the eccentricity of his act by stiffening his right leg and extending his left arm with a beckoning gesture of his hand which corresponded to the naughty one of his partner (see Illustration 20).

Arms and hands formed a most expressive part of the dancer's performance. According to its character, they were intense or relaxed, held over the head or extended in front, with the fingers usually spread wide apart (see Illustration 21). When the forearms were held out in front, the hands were droopy (see Illustration 22). T. D. Rice was especially inventive in such nonchalant gestures (see Illustration 23).

David Reed, a dancer known after the middle of the century, varied an early gesture "by placing his elbows near his hips and extending the rest of his arms at right angles to his body, with the palms of his hands down . . . ." He is reported to have learned this

---

[18] J. Kierman, "Forty Hosses in de Stable," *The Ethiopian Serenaders Own Song Book* (New York, n.d. [forties]).

[19] "Amusement Annals," *The New York Clipper* (July 14, 1877).

[20] "Stop Dat Knocking" in Gumbo Chaff [Elias Howe], *The Ethiopian Glee Book* (Boston, 1849).

Illustration 20. The minstrel dancer added to the eccentricity of his act by stiffening his right leg and extending his left arm with a beckoning gesture of his hand which corresponded to the naughty one of his partner. From a playbill of the Buckley's Serenaders (New York, December 16, 1853).

trick "from the negroes when he used to dance on the steamboat 'The Banjo' on the Mississippi River."[21]

The various gestures and postures were often meaningfully co-ordinated. In one movement (see Illustration 24) the dancer's left hand and knee and his right hand held across his head created a grotesque sidewise motion which counteracted the stressed frontal aspect of his body. Note that here too the elbow, though pulled in a little, was pressed against the hip. In a variant (see Illustration 25) the straight right arm with its intensely pointing finger and the stren-uously bent left arm complemented each other. As a consequence the motion of the right arm was led back and onward through the curve to the broad-brimmed hat and the head of the dancer, which was lowered between hunched shoulders. The hat figured also in another scene, again convincingly integrated into the stance of the performer (see Illustration 26). It served to lift his body and to

[21] From a newspaper clipping, "Negro Minstrels and their Dances" (August 11, 1895, Harvard Theatre Collection and the New York Public Library).

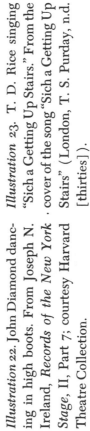

Illustration 21. Master John Diamond; courtesy of the Harvard Theatre Collection.

Illustration 22. John Diamond dancing in high boots. From Joseph N. Ireland, *Records of the New York Stage*, II, Part 7; courtesy Harvard Theatre Collection.

Illustration 23. T. D. Rice singing "Sich a Getting Up Stairs." From the cover of the song "Sich a Getting Up Stairs" (London, T. S. Purday, n.d. [thirties]).

Illustration 24. A characteristic movement of the minstrel dancer. From a playbill of the Huntley's Minstrels (possibly the early sixties).

Illustration 25. Another characteristic movement of the minstrel dancer. From the cover of the song "Jumbo Jum" (Boston, 1840).

Illustration 26. The hat figured prominently in the minstrel dance. From *The Jim Crow Song Book* (Ithica [*sic*], 1847).

Illustration 27. The twist of the torso and the finely balanced weight of the arms and hands gave the minstrel dance its fluency. From the cover of the song "Ginger Blue" (New York, 1841).

Illustration 28. The restrained posture of the dancer as it appeared in some dances from the sixties on. From the cover of the song "Sally Come Up" (Boston, 1863).

add to his already exaggerated ceremoniousness. In an even more intriguing pattern, the widely spread legs and the upward bent feet of the dancer suggested muscle-bound effort, but the twist of the torso and the finely balanced weight of the arms and hands resolved this into fluency (see Illustration 27).

In the sixties, when in some dances "gesticulating movements" of the arms were to be avoided,[22] we observe how elegantly the dancer could match with his hands the easy motion of his legs and feet (see Illustration 28).

[22] Clifford, *Jig and Clog Dancing*, 3.

While the dancer was in action, he often sang or made some kind of pungent exclamations (see Chapter 9). Juba was very successful in synchronizing rapid vocalization with a rapid tempo as Negroes did at corn-shuckings.[23] Laughter and chuckles also punctuated his performance.[24] Everything about a dancer was in motion, even his eyes:

> Oh! it made me dance, it made me tremble,
> I golly it made my eye-balls jingle[25]

Aside from various details, what was typically Negrolike about dances of minstrels was the intensity which animated the dancers' faces and bodies. An eighteenth-century observer already noticed what appeared to him "most violent" about Negro dances in Virginia and he disapproved of it by calling them "so irregular and grotesque."[26] Soon, however, one learned how to interpret the tribal ecstasy which was so alien to European or Europeanized culture. Fanny Kemble, for example, found the slaves' complete lack of self-consciousness and their sultry concentration most impressive. She was fascinated by what "these people did with their bodies, and, above all, with their faces, the whites of their eyes, and the whites of their teeth, and certain outlines which . . . they bring into prominent and most ludicrous display," and by the "languishing elegance of some—the painstaking laboriousness of others . . . ."[27] And when we read about the "indescribable 'frills' of foot motion"[28] of a Negro dancer in our own time, we know that the vast physical energy of the race is far from being exhausted.

[23] Winter, "Juba," 50. "Negro Minstrelsy—Ancient and Modern," *Putnam's Monthly* (January, 1855), mentions Negroes at corn shuckings who are "pronouncing the words rapidly in a deep tone, and at the same time violently agitating the body in a perpendicular direction."

[24] Winter, "Juba," 48. Dickens, *American Notes,* speaks of Juba's "chuckle of a million of counterfeit Jim Crows . . . ." The minstrel Nelse Seymour was known for faithfully imitating "the manners, gestures and quaint looks, even the laugh of any colored individual"; *The New York Clipper* (May 1, 1875).

[25] Charles White, "Old Bob Ridley" (New York, 1855).

[26] *The Journal of Nicholas Creswell* (1774, republished New York, 1924), 19.

[27] Kemble, *Journal,* 96–97.

[28] Thomas W. Talley, *Negro Folk Rhymes* (New York, 1922), 259.

Illustration 29. Negro Methodists holding a meeting in Philadelphia. Watercolor by Pavel Petrovich Svinin (1812); courtesy The Metropolitan Museum of Art (New York).

At times slaves would indulge a "swaying motion of the hips."[29] Others, on a Mississippi plantation, did "a double shuffle in a thumping ecstasy, with loose elbows, pendulous paws, angulated knees, heads thrown back, and back arched inwards—a glazed eye, intense solemnity of mien."[30] And when religious emotion seized upon their minds, they would think nothing of throwing themselves into convulsions, or of wallowing on the ground and propelling themselves into the air (see Illustration 29). The old Negro at a church service who was observed jumping up as often as "eighty-nine times . . . with-

[29] Sass, *Carolina Rice Plantation,* 76.
[30] Russell, *My Diary,* Chap. 32.

out moving a muscle of his thin, parchment-like face, and without disturbing the meeting" was no unusual occurrence.[31] It is obvious that movements like these, frenzied as they were, were not in keeping with Anglo-Saxon decorum, but they nevertheless found their way into the outer world through the frontiersmen and, above all, through the Negro minstrels.[32]

While the Negroes often danced with ceremonial introversion, even if the occasion was not religious, they were also apt to show brighter moods, especially in the Northern cities. Dickens tells about "a lively young negro [presumably Juba], who is the wit of the assembly, and the greatest dancer known. He never leaves off making queer faces, and is the delight of all the rest, who grin from ear to ear incessantly."[33] It was this facial expression which was seen customarily in minstrel acts.

How much variety was possible in minstrel dances is shown in John Diamond's "Rattle Snake Jig." It consisted of as many as 120 different steps.[34] Juba's performance must have been breath-taking. Something of its whirlwind style animates a description of an English critic. "[Such] mobility of muscles," he exclaims, "such flexibility of joints, such boundings, such slidings, such gyrations, such toes and heelings, such backwardings and forwardings, such posturings, such firmness of foot, such elasticity of tendon, such mutation of movement, such vigor, such variety . . . such powers of endurance, such potency of pastern [ankle]." There was no effort; everything came with ease and "natural grace.[35]

An important step was the "double shuffle."

Oh! de long Island nigger
He good at de dance,—

[31] William E. Barton, *Old Plantation Hymns* (Boston, 1899), 41.

[32] After the Civil War, the plantation dances continued to exist in the cities. See the vivid description of dances of colored roustabouts and their girls in Cincinnati during the seventies in Lafcadio Hearn, *Levee Life* (1876), as quoted in Gilbert Chase, *America's Music* (New York, 1955), Chap. 21.

[33] Dickens, *American Notes*, Chap. 6.

[34] Playbill of the Ordway's Aeolians (Boston, January 2, 1852).

[35] Winter, "Juba," 50.

In de double shubble figger
He beat the man from France[36]

Your applause you wouldn't muffle,
Did you see our double shuffle
On de ole oak plank.[37]

The step also occurred in dances of Negroes and whites in the
South, and in those of the frontiersmen as well.[38] It was originally,
no doubt, some kind of repeated brush with the foot. Specific explanations of it exist only in later times and refer then only to the
shuffle. Moreover, they are not quite consistent. In a description of
a frontier dance in Tennessee in the thirties, shuffling was associated
with "knocking it off," which implies noisy foot work.[39] An explanation of 1864 gives the following instructions: "spring up with both
feet; strike with the ball of the left foot, and at the same time slide
the right foot forward and back without raising it from the floor.
Reverse."[40] This however, according to a source of 1874, was a variant of a "spring." Notating the shuffle musically in triplets, it advises
the dancer (if the wording is interpreted correctly) to brush the
floor slightly with the left (or the right) foot in a forward direction
and then backwards, with a final tap at the end.[41] A double shuffle

[36] "De Long Island Nigger," *Emma Snow Song Book* (New York, n.d. [c.1848]).
[37] "The Band of Niggers! From 'Ole Virginny State'" (Boston, 1844).
[38] The double shuffle is mentioned in W. T. Thompson, "Great Attraction," *Chronicles of Pineville* (Philadelphia, 1843); in Eugene V. Smalley, "Sugar Making in Louisiana," *Century Magazine* (November, 1887); in Augustus Baldwin Longstreet, "The
Dance" (1833), and *Georgia Scenes* (New York, 1840); and in Henry Howe, *Historical
Collections of Ohio* (Cincinnati, 1847), 274.
[39] *Sketches and Eccentricities of Col. David Crockett of West Tennessee* (New
York, 1833), 39; ". . . both began to shuffle. Soon the whole house was knocking
it off . . . ."
[40] Clifford, *Jig and Clog Dancing*, "8th Step—Shuffle."
[41] Henry Tucker, *Clog Dancing Made Easy* (New York, 1874), 2: Spring: "Leap
or spring up from both feet at once; coming down, strike the feet almost, but not quite
at the same time . . . . Shuffle: First draw two diagrams . . . on the floor similar to
these, viz.:
Left $1_{\vee}2$ foot   Right $1_{\vee}2$ foot
leaving the ends about three inches apart . . . . Place the heels on the angles of the
diagram and then with both feet 'tap,' first No. 1, then No. 2; making the sounds
nearly at the same time." In Eddie Russell, *The Art of Buck and Wing Dancing* (New
York, 1924), "shuffle" and "triple shuffle" are identical, but there is this extension:
the final tap of the foot at the bottom of each diagram.

might be the same motion done twice. When a traveler in the West reported of a "powerful toone" which "was done . . . in first rate double-shuffle style, with very curious extempore variations, and very alarming embellishments,"[42] he must have referred to a rhythmical pattern of triplets which continued throughout the music, and to the insertions of tones which it necessarily produced.

The "double trouble" may very well have been another name for the "double shuffle," or else it was a variant of it. In the following lines it remains obscure:

> Den go ahead wite fokes
> Dont be slow,
> Hop ober dubble trubble
> Jump Jim Crow.[43]

But it becomes more meaningful in a statement about a colored dancer by Washington Irving in 1807: "No long Island negro could shuffle you 'double trouble,' or 'hoe corn and dig potatoes' more scientifically."[44] This ties in with a description of a frontier dance so that it seems that "double trouble" involved some kind of furious digging motion with the foot similar to "scratching gravel." When the Negro banjoist at this dance, called out, "Now, weed korn, kiver taters, an' double shuffle," the following scene ensued: "They spin round—they set to—they heel and toe—they double-shuffle—they weed korn—they kiver taters—they whoop and stop." After this wild motion, one of the girls said: "Now Dick, . . . didn't I go my death?" Her partner confirmed her exertions and thus the Negro style of her dance by replying: "Yes, you did, Sal. You are the yallerest flower of the forest."[45]

In the "pigeon wing"[46] the dancer jumped up and kicked his legs together in mid-air—sometimes, more specifically, his heels or his ankles:

[42] Robert Carlton [Baynard Rush Hall], *The New Purchase or Seven and a Half Years in the Far West* (New York, 1843), I, Chap. 28.

[43] "James Crow" (Philadelphia, 1832).

[44] Irving, *Salmagundi*, Chap. 5.

[45] *Sketches and Eccentricities*, 40.

[46] Sir William A. Craigie and James R. Hulbert (eds.) *Dictionary of American English* (Chicago, 1938–44). Bacon, *Complete Dancing Instructions*, 2nd step. Tucker, *Clog Dancing*, 11th step.

An when I cut de pigeon wing,
I fan de ceilin wid my fling[47]

White folks, I'm a going to sing,
And dance a fancy pigeon wing;
I really feel first rate to-night,
I'll throw myself clar out of sight.[48]

I no mind a snuff what care I hab to feel
While I can sing and dance de breakdown nigger reel,
I cum de pigeon wing please Diana Moon,
Catch de fat Oppossum kick de sly Racoon[49]

At the beginning of the nineteenth century the "pigeon wing" was a fine point in eastern ballroom dancing, perhaps derived from the classical *entrechat*.[50] While the minstrels made an acrobatic fling out of it, it became in the outdoors, as executed by two Mississippi raftsmen, a wild ceremony accompanied by curses and yells—the overture to a bloody hand-to-hand fight. To Mark Twain's Negro Jim, whose liberty is in sight, it was the spontaneous expression of jubilance. "We's safe, Huck, we's safe!", he shouts, "Jump and crack yo' heels . . . ."[51] It might be mentioned here that in minstrel as well as in frontier dances, the heels were clicked together not only in mid-air but, at times, also on the ground.[52]

The "chicken flutter," to judge by its name, was either a jump with

[47] "Dandy Jim ob Caroline" (Boston, 1844).
[48] "Do Fare You Well Ladies," *The Negro Singer's Own Book* (Philadelphia and New York, n.d. [forties]).
[49] "Jim Along Josey" (London, Duncombe, n.d.).
[50] Irving, *Salmagundi*, Chaps. 1 and 5.
[51] Mark Twain, *Life on the Mississippi* (1883), Chap. 3; and *The Adventures of Huckleberry Finn* (1884), Chap. 16.
[52] Clifford, *Jig and Clog Dancing*, 14th step. Tucker, *Clog Dancing*, 4th step. J. F. H. Claiborne, "A Trip through the Piney Woods" (1841–42), as reprinted in *Publications of the Mississippi Historical Society*, Vol. IX: at a Mississippi frontier wedding, the dancers "commenced shuffling, cracking their heels together and cutting the pigeon wing."

wing motions of the arms or simply the popular name of the "pigeon wing." It appears in this context:

> De niggers dey come all around and kick up a debil of a splutter;
> Dey eat de coon and clar de ground to dance de chicken flutter[53]

And the Tennessee frontiersman David Crockett, when speaking of the dances in his country, mentioned with gusto "a regular sifter, cut-the-buckle, chicken-flutter set-to."[54]

Although T. D. Rice's act has been described before (see Chapter 4), one little detail may be added here. When Rice sang his refrain: "Weel about and turn about and do jis so," he made a full turn while resting on one of his heels. That he rested very heavily on it is confirmed in these lines:

> He twist round de ancle,
> And he flatten on de heel,
> And he makes a mighty hole—
> When his foot gib a wheel.[55]

The posture of the younger Pelham (see Illustration 17) is rare on the minstrel stage, but if it fits a description of a dance of frontiersmen in Georgia, it was practiced by white Southerners and possibly by the slaves as well. We are told that, to the sound of a Negro fiddler, "Bill Martin always set to his partner with the same step . . . . He brought his right foot close behind his left, and with it performed precisely the motion of the thumb in cracking that insect which Burns has immortalized; then moved his right back, threw his weight upon it, brought his left behind it, and cracked with that as before; and so on alternately."[56] This motion, in which the knees were clicked together, is reminiscent of the modern Charleston. Moreover, a pose

---

[53] "Uncle Gabriel" (New York, 1848).

[54] *An Account of Col. Crockett's Tour to the North and Down East in the year of our Lord 1834 . . . written by himself* (Philadelphia, 1835), 34.

[55] "De Long Island Nigger."

[56] Longstreet, "The Dance."

of the sixties may well be the variant of another phase of it (see Illustration 30).

New choreographic aspects are revealed in the following minstrel lines:

> I set down, didn't know what to do,
> He cruck his heels, den smack his shoe,
> Jumped on de carpet, cut de long J bow
> Den I gib him a quarter to go to de show[57]

> Here is the Jay Bird wing!
> And the back action spring[58]

> My fortune I shall surely make
> Wid some ob dem new steps you take.
> De two best steps you hab forgot—
> De "long-jay-bow" an' "turkey trot."[59]

> I'll be dere on de spot
> Wid "wing" and "turkey trott"[60]

> Walk Jaw Bone wid your turkey too
> Nebber mind dat bugerbu[61]

> Dey all got drunk, but me alone
> I make ole Tucker walk jaw-bone[62]

> An when old master goes from home,
> My missus make me walk jaw bone.[63]

[57] "New York Gals," *Emma Snow Song Book*.
[58] "Jumbo Jum" (Boston, 1840).
[59] D. D. Emmett, *Hard Times* (New York, 1874), performed in 1855.
[60] D. D. Emmett, *Mr. Per Coon* (MS, 1862).
[61] "De Ole Jaw Bone" (Boston, 1840).
[62] "Old Dan Tucker" (New York, 1843).
[63] "Walk Jawbone, Original Verses by Dan Emmitt," *The Negro Singer's Own Book* (Philadelphia and New York, n.d. [forties]).

Illustration 30. A dance step reminiscent of the Charleston. From thc cover of the song "Shew Fly" (Boston, 1869).

T. D. Rice, when dancing on the English stage, gave out the following comment:

This is the style of Alabama
What dey hab in Mobile,
And dis is Louisiana
Whar dey track upon de heel . . . .

Here's Virginia double trouble,
Where dey dance de corn chuck,
And here's de real scientific,
What dey hab in Kentuck . . . .

Here's the Long Island juba,
Or de hunck over dee,
And here's de Georgia step,
By de double rule of three . . . .

Here's de kneel in Carlton's daughter,
What dey hab in Indian,
And here's de ol Missisip
S[t]ep and fetch it if you can[64]

How "cutting the long J bow" was performed may be shown in Illustration 31. The dancer in the foreground—and particularly the one behind him on the left—slides his right leg forward on the ground and thus, with the foot at a sharp angle, forms a tilted "J." Let us add at this point that sliding steps, both forward and backward, were not uncommon on the popular stage.[65]

The "backaction spring" probably was what was called a "back

Illustration 31. The "long J bow" as performed by the second dancer from the left and the one in the foreground. From the cover of the song "Ole Virginny Break Down" (Boston, 1841).

---

[64] From an English broadside [probably thirties] featuring a woodcut of T. D. Rice and many stanzas of "Jim Crow" (Harvard Theatre Collection).
[65] Bacon, *Complete Dancing Instructions.* Clifford, *Jig and Clog Dancing,* 16th step.

hop" in the British jig of the eighteenth century.[66] If the "jaybird wing" was identical with a frontier dance of practically the same name, it was considered highly indecent for someone with skirts on. A story is told of a woman at a country frolic in Tennessee who asked "for her favorite tune of jaybird; but she was admonished that she had once been before the church for the same profanity, and was ordered to be seated."[67] As a milder alternative, the tune of Jim Crow was struck up by the colored banjoist, at the end of which "every woman in the house was on the floor [that is, sitting or crouching], being afraid of the consequence of the last line"—the jump.

There is equally sparse data available on "turkey trot" and "walking jawbone." If the "turkey trot" referred to the motion of that bird, it can be tied in with the lines from a song by Emmett:

Possum up a gum tree, sarcy, fat an dirty;
Come kiss me gals or I'll run like turky[68]

The latter image was also used by someone who described a cotillion of three white southern ladies. Their motion appeared to him like those "of a turkey-cock strutting, a sparrow hawk lighting, and a duck walking . . . ."[69] "Walking jawbone" must have been a very strenuous step. It is likely that it consisted of quick taps reminiscent of the rattle of the teeth of a jawbone when used as an instrument. "Tracking upon the heel" can be assumed to be identical with the "running forward on the heels" in a hornpipe as performed on the stage around the middle of the century.[70]

The "Juba" was a dance common among Negroes, especially among those in Georgia and the Carolinas.[71] It is still danced on the

---

[66] Baskervill, *Elizabethan Jig*, 361.

[67] *Sketches and Eccentricities*, 40. See also Dan Emmett's walk-around "High Daddy" (1863), Stanza 5: "The black man is a very curious thing, / His jay-bird heel can shuffle cut and wing."

[68] Dan D. Emmit, " 'Twill Nebber Do to Gib it up So" (Boston, 1843).

[69] Longstreet, "The Ball," *Georgia Scenes* (published separately in 1832).

[70] C. Durang, "Pas de Matelot. A Sailor Hornpipe—Old Style," *The Ball-Room Bijou* (Philadelphia, n.d. [fifties]).

[71] G. W. Cable, "Creole Slave Songs," *Century Magazine* (April, 1886).

Georgia Sea Islands.[72] Haitians believe it to be, rightly or wrongly, "one of the first African dances in the New World."[73] That its present style emphasizing vigorous foot and leg work is basically similar to that of the past is confirmed by these minstrel lines:

> Five thousand niggas dancing Juba to de Cymbal,
> Oh, dear Moses, how dar toe nails jingle.[74]

A traveler in the thirties said that someone having "his teeth, and his hands, and his feet all in motion . . ." looked to him like "a Negro dancing 'Juba.' "[75] Sometimes "pennies [were] screwed on the heels of . . . [the] boots" of the dancer in order to strengthen with sound the impetuousness of the performance.[76]

Of a Carolina Negro taking part in a dance, it is said that he took "three or four steps, and then down on one knee he fell. A pleading look, and up he bounced; then a few steps and down on the other knee he fell . . . ."[77] Thus the "kneel," which according to Rice belonged to Indiana, existed also on the southern plantation.

Any dance in Negro style was called a "breakdown," always a favorite with the white river boatmen. Ohio flatboatmen were observed as early as 1819 indulging in a "Virginia 'breakdown' " at a landing.[78] And Mark Twain gives us this picture of Mississippi keelboatmen: "Next they got out an old fiddle and one played, and another patted juba [juba was here merely a rhythmic pattern], and the rest turned themselves loose on a regular old-fashioned keelboat breakdown."[79] Rice mentions the "Louisiana Track Upon the Heel,"

---

[72] Lydia Parrish, *Slave Songs of the Georgia Sea Islands* (New York, 1942), 116, Plate No. 11.

[73] Harold Courlander, *Haiti Singing* (Chapel Hill, 1939), 160.

[74] "Rob Ridley," *Phil. Rice's Correct Method for the Banjo* (Boston, 1858), Stanza 3.

[75] William A. Carruthers, *The Kentuckian in New York* (New York, 1834), I, 113.

[76] Ralph Keeler, *Vagabond Adventures* (Boston, 1870), 101–102.

[77] Sass, *Carolina Rice Plantation*, 76.

[78] Claiborne, *Life of Quitman*, I, 42.

[79] Twain, *Life on the Mississippi*, Chap. 3. J. M. Field, "The Death of Mike Fink," *St. Louis Reveille* (October 21, 1844), as republished in Walter Blair and Franklin J. Meine, *Mike Fink* (New York, 1933), reports of the river boatmen's fondness of "river yarns, and boatman songs, and 'nigger break-downs,' interspersed with wrestling-matches, jumping, laugh, and yell, the can circulating freely . . . ."

the "Virginia Double Trouble," the "Long Island Juba," the "Georgia Step," the "Indiana Kneel," the "Ol Missisip," and the styles of Alabama and Kentucky. To these names we can add the following: "Virginny (or Ole Virginny) Breakdown," "Louisiana Toe-and-Heel," "Alabama Kick-Up," "Long Island Troubles," "Tennessee Double-Shuffle," "Dandy Nigger Flourishes," "Heel and Toe Tormentos," "Grape Vine Twist," "Grand Congo Dance," "Alligator Reel," "Nebraska Reel," "Breakdown Nigger Reel," "Camptown Hornpipe," "Breakdown Hornpipe," "Negro Camptown Hornpipe," "Rattle Snake Jig," "Smoke House Dance," and "Five Miles out of Town."[80] Some of these are fancy titles; others may refer to local variants and to dances of which we have no information. All of them, however, can be assumed to contain some of the steps and gestures which have been described above.

Motion in minstrel dances was usually rapid. However, there were also slow steps of distinct character,[81] which means that the modern differentiation between foxtrot (or something similar to it) and blues, at least in principle, existed about one hundred years ago. To the slow or moderately slow movements belongs no doubt the one in which the dancer treads the ground, walking at once on the toe of one foot and the heel of the other. Another one, we are informed, included "the saltatorial efforts of genuine old negroes of both sexes," which Frank Brower is said to have introduced.[82] Dances featuring such jumps and leaps were called "essences" from about the fifties on, of which the "Essence of Old Virginny," frequently accompanied by Emmett's tune "Root, Hog or Die," is the best known example (see Illustration 32).[83] Dan Bryant's famous rendition must have been highly realistic, for the press referred to it as "a dance

[80] The names are from American playbills and songsters, as well as from an article on Juba in *The Illustrated London News* (August 5, 1848).

[81] Winter, "Juba," 47, publishes a contemporary report on the dancer Diamond that says: "he executed in an extremely neat and slow fashion"; on page 52 of the same work an account of Juba reads: "he dances demisemi, semi, and quavers, as well as the slower steps."

[82] "Negro Minstrels and Their Dances." *Ryan's Mammoth Collection* (Boston, 1883) includes four "essences," two of which are slow. The "quintessences" mentioned are dances "done in rather fast time."

[83] See "Root, Hog or Die" in the Bibliography of Emmett's Works.

Illustration 32. One phase of the "Essence of Old Virginny," presented by Dan Bryant. From a playbill of the Bryant's Minstrels (New York, October 1, 1860).

characteristic of the rude and untutored black of the old plantation."[84] In "essences" the dancer sometimes held his "palms . . . at right angles with the wrists, while the arms were extended in a sort of pushing gesture . . . ." but this was apparently at a later time.[85]

Mixing realism with parody, the minstrels were inspired by anyone, black or white, who looked unusual and thus could easily be made to appear ludicrous. When Alpine singers traveled through America, it was they who were burlesqued.[86] When public interest was drawn to the religious sect of the Shakers and to their strange costumes and dances, it was they who proved irresistible.[87] How the

[84] *The New York Clipper* (May 22, 1858). See also "Negro Minstrels and Their Dances."

[85] Charles R. Sherlock, "From Breakdown to Rag-Time," *The Cosmopolitan* (October, 1901).

[86] Hans Nathan, "The Tyrolese Family Rainer, and the Vogue of Singing Mountain-Troupes in Europe and America," *The Musical Quarterly* (January, 1946).

[87] Edward D. Andrews, *The Gift to be Simple* (New York, 1940), 158, reprints a playbill of the forties of a public performance of Shaker songs and dances on a New York stage. Performances of this kind also existed earlier. For example, a playbill of the American Theatre (New York, December 12, 1835), reads: "A Lebanon Shaker will make his 1st appearance before the public, late from that people, resident of New Lebanon . . . State of New York . . . member of their community for 15 years—he will exhibit the following peculiarities of the Society: 1. Circular March. 2. Square Order. 3. Shuffling Manner. 4. Square Order Step Manner. 5. Square Order Square. 6. Square Hollow Dance. 7. Round Shuffling Manner. 8. Circle Quick Step."

Illustration 33. An almost surrealist interpretation of a Shaker dance on the minstrel stage by C. Winter, painted perhaps before the middle of the century. Courtesy M. and M. Karolik Collection, Museum of Fine Arts (Boston).

minstrels interpreted their square-order dance is shown by Illustration 33.

In spite of strong Negro influence, the minstrels used various steps of the folk dances of the British Isles. These they had borrowed from the plantation itself, the frontier, and, above all, from theatrical tradition. At times, such dances would even be performed in white face. John Diamond, for example, danced thus the "firemen's hornpipe," an Irish jig, and the "naval hornpipe in the character of a Yankee sailor."[88] To judge by a famous hornpipe presented on the urban stage in the first half of the century, his version may have included steps which we have already met in minstrel dances, such as the "double shuffle," the "heel and toe," the "pigeon wing," and the "running forward on the heels."[89]

The display of physical skill on the minstrel stage led to competitive performances.[90] One such example of the early forties has been mentioned before (see Chapter 4). Another of the late fifties and early sixties is illustrated here (see Illustration 34). Dances of this kind became real sporting events, especially when presented in white face, and newspapers reported on them in an appropriate style, of which the following is a sample: "Charles M. Clarke, a professional jig dancer . . . had a contest on the evening of the 3rd inst. at Metropolitan Hall . . . for a silver cup valued at $12. Clarke did a straight jig with eighty-two steps and won the cup. Edwards broke down

Illustration 34. A "challenge dance" of the late fifties and early sixties. From a playbill of the Bryant's Minstrels (January 24, 1859).

[88] Announcement of Vauxhall Gardens in the *Morning Herald* (New York, July 29, 1840); a playbill of the New Theatre (Mobile, February 24, 1841).
[89] Durang, "Pas de Matelot."
[90] Winter, "Juba," 47.

after doing about sixty-five steps . . . ."[91] Announcements of dances sometimes read like this one: "Challenge for three hundred dollars! —Whereas some interlopers and boasters have, in order to get an engagement, bragged that they could beat any man in America in a Sailor's Hornpipe, I now challenge one or all of them to meet me in public, and dance a hornpipe for a sum of $100 to $300. Come braggers, down with your dust [lay down your money] or 'haul in your horns.' Henry Manning."[92] In 1861 a Union soldier in Virginia observed two "darkies" in his barracks, who interested him not only because, as he oddly put it, they "look exactly like our minstrels . . ." but because of their doings. "One tried to outdance the other; neither would 'gib up.' They danced until the perspiration ran from them."[93] It seems then that competitive dances, though not indigenous to the plantation, were known among southern Negroes, perhaps suggested by matches of frontiersmen, and no doubt encouraged by the urban stage.

[91] *The New York Clipper* (April 11, 1868).
[92] *Morning Herald* (New York, July 23, 1840).
[93] *Passages from the Life of Henry Warren Howe* (Lowell, Mass., 1899), 91.

Chapter 6

DAN EMMETT'S YOUTH

———◆———

I<small>T SEEMS THAT THE NAME</small> of Daniel Decatur Emmett, which was once on the lips of millions of Americans, is now forgotten. And yet many of the best-known songs, dances, and banjo tunes of the forties, fifties, and sixties—"Dixie" among them—came from his pen. He was a force in nineteenth-century Negro minstrelsy, entertaining urban and rural audiences as a banjoist, fiddler, singer, and comedian.

His contributions not only include music but lyrics, stump speeches, and plays. It is not that they are merely important in the history of the early American popular theatre and of early popular music. Their hard-bitten humor, their naïve freshness, and their native flavor lend them an intrinsic value. Like the oils and water colors of itinerant American painters, Emmett's is a folk art. It speaks only to those who, either out of naïveté or sophistication, are capable of delighting in something that is unpolished and of limited means, but sharply defined and direct.

Daniel's father, Abraham, was among the earliest settlers in Mount Vernon, Ohio, a hamlet northeast of Columbus. He had come from Staunton, Virginia, at the very foot of the Allegheny Mountains, allured by the promises of a new life in the wilderness beyond the Ohio River.[1] The trip from Virginia to Ohio was a venture by itself; it called for courage and endurance, for "it had to be made on pack-horses, through an unsettled region, without suitable roads or stopping places."[2] He arrived in Mount Vernon some time before 1812. Perhaps he came with his sister Rebecca, her husband, James Smith, and their child, who reached the hamlet in 1806.[3]

Abraham found Mount Vernon "a rough, ragged, hilly spot, with a thick growth of hazel and other bushes . . . ," inhabited by only a handful of people. Even "Main Street was full of stumps, log heaps and trees, and the road up the street was a poor crooked path winding round amongst the stumps and logs."[4] Dense forest was dangerously near and remained so for many years to come. By day and night wolves circled the log houses, and legions of squirrels often descended upon the crops. Hostile encounters with the Indians were not infrequent. But Mount Vernon soon ceased to be a desolate frontier outpost. In 1808 it was made the county seat, and new opportunities for trade opened up without delay (see Illustration 35).

Abraham was a blacksmith by trade.[5] In the beginning he no

---

[1] According to the Federal Census of St. Paul, Minnesota, which was taken on July 30, 1860, Abraham Emmett, then a resident of St. Paul, was seventy-two years old (information from the Minnesota Historical Society). He was therefore born in 1788. According to his son Daniel Decatur's statement of July 31, 1895 in *The Confederate Veteran* (Nashville, September, 1895), his birthplace was Staunton, Virginia. The various sources disagree on the spelling of his name; they list it as Emit, Emmitt, Emmet, and Emmett. According to Robert Sheerin, "Dixie and Its Author," *The Century Magazine* (October, 1895), Abraham's father was "an Irishman. He came to this country before the Revolutionary War, in which he served a regiment as surgeon and chaplain at the same time." Charles Burleigh Galbreath, *Daniel Decatur Emmet / Author of "Dixie"* (Columbus, 1904), 7, reports that he lived in "Augusta Co., Virginia . . . followed various vocations, including that of local Methodist preacher. He died at Utikah, Ohio. The stone at the head of his grave simply bears the inscription, Rev. John Emit . . . ." The records of the Court House in Staunton, Virginia, contain a few references to a John Emmitt, dated 1786 (when he bought land) and 1789. See additional, though undocumented, facts on "Emmett's Ancestry and Boyhood" in H. Ogden Wintermute, *Daniel Decatur Emmett* (Mount Vernon, Ohio, 1955), Chap. 1.

[2] N. N. Hill, *History of Knox County* (Mount Vernon, Ohio, 1881), 806.

[3] *Ibid.*

[4] A. Banning Norton, *A History of Knox County, Ohio* (Columbus, 1862), 31–32.

[5] Newspaper clipping (Chicago, January 24, 1880), as quoted in Charles C. Moreau (ed.), *Negro Minstrelsy in New York* (New York, 1891), II, Harvard Theatre Collection. Galbreath, *Daniel Decatur Emmett*, 7.

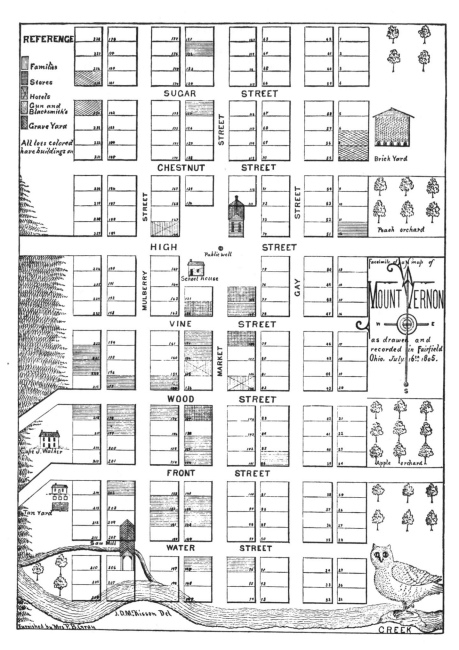

Illustration 35. An early map of Mount Vernon, Ohio. From N. N. Hill, *History of Knox County* (Mount Vernon, Ohio, 1881).

doubt worked for the local gunsmith, who in his "pole shantee . . . had a little pair of bellows in one corner, and tinkered gunlocks for the Indians."[6]

In early June, 1812, when the war with England called for fighting men, the local militia of Mount Vernon, consisting of forty-one men, volunteered for service, signing up for one year; Emmett, then twenty-four years old, was one of the privates. But the war proved short and bloodless for them. When their regiment arrived near Detroit in mid-August, they were informed that the American army under General Hull had surrendered. There remained nothing else for them to do but to proceed to the city and hand over their arms, whereupon the English allowed them to return home.[7]

Four years later, Abraham had become the captain of the militia, a promotion which testifies to his energy and his talent for organization.[8] That he was one of those fearless, roughhewn pioneers is shown by the following incident:

"The Indian chief, Armstrong, from Greentown, came frequently to town and often got drunk at Butler's tavern. On one occasion, while 'Abe' Emmett was drilling his company of militia, Armstrong got in his way and annoyed him very much. After telling the chief many times to keep out of his way without effect, Emmett finally knocked him down. This had the desired effect, but the chief never forgot it. Sometime after this, Armstrong, accompanied by three other Indians, met Emmett and Riverius Newell in the woods, when Armstrong asked 'Is your name Emmis?' 'Yes, sir, my name is Emmett!' 'What for you fight Indian?' said the chief. 'Because you kept getting in my way.' 'You fight Indian now?' said the chief, making a motion to draw his tomahawk. 'Yes!' said Emmett, with an oath, and immediately drew his tomahawk, while Newell cocked his gun and brought it to bear upon one of the other Indians. This determined attitude not being relished by the Indians, a truce was called and the parties separated."[9]

[6] Norton, *History of Knox County*, 60.

[7] *Ibid.*, 143, 145. Caleb Atwater, *A History of the State of Ohio* (Cincinnati, 1838), 189, 190, 193.

[8] Norton, *History of Knox County*, 213.

[9] Hill, *Knox County*, 356.

Early in 1817, Mount Vernon experienced what larger communities would call a revolution. No blood was shed, but the life of the village was shaken out of its customary routine. It happened this way. A well-off citizen, who owned a good deal of land, had it all fenced in with the result that passage for his neighbors and other commuters was made exceedingly difficult. Thereupon fifty-five Mount Vernoners—Emmett among them—banded together and handed a petition to the court asking "in order that we may have all obstructions removed out of Each of the Streets and alleys . . ." that "the whole of the . . . Premises may be Incorperated [*sic*] according to Law . . . ."[10] When the court rejected their plea, fifteen of the petitioners —and it is more than likely that Emmett had joined them—decided to take matters into their own hands. "Meeting on the public square, they faced west, locked arms, and started on their march to secure justice for themselves. As they came to an obstruction they began levelling the fences to the ground, scattering rails hither and thither with all the glee of schoolboys bent on mischief. From one obstruction to another the 'regulators' marched. A tornado could not have made more havoc in its route than did the 'laughing and shouting fifteen.' "[11] The rebellious citizens had finally to answer for their action, but the court merely fined each of them a nominal charge of "one dollar and cost."

One day the *Ohio Register*, a newspaper in Clinton near Mount Vernon, ran the following announcement: "Married—On Tuesday, January 22, 1815 by Joseph Walker, esq., Mr. Abraham Emmett to Miss Sally Zerick, both of Mount Vernon."[12] Abraham and his wife Sarah (see Illustration 36) settled at the corner of Mulberry and Front Streets, not far from the sawmill and the Owl Creek Stream.[13]

[10] *Ibid.*, 352.

[11] *Ibid.*, 353. According to Albert B. Williams, *Past and Present of Knox County, Ohio* (Indianapolis, 1912), 276, Abraham occupied in 1849 the position of a marshall in Mount Vernon.

[12] Hill, *Knox County*, 359. Daniel Decatur Emmett wrote in the *Confederate Veteran* (Nashville, September, 1895), "My mother Sarah Zerick [was a native] of Fredericktown, Md."

[13] Galbreath, *Daniel Decatur Emmett*, 7, mentions this address as the place where Dan was born later.

Illustration 36. An oil painting, reported to be Dan Emmett's mother, by an itinerant painter. Courtesy Mr. Ogden Wintermute (Mount Vernon, Ohio).

On October 29, 1815, a son was born to them and named Daniel Decatur.[14]

The sparse details of Dan's youth and adolescence can be told briefly. The little schoolhouse, which was open only three winter months during the year, offered him an education of the most rudimentary kind; it consisted of writing, reading, and ciphering.[15] He must have excelled in writing, for his manuscripts throughout his life show clear, well-rounded letters and notes, carefully drawn with a quill.[16] Later on he learned the trade of a printer, and it is hardly to be doubted that he served an apprenticeship with a newspaper in or near Mount Vernon. When he was about eighteen, he left the village.[17]

Dan recalled in his old age that "it was a fashion in those days [in Mount Vernon] among the young people to try their skill at making verses, and sing them to some popular tune."[18] "In this way," it is said, "he formed a taste for verse-making and singing . . . ."[19] Adapting new words to old tunes, especially on the occasion of presidential elections, was even then a time-honored custom; but there existed in Mount Vernon also an interest in poetry for its own sake. The man who, by way of a newspaper notice, threatened to retrieve a collection of poetry from a borrower "peaceably if I can, forcibly if I must"

[14] There are no primary sources to confirm this date, but Dan Emmett himself never contradicted it. Abraham and Sarah had three more children: Lafayette, born May 8, 1822; Derada Jane, birth date unknown; and Martha Ellen, born in 1834. See Galbreath, *Daniel Decatur Emmett*, 8; and the Federal Census, St. Paul.

[15] Hill, *Knox County*, 221.

[16] This practice was mentioned by William E. Hull, "D. D. Emmett," as published in Williams, *Past and Present*.

[17] The date is only approximate, but we know definitely that Dan was in Cincinnati in the spring of 1834. He was then eighteen years old, and his profession was that of a printer. In what is apparently a very late interview, Emmett himself remembered having been in Mount Vernon at least up to the age of fifteen or sixteen. See Galbreath, *Daniel Decatur Emmett*, 9. *The Daily Banner* (Mount Vernon, June 29, 1904), wrote: "His first work was in a printing office where he served an apprenticeship until his 18th year when he went out into the world as a jour printer." Galbreath, *Daniel Decatur Emmett*, 8, mentions the newspapers *Huron Reflector* (Norwalk, Ohio), and *The Western Aurora* (Mount Vernon), where Dan was supposed to have worked; but there is no additional evidence to corroborate these statements.

[18] Sheerin, "Dixie."

[19] *Ibid.*

[20] Norton, *History of Knox County*, 225.

was surely one of those whose enthusiasm for literature was genuine.[20] "In those early times," declares a local historian with solemnity, "there were many who courted the Muses . . . ."[21] Some poured their talents into rhymes which appeared in the press on the occasion of weddings, of which the following are two examples:

> There seems no goose so gray, but soon or late
> She finds some honest gander for her mate.

> What joys they both receive and both bestow,
> Virgins may guess but wives, experienced, know.[22]

Dan's early verses could not have been much different.

The music which Dan heard in his youth was typical of a remote frontier village: there were the slow, staid church hymns on Sundays, the lusty fifing and drumming of the militia, particularly on the Fourth of July, and, above all, the jolly, restless fiddler's tunes to which people danced "three or four handed reels, or square sets, and jigs."[23] It was these tunes which Dan played on his fiddle after he had learned this instrument, as he claimed later, all by himself.[24]

Most of the tunes which impressed themselves on the boy's mind were of Scottish, Irish, and English origin, with a sprinkling of early American Negro minstrel music.[25] They were characterized by small intervals, short-winded recurrent phrases, and an occasional pentatonic arrangement of the melody. This style was to guide the boy's musical thinking throughout his career.

While Dan was growing up, Mount Vernon expanded into a respectable little town. But its inhabitants were not much affected by this change in their environment. They remained frontiersmen, full of hard-driving vigor and boyish exuberance. As a pastime they

[21] *Ibid.*, 245.
[22] *Ibid.*, 231.
[23] Hill, *Knox County*, 220.
[24] Moreau, *Negro Minstrelry*. Sheerin, "Dixie."
[25] *Ibid.*

wrestled and fought, taking a few broken limbs in their stride if these resulted from the exercise. They gulped pure whiskey with the ease with which others sipped tea.[26] Impressed by physical skill, they decided to choose the one as a postmaster who could throw a coon's tail over a wire strung up high between the crowns of two trees.[27] An odd, colorful lot they were: stubbornly independent, pugnacious, and bigoted, but always ready for uproarious laughter. Dan Emmett, who lived among them, inherited their simplicity and directness and, above all, their tough humour.

Mount Vernon counted a highly unconventional, droll character among its citizens—Seeley Simpkins. Dan must have known him and been impressed by his antics, because he set him a "monument," many years later, by naming after him one of the tunes in his *Fife Instructor*.[28] This Simpkins was as grotesque as the Ohio wilderness itself: a musician, dancer, self-styled actor, and backwoodsman all at once. While others were content to ride on horseback, he proudly perched on the neck of a bull, taking "an airing around the town, whistling as he went." In the words of a pioneer history, he was "a great favorite with the squaws and pappoes, by reason of his uncommon musical talent. He could mimic any sound of varmint or human, surpassed the lute of Orpheus, and outwhistled all creation. He furnished *the* music for early musters, and when it took four counties to make a regiment, he gave a challenge to outwhistle any man within them . . . . He frequented race tracks, and drew crowds and supplied hoe-downs on demand."[29]

[26] Hill, *Knox County*, 211.
[27] *Ibid.*, 357.
[28] Another tune in the same publication is entitled "Owl Creek," named by Emmett after the stream in Mount Vernon.
[29] Norton, *History of Knox County*, 422–23.

Chapter 7

EMMETT'S CAREER IN THE THIRTIES

———◄❖►———

IN 1834 EMMETT WAS IN CINCINNATI, and, on May 2, he signed up for three years with the United States Army.[1] To the sober eyes of the enlistment officer he looked as follows: "eyes, gray; hair, dark; complexion, fair; height, 5 feet 8½ inches." His occupation was recorded as that of a "printer" and his age as "21 years," although he was actually only eighteen and not yet eligible for military services. We don't know what attracted him to army life, but it must have been the chances of a musical rather than a military career.

At Newport Barracks in Kentucky, where he was at first stationed,[2] his talents were soon given full play. "I practiced the drum incessantly under the tuition of the renowned John J. Clark (better known as 'Juba')," he reported later, "and made myself master of the 'Duty' and every known 'side beat' then in use."[3] "Duty" included all the

---

[1] Information from the War Department (Washington, D. C.). According to several reports, Emmett traveled with circus bands before entering the army. See Charles T. White, "Old Time Negro Minstrels," *The World* (New York, June 23, 1889); a newspaper clipping of January 24, 1880, in Moreau, *Negro Minstrelsy*, II; and Sheerin, "Dixie."

[2] See Emmett's Preface to "Emmett's Standard Drummer" in Galbreath, *Daniel Decatur Emmett,* 47–48. The records of the War Department do not mention Emmett's stay in Newport. See, however, the titles of the following tunes in Emmett's *Fife Instructor:* "No. 11, 'Newport'"; "Seely Simpkins, No. 19, Drum-major 'Juba Clark's' Army"; and "Here's To Our Friends, No. 20, Drum-major 'Juba Clark's' Army."

various drum beats which accompanied the activities of the infantry at camp: starting with "reveille" at six in the morning or earlier; proceeding to "pioneer's call" which was a summons to "fatigue parties" "to police the quarters, clean [the] parade ground . . ." and, if a fife was used in addition, "to drum disorderly women out of camp . . ."; and ending, after many exercises during the day, with "tattoo" at nine o'clock in the evening.[4] Emmett also practiced the fife. Throughout his life he preserved a sheet of paper on which a few tunes were scribbled and to which he had later added the remark, "Copied by my old fife instructor Sandie McGregor—at Newport Barracks Kentucky—in the year 1834. D.D.E."[5]

On March 3, 1835, he joined the Sixth United States Infantry, which was stationed at Jefferson Barracks, Missouri.[6] "I was retained as 'leading fifer' until discharged," he said of this period. "In the meantime I continued my drum practice, which was then taught according to the *School of Ashworth*."[7]

His stay in the army was to come to a sudden end. As soon as it was discovered that he was underage, he was discharged "by process of civil authority by reason of minority."[8] The day of his official release was July 8, 1835, but this time the army records listed him as "a musician."

Had his parents informed the army authorities of his true age? Had he run away from home?[9] These and many more questions concerning his career during the next four years remain unanswered for want of reliable documents. It is likely, however, that he now divided his time between his old and his new professions: working as a printer

[3] Galbreath, *Daniel Decatur Emmett,* 47–48.

[4] Emmett, "Camp Duty," *Fife Instructor,* 28–46.

[5] Manuscript in the State Library (Columbus, Ohio). A quickstep is called "Sandy McGregor's," in *Fife Instructor,* 59.

[6] Information from the War Department. Galbreath, *Daniel Decatur Emmett,* 47–48.

[7] *Ibid.* On the frontispiece of the *Fife Instructor,* Emmett calls himself "Late Principal Fifer, 6th Infantry U. S. Army."

[8] Information from the War Department.

[9] Moreau, *Negro Minstrelsy,* II. William D. Hall, "Does It Pay to be Famous," *The Lamp* (January, 1905). About Emmett's discharge from the army, Hall says, "He brought influence to bear that eventually led to his being released . . . ."

in Cincinnati in wintertime and traveling as a musician with circus companies in the summer.[10]

During the late thirties he turned up in Cincinnati as a member of a circus. One of his manuscripts verifies his being there: "This is the first negro song that I wrote—twas written in Cincinnatti [*sic*], Ohio, for Mr. Frank Whitaker (Equestrian and negro singer) about the year 1838 or 9. D. D. Emmett." Its title was "Bill Crowder."

Emmett forgot to indicate to which tune his words were sung, but it is easy to see that it was the one of "Gumbo Chaff," a minstrel song of the thirties, republished by him (with new words) as "De Wild Goose-Nation" in 1844.[11] That "Bill Crowder" was presented by a performer in blackface from the back of a horse, as we may assume it was, was nothing unusual in the circus at that time.

This first sample of Emmett's literary talents is by no means remarkable. Its language is crude rather than primitive, and its story conventional. However, the song is of biographical interest: it shows familiarity with stage Negro dialect, and it marks Emmett's awakening interest in Negro minstrelsy. The following is the complete text except for the final two stanzas:

I 'ribed at Cincinnati and I gits upon de landin
De first place I foun mysef was fotch up a standin,
I heard a great noise like a rassle jack brayin.
Tinks I to mysef dis is no place for stayin.

Den I cast my eyes aroun,
In de rection ob de soun.
Twas noting but a Jew sellin close by de poun.

He sez "Kum here Bill. Ibe somting for to tell y'e.
I'ze got an old koat dat I wants for to sell y'e."
Sez I you shant tawk to me in dat sort ob fashion.
Besides I hab a mine for to gib you a slashin.

---

[10] White, "Old Time Minstrels." Moreau, *Negro Minstrelsy.*

[11] The two opening lines of the third stanza of "Bill Crowder" are used again by Emmett in "De Wild Goose-Nation," and the first two lines of the first stanza in a slightly varied form are used in "My Old Aunt Sally."

Den he gin for to grin
[*illegible*]
He sez clar de trac an I'll bark de niggars shin.

I 'spose y'e all noes dat for spunk I isnt lackin
But when I gwine to fight I always want backin,
I noed berry well dat I hadn't time to skeer 'im
More so in ticlar when he had his frens near 'im.

Den I fotch im sich a cuff
Jis whar he take de snuff
Dat he soon gin to holler 'nuff! 'nuff!! 'nuff!!![12]

The text describes the adventures of a Negro who, after having arrived in Cincinnati, picks a fight with a Jewish old-clothesman. If we replace the name of "Bill Crowder" with "Jim Crow" or "Gumbo Chaff," we have the hero of popular minstrel songs of the thirties, who sails down the Mississippi or Ohio River and, on stepping ashore, enjoys his first brawl. The ludicrous figure of Emmett's Jewish old-clothesman, however, was suggested by English stage music; it does not exist in early American Negro minstrel songs.

Emmett's new interest in Negro impersonation soon led to his own debut as a banjo player and singer in the circus ring, undoubtedly in blackface. How and when this happened is told by the circus manager C. J. Rogers: "The 'Cincinnati Circus Company' was started in the spring of 1840 . . . . We opened in Cincinnati soon after our arrival, and spent the season traveling in Ohio, Indiana, Virginia and Kentucky . . . . [Emmitt] during the season of 1840, was a member of our orchestra, and while we were traveling in Western Virginia found a banjo player by the name of 'Ferguson,' who was a very ignorant person, and 'nigger all over' except in color. Emmitt wanted us to engage him, but my partners objected to increasing our expenses. We were only giving an afternoon performance that day, on account

---

[12] "Bill Crowder," manuscript in the State Library (Columbus, Ohio).

of a long route ahead; the wagons were about starting, when Emmitt ran up, shouting: 'Ferguson will work on canvas, and play the banjo, for ten dollars a month.' I answered, 'Tell him to jump on a wagon,' which he did, and when we reached Lexington, Kentucky, in the fall . . . 'Ferguson' was the greatest card we had and 'Brower and Ferguson' were the talk of the town . . . . During this season Dan Emmitt learned to play the banjo . . . . In the spring of 1841 Frank Brower again joined us, and Dan Emmitt, after a good deal of persuasion, agreed to play in the orchestra and assist Frank in the ring with the banjo. This was the beginning of that popularity which continued so many years, and made Frank Brower and Dan Emmitt famous. At Lynchburg, Va., during Fourth-of-July week, 1841, Frank Brower first introduced 'bone playing' before an audience, accompanying Emmitt in the new song of 'Old Tar River'."[13] When the company played in Charleston, South Carolina, in early November, 1841, its playbills announced Emmett as a performer.[14]

His next engagement was with Raymond and Waring's Circus "about 1841–42." All we know is that the company appeared in Philadelphia in a building on Walnut Street which was later called the Grand Central Variety Theatre. Among its members was also Frank Brower.[15]

During 1842, Emmett was employed as a musician by Spalding's North American Circus, traveling through Michigan in the early fall and performing, between the eighteenth and twenty-third of September in Detroit, Mount Clemens, Utica, Pontiac, and Farmington. The company, to which Emmett's old friend C. J. Rogers belonged, consisted of as many as "200 Persons and Horses," and its brass band

[13] Published in *The New York Clipper* (June 20, 1874), as a letter to the editor, signed "C. J. R." A playbill of the Cincinnati Circus (Cincinnati, April 23, 1841), mentions that "Mr. Brower, The celebrated negro Dancer and Singer will sing and dance 'Jim Along Josey' " and the "Negro Extravaganza—Zip Coon." Emmett's name, however, is not listed.

[14] Statement by Al. G. Field as quoted in Dailey Paskman and Sigmund Spaeth, *Gentlemen Be Seated* (New York, 1928), 186: "The earliest authentic announcement I have of his [Emmett's] appearance as a performer is a bill which he gave me in 1897. The bill advertises a performance of the Cincinnati Circus in Charleston, S. C., on November 2, 1841."

[15] Obituary of Frank Brower in *The New York Clipper* (June 13, 1874).

comprised fifteen musicians.[16] Emmett himself tells us that he "traveled as small Drummer with the celebrated Edward Kendall while he was leader of Spalding and Rogers' Circus Band. I benefited from his superior qualifications as a drummer . . . ."[17]

The time had now come when Emmett could show himself before an exacting audience. With his friend Frank Brower, he thus turned to New York. There, the two young versatile performers stood a good chance of being welcomed.

[16] Playbill of 1842 as republished in *The New York Clipper* (September 6, 1884). The playbill mentions "Kendall's Brass Band."
[17] Galbreath, *Daniel Decatur Emmett*, 47–48.

Chapter 8

THE VIRGINIA MINSTRELS
IN NEW YORK AND BOSTON

F RANK BROWER, WHOSE FULL NAME WAS Francis Marion Brower, was eight years younger than his friend Emmett. He was born on November 30, 1823, in Baltimore.[1] About 1838 he made his first public appearance in song and dance acts in Philadelphia. Soon he had established himself as a comedian, a singer, a bone player (one of the earliest),[2] and a dancer; by the middle of the forties he was considered one of the foremost blackface dancers of his day.[3] By imitating the typical jumps and leaps of old Negroes, he is said to have initiated a new trend in minstrel dancing.[4]

Emmett and Brower quickly gained a foothold in New York. By late November, 1842, they performed at the Franklin Theatre on Chatham Square, which had opened as a variety theater about two

---

[1] Obituary of F. M. Brower in *The New York Clipper* (June 13, 1874).

[2] A letter to the editor, signed C. J. R., *The New York Clipper* (June 20, 1874), mentions that Brower, engaged with the Cincinnati Circus Company in 1841, "introduced 'bone-playing' before an audience . . . ," stressing that this was a novelty at that time.

[3] The playbill of "Master Juba . . . and the Ethiopian Minstrels" of 1845 mentions that Juba will imitate "all the principal dancers in the United States," listing them in the following order: 1. Richard Pelham, New York; 2. Francis Brower, New York; 3. John Daniels, Buffalo; John Smith, Albany; James Sanford, Philadelphia; Frank Diamond, Troy; and John Diamond, New York.

[4] "Negro Minstrels and their Dances."

113

weeks earlier.[5] Following the latest trend in their profession, they appeared along with a third performer, the young dancer Pierce. Thus it can be assumed that Brower and Pierce, jointly as well as separately, danced to Emmett's banjo accompaniment, which was occasionally enlivened by a vocal rendition of the songs by one of the three minstrels. Doubtless, Emmett was also heard in song-banjo solos. The talents of the group were warmly recommended to New Yorkers by newspaper notices which called Emmett "the great Southern Banjo Melodist," Brower "the perfect representation of the Southern Negro characters," and Master Pierce "the great heelologist."[6]

By the middle of December, Brower left the Franklin while Emmett and Master Pierce continued until the end of the first week of January, 1843. Billed as "the renowned Ethiopian Minstrel and his Little Darkey Ariel," the two also appeared for about a week, starting December 19, at a circus in the Amphitheater of the Republic (37 Bowery), where they gave "an exhibition of their enlivening Banjo melodies and Negro Dances," including the "Ethiopian Serenade."[7] During the last days of December, Emmett and his old partner Brower are listed among the attractions at the same place, but whether they performed together is not known. On these occasions, Emmett acted not only as a banjoist and singer but as a dancer, thus exhibiting a talent which he usually neglected. On January 1-2, 1843, the two did perform jointly in what was called "Negro Holiday Sports in Carolina and Virginia," and on January 13 Emmett participated in a benefit performance. In a bill which included four bands, a Chinese nondescript, and eight clowns, he impersonated the role of "Old Dan Tucker," perhaps singing his own text to the then popular tune.[8]

In a few weeks' time, Emmett and Brower joined with two other blackface comedians, Bill Whitlock and Dick Pelham, in a venture which was to open up a new chapter in the history of the American popular theater.

[5] Notices in *The New York Herald* (November and December, 1842). See also "Among the Minstrels of the Past," *The New York Clipper* (November 4, 1876).
[6] *The New York Herald* (December 5, 1842).
[7] Notices in *The Evening Post* and *The New York Herald* (December, 1842).
[8] *The Evening Post* (January 13, 1843).

Of the four minstrels it was William M. Whitlock who was best known in the East. Born in New York in 1813, he was originally a printer, a compositor to be exact, on a religious journal and, later, on the *New York Herald*.[9] It is said that in 1838, when traveling as a Negro singer with a circus company through the South, he met Joe Sweeney, the famous banjoist, and received a few lessons from him. It did not take long until he mastered the banjo himself. In 1839, P. T. Barnum recognized his talents and took him under his management. From then on Whitlock began to establish his reputation, first in conjunction with the young dancer John Diamond and later with the young Frank Lynch, who also called himself Diamond. He frequently appeared in New York.[10] Though mainly known as a highly skilled banjoist and singer, he also excelled in dancing, if we care to believe the grotesque statement of a playbill of 1840: "Not dat Massa Whitlock plays so partic'lar combustious, and will sing dat 'fecting song of Jinny git your Hoe Cake done! and dat first rate ballad of Jim Along Josey! defying all de niggers in de world to charm de people after dat same manner. Dis very partic'lar nigga will jump, dance, and knock his heels in a way dat Mademoiselle Fanny Elssler [the famous European dancer who had just made her American debut] neber did, neber can and neber will do."[11] He is said to have acquired "his accurate knowledge of the peculiarities of plantation and cornfield negroes" by close observation of southern life when he was on tour.[12]

Richard Ward Pelham was born in New York on February 13, 1815.[13] He frequently performed with his younger brother, Gilbert W., in "Negro Peculiarities, Dances, and Extravaganzies." Not only was he, like many minstrels, a capable dancer, but he was one of the very first rank.[14] During the early forties he was often seen on New York stages in solos and in ensembles of two and three.[15]

[9] An article in *The New York Clipper* (April 13, 1878), based on the manuscript autobiography of Whitlock.
[10] George C. D. Odell, *Annals of the New York Stage* (New York, 1928), IV, mentions him frequently when discussing the period of the late thirties and the early forties.
[11] Playbill of the National Theatre (Boston, June 5, 1840).
[12] An article on Whitlock in *The New York Clipper* (April 13, 1878).
[13] *The New York Clipper* (March 2, 1912).
[14] Playbill of "Master Juba . . . ."
[15] Odell, *Annals*, IV.

One day toward the end of January, 1843, Emmett, Brower, Whitlock, and Pelham, then among the stars of the minstrel profession in New York, conceived the idea of forming a novel kind of ensemble consisting of fiddle, bones, banjo, and tambourine. So well did they exploit its theatrical and musical possibilities that they turned an experiment into a new medium—the jazz band of the nineteenth century, as it might be called by analogy. Whitlock claimed to have invented it, but the idea itself (strongly suggested by circumstances) was much less original than its actual realization.[16] And to this all four minstrels contributed equally.

The earliest session of the "band" has been described by eye witnesses: by Whitlock, by Emmett, as well as by George B. Wooldridge, who was to become their agent. Whitlock's and Emmett's accounts roughly complement each other but do not agree in all details, nor can any of their data be verified at this point. However, their reports have documentary value in conveying the liveliness of these early sessions and the daredevil attitude of their participants.

According to Whitlock and Wooldridge, the first rehearsal was held in Emmett's room in New York, in Mrs. Brooke's boarding house at 37 Catherine Street,[17] and the three observers state or imply that it came about by chance. Wooldridge said the four were together in one room, and that "the banjo, bones, violin and tambourine lying around loose, as if by accident, each one picked up his tools and joined in a chorus of 'Old Dan Tucker,' while Emmett was playing and singing. It went well, and they repeated it without saying a word. Each did his best, and such a rattling of the principal and original instruments in a minstrel band was never heard before."[18] The story is told in a more detailed manner by Whitlock himself: "One day I asked Old Dan Emmett, who was in New York at the time, to practice the fiddle and the banjo with me at his boarding house in Catherine Street. We went down there, and when we had practiced two or three tunes, Frank Brower called in (by accident). He listened to our music,

---

[16] In *The New York Clipper,* (April 13, 1878), Whitlock said, "The origination of the [Virginia] Minstrels I claim as my own idea, and it cannot be blotted out."

[17] Address from "Among the Minstrels of the Past."

[18] *The New York Clipper* (April 13, 1878).

charmed to the soul. I told him to join us with the bones, which he did. Presently Dick Pelham came in (also by accident), and looked amazed. I asked him to procure a tambourine and make one of the party, and he went and got one. After practicing for a while, we went to the old resort of the circus crowd—the 'Branch,' in the Bowery— with our instruments, and in Bartlett's Billiard-room[19] performed for the first time as the Virginia Minstrels."[20]

The substance of Emmett's description of the beginning of the troupe is recounted by *The New York Clipper:*

All four were one day [in the winter of 1842–43] sitting in the North American Hotel, in the Bowery,[21] when one of them proposed that with their instruments they should cross over to the Bowery Circus and give one of the proprietors (Uncle Nate Howes) a "charivari" as he sat by the stove in the hall entrance. Bringing forth his banjo for Whitlock to play on, Emmett took the violin, Pelham the tambourine, and Brower the bones. Without any rehearsal, with hardly the ghost of an idea as to what was to follow, they crossed the street and proceeded to "browbeat" Uncle Nat Howes into giving them an engagement, the calculation being that he would succumb in preference to standing the horrible noise (for they attempted no tune) they were making with their instruments. After standing it for a while, Uncle Nate said: "Boys, you've got a good thing. Can't you sing us a song?" Thereupon Emmett, accompanying himself on his violin, began to sing "Old Dan Tucker," the others joining in the chorus. The four minstrels were as much surprised at the result as was Uncle Nate. After singing some more songs for him, they returned to the North American, where they resumed their "horrible noise" in the reading room, which was quickly filled with spectators. . . . [Later on they] rehearsed a few songs in Emmett's room . . . .[22]

---

[19] According to *The Great Metropolis or Guide to New York for 1845* (New York), Jonas Bartlett was the owner of the Branch Hotel at 36 Bowery. The hotel was "opposite the Bowery Amphitheater, and for many years a leading sporting-house on the east side, and at one time kept by Thomas Hyer, the pugilist" (*The New York Clipper,* November 4, 1876).

[20] *The New York Clipper* (April 13, 1878).

[21] According to *The Great Metropolis,* this hotel was located at 30 Bowery.

[22] *The New York Clipper* (May 19, 1877).

Emmett, Whitlock, and Pelham claimed that their ensemble appeared for the first time in public at a benefit performance for Dick Pelham at the Chatham Theatre. If so, this must have been on January 31.[23] Since it had not been announced previously, it found no echo in the press.

The first confirmed appearance of the four minstrels occurred a few days later, on February 6, at the Bowery Amphitheatre—at the same place where they had previously tried so hard to get an engagement. The première was announced by the *New York Herald* as the "First Night of the novel, grotesque, original, and surprisingly melodious Ethiopian band, entitled the *Virginia Minstrels*, being an exclusively musical entertainment combining the banjo, violin, bone castanets, and tambourine, and entirely exempt from the vulgarities and other objectionable features which have hitherto characterized negro extravaganzas." Staying for one week, the minstrels presented, in the midst of the usual attractions of a circus, what they called a "Negro Concert," in which they played and sang together. They also performed two scenes: "Dan Tucker on Horseback," with Pelham as a Negro riding master, Brower as a Negro clown, and an equestrian; and "The Serenade," enacted by a lover (probably Whitlock) and a female impersonator.[24]

The troupe appeared next on February 16 at the Cornucopia, a "sporting saloon" at 28 Park Row.[25] This seems to have been their first solo appearance, although they may not have had the entire evening to themselves. From the Cornucopia they moved on to the nearby Olympic Circus at the Park Theatre, where they played from February 17 to March 1. Among new scenes they offered were "Negro Lecture on Locomotives" presented by Whitlock, "A Definition of the Bankrupt Laws" by Brower, "A brief Battering at the Blues" by

[23] This benefit performance is mentioned in Odell, *Annals*, IV, 675. For a discussion of this and other dates, see *The New York Clipper* (November 4, 1876). It is mentioned there that the two Pelhams believed, "as indicated in a note now before us that the Virginia Minstrels made their initial bow on February 17, 1843, at the Chatham Theatre, for the benefit of Richard." This date is obviously too late.

[24] *The New York Herald* (February 6–11, 1843).

[25] *The New York Clipper* (November 4, 1876 and May 19, 1877); a clipping from a Chicago newspaper (January 24, 1880), based on an interview with Emmett, as quoted in Moreau, *Negro Minstrelsy*, II.

Pelham, and conundrums by Emmett.[26] "Dan Tucker on horseback" was now expanded into a scene with four characters, consisting of "Smarto Swivelwhip" (Pelham), "Merryman" (Brower), "Mungo" (Whitlock) and "Dan Tucker" (impersonated by the equestrian B. Carrol). It was approximately at this time that the press mentioned the virtuosity of each player and the rhythmic unanimity of the four: "the harmony and skill with which the banjo, violin, castanets [meaning bones] and tambourine are blended . . . ."[27]

Plans of touring the European theaters flashed through their minds,[28] but they finally decided to go to Boston first, where Negro minstrels were always welcome. Before Howes' Circus (now renamed Great Olympic Circus) left New York, the minstrels had offered themselves for "ten dollars apiece" weekly, but Howes had found this exorbitant.[29] Whereupon the minstrels made themselves independent and hired George B. Wooldridge as their agent.

On March 7 and 8, they opened at the Masonic Temple in Boston. Their "Ethiopian Concert," a full evening with minstrel music and scenes centered on a minstrel band, was what was later called a *minstrel show*—the first of a new type of entertainment. This was their program:

PART I

AIR — JOHNY BOWKER . . . . by the Band

SONG—OLD DAN TUCKER, a Virginian Refrain,

    in which is described the ups and

    downs of Negro life . . . . Full Chorus by the Minstrels

SONG—GOIN OBER DE MOUNTAIN, or the difficulties

    between Old Jake and his Sweet Heart . . . Full Chorus

SONG—OLD TAR RIVER—or the Incidents

    attending a Coon Hunt . . . . Full Chorus

---

[26] Playbills of the Olympic Circus, conducted by Rufus Welch, and a notice in *The New York Herald* (March 1, 1843).

[27] Notice in the *New York Courier*, reprinted on the playbills of the Virginia Minstrels (March 7, 8, 1843).

[28] See the playbill of the Olympic Circus at the Park Theatre (February 24, 1843), which mentions that "terms have been offered them for the European Theatres and concerts."

[29] *The New York Clipper* (May 19, 1877). Moreau, *Negro Minstrelsy*, II.

A NEGRO LECTURE ON LOCOMOTIVES . . . . by BILLY WHITLOCK
in which he describes his visit to the Wild
Animals, his scrape with his Sweetheart,
and show[s] the white folks how the
Niggers raise Steam.

PART II

SONG—Uncle Gabriel—or a chapter on Tails . . . . Full Chorus
SONG—BOATMAN DANCE—a much admired Song, in
imitation of the Ohio Boatman . . . . . . Full Chorus
SONG—LUCY LONG—a very fashionable song
which has never failed to be received
with unbounded applause . . . . Full Chorus
SONG—FINE OLD COLORED GEMMAN—a Parody, written by
Old Dan Emmet, who will, on this occasion,
accompany himself on the BANJO, in a manner
that will make all guitar players turn pale with delight.

The review in the *Evening Transcript,* one day after their first appearance, was brief but positive: "The Virginia Minstrels made a 'great hit' at the Temple last evening. They are rare boys—'full of fun' and music."

Since they appeared in Worcester, Massachusetts, on March 20, 21, and 22, they may have played in other towns in the vicinity of Boston as well. Making the most of the native "folk" style of their scenes, they stressed their use of the "songs, refrains, and ditties as sung by the southern slaves at all their merry meetings such as the gathering in of the cotton and sugar crops, corn huskings, slave weddings, and junketings."[30]

The Great Olympic Circus (June, Titus, Angevine and Co., and N. A. Howes, proprietors) had been playing at the Tremont Theatre since February 20. Only a few days after the successful first appearance of the Virginia Minstrels which had revitalized in the city the interest in Negro minstrelsy, blackface banjo-dance acts were introduced into the circus show. Finally, on March 13, an entire minstrel band consisting of banjo, fiddle, bones, and tambourine (hur-

[30] See playbills of Brinley Hall (Worcester, Mass., March 20, 21, 22, 1843).

riedly styled "The Kentucky Minstrels") was formed.[31] And for the last week which the circus spent in Boston (March 23–29), the Virginia Minstrels themselves were called in, no doubt on their own financial terms. They were announced, without undue emphasis, as the "able delineators of the sports and pastimes of the Sable Race of the South . . . who have won for themselves a popularity unprecedented and the patronage of the elite of Boston . . . ."[32] At the last night of the circus, the four minstrels offered, in addition to their usual songs and dances, Whitlock's locomotive lecture and two scenes which Bostonians had not seen yet: "The Elssler Serenade or—Two Strings to one Beau," with "Fanny Dinah Valbrina" (D. Gardner, clown at the circus), "Sambo Paganini in love with Fanny" (Whitlock), and "Penny Post" (Brower); and "Dan Tucker on Horseback," in which the ringmaster, clown, and groom were acted by Pelham, Brower, and Emmett, respectively, and "Dan Tucker" was impersonated by the equestrian H. Madigan.[33] "By this time Emmett's Old Dan Tucker had given him considerable notoriety, and he began to be identified by that name. Old Dan Tucker was on the end of everybody's tongue . . . ." When in a street parade Madigan was seen "dancing, jumping through hoops, and turning somersaults on the horse's back . . . ," everybody mistook "him for Uncle Dan, [and] wondered what that man couldn't do . . . ."[34]

The manager of the Tremont Theatre, impressed by the "Overflowing Houses drawn by the Original and Unrivaled Virginia Minstrels"[35] held them over for the beginning of the spring season "previous to their departure for Europe." Thus, sandwiched between dramas and burlettas, they frolicked in a "Grand Ethiopian Olio" from the third of April to the fifth. A few days later, on April 7, Emmett, as the most prominent member of the ensemble, volunteered

[31] See Playbills of the circus (February and March) as well as notices in the *Evening Transcript.*

[32] Playbill of the Great Olympic Circus (March 27, 1843).

[33] Playbill of the Great Olympic Circus (March 29, 1843).

[34] Moreau, *Negro Ministrelsy*, II. In the notice of the *Plebian*, reprinted on the playbill of March 7 and 8, the Virginia Minstrels are dubbed "Old Dan Tucker & Co."

[35] Playbills of the Tremont Theatre (April 3–5, 1843), as well as notices in the *Evening Transcript.*

for a benefit concert at the Melodeon, which had been arranged for a Mr. Armour, a needy trumpet player.[36]

Back in New York, the four minstrels bade good-bye to their admirers in entr'actes at the Park Theatre on April 17.[37] Their popularity was unquestioned except by one old fogey of a critic. "We venture to say," he wrote indignantly, "that nothing upon a par with these gentry has ever appeared upon the boards of Old Drury. It is painful to see this theatre so reduced—even to a level with the Five Points [a low-class section of New York]. They had much better shut [it] up, and write for its motto 'Fuit Slium.'[38] Can it be that this theatre can have no success without such pitiful resorts? And yet Hackett [the famous actor] is obliged to play within the same walls around which the sound of the banjo and the tune of 'Lucy Long' are still echoing."[39]

Undaunted, the minstrels left the United States on April 21, on the packet ship *New York*, headed for Liverpool and new adventures in the British Isles.[40]

[36] Notice in the *Evening Transcript* (April 7, 1843).

[37] *The New York Clipper* (November 4, 1876 and May 19, 1877); Odell, *Annals*, IV, 618.

[38] Could this be a parody of "Fuit Troia" from Virgil's *Aeneid?*

[39] Reprinted in *The New York Clipper* (November 4, 1876).

[40] The *Morning Courier and New York Enquirer* (April 21, 1843), and *The New York Clipper* (August 8, 1874), which quotes from a letter by Pelham published in *Hague's Minstrel and Dramatic Journal* (Liverpool).

Chapter 9

THE PERFORMANCE
OF THE VIRGINIA MINSTRELS

———⬗———

The four virginia minstrels sat on the stage in a semicircle, partly turned to the audience, partly to each other to ensure rhythmic co-ordination. In the center were Emmett with his fiddle and Whitlock with his banjo, flanked by Pelham pounding his tambourine and Brower who furiously rattled the bones (see Illustration 37).

Their ill-assorted garments, their oddly shaped hats, and their gaudy pants and shirts were in the traditional style of the stage plantation Negro. But the effect of their costuming was heightened by almost frightening countenances which were distinguished by wide-open mouths, bulging lips, and eyes that shone like full moons. When the minstrels addressed themselves on their playbill "To the most sensitive and fastidious beholder" with the promise to be "chaste and elegant," they may have been sincere in their intentions, but they modestly understated their case. For in their efforts to be both laughable and characteristically Negrolike, they went much further than other minstrels before them. Composure indeed was not a part of their temperament; they were boisterous to the point of grotesqueness. When they could force themselves to remain seated, they would stretch out their legs toward their audience in rowdy fashion and

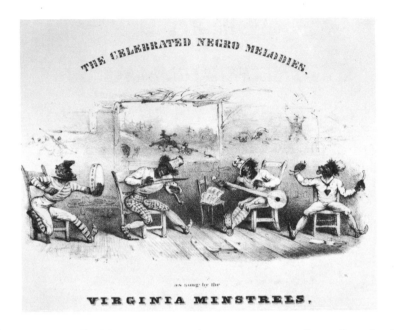

Illustration 37. The Virginia Minstrels in action; notwithstanding the decorative music book, they performed their music by ear. In the center are Dan Emmett with his fiddle and Bill Whitlock with his banjo; they are flanked by Dick Pelham, pounding a tambourine, and Frank Brower, furiously rattling the bones. From the cover of Th. Comer (arr.), *The Celebrated Negro Melodies, as Sung by the Virginia Minstrels* (Boston, 1843).

bend their feet and their toes at the sharpest possible angles.[1] They would bob up and down and sway to and fro, sputtering uncouth sayings, shouts, and hoarse laughter. The endmen, Pelham on the left and Brower on the right, were the most unruly of the lot, while the banjoist and the fiddler indulged in as many contortions as the

[1] How realistic the appearance of the Virginia Minstrels was can be seen by comparing them to a Negro banjoist as "drawn from life" in *Sketches and Eccentricities*, 38: "He was seated in a corner upon a stool, holding his instrument . . . . His forehead was low and narrow; his eyes red and sunken; his nose . . . protuberant at the sides; his lips as if in scorn at each other. His teeth were . . . set in at an obtuse angle, which caused them to jut out; and his lower jaw seemed to have a great antipathy to the upper, and when idle, always kept as far off as possible . . . . His leg was placed so nearly in the middle of his foot that, with toes at each end, no one could have tracked him; and the hollow of his feet projected so far outward that it gave them somewhat the appearance of rockers to a chair."

Illustration 38. A close-up of Frank Brower. From the cover of *Old Dan Emmit's Banjo Melodies* (Boston, 1844), Second Series.

handling of their instruments allowed. Pelham exhibited "looks and movements comic beyond conception. He seemed animated by a savage energy; and [the handling of his instrument] . . . nearly wrung him off his seat. His white eyes rolled in a curious frenzy . . . and his hiccupping chuckles were unsurpassable."[2] When Brower "trucked" around a bit, the clicks of his bones would mingle with the heavy thud of his boots. He and Pelham sometimes burst into breakdowns, usually without ceasing to keep their instruments in motion (sec Illustration 38).

Emmett performed like a real country fiddler; he held his instrument in front of his chest and drew his bow across the strings as if it were an unwieldy pole (see Illustration 39). Like a hot bass

[2] An English review in a pamphlet on the Ethiopian Serenaders (1846; Harvard Theatre Collection). Although the quotation refers to the peculiarities of Pelham's performance as a bone player, it may not be amiss to apply it to his tambourine playing as well.

Illustration 39. A close-up of Dan Emmett. From the cover of *Old Dan Emmit's Banjo Melodies*, Second Series.

player of our time, Whitlock played his banjo with complete abandon, roughly striking the strings with the nail of his forefinger.[3] His banjo was of the type customary in the thirties and early forties; it had an extremely long thin neck and only four strings (though a fifth appears to have been soon added).[4] Pelham not only jingled his tambourine but pounced on it vehemently as if it were a drum. The bones, which may have measured ten inches or more, were shaken with a loose wrist and, for greater virtuosity, the entire arm (see Illustration 40).

In order to give the impression of genuine plantation music, the minstrels asserted on their playbills that their "instruments were manufactured by themselves,"[5] which as far as the bones were concerned was undoubtedly true. Moreover, they lent their instruments such picturesque names as "Tuckahoe Violin," "Congo Banjo," and "Cohea Tambourine." "Tuckahoe" and "Cohea" (or rather "Cohee") do not have a direct connection with the Negro; they were, in the early nineteenth century, rural nicknames of the inhabitants of Virginia, the first of those living east of the Blue Ridge, the second of those living west of it. However, if "Tucka" is identical with "Tuckey," it was a Negro name in Jamaica.[6] The word "Congo" was part of a name of a white frontier dance of 1800—a "Congo minuet," which was also observed, as early as the 1780's, at balls given on Haitian plantations.[7]

---

[3] That this was the genuine Negro style becomes clear from a description of a colored banjoist in Kemble, *Journal*, 97: "[he] seemed . . . to thump his instrument with every part of his body at once . . . ." The technical details are explained in Thomas F. Briggs, *Briggs' Banjo Instructor* (Boston, 1855), and in *Buckley's Guide for the Banjo* (Boston, 1868).

[4] On the cover of sheet editions of minstrel music up to about 1844, the banjo is drawn with four strings. See "De Ole Jaw Bone" (Boston, 1840), and "Lucy Neal" (Boston, 1844). However, the instrument already has five strings on the covers of Emmett's London song series (c.1844). "Good Bye Sally Dear" (Boston, *Songs of the Ethiopian Serenaders*, 1849), shows five strings. Gumbo Chaff (Elias Howe), *The Complete Preceptor for the Banjo* (Boston, 1851), gives the tuning as follows: F-c′-e′-g′-c″ (sounding an octave lower).

[5] Playbills of the Olympic Circus (New York, February 24, 1843, and Worcester, March 20–21, 1843).

[6] In *A Dictionary of American English*: see "cohee" and "tuckahoe." "Tuckey" is the name of a slave on a sugar plantation in Jamaica in the English opera *Obi, or Three-Fingered Jack*. Names of such realistic characters were usually not invented.

[7] Cheney, *Travels of John Davis*, 149–50, and Lillian Moore, "Moreau de Saint-Mery and 'Danse,'" *Dance Index* (October, 1946). In Haiti this dance was called "Minuet Congo."

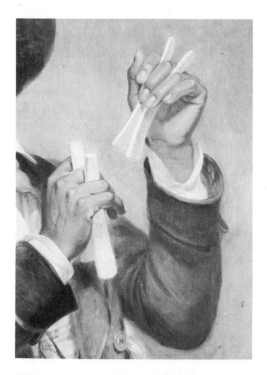

Illustration 40. Detail from *The Bone Player* by William Sidney Mount (1855). Courtesy Karolik Collection.

Although the style of the Virginia Minstrels has not been preserved by tradition, one nevertheless can venture a few guesses concerning its actual sound. The bones produced single clicks as well as "trills" or shakes of short or long duration. Their crispness was varied by dynamic shadings ranging from pianissimo to fortissimo. It was the precision of the clicks which lent articulation to the ensemble.[8] In the main, the bone player followed the meter, but like the banjoist and fiddler, he may have occasionally disturbed it by entering on ordinarily unaccented beats. The tambourine part was similar except that its sound was less clearly defined because of the jingles which prolonged each thump. There were no chords in the ensemble because the banjoist played only a melody; this is evident from banjo

[8] The pamphlet on the Ethiopian Serenaders: "He can put as many notes as you like into a bar, and indicate every variety of emphasis between the extremest point of piano and forte, without losing the crispness and distinctness of the click . . . ."

methods of the fifties which also described an older practice.[9] They show in addition that the banjoist liked to vary the main melody by inserting into it the open tones of his two highest strings. This insertion was frequent after the fifth, the "thumb-string," had been added to the banjo around the middle of the forties, but it may have also occurred earlier. Motion was intensified by omitting tones on accented beats, creating a type of syncopation which existed in print already in the early forties.[10] In some early ensembles other than the Virginia Minstrels, the banjoist, too, tapped out the regular beats of the music with his foot; differing from his solo acts, he used his sole instead of his heel.[11] The fiddler may have played the tune straighter than the banjoist, though with occasional variants including dotted notes and syncopations, and with open strings as drones, as is still the custom in the backwoods.[12] All four minstrels of course played by ear, regardless of the decorative music book in Illustration 37.

The volume of the minstrel band was quite lean, yet anything but delicate. The tones of the banjo died away quickly and therefore could not serve as a solid foundation in the ensemble. On top was the squeaky, carelessly tuned fiddle. Add the dry "ra, raka, taka, tak" of the bones[13] and the tambourine's dull thumps and ceaseless jingling to the twang of the banjo and the flat tone of the fiddle, and the sound of the band is approximated: it was scratchy, tinkling, cackling, and humorously incongruous.

The Virginians often sang and played at the same time. A soloist took the first part of the song while the others joined him in the second, the refrain, singing in one voice, which was considerably closer to the plantation manner than the four-part glee style of other min-

[9] *Rice's Correct Method.*

[10] See Chapter 13.

[11] See illustration 44, the cover of *Songs of the Virginia Serenaders* (Boston, 1844) and the cover of *Songs of the Nightingale Serenaders* (Philadelphia, 1846). See Chapter 13 for the tapping of the banjoist in solo acts.

[12] Samuel P. Bayard, "Introduction," *Hill Country Tunes* (Philadelphia, 1944), p. xv. John A. and Alan Lomax, *Our Singing Country* (New York, 1941), 55–57. Cecil J. Sharp, *English Folk Songs from the Southern Appalachians*, I, p. xxvii, wrote of two fiddlers: "Wherever possible they used the open strings as drones . . . ."

[13] Onomatopoetic description of the sound of the bones in "De Rattle of de Bones," *The Ethiopian Gleebook.*

strel bands.[14] Occasionally, fewer than four musicians accompanied the songs. For example, in Emmett's "I'm Gwine Ober De Mountains," only the bones and the banjo were heard in the interludes.

It is likely that the intonation of minstrels was not the conventional one. In imitating the Negro's manner and speech, they must have also imitated his way of singing which was characterized not only by a specific timbre, but as it still is, by pitches outside our tonal system, "slides from one note to another, and turns and cadences not in articulated notes."[15] Features like these hardly ever appeared in printed editions of minstrel songs. Emmett's "Dar He Goes! Dats Him!" is an exception: the ambiguous pitch of two tones of its melody is here implied (following the example of printed banjo pieces) by the use of two adjacent tones, the first "sliding" from below into the second.

Fully aware of the uniqueness of their musical acts, the Virginia Minstrels always called attention on their playbills to their "concert" or "exclusively musical entertainment," "Ethiopian" or "African."

When they presented a minstrel show, performing all by themselves as they did a few times in Boston, they divided the evening into two parts. The first opened with an instrumental piece and often concluded with a stump speech. In both parts, songs with instrumental background alternated with banjo solo songs. All of their scenes were interspersed and linked with droll conversation in Negro dialect, remarks, shouts, acting, and dancing. There was no fixed "interlocutor" yet, and the repartee was not restricted to him and the "end men," as was customary in later minstrel shows. All four minstrels did the talking spontaneously, "asking and answering quaint questions and conundrums in turn," though it seems that Brower and Pelham were more boisterous and active than the others.[16]

---

[14] A newspaper clipping (Chicago, January 24, 1880), as quoted in Moreau, *Negro Minstrelsy*, II, states that the Virginia Minstrels "all sang in one voice." Kemble, *Journal*, 127, remembered that the plantation Negroes "all sing in unison, having never, it appears, attempted or heard anything like part-singing."

[15] Allen, *Slave Songs*, pp. vi, xx.

[16] Moreau, *Negro Minstrelsy:* "They were then all 'end men,' and all were 'interlocutors' . . . ." On playbills Brower and Pelham were mainly mentioned as offering conundrums.

In the tradition of the English stage, the songs themselves were interrupted by dialogue, usually before the refrain. No such dialogue of the Virginia Minstrels is preserved, but we can gain an idea of its style from a scene which Emmett and Brower performed about 1846. Its text, if taken literally, amounts to no more than foolish babbling in the manner of circus clowns, but it was a mere outline for improvisation on the spot. Also its dialect must have been more genuine, for it is known that Negro minstrels "made a study of Negro dialect a specialty . . . . As a result, no two adopted the same type of darkey for a study . . . . The Kentuckian differed as much from [the] Virginian, as the South Carolinian did from the Alabamian, or the 'field hand' from the genteel house servant."[17] The song around which Emmett and Brower built their scene was "Lucy Long," which had been a favorite of their Boston audiences.[18] Here is a part of the scene; after the odd beauty of Miss Lucy Long had been commented on, Emmett reported his amorous adventures while singing:

> Pray turkey buzzard lend to me your wing
> Till I fly over de river to see Miss Sally King.
> When I got over de river, Miss Sally she was gone.
> If I had known she'd sarved me so, I stop wid Lucy Long.
>
> [Dialogue.]
> *Frank.* She had a ticklar gagement to go to camp me[e]tin
>   wid dis child.
> *Dan.* hah! You went down to de fish Market to daunce arter
>   eels. mity cureous kind ob camp meetin dat!
> *Frank.* I[t] wasnt eels, it was a big cat fish.
> *Dan.* What chune did you dance?
>
> Chorus [both singing].

---

[17] H. B. White, "The Origin of Ethiopian Minstrelsy" (Harvard Theatre Collection, newspaper clipping of the early twentieth century).

[18] Whitlock, unduly proud of a nondescript tune, asserted in his autobiography: "I composed . . . 'Miss Lucy Long' (the words by T. G. Booth) in 1838." An 1842 edition of the song without designation of author or composer appears in Damon, *Old American Songs.*

Take your time Miss Lucy
Take your time Miss Lucy Long
Rock de cradle Lucy
Take your time my dear.

[Dialogue.]
Frank. I trade her off for bean soup.
Dan. Well, you is hungryest nigger eber I saw. You'r neber
   satisfied widout your tinken bout bean soup all de time.

Chorus [both singing].[19]

In Boston "Lucy Long" had been enacted with a different text
which appeared in a sheet music edition and in a slender booklet,
Songs of the Virginia Minstrels, both published by C. H. Keith (Boston, 1843), under the heading "Miss Lucy Long and Her Answer."
The song consisted of four stanzas for Lucy's bridegroom and four
for herself in which she denied to know "de gemman Dat wrote dat
little song, Who dare to make so public De name ob Lucy Long" and
expressed her preference for "De 'stinguished Jimmy Crow." Here
was what was called a "wench performance"—an impersonation of
a colored lady by a male minstrel—although it seems to have been
done by the Virginians without the appropriate costume. The earliest
impersonators of Lucy Long, doubtless in skirts and pantalettes, are
supposed to have been George Christy and Dan Gardner (see Illustration 41).[20] In another lively scene, the "Boatman's Dance," the
minstrels impersonated "the negro boatmen on the Ohio River."[21]
Assuming that their representation of the crude voices and insolent
manner of these boatmen was totally realistic, they must have gone

[19] This scene, in Emmett's handwriting, was found among his manuscripts. It is
not dated, but since it refers to "Santa Anna" and thus to the Mexican War, it was
probably written about 1846.
[20] *The New York Clipper* (December 8, 1866): "George |Christy] was the first
to do the wench business; he was the original Lucy Long . . . ." However, the newspaper clipping "Negro Minstrels and their Dances" maintained that the " 'Lucy Long' act
was first presented by Dan Gardner and afterward had many and able exponents . . . .
George Christy was the second one of those who tried it . . . ."
[21] Playbill of the Masonic Temple (Boston, March 11, 1843).

131

Illustration 41. A "wench performance" of a male actor. From *White's New Illustrated Melodeon Song Book* (New York, 1848).

to the limit of what was permissible on a public stage. An observer in the twenties and thirties remembered having heard Ohio boatmen sing:

> Dance, boatmen, dance
> Dance, dance away
> Dance all night till broad day light
> And go home with the gals in the morning.[22]

These words are almost identical with the refrain of the sheet music edition of the song which Emmett published in 1843; the tune was possibly similar in both cases.

"Virginia Breakdowns," mainly performed by the endmen Pelham and Brower, were not only accompanied by music but spiced with brief, pungent interjections. Among these "sayings"—preserved in Emmett's handwriting, though neither signed nor dated—the following may have been used:

[22] W. P. Strickland, *The Pioneers of the West* (New York, 1856), 198; the author lived in Ohio in the twenties and thirties.

Dats de heel what neber told a lie.

Dars musick in dem ole heels.

Dat deaph to creepin insects.

Dem ole legs is hung on a swibbel.

Wade in Moses.

De nigger gins to sweat to perfection.

O gosh, I kick like an ole warginny hoss wid four shoes on one foot.[23]

Not the least attractive part of the minstrels' performance were comical stump speeches in Negro dialect. Brower's "Definition of the Bankrupt Laws" was a burlesque of a timely financial topic, whereas Pelham's "A brief Battering at the Blues" may have been nothing but a nonsensical, merrymaking speech. Whitlock's "Locomotive Lecture" was probably full of pseudoscientific explanations of the steam engine, the wonder of the age. It was customary in this kind of oratory to ridicule, by means of highfalutin expressions and malapropisms, the attempts of the Negro to imitate the language of their educated white masters.

Conundrums, no doubt identical with what the Virginians called "explanations," were delivered with infectious comicality, though alone they were nothing but trite puns. Evidently this type of humor came from the circus; it was far removed from the humor of the real Negro and the backwoodsman.[24]

Dan Emmett played a prominent part in the ensemble of the Vir-

[23] These "sayings" were no doubt used by other minstrels also. See, for example, the song "Who's Dat Nigga Dar A Peepin" (Boston, 1844): ". . . persipitating dat foot ob hers up so high dat when it dropt it was death to all creeping insects . . . ."

[24] "Negro Minstrelsy—Ancient and Modern": "The negro is humorous rather than witty, and his comic songs consist of ludicrous images instead of witty conceits. I do not remember in the whole course of my investigations, to have met with anything like a pun in a genuine plantation melody." The backwoodsman David Crockett in *Col. Crockett's Tour*, 32, thought it ridiculous that Philadelphians were "eternally cutting up jokes on words." The Virginia Minstrels held a conundrum competition at the Tremont Theatre (Boston); the *Evening Transcript* (March 30, 1843), published the conundrum that received a prize. Among Emmett's manuscripts are the conundrums "submitted to the Committee for the Minstrels, Tremont Theatre."

ginia Minstrels. He, in fact, was called their "leader."[25] He wrote many of their lyrics, composed some of their tunes, and even appeared as a solo singer accompanying himself on the banjo. Since Whitlock was a virtuoso on this instrument, Emmett must have been very skillful to hold his own. One of his favorite songs was "The Fine Old Colored Gentleman," originally an English tune to which he had adapted his own text. It was the story of the Tennessee Negro Sambo —in type a backwoodsman—who was distinguished by his enormous height ("'leven feet"), by his banjo playing, by his singing ("He sung so long and sung so loud, he scared the pigs and goats"), by his jumping, racing, and hopping, and finally by his swallowing of "two small railroads wid a spoonful of ice cream . . . and a locomotive bulgine while dey blowin off de steam." When he died in the end, it was "for want of breath."

The Virginia Minstrels became famous overnight. In fact, their name became a symbol of high standards in minstrelsy. Without compunction it was borrowed not only by other minstrel bands but by publishers as well, who realized that their song sheets would recommend themselves to the public with the remark on their cover: "sung by the Virginia Minstrels."

[25] See notes on playbills (March 7, 8, and 11, 1843), and on Emmett's edition of "De Boatman's Dance."

Chapter 10

THE VIRGINIA MINSTRELS
IN GREAT BRITAIN

———◆———

T HE BOAT ON WHICH the Virginia Minstrels sailed to the Old World arrived in Liverpool on May 21, 1843. Nothing unusual happened on board, except a short-lived quarrel which "caused a separation, Brower and Emmett sticking together, while Whitlock clung to Pelham; but Emmett's song 'Dandy Jim' was the means of speedily bringing the four into harmony again." Their finances, already at low ebb at the beginning of their trip, unexpectedly improved when "a German with a fondness for poker had an hour's sitting with Pelham who won all his money . . . ." This filled the minstrels with an unaccustomed sense of security so that they "were in no hurry to begin operations after reaching Liverpool, especially as all had heavy colds." Not long, however, did they enjoy their riches. At the inn where they were lodged, Pelham let himself in for another game and lost all he had won before.

They gave two evenings at the Concert Rooms on Concert Street —the first performance of a Negro minstrel band in Europe, preceded only by the Negro impersonations of T. D. Rice in London during the thirties and by the popularity of the published American minstrel songs. Whether the citizens of Liverpool were impressed by the historic significance of the occasion is not known, but it may be doubted, because the four minstrels did not stay long in that city. In fact, they "made just money enough to transport them to Manchester . . . ," where they performed six times at the Athenaeum and subsequently at the Queen's Theatre.[1]

It seems that they had met so far with no appreciable response, but as soon as they came to London their fortunes changed. There the magician Anderson engaged them to appear with him at the Adelphi Theatre and proceeded to announce on his playbills that he had, "At The Expense Of One Hundred Pounds Per Week Secured The Greatest Novelty ever brought from America." They were also helped along by a favorable press which, twisting the facts a little, reminded the public that the Virginia Minstrels were "the only representatives of the Negro that have appeared in this country . . . ."[2] On June 19 (see Illustration 42) they made their debut in a "Grand Ethiopian Concert," which consisted of their well-tried songs, instrumental pieces, conundrums, and at the end, "grapevine twisting, with unconquerable jigs by Brower and Pelham." All this, according to the playbill, was "a true copy" of the life of the Negro slaves.[3]

At one of their early performances an incident occurred, according to Emmett, that almost broke up their engagement.

> As they came upon the stage, a rebuff staggered them. Pennsylvania had recently repudiated her indebtedness. An officer in the first tier of boxes saluted them: "Go home! You d—d humbugs! Go home, I say." While the disconcerted minstrels were debating as to whether they should "go home" or begin their entertainment, a white-haired old gentleman arose to their relief: "Gentlemen Americans, go on with your performance. There is but one fool in this house. He sits up there, with a soldier's coat on." The father of the officer had lost money through Pennsylvania's act of repudiation. The officer essayed to retort, the old gentleman began to hiss him, the whole house joined

[1] The above quotations are from an account by Emmett which, rephrased by the editor, appeared in *The New York Clipper* (May 19, 1877). Additional facts are taken from a letter by Pelham as published in *Hague's Minstrel and Dramatic Journal*, Liverpool, and republished in *The New York Clipper* (August 8, 1874). These two documents have furnished material for the entire chapter.

[2] *The London Times* (June 26, 1843).

[3] Playbill of the Adelphi Theatre (June 19, 1843), as reprinted in *The New York Clipper* (October 25, 1873).

ETHIOPIAN CONCERT

On MONDAY EVENING, JUNE 19, 1843.

Illustration 42. From the playbill of the first performance of the Virginia Minstrels at the Adelphi Theatre (London, June 19, 1843).

in, the officer was ejected, and there was no further interruption throughout the minstrels' engagement in London . . . .

The popular acclaim which the minstrels received nightly increased as their engagement proceeded. While the *Era* called their performances "on the whole a capital one," though, for some inexplicable reasons, finding fault with the selection of their songs,[4] the *London Times,* relaxing its traditional reserve, published a most enthusiastic review only one week after the debut of the Americans.[5] Contrary to expectations, the fastidious critic, conditioned by the Mozart-Beethoven school and his own contemporaries, Rossini, C. M. von Weber, and M. W. Balfe, was greatly intrigued by the crude, unadorned antics of the four blackface comedians, of course blindly taking their primitive originality for "aboriginality." This is what he wrote:

In addition to the conjurations of the celebrated individual who has assumed the title of the Wizard of the North, and whose performances fully justify the assumption of such an addition to his name, the spectators and auditors of the wonders exhibited at this theatre have during the week been amused by what is called an Ethiopian concert, by four Virginian minstrels, in which some of the aboriginal airs of the

[4] The *Era* (June 25, 1843), as quoted in Harry Reynolds, *Minstrel Memories* (London, 1928), 84.
[5] *The London Times* (June 26, 1843).

137

interior of Africa, modernized if not humanized in the slave states of the Union, and adapted to ears polite, have been introduced by the musical conductor of the theatre. This interpolation upon the Italian, German, and English schools of composition has at least the merit of originality, and is some relief from the tiresome repetitions inflicted upon those who attend the regular theatres. The performance in itself has great merit, and is characteristic and peculiar. It could be very difficult to describe it in libretto, and [a] musical score would not do it justice. Those who want an evening's relaxation, a hearty laugh and matter for speculation how certain strange feats are performed, will find ample opportunity for such indulgences by visiting the pit or boxes.

On July 14, the minstrels appeared for the last time.[6] Whitlock, along with Wooldridge, the agent of the troupe, immediately returned to New York, possibly because he was discouraged by the poor financial results of the engagement. Emmett maintained that the minstrels "did not get enough [money] to pay [even] their board." Whether this was because of dishonesty on the part of the "Wizard of the North" or because of the falling off of attendance which forced him (contrary to the announcement on the playbill of June 19) to have "the house . . . filled nightly with orders [passes]" is uncertain.[7] In any case, the career of the original troupe had unceremoniously come to an end.

If they had done considerably less in Great Britain than amassing a fortune, as they perhaps had hoped for, they had at least successfully transplanted the characteristically American minstrel band and show, refreshing in their primitive hilarity, to the jaded atmosphere of Europe. Whatever can be told of the rest of the troupe is hardly more than an epilogue.

Emmett, Brower, and Pelham remained in England, the first two until September 1844, the latter permanently.[8] The three parted for

---

[6] See notices in *The London Times* from June 19 to July 14.

[7] The two quotations are from Emmett's account in *The New York Clipper* (May 19, 1877). Years later in a newspaper clipping (Chicago, January 24, 1880), as quoted in Moreau, *Negro Minstrelsy*, II, Emmett claimed that Anderson had "swindled the party." See the playbill of the Adelphi Theatre (June 19, 1844): "All Orders Suspended, the Public Press excepted."

some time. Emmett was immediately engaged at Astley's, a fashionable circus at Westminster Bridge. On July 17, he made his bow in the sawdust ring as the "Real Old Virginia Negro Banjo Melodist," singing his version of "De Fine Old Coloured Gemman" as well as the racy "Walk Along John."[9] His engagement did not last long, and he later remembered of it only a nagging stage manager. For the rest of the summer he traveled with June and Sand's American Circus.

In November Pelham performed at the Sadler's Wells Theatre in London, delighting his audiences with song and dance for two months as the "Genuine Yankee Nigger of the U.S." The whirlwind style of his dances had suggested the following warning on the programs, "den he will dance his Slave Wedding Jig! Knocking out all de leaves from de note books of de musicianers so dat dey will nebber be ob no use to nobody no more."[10]

Brower went to Scotland at the end of July to join the American banjoist Sweeney, who had been playing in entr'actes at the Adelphi Theatre in Edinburgh. On his last night, July 24, Brower with his bones appeared too, and the two excelled in "New Songs, Duets, and Dances interspersed with a pretty considerable sprinkling of Transatlantic Sayings and Doings . . . ."[11] Staying together as a team, they turned up in early October in the Theatre Royal in Birmingham and, late in the month, with a circus in Leicester.[12] Their tour was apparently interrupted for some time, for "Emmett and Brower joined fortunes again, performing in Manchester and Nottingham, after which Brower rejoined Sween[e]y . . . ."[13]

[8] "Pelham . . . married an actress, wished to remain in England, did so, and died there last October [October, 1876]," according to *The New York Clipper* (May 19, 1877). He appeared with various Negro minstrel bands all over Great Britain, his final engagement being in Birmingham on August 19, 1856, according to *The New York Clipper* (August 8, 1874).

[9] Playbill of the same date. On the few available playbills for July and August, Emmett's name does not appear again.

[10] Playbill (November 6 and 13, 1843).

[11] Playbill (July 24, 1843), and earlier playbills.

[12] Playbills of Birmingham (October 4, 1843), and of Batty's Amphitheatre, (Humberstone Gate, "printed in Leicester," October 28, 1843).

[13] Quotation from *The New York Clipper* (May 19, 1877). A playbill of the Victoria Rooms (Hull, October 21, 1843), referring also to a performance the day before and to one in Birmingham on October 23, announces "the last night of the Virginia Minstrels" without listing their names. The troupe may have included at least the two original members that were available at the time: Brower and Emmett.

In the spring of 1844, Pelham was instrumental in reviving the old troupe, as far as this was possible without Whitlock. He had an engagement at the Theatre Royal in Dublin which was to start in late April. While passing through Liverpool, he says, he met Brower and Sweeney, "told them where . . . [he] was going, talked over old times, and agreed to form the band again . . . ."[14] Emmett who had been appearing in nearby Bolton was called in to play the fiddle again, but he had to relinquish his place as a "leader" to the banjoist Sweeney. The four traveled then under the name of "The Virginia Minstrels" to Dublin where they appeared at the Theatre Royal from April 24 to May 7, adding a worthy sequel to the career of the original troupe.[15]

Their entr'actes punctuated a rich bill, which not only included farces and ballets but also such a respectable item as Bellini's *Sonnambula* with the prima donna Eugénie Garcia. After a visit to Cork, they traveled north to Belfast and from there back to Scotland. At the end of May they appeared several times at the Theatre Royal, Adelphi, in Glasgow, then in the Waterloo Rooms in Edinburgh, and "for one night only" on June 15 again in Glasgow, but this time in City Hall.[16] At the Adelphi their program consisted not only of their usual musical acts with choreographic and conversational trimmings but of two comical skits. One was the old minstrel play *The Virginia Mummy,* in which Brower impersonated "Ginger Blue, a regular Virginia Nigger with the usual characteristics of his race and an uncommon love of wittles," and the other was "Mr. W. R. Pelham's *Masquerade Ball or Tickets on Tick.*" The latter was evidently a Shakespearean parody. The list of its characters was comprehensive, to say the least. It included such notables as Richard III, Hamlet, Ophelia, Falstaff, Othello, and Lady Macbeth, who rubbed elbows with "Sambo Hit-Em-Hard, a negro doorkeeper" (Pelham), "Spruce Pink and his Love" (Emmett and a Mrs. Wood), and "Joe Break-Em-All, the Virginia

[14] *The New York Clipper* (August 8, 1874 and May 19, 1877).

[15] Playbills (April 24 to May 7, 1844). The playbill of April 29, 1844 was republished in *The New York Clipper* (February 10, 1877).

[16] A playbill (Glasgow, May 31, 1844), as republished in *The New York Clipper* (December 13, 1873), announces the "last appearance of the Virginia Minstrels" as well as appearances on June 1 and 3. A playbill of Glasgow (June 15, 1844), as republished in *The New York Clipper* (January 10, 1874), speaks of a previous performance in Edinburgh.

140

Illustration 43. The only cover of Emmett's publications in London which shows him with his companions. At the bottom are Brower and Pelham performing "grapevine twisting." The representation of castanets and jawbone is no doubt merely a decorative device of the lithographer. From "Dandy Jim from Caroline" (London, D'Almaine & Co., [c. 1844]).

Paganini" (Sweeney). These names alone spell out fairly the action
of the play. Emmett was mentioned on the playbill not merely as a
banjoist and singer but as a "composer of negro music."

At least one performance, the final one in Glasgow, was given
by the minstrels all by themselves—that is as a minstrel show, except
for a few (undoubtedly white-faced) presentations of Mr. W. G.
Ross, the Irish singer and "representative of eccentric characters."
Besides well-known items, on the playbill were an "Introductory Air"
—sufficiently characterized by the line: "Merely to get the instruments in tune"—Brower's "Marriage Festival Dance," Pelham's "Corn-
Husking Jig," and Brower's "Locomotive Lecture." Following Whitlock's example in London, Brower gave, among other items, "a correct
imitation of a locomotive in operation, with the steam whistle accompaniments . . . ."

The exploits of the Virginia Minstrels were now a thing of the
past. In September, after a brief tour with Brower as a member of
Cook's Circus, Emmett and his companion returned to America.

Evidence of Emmett's popularity in England is a series of thir-
teen songs from his repertoire which were published during or shortly
after his stay there. They appeared as *Emmit's Celebrated Negro
Melodies, Or Songs Of The Virginny Banjoist.*[17] On almost every front
cover he is depicted with his banjo as the protagonist of his musical
narrative (see Illustration 43). These illustrations, lacking the freshness of corresponding American lithographs and woodcuts, lend the
minstrel gestures and faces a touch of freakishness. Moreover, some
of the piano arrangements do not use the simple harmony appropriate
to the simplicity of the tunes. It is likely that more than one Englishman was puzzled by the style of American minstrels, *outré* as it was.
On the front cover of "De Old Banjo" of Emmett's series, there is indeed an elderly gentleman of the John Bull type, who is gazing in
speechless amazement at the blackfaced banjoist before him; yet the
younger folks around him seem quite happy.

[17] Published by D'Almaine (London, n.d., [c.1844]).

Chapter 11

THE FIRST NEGRO MINSTREL BAND
AND ITS ORIGINS

THE QUESTION OF THE BEGINNINGS of the Negro minstrel band was heatedly debated in the nineteenth century, for to professionals at that time, the claim of priority was not only a matter of pride but of reputation as well. The honor of having been the first minstrel band was often conceded to the Virginia Minstrels, as it was also often violently denied them. Finally, an attempt to end the quarrel once and for all was made by Emmett, Brower, and Whitlock in 1859 by sending a "certificate" to the editor of *The New York Clipper*, in which they asserted that they were the "pioneer troupe."[1] This certificate was afterwards endorsed by Pelham who was then living in England.

A serious claimant was E. P. Christy, whose minstrel company ranked among the foremost from the middle of the forties on. Early in his career he called his troupe "Christy's Original Band of Virginia Minstrels,"[2] thus not only plagiarizing a very popular name, as had others, but with the word "original" implying an unproved priority. Soon dropping the name, Christy became even more outspoken. His announcements read: "Organized 1842. The oldest established company in existence. The model troupe of the world. The first to

---

[1] "The Late Eph Horn" in *The New York Clipper* (January 13, 1877). The date of the "certificate" was July 29, 1859.

[2] Playbill (New Orleans, December 16, 1843, in the collection of the New York Historical Society).

harmonize negro melodies, and originators of the present popular style of Ethiopian entertainments . . . ."[3] Christy was fortunate enough in later years to have 1842 as the year of the origin of his troupe (thus antedating the Virginia Minstrels) endorsed by the Supreme Court of New York. However, whether this endorsement referred specifically to a "Negro minstrel band" was not made clear, since the court decision spoke rather vaguely of a "band of performers of Negro minstrelsy."[4]

Let us examine the available facts. An article on the Christy Minstrels which appeared in the Buffalo *Morning Express* of January 15, 1846, contained this sentence: "It was our lot to witness their earliest efforts to entertain an audience, four years since, in the 4th story of a brick block on Water Street . . . ."[5] This was in 1842, several months before the Virginia Minstrels made a name for themselves. That the company indeed existed at this time is credible, because Christy was able later to show his business receipts which dated back to June of the same year.[6] However, the writer of the newspaper article did not explain what kind of entertainment he had witnessed. He merely stated that he was "more amused by their caricatures than charmed by the power or sweetness of their music."

A considerably more detailed description of the Christys is available, but it refers to a later performance. In the fall of 1843, the English actor H. P. Grattan visited Buffalo and, as he reported, dropped in at "a lake-side house of entertainment, chiefly frequented by the Erie steam boatmen and those . . . mariners who ride the horses of the passenger boats on the towing-path . . . ."[7] Sitting with "their ladies" at tables, they enjoyed their drinks and the antics of three

---

[3] Playbill (New York, September 5, 1853), as reprinted in *The New York Clipper* (May 4, 1872).

[4] Republished in *Christy's Plantation Melodies* (Philadelphia, 1851).

[5] Information obtained from Margaret M. Mott (The Grosvenor Library, Buffalo, New York).

[6] Published in the New York *Sunday Age* (January 30, 1848, clipping in the Harvard Theatre Collection), and in the preface of *Christy's Plantation Melodies No. 4* (Philadelphia, 1854).

[7] H. P. Grattan, "The Origin of the Christy's Minstrels," *The Theatre* (London, March, 1882). He remembered having been in Buffalo in the "fall of 1842 after playing an engagement . . . in New York . . . ," but he meant 1843. His first appearance in America occurred in New York as late as May 11, 1843: see Odell, *Annals,* IV, 620.

Negro minstrels. One of these minstrels was "tall" Ned Christy [E. P. Christy], "the next to him, whom all called 'George' [George N. Harrington], was some years younger . . . . He was the son of the hostess, though he afterwards took the name of Christy and became justly celebrated as the very best 'end man and bones' ever seen in a nigger troupe. The third performer was a slightly-built young man, I believe of the name of Vaughn [T. Vaughn, a banjoist]." Grattan goes on to describe the performance of the three minstrels: "The orchestral implements of the troupe (they all played double) were a banjo, a violin, a tambourine, a triangle, and the immortal bones." "I am stating a simple fact when I say," he continues enthusiastically, "that so droll was the action, so admirable the singing, so clever the instrumentation, and so genuine was the fun of these three nigger minstrels, that I not only laughed till my sides fairly ached, but that I never left an entertainment with a more keen desire to witness it again than I did the first Christy Minstrel concert I had had the pleasure of assisting at . . . . The staple of E. P. Christy's entertainment was fun—mind, genuine negro fun . . . the counterfeit presentment of the southern darkies [whom] they personally wished to illustrate, and whose dance and songs, as such darkies, they endeavored to reproduce."

The Christys, evidently, were experts at the true style of the minstrel band. But this was in late 1843, and it would be hazardous to assume that their manner of performance was the same a year earlier. Nor is there any reason to believe that they employed then as many as four musicians—not a negligible feature which distinguishes them from the Virginia Minstrels. In 1842 and early 1843 they may very well have acted out many of their scenes in duos, and they surely must have often interrupted their performances to give their restless audience a respite to indulge in alcohol and conversation. Whatever their style was, additional evidence does not add to the probability that, in 1842, theirs was the performance of a true minstrel band.[8]

---

[8] Remarks attached to the open letter by A. P. Durand, *The New York Clipper* (March 10, 1877), indicate that Christy's early troupe "may have been not exactly a minstrel band, but a party similar to that which P. T. Barnum had about 1841, and to that which Charley Jenkins had in the New England States about 1841–42. Both had four or five members . . . ."

Many years later a Mr. A. P. Durand claimed in *The New York Clipper* that the Christys were organized in Buffalo as early as 1839.[9] It is obvious that Mr. Durand's memory was faulty. First of all, his statement about the year of the origin of the band does not tally with E. P. Christy's which ought to be more trustworthy. Secondly, Durand's description of the band in its very early days as consisting not only of the two Christys and Vaughn but of three additional musicians, himself included, is contradicted by Grattan's experience.

Emmett promptly refuted Durand's claims.[10] His arguments were unfortunately based on hearsay only, but in the light of all other data, they may have more than a grain of truth in them. They said in essence that Christy's place on Water Street was originally a "dance-house"[11] and that his "dancers and fiddlers" were trained in the manner of the "new-fashioned nigger shows" some time after the Virginia Minstrels had established their style in New York and Boston.

It seems most likely then that the Virginia Minstrels deserve to be called the first minstrel band—one consisting of four blackface musicians playing the violin, banjo, tambourine, and bones.[12] And it is certain that they were the first to give this particular ensemble the most widespread popularity. Finally, by making the ensemble the nucleus of continuous "Ethiopian" scenes during an entire evening, they actually created the minstrel show—a type of performance

[9] March 10, 1877.

[10] Open letter of May 1, *The New York Clipper* (May 19, 1877).

[11] Remarks attached to the open letter by Emmett, *The New York Clipper* (May 19, 1877): "To a well known comedian he [E. P. Christy] gave a copy of the alleged yearly receipts of his troupe from 1842 (inclusive) forward, yet there has never been much doubt in our mind that the first year's receipts were those of his dance-house in Buffalo."

[12] There were additional minstrel troupes that were thought to antedate the Virginia Minstrels. "Negro Minstrelsy," *The New York Clipper* (January 13, 1877), mentions one of them: "The theory as to the existence of a band of minstrels in Philadelphia in 1837, of which the late Eph Horn was a member . . . seems to be thoroughly exploded . . . ." Another band was the New Orleans Serenaders, claiming to have been "organized in the late fall of 1841": see playbill (Philadelphia, probably of 1850). However, well-known minstrels like Sam S. Sanford, writing in *The New York Clipper* (April 3, 1880), and Charles White finally decided the question in favor of the Virginia Minstrels. White, in an undated newspaper clipping now in the Harvard Theatre Collection, wrote: "From all the researches I have made I have been unable to discover any minstrel organization as early as 1842 . . . . It is quite impossible to prove that he [Christy] had any . . . minstrel band prior to the original founders of that credited amusement [meaning prior to the Virginia Minstrels]."

which was to dominate theatrical entertainment in America for more than half a century.

Original as the performances of the Virginia Minstrels were in setup and style of presentation, they were based in various details, however, on traditional ideas. For example, the instrumental introduction, acting like an overture, came from variety programs, as did the division of the evening into two parts. The scenes themselves were variations of well-known types. Vocal solos with banjo accompaniment had been popular in minstrel entertainments since the end of the thirties, whereas topical, humorous speeches date back even to an earlier time. Nor were Whitlock's locomotive imitations novel; they were tried out first by the Yankee comedian, "The Great Western."[13] Finally, the boatmen's dance of the Virginia Minstrels was an ensemble version of such early solo impersonations of the river boatman and backwoodsman as "Gumbo Chaff" and "Jim Crow."

As soon as the Virginia Minstrels had tested the possibilities of the minstrel band and the minstrel show, they were faced with a host of imitators and competitors. Among the earliest troupes roaming the country were the Alabama Minstrels, the Christy Minstrels, the Columbia Minstrels, the Congo Minstrels, the Ethiopian Minstrels, the Ethiopian Serenaders, the Georgia Champions, the Harmoneons, the Kentucky Minstrels, the Kentucky Rattlers, the Missouri Minstrels, the Nightingale Serenaders, the Sable Harmonists, the Southern Minstrels, the Virginia Serenaders, and the Virginia Vocalists, to mention only a few (see Illustrations 44–46).[14]

The minstrel band of the forties customarily consisted of four or five instruments and occasionally of six. Banjo, tambourine, and bones formed the nucleus of the ensemble, complemented by either a fiddle, an accordion, or perhaps a second banjo. In order to obtain an ensemble of five or six, any instrument could be doubled—except, as a rule, the bones, the tambourine, and the accordion—and any instrument could be added. Among the latter were the triangle and other percussion instruments. The accordion, frequently substituting for

[13] "Among the Minstrels of the Past," *The New York Clipper* (November 4, 1876).
[14] More minstrel bands are listed in "Among the Minstrels of the Past," and in "Negro Minstrelsy's Origin," based on Charles White's diary in the *New York Sun* (April 20, 1902).

Illustration 44. The Virginia Serenaders. From the cover of *Songs of the Virginia Serenaders* (Boston, 1844).

Illustration 45. The Harmoneons—all male actors as was customary on the minstrel stage. From the cover of *Harmoneons/Carolina Melodies* (Boston, 1845).

Illustration 46. The Congo Minstrels employed a cymbalist in the place of a bone player; the appearance of a boy was nothing unusual in minstrel acts, nor in the circus where the custom originated. From the cover of *The Celebrated Congo Minstrels' Songs* (Boston, 1844).

the fiddle, probably played no chords but merely the main melody.[15] Of other instruments we find the jawbone and, though rarely, the firetongs and the dulcimer.[16] The jawbone was taken from a horse, ox, ass, or sheep (see Illustration 47). Its teeth were rattled, scraped, or struck, producing what someone called a "tremolo"—a quick suc-

[15] The accordion methods of 1843 and 1846 by Elias Howe (Boston), have no reference to chords. It should also be noted that the banjoist in early minstrel bands hardly ever played chords.

[16] Firetongs were used by the Ethiopian Serenaders (see Illustration 48). In "Old Joe's Sermon to de Skientific Singer," *The Negro Singer's Own Book* (Philadelphia and New York, n.d. [probably forties]), the following quotation from a minstrel stump speech undoubtedly reveals a not uncommon practice among Negroes, "dis nigga . . . will nebber stop playing on de banjo or soundin' on de tongs . . . ." A playbill of the circus Messrs. Howes and Co. (March 27, 1848), mentions a band consisting of dulcimer, banjo, tambourine, and bones.

Illustration 47. A Negro minstrel singing to his jawbone on the wall; on the floor lies a typical long-necked banjo with four strings. From the cover of "De Ole Jawbone" (Boston, 1840).

cession of dry staccato clicks not dissimilar to those of the bones.[17] The Virginia Minstrels, surprisingly, never made use of this primitive and grotesque instrument.

At times smaller combinations of instruments were favored, such as banjo, fiddle, and tambourine; fiddle, jawbone, and tambourine; banjo and fiddle; two banjos; and accordion and bones.

The program pattern of the Virginia Minstrels was soon varied. The ragged, Southern plantation type of Negro was frequently relegated to the second part of the show, while the more formal, Northern type, the dandy, was introduced into the first part (see illustration 48). In consequence the Negro atmosphere of the first part of the show paled during the forties and led eventually to the use of sentimental ballads and the addition of a flashy middle section, the olio, which was characterized by musical virtuoso acts. Thus, in the fifties it was mainly the last (third) part which retained a pronounced and genuine Negro atmosphere. The trend away from simplicity and primitive realism in minstrelsy which began immediately after the appearance of the Virginia Minstrels—to be arrested, for a time, in the late fifties—reveals itself not only in the use of the accordion but in the adoption of four-part harmony by various troupes.[18]

The placing of the bone and tambourine players at either end of the band, introduced by the Virginia Minstrels, was imitated by many troupes in the forties, though not by all. It finally became the standard pattern in minstrel shows. While the Virginia Minstrels carried out their comical conversation jointly with only a slight emphasis on the "end men," this emphasis grew and soon made the tambourine and bone players the center of attention. Moreover, to judge by the example of the Ethiopian Serenaders in the middle forties, one of

[17] "Negro Minstrelsy," *The New York Clipper* (January 18, 1868), refers to the jawbone as the "horse's lower jaw . . . [which] was the 'tremolo' . . . ." Further information comes from the following lines: "We made de 'lodious sheep-bone rattle," in "Ahoo! Ahoo!" *White's New Book of Plantation Melodies* (New York, 1849); "And beat on de old jaw-bone," in Stephen Foster, "Angelina Baker" (1850). *Sanford's Plantation Melodies* (Philadelphia, 1860), 16, contains a picture of a banjoist, a dancer, and a jawbone player.

[18] In contrast to Christy's claims, *The New York Clipper* (July 5, 1879), stated that the Congo Minstrels "were the first company to introduce harmony . . . .", which was in 1842–43. Four-part harmonizations of Negro minstrel songs appear in *The Ethiopian Glee Book*.

Illustration 48. The Original Ethiopian Serenaders or Boston Minstrels appearing as dandies and as plantation hands. One of the minstrels (the first, second row) holds firetongs in his hands. From the cover of a song sheet of the troupe (New York, C. G. Christman, 1843).

these end men assumed the role of master of ceremonies, a role which in later years was shifted to the so-called "interlocutor" in the center of the band. The tambourine player of this troupe is reported to have been "the spokesman of the parts . . . [announcing] the successive performances . . . [and diversifying] them by a species of 'clown in the ring' humor . . . ."[19] It was undoubtedly also his role to lead off the comical dialogue with his opposite, the bone player.

The minstrel band originated as a form of urban entertainment, but its roots lay deep in the lower strata of American society. The instruments of the early minstrel band—banjo, bones, tambourine, triangle, and fiddle—with the exception of the accordion, were a part of the life of southern slaves. On the plantation these instruments served the slaves well when at the end of the day "they would assemble in little parties and pass some hours in singing and dancing to the accompaniment of music from rude instruments they had themselves constructed."[20] Musical merrymaking was indeed encouraged by the white planters because it was thought, perhaps a little naïvely, that a "laughing, singing, fiddling, dancing negro is almost invariably a faithful servant . . . ."[21]

The Negroes often cut their banjo, an old plantation instrument known to slaves in Jamaica as early as the seventeenth century, out of a long-necked gourd, the bowl of which they covered with coonskin.[22] They used only four strings, and this number prevailed on the minstrel stage until the late forties. If we may believe an early min-

[19] An English pamphlet on the Ethiopian Serenaders (1846, Harvard Theatre Collection).

[20] "Negro Minstrelsy," *The New York Clipper* (May 6, 1871).

[21] J. Kinnard, Jr., "Who Are Our National Poets?" *The Knickerbocker Magazine* (October, 1845). "I have heard that many of the masters and overseers on these plantations," said Kemble, *Journal,* 129 "prohibit melancholy tunes or words, and encourage nothing but cheerful music and senseless words, deprecating the effect of sadder strains upon the slaves, whose peculiar sensibility might be expected to make them especially excitable by any songs of a plaintive character, and having any reference to their peculiar hardships."

[22] Scarborough, *On the Trail,* 101, in referring to the very early banjo, said that its "head was covered with rattlesnake skin." *The Journal of Nicholas Creswell,* 18–19, confirmed that the banjo of the Negroes in Virginia was made "of a Gourd something in the imitation of the Guitar, with only four strings and played with the fingers in the same manner . . . ." Jekyll, *Jamaican Song,* 283, referred to the Jamaican banjos that were used at the beginning of the eighteenth century as "gourds with necks and strung with horse-hair." According to Cable, "Place Congo," New Orleans Negroes in the eighties still used a banjo with four strings only.

strel song, there existed also a slightly different type of banjo which is described as "a gourd, three string'd, and an old pine stick."[23] Bones, two for each hand, were made of "rib-bones of cattle" like their African models. They became common among minstrels from the early forties on, although they were found in urban Negro dance halls, if we may generalize from a report on Cincinnati, about ten years earlier.[24] The tambourine, too, was well known. A Negro tambourine player, who with five other musicians played at a white ball in Georgia in the thirties, produced intricate rhythms—"the rattlesnake note"—with his fingers on the instrument.[25] Further information comes from the northern United States. Charles Dickens witnessed in 1842 two Negro musicians in a New York saloon, one playing the fiddle and the other the tambourine as an accompaniment to a "negro breakdown."[26]

The primitive plantation Negro, fascinated by anything percussive, did not overlook the white man's triangle. If this was not available, he took "the U-shaped iron clives [clevis] which . . . was used

[23] "Picayune Butler's Come to Town," *Rice's Correct Method*. The song also appeared separately as early as 1847 (Baltimore, F. D. Benteen), but without the line that has been quoted.

[24] Percival R. Kirby, *The Musical Instruments of the Native Races of South Africa* (London, 1934), 10. Frank Brower's bone playing in 1841 is reported to have been something of a novelty: see the letter to the editor by C. J. R. in *The New York Clipper* (June 20, 1874). A story in Charles Cist, *The Cincinnati Miscellany* (Cincinnati, 1845), I, 14, tells of a man who in 1830 attended "a Nigger dance . . . at a dance house on Columbia St., with his slippers off, dancing and playing the jaw bones [a misnomer for bones] or Castanets." Bones also existed in Europe. A passage in Shakespeare's *Midsummer Night's Dream*, Act IV, Scene I, proves that they were in use among the English peasants of the sixteenth century. When Nick Bottom, the weaver, said: "I have a reasonable good ear in music. Let's have the tongs and the bones," a stage direction in an early text adds: "Musicke Tongs, Rurall Musicke": see Sir Arthur Quiller-Couch and John Dover Wilson, *The Works of Shakespeare* (Cambridge, England, 1924). Tongs were evidently not fire-tongs, but similar to bones—both of them castanetlike instruments.

[25] "The [coloured] tambourine player . . . performed the rattlesnake note with his middle finger which threw Miss Crump entirely in the shade," in *The Ball* (publisher separately in 1832) in Longstreet, *Georgia Scenes*. It is also reported that the tambourine, along with two fiddles, was played at dances of Negro slaves on Haitian estates in the late eighteenth century; see Moore, "Moreau de Saint-Mery."

[26] Charles Dickens, *American Notes*, Chap. VI. The cover of the minstrel song "Ole Virginny Break Down," (Boston, 1841), depicts realistically an outdoor dance of Negroes to the accompaniment of a banjo (see Illustration 31 on page 90). On the cover of "Backside Albany" (New York, 1837) there is a similar scene, although without a banjo.

for hitching horses to a plow. The ante-bellum Negro often suspended [it] . . . by a string and beat it with its pin . . . ."[27]

The jawbone was among his favorite instruments.[28] Macabre in shape, it must have particularly appealed to his tribal sense of magic. No wonder then that the instrument lived on the plantation much longer than on the minstrel stage and has survived in our century up to the present among the Negroes in Jamaica, the Georgia Sea Islands, and in certain parts of Cuba, being a part of South American dance bands as well.[29]

The fiddle, a typical instrument of the backwoods, was frequently heard on the plantation as well as on the early river boats which customarily had a fiddler on board. The fiddler was often accompanied by a tambourine player,[30] a practice reflected in these lines of an early minstrel song:

He jump into a boat wid his old Tambourine
While schoonerhead Sambo play'd de Violin.[31]

The slaves were fond of playing on their rude instruments in small groups which, as a rule, included at least one percussion instrument. There existed then ensembles of various kinds: banjo and drum (see Illustration 49); banjo and tambourine; fiddle, triangle, and "patting" (beating time with hands and feet); fiddle, bones, and sticks hitting the floor; banjo, jawbone, and bones; and so forth.[32] Thomas Ashe

[27] Talley, *Negro Folk Rhymes,* 307. See also Parrish *Slave Songs,* 16.

[28] Kennard, "National Poets," mentions that the "sound of the violin, banjo, or jawbone lute" [meaning the jawbone] was frequently heard on Southern plantations. See also Scarborough, *On the Trail,* 102.

[29] The song of a colored banjoist at a white frolic in the thirties included the following lines: "My old horse died in Tennessee / And will'd his jawbone here to me"; *Sketches and Eccentricities,* 39. See also Jekyll, *Jamaican Song,* 216–17; Helen H. Roberts, "Possible Survivals of African Song in Jamaica," *The Musical Quarterly* (July, 1926); Parrish, *Slave Songs,* 16; Harold Courlander, "Musical Instruments of Cuba," *The Musical Quarterly* (April, 1942); and *Meet Mr. Cugat* (New York, 1943).

[30] Leland D. Baldwin, *The Keelboat Age on Western Waters* (Pittsburgh, 1941). The minstrel song "Sich a Gitting Up Stairs" (Baltimore, n.d. [thirties]), dealing with a Negro boatman, has this line: "On a Suskehanna raft I come down de bay, And I danc'd and I frolick'd, and I fiddled all de way." The picture *Jolly Flatboatmen* by the Missouri artist George Caleb Bingham, painted in 1844, shows three white boatmen, one dancing, another banging a tin-pan in lieu of a tambourine, and a third fiddling.

[31] "Gumbo Chaff" (Baltimore, 1834).

[32] See the cover of the minstrel song "Ole Virginny Break Down"; "Management of Negroes upon Southern Estates," *De Bow's Review* (New Orleans, 1851), as repub-

in his *Travels in America performed in 1806*[33] observed, in a back-woods inn in Virginia, a group which included an Indian: "The music consisted of two bangies [banjos] played by negroes nearly in a state of nudity, and a lute [probably a guitar or some such instrument] through which a Chickesaw breathed with much occasional exertion and violent gesticulations . . . ," but "the music of Ethiopia was with difficulty heard" because of the "clamour of the card tables." Here a percussive quality was maintained by the accumulated, incisive sound of sharply plucked strings. A more elaborate ensemble of three fiddles and clarinet supported by a tambourine and a triangle at a white ball in Georgia in the thirties can be accounted for by the formal occasion which demanded a toning down of primitive sonorities.[34]

Before the Virginia Minstrels joined in a "quartet," they had already tried out smaller ensembles. Whitlock remembered that in about 1840 while in Philadelphia he "practiced with Dick Myers, the violinist, and on our benefit night we played the fiddle and the banjo together for the first time in public," adding with exaggerated emphasis: "I retained this novel idea in my memory for future reference."[35] Two other members of the band had also been active. Brower is reported to have rattled the bones in 1841 to a minstrel song rendered by Emmett in the circus ring and undoubtedly accompanied by him on the banjo.[36]

It was perhaps only a small and inevitable step to proceed from such smaller ensembles to a larger one which then constituted the so-called minstrel band. All that Emmett, Brower, Whitlock, and

lished in A. P. Hudson, *Humor of the Old Deep South* (New York, 1936); Smith, "Plantation Boyhood"; and Scarborough, *On the Trail,* 102. The slaves patted sometimes "by striking the hands on the knees, then striking the hands together, then striking the right shoulder with one hand, the left with the other—all the while keeping time with the feet and singing": Solomon Northup, *Twelve Years A Slave* (Auburn, 1853), as quoted in B. A. Botkin, *A Treasury of Southern Folklore* (New York, 1949), 708.

[33] London, 1808, 100.

[34] Longstreet, *Georgia Scenes.* A similar Negro ensemble playing "white" dance music was described by Caroline Gilman in *Recollections of a Southern Matron* (New York, 1838), 76: The musicians were seen "sawing violins, [playing] harsh clarinets, jingling tembarines [*sic*], crashing triangles, with the occasional climax of a base [*sic*] drum . . . and then, overtopping even that climax, comes the shout of a voice with the negro dialect, calling out the figures . . . ."

[35] From Whitlock's autobiography, as quoted in *The New York Clipper* (April 13, 1878).

[36] Letter to the editor by C. J. R. in *The New York Clipper* (June 20, 1874).

Illustration 49. Primitive water color of a southern plantation (c. 1800). Courtesy Ludwell-Paradise House (Williamsburg, Virginia).

Pelham had to do, one might argue, was to draw on their previous experiences by pooling their resources (fiddle, banjo, and bones) and adding the tambourine which the river boatmen so often combined with the fiddle. However, this idea might never have materialized, had not several circumstances occurred simultaneously.

There was, first, a trend in Negro minstrelsy towards larger ensembles of two or three performers, which, beginning in the late thirties with banjo-dance acts, made itself strongly felt in the early forties. The following combinations, we may remember, existed: two banjoists and one dancer; one banjoist and two dancers; one fiddler and two dancers; and one banjoist, one dancer, and a singer. Finally, a

157

few weeks before the founding of the minstrel band, as many as four minstrels (one banjoist and three dancers) may have performed together in January, 1843 (see Chapter 4).

The second circumstance was the arrival of the Tyrolese Family Rainer in America in 1838. The group consisted of two female and two male singers—one of many Alpine troupes which roamed all over Europe in the twenties and thirties.[37] The Rainers soon popularized ensembles of their kind and their number. In their wake, that is about 1842–43, American "singing families," usually quartets, sprang into existence; the New Hampshire Hutchinson family was the best known. It is noteworthy that at this moment, blackface comedians, too, banded together in groups of four. This is as unlikely to have been mere coincidence as the fact that most of them styled themselves "minstrels"—"Ethiopian Minstrels," to be exact—replacing the former designation, "Ethiopian delineators." The new name was clearly suggested by the Rainers who also appeared as "Tyrolese Minstrels." The success of their concerts encouraged the introduction of part singing into minstrel performances, as revealed by the following playbill of the Congo Minstrels of 1844: "Their songs are sung in Harmony in the style of the Hutchinson Family."[38]

The third element which led to the creation of the minstrel band in 1843 was the financial crisis which befell the New York theaters during the 1842–43 season. In order to attract the public, programs were sensationalized, prices were reduced, and, in consequence, the salaries of actors were decreased as well.[39] Even such successful performers as Emmett, Whitlock, Brower, and Pelham had to make special efforts to arouse the interest of cautious theatrical managers and of listless audiences. Emmett remembered that "their business became stale and they were no longer attractive. They were all at sea for a new idea . . . ."[40] To find the idea they had merely to open their eyes, as it were; but to make it work, all their daring and imagination were required.

[37] See Nathan, "The Tyrolese Family Rainer."
[38] Playbill (Baltimore, May 31, 1844).
[39] Odell, *Annals*, IV, 603.
[40] From an interview with Emmett in a Chicago newspaper (January 24, 1880), as quoted in Moreau, *Negro Minstrelsy*, II.

Chapter 12

EARLY MINSTREL TUNES

———◄◦►———

THE INDIGENOUS CHARACTER OF EARLY MINSTREL ACTS revealed itself mainly in the type of acting as well as in both the style and content of the texts. Appropriate tunes existed of course, and they indeed contributed greatly to the popularity of the genre. But although they seemed original at the time, most of them turned out to be variants of stage and folk music of Great Britain. The emergence of a more independent song literature did not occur until about the early forties. Only then did the production become continuous and stylistically coherent, whereas no more than a handful of minstrel tunes of diverse character appeared in the twenties and thirties.

Of the tunes of the twenties "Bonja [Banjo] Song" and "Coal Black Rose," in keeping with the origin of American minstrelsy and the prevailing taste of the early years of the nineteenth century, continued the idiom of the English stage music of the eighteenth century. "Do I Do I Don't Do Nothing," too, is essentially a "patter song" in the same vein (see Musical Examples 9–11).[1]

---

[1] "Bonja Song" (n.d. [*c.*1820]), and "Coal Black Rose" (n.d. [early thirties]), appear in facsimile in Damon, *Old American Songs*. The latter song was performed in the late twenties: see Damon, "Early American Songsters." "Do I Do I Don't Do Nothing" (Baltimore, G. Willig, 1825). See also "Massa Georgee Washington and General Lafayette" (New York, 1824): see Chapter 3.

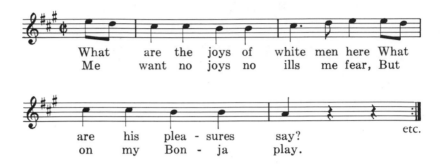

What are the joys of white men here What
Me want no joys no ills me fear, But

are his plea - sures say?
on my Bon - ja play.

etc.

Musical Example 9
"Bonja Song" (c. 1820)

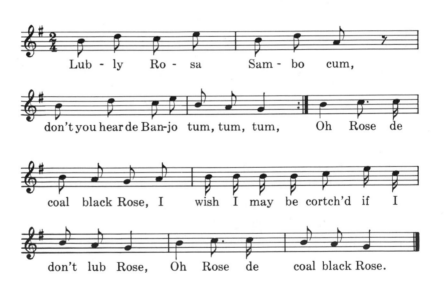

Lub - ly Ro - sa Sam - bo cum,

don't you hear de Ban-jo tum, tum, tum, Oh Rose de

coal black Rose, I wish I may be cortch'd if I

don't lub Rose, Oh Rose de coal black Rose.

Musical Example 10
"Coal Black Rose" (late 1820's)

From the late twenties on, and especially during the thirties, the influence of British folk music, in contrast to that of the theater, makes

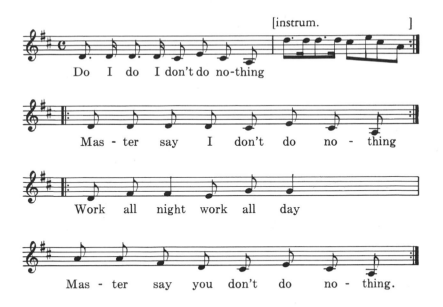

Musical Example 11
"Do I Do I Don't Do Nothing" (1825)

itself increasingly felt. It marks the beginning of a trend toward a more genuine idiom, although some of its first results were only tentative. Examples are "Long Time Ago" (see Musical Examples 12 and 13),[2] "The Bee-Gum" (see Musical Examples 14 and 15),[3] Clare De Kitchen" (see Musical Examples 16–18),[4] and "Settin' on a Rail" (see Musical Examples 19–21),[5] which consist of modified Scottish, Irish, and English elements.

[2] "Long Time Ago" (Baltimore, John Cole, 1833); the facsimile of an 1836 edition appears in Damon, *Old American Songs.* See "Our Guidman Cam Hame at E'en," in Robert Chambers, *The Songs of Scotland Prior to Burns* (Edinburgh and London, 1880).

[3] "The Bee-Gum (Baltimore, G. Willig, 1833). See "The Hon. Miss Rollo," in John Glen, *The Glen Collection of Scottish Dance Music* (Edinburgh, 1891), Book I.

[4] "Clare De Kitchen" (n.d. [early thirties]); the fascsimile appears in Damon, *Old American Songs.* See "The Star of the County Down," in Herbert Hughes, *Irish Country Songs* (London, 1936), IV; and "Lady Shaftsbury's Reel," in Elias Howe, *The Caledonia Collection* (Boston, 1860).

[5] "Settin' on a Rail" (Philadelphia, G. E. Blake, n.d. [thirties]). See "O! A-Hunting We Will Go," in Alice B. Gomme and Cecil J. Sharp, *Children's Singing Games* (London, 1909); and "The Countess of Percy," in Glen, *Scottish Dance Music,* Book I.

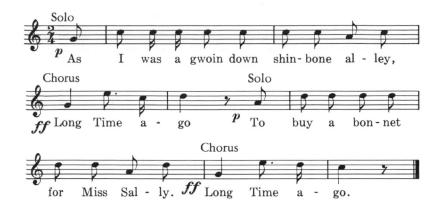

As I was a gwoin down shin-bone al-ley,
Long Time a-go To buy a bon-net
for Miss Sal-ly. Long Time a-go.

Musical Example 12
"Long Time Ago" (1833)

Musical Example 13
"Our Guidman Cam Hame at E'en" (Scottish folk tune)

Musical Example 14
"The Bee-Gum" (1833)

Musical Example 15
"The Hon. Miss Rollo" (Scottish reel)

In old Ken-tuck in de ar - ter - noon, We

sweep de floor wid a bran new broom, And

ar - ter dat we form a ring, And
dis de song dat we do sing, Oh!

Clare de kit - chen old folks young folks

Clare de kit - chen old folks young folks

Old Vir - gin - ny ne - ver tire.

Musical Example 16
"Clare De Kitchen" (early 1830's)

164

etc.

Musical Example 17
"The Star of the County Down" (Irish)

etc.

Musical Example 18
"Lady Shaftsbury's Reel" (Scottish)

I   walkd out   by   de   light ob de moon, So

mer - ri - ly   sing - ing   dis same tune;   I

cum   a   cross   a   big   Ra - coon, A

set - tin' on   a   rail,   Set - tin' on   a

rail,   Set - tin' on   a   rail,

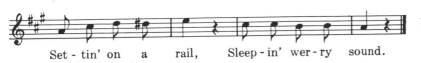

Set - tin' on   a   rail,   Sleep - in' wer - ry sound.

Musical Example 19
"Settin' on a Rail" (1830's)

Musical Example 20
"O! A-Hunting We Will Go" (English)

etc.

Musical Example 21
"The Countess of Percy" (Scottish reel)

Of greater interest are the remaining tunes of the period. Also leaning heavily on foreign models, they nevertheless reveal a certain originality in their variants. "Zip Coon" is related to two Irish hornpipes (see Musical Examples 22–24),[6] "Sich a Gitting Up Stairs" is a slightly but significantly changed English Morris dance tune (see Musical Examples 25 and 26),[7] "My Long Tail Blue" follows a Scottish folk song (see Musical Examples 27 and 28),[8] and "Jim Crow" is partly related to an Irish folk tune and partly to one of the eighteenth-century English stage (see Musical Examples 29–31).[9] But unlike "Gumbo Chaff" (see Musical Example 32),[10] which is practically

[6] "Zip Coon" (Baltimore, G. Willig, n.d. [early thirties]); the facsimile of an 1834 edition appears in Damon, *Old American Songs.* "The Glasgow Hornpipe" and "The Post Office" (a hornpipe), in Francis O'Neill, *O'Neill's Music of Ireland* (Chicago, 1903).

[7] "Sich a Gitting Up Stairs" (Baltimore, G. Willig, n.d. [early thirties]). "Getting Upstairs," in Winston Wilkinson, "Virginia Dance Tunes," *Southern Folklore Quarterly* (March, 1942).

[8] "My Long Tail Blue" (n.d. [early thirties]); the facsimile appears in Damon, *Old American Songs.* "Jenny's Babee," in Chambers, *Songs of Scotland.*

[9] "Jim Crow" (n.d. [early thirties]); the facsimile appears in Damon, *Old American Songs.* "I Wish the Shepherd's Pet Were Mine," in P. W. Joyce, *Irish Folk Music and Song* (Dublin, 1888). "The Old One Outwitted / In the Honest Yorkshire Man" (on an English eighteenth-century broadside in the Boston Public Library).

[10] "Gumbo Chaff" (Baltimore, G. Willig, n.d. [early thirties]).

Musical Example 22
"Zip Coon" (1834)

Musical Example 23
"The Glasgow Hornpipe" (Irish)

Musical Example 24
"The Post Office" (Irish hornpipe)

identical with the English "Bow Wow Wow" (see Musical Example 33),[11] "Jim Crow" manages to preserve a degree of independence.

[11] "Bow Wow Wow," in W. Chappell, *Popular Music of the Olden Time* (London, 1859), II, and in William Shield, *Love in a Camp, or Patrick in Prussia / A Comic Opera* (see Musical Example 33). An American eighteenth-century edition of "Bow Wow Wow" is listed in O. G. Sonneck and W. T. Upton, *A Bibliography of Early Secular American Music* (Washington, D.C., 1945).

Musical Example 25
"Sich a Gitting Up Stairs" (early 1830's)

Musical Example 26
"Getting Upstairs" (Morris dance tune)

169

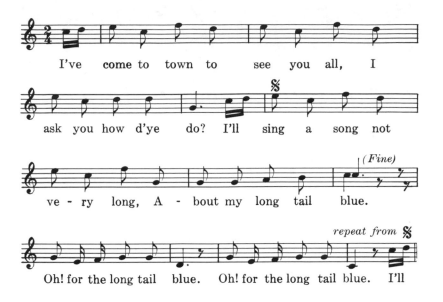

I've come to town to see you all, I ask you how d'ye do? I'll sing a song not ve-ry long, A-bout my long tail blue. Oh! for the long tail blue. Oh! for the long tail blue. I'll

Musical Example 27
"My Long Tail Blue" (early 1830's)

Musical Example 28
"Jenny's Babee" (Scottish)

Come lis - ten all you galls and boys, I'm just from Tu - cky - hoe; I'm goin to sing a lee - tle song, My name's Jim Crow. Weel a - bout, and turn a - bout, And do jis so; Eb' - ry time I weel a - bout, I jump Jim Crow.

Musical Example 29
"Jim Crow" (early 1830's)

etc.

Musical Example 30
"I Wish the Shepherd's Pet Were Mine" (Irish)

(transposed)

Musical Example 31
"The Old One Outwitted" (English) [transposed]

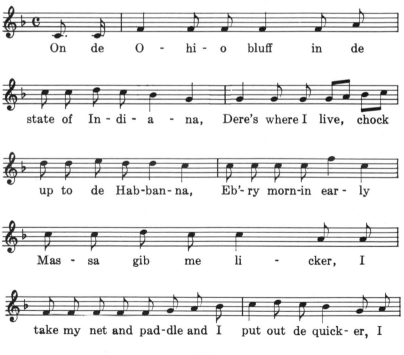

On de O - hi - o bluff in de
state of In - di - a - na, Dere's where I live, chock
up to de Hab-ban-na, Eb'- ry morn-in ear - ly
Mas - sa gib me li - cker, I
take my net and pad-dle and I put out de quick- er, I

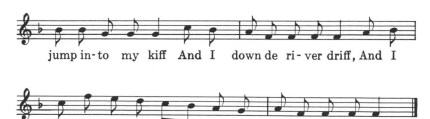

jump in-to my kiff And I down de ri-ver driff, And I

cotch as man-y cat fish as ev-er nig-ger liff.

Musical Example 32
"Gumbo Chaff" (early 1830's)

(transposed)

Musical Example 33
"Bow Wow Wow" (English) [transposed]

"My Long Tail Blue"

"Sich a Gitting Up Stairs"

"Jim Crow"

"Zip Coon"

Musical Example 34
Passages from early minstrel tunes, prior to 1840,
revealing an indigenous melodic idiom

It is not surprising that the above four tunes, in particular "Zip Coon" and "Jim Crow," enjoyed great popularity, which the first (known since the sixties as "Turkey in the Straw") has kept to the present. There is a jollity and homespun simplicity about them which fits the life of the frontier. The melodic design of the tunes—their variants and new sections—is clear-cut, sober, and animated. One can indeed single out a few passages which form the nucleus of an indigenous vocabulary (see Musical Example 34). They are sustained by firm, noncantabile intervals, operating vigorously within an unlyrical context. To this style corresponds a heavy-footed motion, partly resulting from accentuated endings of brief phrases, which has nothing in common with old world dances. The tunes possess sporadic modal and pentatonic features; generally, however, they tend to the major tonality, especially when they vary Anglo-Celtic material. As far as their formal organization is concerned, "Jim Crow" and "Sich a Gitting Up Stairs" end in a lusty refrain, but this is not the rule yet at this time.

From the beginning of the forties on, the publication of minstrel songs proceeded at an ever increasing rate. Aside from adaptations of texts to well-known tunes, taken even from operas, there appeared within one decade about two dozen songs which constitute the most indigenous American music apart from somewhat earlier southern folk hymns and the New England hymn tunes and their settings of the late eighteenth century.

The new idiom emerged only by stages. Even the influence of English eighteenth-century theater music, though clearly on the wane, did not cease immediately. For example, the tune of "My Old Aunt Sally" (see Musical Example 35) is a variant of Dibdin's "Peggy Perkins" (see Musical Example 36); the same type of element went into "Jim Along Josey" (see Musical Example 37), but the style of the refrain belongs to the new vocabulary (see also Musical Example 38).[12]

Minstrel music now began to acquire a measure of coherence by drawing on its own past. For instance, the opening section of "My Old Dad" (see Musical Example 39)[13] stems from preminstrel material, the serious "A Negro Song" (see Musical Example 40)[14] by Benjamin Carr of about 1801. Measures one, two, nine, and ten of "De Ole Jaw Bone" (see Musical Example 41)[15] are reminiscent of "Sich a Gitting Up Stairs" and "Coal Black Rose."

The motion of the songs of the forties is the steady one of equal notes within duple time as in the pattern | ♪♪♪♪ |. It occurs mainly in the first section, while in the last, the refrain, it is usually less regular. The melodic line as a whole consists of very brief phrases, as a rule two measures long, or, in the refrain, one measure long. It gives the impression of primness and compactness, for its tones are close together within a narrow range and each tone is hardened by a

[12] Facsimiles of "My Old Aunt Sally" (1843), and "Jim Along Josey" (1840), appear in Damon, *Old American Songs.* "Peggy Perkins" is a song of the English composer Charles Dibdin, used in his *The Oddities* (1790); an American edition is listed in Sonneck and Upton, *Bibliography of Early Music;* Musical Example 36, "Peggy Perkins," is from *The Songs of Charles Dibdin* (London, 1848). See also "Four and Twenty Fiddlers / A favorite Song sung by Mr. Edwin at the Theatre Royal at Covt. Garden," (on an English broadside in the possession of the Boston Public Library).
[13] "My Old Dad" (Boston, 1844).
[14] "A Negro Song" (Baltimore, J. Carr, n.d. [*c.*1801]).
[15] "De Ole Jaw Bone" (Boston, 1840).

A - gwine down to New Or - leans I
a - la - mode de duck soup, de

got up - on de land - in, I
cor - ner ob an al - ley; I'll

ran a - gin a cot - ton bag, it
tell you ob a scrape I had

foch me up a stand - in It's
wid my lub - ly Sal - ly.

O Sal - ly, O Sal - ly, my old aunt Sal - ly, etc.

Musical Example 35
"My Old Aunt Sally" (1843)

(transposed)

Shall loud - ly sing, like a - ny - thing; 'Tis

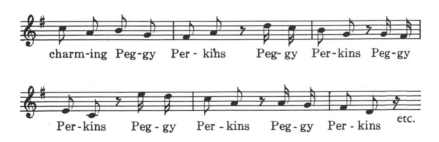

charm-ing Peg-gy Per - kihs   Peg- gy Per - kins Peg-gy

Per - kins   Peg - gy   Per - kins   Peg - gy Per - kins   etc.

Musical Example 36
"Peggy Perkins" (Charles Dibdin) [transposed]

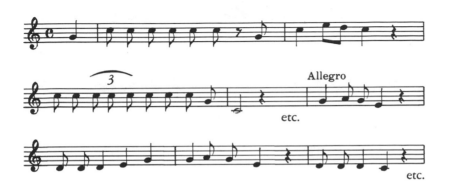

Musical Example 37
"Jim Along Josey" (1840)

Musical Example 38
"Four and Twenty Fiddlers" (English)

177

Musical Example 39
"My Old Dad" (1844)

Musical Example 40
"A Negro Song" (c. 1801) [transposed]

Musical Example 41
"De Ole Jaw Bone" (1840)

Musical Example 42
"Ole Pee Dee" (1844)

Musical Example 43
"Old Dan Tucker" (1843)

syllable. Among seconds (more major than minor ones), interspersed with thirds and fourths, it is especially the latter interval which acts as a rigid skeleton. Only a few tunes are modal. The majority, avoiding the ambivalent style of the thirties, merges elements of modality, including pentatonic ones, with the major tonality.

As soon as the melody begins to move in one direction, frequently upwards, it returns to its starting point or to a point near it, or else it is led back to it by a subsequent phrase (see Musical Example 42).[16] Thus the line is punctuated by constant starts and stops. Another prominent feature is the frequency of repeated tones, sometimes as extreme as in "Old Dan Tucker,"[17] perhaps the most popular song of its time (see Musical Example 43).

The direction of the melody and the use of small intervals favor the recurrence of two or three adjacent tones. Note for example how

[16] "Ole Pee Dee" (Boston, 1844).
[17] "Old Dan Tucker" (Boston, 1843), was said at the time to have "been sung, perhaps, oftener than any melody ever written": "Negro Minstrelsy—Ancient and Modern."

Musical Example 44
"De Blue Tail Fly" (1846)

often the tones *b*-flat, *c*, and *d* appear merely in the first phrase of
"De Blue Tail Fly" (see Musical Example 44).[18] Such tones, through
the multiple repetition of phrases, become the center of the entire
first or second section of a tune. This indeed is the chief structural
principle of the style of the forties. One might say that the repetition
of brief motives existed earlier, namely in British reels; however, there
the recurrent tones are part of a coherent, rapid, and, above all, sin-
uous melodic line with the result that they are less noticeable.

Even the slightest deviation from repetition in minstrel tunes becomes conspicuous. In "Ole Pee Dee" (see Musical Example 42), the
first two-measure phrase ends on *f*-sharp and the second identical
one on *d*. The difference between the two tones looks small, but to
the ear it seems unexpected and thus large.

Most of the minstrel songs of the forties end in a lively refrain.
Usually contrasting with the first section, though often using some
of its phrases, the refrain acquires energy through greater brevity of
phrases, shorter and more varied note values, and larger volume (occasional markings like "chorus" indicate a group performance). The
element of pure motion is sometimes strengthened through inserted
instrumental passages. These are thrown into relief, by way of contrast, when, as was customary, they are subsequently repeated with

18 "De Blue Tail Fly" (Boston, 1846).

Musical Example 45
"O Lud Gals, Gib Me" (1843)

words adapted to them (see Musical Example 45). The same features appear in "My Old Dad," but there are also other aspects which
deserve a comment. The two-tone phrase to the words "Old Dad" has
a special vigor: supported by slangy words and set off against rapid,
persistent motion, it resembles the humorously vulgar shout as we
know it from twentieth-century dance music. In addition, the second
tone (*d*) has a stress—unexpectedly so, since the interval to which it
belongs had an accent on the first tone in the preceding section. This
is a syncopation, and it affects the subsequent music. Finally, the
emphasis on the minor tonic produces a lugubrious, "bluesy" flavor
so that, all in all, one can say that the refrain anticipates certain aspects of modern jazz.

The minstrel tunes of the forties are no longer mere echoes of the
Old World. After a growth of about twenty years, they have attained

a character all their own, though their vocabulary remains limited. Like true folk songs, they are genuine and straightforward, but in contrast to European styles, there is nothing idyllic or pathetic about them. Instead they combine the blandness and charm of children's songs with the rigidity and rhythmic persistence of ethnically primitive music. They are jolly (if tune, text, and theatrical purposes are considered together), but they make their point with reticence. The result is a dead-pan quality which is wholly in the tradition of American humor.

The influence of British folk music, which was of intense formative value at an earlier stage, has now weakened, though it has not vanished. For one thing, Scottish and Irish reels are responsible for the organization of the first section of most minstrel tunes of the forties: the use of four two-measure phrases, each of which starts in the same manner. To this the following instances may be added. The English song "The Spinning Wheel,"[19] or some such tune (see Musical Example 46), was the model of the initial phrase of "I'm Going Ober De Mountains," "O Lud Gals Gib Me,"[20] and other songs. However, the American variants are plain and robust in contradistinction to the suppleness and the cantabile character of the English melody. The typical ending of Scottish reels and strathspeys and of Irish reels reappears in measures seven and eight of "De Ole Jaw Bone" (see Musical Example 41) and as the main motive, along with a variant, in "Dandy Jim from Caroline" (see Musical Examples 47 and 48).[21] In the latter case, the original element is again slightly modified: it is more angular because of the emphasis on the fourth. Finally, the influence of Irish and Scottish reels appears in the refrain of " 'Twill Nebber Do to Gib It up So," the initial phrase of "De Blue Tail Fly" (see Musical Example 44), and the instrumental sections in the refrain of "My Old Dad" (see Musical Examples 49 and 50);[22] but

---

[19] "The Spinning Wheel," in Frank Kidson, *et al.*, *Folk-Songs of the North-Countrie* (London, 1927).

[20] "O Lud Gals Gib Me" (Boston, 1843).

[21] "Dandy Jim From Caroline" (London, D'Almaine & Co., n.d. [*c*.1844]). See also "The Miller's Maid," in O'Neill, *Music of Ireland*.

[22] "Take Her Out and Air Her," in George Petrie and Charles Villiers Stanford, *The Complete Collection of Irish Music* (London, 1902 and 1905). "Capt. Lockhart of the Tartar," in Glen, *Scottish Dance Music*, Book I.

while it is usually not literal here, it is again undisguised from the forties on in preludes and postludes. For example, notice the use of the Scottish "Miss McLeod's Reel" in "My Old Dad." At times one sees evidence of the popularity of the polka, the craze of the forties. Its traces can be found in Emmett's "Dar He Goes! Dats Him!" but it is combined with Scottish folk song elements in the refrain (see Musical Examples 51 and 52).[23]

Negro minstrel music stirred popular imagination in the nineteenth century, particularly in the first half, with the same intensity as jazz does in our own time. Disseminated by circuses and by the

Musical Example 46
"The Spinning Wheel" (English)

Musical Example 47
"Dandy Jim from Caroline" (c. 1844)

Musical Example 48
"The Miller's Maid" (Irish reel) [transposed]

[23] "Dar He Goes! Dats Him!" (Boston, 1844). "Duncan Gray," in Alfred Moffat, *The Minstrelsy of Scotland* (London, 1894 and 1896).

etc.

Musical Example 49
"Capt. Lockhart of the Tartar" (Scottish reel)

etc.

Musical Example 50
"Take Her Out and Air Her" (Irish reel)

etc.

Musical Example 51
"Dar He Goes! Dats Him!"

etc.

Musical Example 52
"Duncan Gray" (Scottish)

urban and rural stage and published in inexpensive sheet editions for voice and piano, it made its way into every walk of life. The "appearance of a new melody," according to an observer in the fifties, "was an event whose importance can hardly be appreciated by the coming generation. It flew from mouth to mouth, and from hamlet to hamlet, with a rapidity which seemed miraculous."[24] And a continental encyclopedia even spoke of "a very characteristically national music, if the Americans will allow us to call it so."[25] It was just that; but the apologetic ending of the statement was appropriate, for few Americans would have been wont to dub "national" what was so ephemeral and of so little social prestige.

On the sheet covers the tunes figured as "Negro Melody" or "Plantation Refrain." Only from the forties on do names of composers appear occasionally, and even then there were conflicting claims and attributions. Sometimes the information on the origin of the music was more specific, as in the edition of "The Bee-Gum," which explained the title of the song as a Negro word for "the hive of the wild bee" and called the tune "genuine, being one of a collection of melodies obtained in South Carolina." And a minstrel publication of the fifties, containing much early material, spoke of "plantation melodies which the author learned when at the south from the Negroes."[26]

It was true indeed that the slaves knew many minstrel songs.[27] This fact, supported by the Negro character of the texts, led to the theory that the slaves had also created the tunes.[28] A little later the same theory was extended to the spirituals.[29]

[24] "Negro Minstrelsy—Ancient and Modern."
[25] "Negro Minstrelsy," *Chamber's Encyclopaedia* (Philadelphia, J. B. Lippincott & Co., and Edinburgh, W. and R. Chambers, 1864).
[26] Preface to Briggs, *Banjo Instructor.*
[27] Allen, *Slave Songs*, p. x, "all the world [the Southern Negroes] knows . . . the 'Jim Crow' songs of thirty years ago." "Settin' on a Rail," to cite only one of many examples, was sung by opossum-hunting slaves while chopping down the tree into which the animal had fled, according to T. B. Thorpe, *The Hive of the Bee-Hunter* (New York, 1854), 260–61.
[28] See the preface to Allen, *Slave Songs.* "Negro Minstrelsy—Ancient and Modern," speculating about the origin of "Jim Crow," says: "Whether it was first sung upon the banks of the Alatamaha, the Alabama, or the Mississippi; or whether it is pre-American and a relic of heathen rites in Congo, or in that mysterious heart of Africa, which foot of civilized man has never trod, is a problem whose solution must be left to the zeal and research of some future Ethiopian Oldbuck."
[29] Refuted by Professor George Pullen Jackson in various publications.

One thing is certain: the anonymity of the early minstrel tunes, their vigor, and their lack of sentimentality, which set them off against the urban middle-class "ballads" of the day, suggest that they originated, for the most part, outside the city, and, above all, in a rough, realistically minded social stratum. This is confirmed by information on the career of a few tunes prior to their publication. "Possum up the Gum-Tree" (see Chapter 3) was known to South Carolina Negroes and to white boatmen. "Clare De Kitchen" is said to have been a song of "negro firemen on the Mississippi River,"[30] and "De Ole Jaw Bone" was probably played and sung by a Negro banjoist at a white frontier frolic in Tennessee in the early thirties.[31] "Zip Coon" is reported to have been "taken from a rough jig dance, called 'Natchez under the hill,' where the boatmen, river pirates, gamblers, and courtesans congregated for the enjoyment of a regular hoedown . . . ."[32] Finally, it seems that in the thirties or somewhat earlier, Ohio boatmen chanted "De Boatman's Dance" (see Chapter 9). That some of these tunes, including "Jim Crow" (see Chapter 4), were credited to the Negro and others credited to the white backwoodsman is overshadowed by the fact that all tunes drew on a heritage of Anglo-Saxon songs and folk dances. Moreover, though this heritage was reflected differently in each case, there existed a constant musical intercourse between the slave and white society. His own musical peculiarities he usually communicated to the world outside the plantation when he played as a banjoist or fiddler, often singing as well, at white frontier dances. From this intercourse resulted a blend of European and primitive melodic styles, of which the earliest example known to us is an eighteenth-century "Negroe Jig," probably of the British colonies in the New World, entitled

[30] T. Allston Brown, "The Origin of Negro Minstrelsy," in Charles H. Day, *Fun in Black* (New York, 1874).

[31] With regard to the origin of "De Ole Jaw Bone," compare its first and second stanzas with lines quoted in *Sketches and Eccentricities*, 39: "I started off from Tennessee, / My old horse wouldn't pull for me . . . / He began to fret an' slip, / An' I begin to cus [*sic*] an' whip; / Walk jawbone from Tennessee . . . / I feed my horse in de poplar trof. / It made him cotch de hoopin' cof; / My old horse died in Tennessee . . . ."

[32] Brown, "Origin of Negro Minstrelsy."

Early Minstrel Tunes

*repeat sign not in the original

Musical Example 53
"Pompey Ran Away" ("Negroe Jig," c. 1775; no text)

"Pompey Ran Away" (see Musical Example 53).[33] It consists of English and Scottish folk song elements, but the frequent reiteration of a short-winded motive is the contribution of the slave.

The minstrel tunes of the late thirties and the forties present a similar picture. Excessive repetition of single tones and of phrases of narrow compass derives from the Negro; on the other hand, the symmetry of phrase structure is a white concept. The rhythm, too, is far removed from the Negroid complexities of banjo-fiddle music. As a matter of fact, the frequent use of equal note values, as well as tone repetitions in the opening phrase, seems to reveal the influence of white hymns. Thus it is not surprising that the influence of Negro hymns is slight.[34] Their characteristic offbeat pattern—the succession

[33] See tune No. 163, *A Selection of Scotch, English, Irish, and Foreign Airs* (Glasgow, printed and sold by James Aird, n.d. [*c.*1775]), I. Note that tunes No. 148, "Old Plantation Girls," and No. 153, "Sam Jones," are called "Virginian."

[34] The relationships that do exist between minstrel tunes and early Negro hymns are due merely to the fact that both are heavily indebted to white music. Two specific examples of the relationship between minstrel tunes and southern folk hymns may be mentioned at this point. "Long Time Ago" (published as sheet music in 1833), is identical to a hymn tune of the same name but different words in *The Southern Harmony* (1835, republished in facsimile, Boston, 1939); this was pointed out by Chase, *America's Music*, 279–80. According to Allen, *Slave Songs*, the tune was believed, in the sixties, to be of Negro origin. The tune of the hymn "Disciple," appearing in *The Southern Harmony*, is very similar, especially in its rhythm, to "Ole Tare River" (published as sheet music in 1840)'. It seems impossible to determine the actual year of origin of these tunes.

187

of a short and long note, often aided by an unexpected accentuation of the accompanying words (see Chapter 13)—does not appear in early minstrel tunes, except for a few tunes in the forties.

From the foregoing facts, stylistic and biographical, one cannot possibly conclude that the early minstrel tunes were "created" by the Negroes. However, one can state with some certainty that they are, as one contemporary observer suggested, "backwoods melodies" which were "brought into general circulation by stage-drivers, wagoners, cattle drovers and other such itinerants . . . ,"[35] including the boatmen. As far as the tunes of the forties are concerned, once their style was established by the frontier, it could easily be imitated and developed by urban minstrels who needed a musical accompaniment for their acts. The dialect of their texts they of course borrowed from the Negro and they often described characteristic scenes of Negro life. But they also retained a white flavor, especially in topical passages, and, in any case, in the taunting over-all character of the songs.

That only cheerful tunes and words were associated with the Negro is explained by the purpose of minstrelsy. At the same time, it confirms a white prejudice, for the slaves were believed to be perfectly contented with their fate. "No hardships or troubles," it was said, "can destroy, or even check their happiness and levity."[36] And the historian Francis Parkman, who in 1846, while traveling through the Middle West, watched two slaves dance to the accompaniment of a banjoist, declared with callous naïveté: "None are more gay and active then [*sic*] the two fellows chained together. They seem never to have known a care. Nothing is on their faces but careless, thoughtless enjoyment. Is it not safe to conclude them to be an inferior race?"[37]

[35] Robert P. Nevin, "Stephen Foster and Negro Minstrelsy," *The Atlantic Monthly* (November, 1867). The quotation contains also this phrase: ". . . backwoods melodies, such as had been invented for native ballads by 'settlement' masters . . . ."

[36] "Negro Minstrelsy—Ancient and Modern."

[37] Mason Wade, *The Journals of Francis Parkman* (New York, 1947), II, 483.

Chapter 13

EARLY BANJO TUNES
AND AMERICAN SYNCOPATION

———◆———

I N EARLY MINSTREL MUSIC there are a sizable number of banjo tunes which quite undeservedly have fallen into oblivion. They made their first appearance at the beginning of the forties when the blackface banjoist, playing as a soloist, and often singing as well, or accompanying a dancer established himself in the popular theater. The tunes continued to be written for about fifty years without essentially deviating from their original style.

From the fifties on, banjo tunes were made available to the public in "Methods" for the instrument. Forty-eight tunes have been preserved in a comparatively early manuscript collection written and compiled by Dan Emmett; they are undated, but originated approximately between 1845 and 1860.[1]

Banjo tunes were customarily called "jigs," a designation that refers to minstrel dances, having no relation to the music itself. Nor do the additional titles (many of them fancy) serve any other purpose than to enhance the uniqueness of each melody, a usage that

---

[1] The manuscript is in the possession of the State Library, Columbus, Ohio. Several of its tunes are included in *Ryan's Mammoth Collection.* Five tunes of the manuscript, all by Emmett, appeared in *Kendall's Clarinet Instruction Book* (Boston, 1845); for an additional one—"Root Hog or Die Jig" by Emmett—the composer wrote words which he dated 1853. Various other tunes were published, in part slightly altered and under different titles, in James Buckley, *Buckley's New Banjo Book* (New York, 1860).

survives in jazz. Although the jigs were mainly performed on the instrument for which they were written, they were probably played also by the fiddler who at times accompanied a dance on the minstrel stage.[2]

According to their published versions, the tunes had no accompaniment, but their actual performance was different. A description of it appears in a note in *The Complete American Banjo School* by S. S. Stewart (Philadelphia, 1887), which is added to a piece called "Darkies' Pastime": "The time in above Jig may be tapped with the foot, 4 taps to each measure—which is the method generally adopted in playing jigs." This type of accompaniment was not new in the late nineteenth century; it was indeed part of a tradition that traces back to the early forties, when it appeared in the early minstrel band (see Chapter 9). Further evidence comes from the cover of a minstrel song of 1840 (see Illustration 13).[3] It shows a minstrel banjoist in the sawdust ring of a circus: his knees are slightly bent outward and the heel of his left foot is raised. When he brought it down (as we assume he did), a tap was heard, reinforced by the wooden board on which he was standing.

It seems that the practice of tapping to banjo tunes came from the Negro, who still today considers a metronomic, percussive background indispensable to the vigorous rhythm he wishes to produce, be it for a dance or a prayer. There is indeed, in a book of 1833, a significant description of a frontier frolic in Tennessee which supports our argument. Referring to the colored banjoist who played for the white dancers, it reads: "[he] thrummed his banjo, beat time with his feet and sung [*sic*] in haste the following lines . . . ."[4]

Although the number of banjo tunes of marked individuality is not inconsiderable, it is nevertheless true that the vocabulary of the genre is limited. It is thus easy to distinguish three melodic types, the first two mainly modes of variation that were applied to borrowed material.

[2] Buckley, *New Banjo Book:* "Many of the Jigs, Reels, and other Dances in this book can be played upon the violin." In *Ryan's Mammoth Collection* (Boston, 1883), they are edited with indications for bowing and fingering.
[3] "Jenny Get Your Hoe Cake Done" (New York, 1840).
[4] *Sketches and Eccentricities,* 39, 40.

The style of the first type, which is clearly set off against the others, is determined by the unstopped tones of the two highest strings. This is explained by the fact that, as outer strings, they are in easy reach of the two most active fingers of the player—the thumb and the index finger. If, for example, the instrument is tuned as in Musical Example 54, it is *e'* and *b* and sometimes *g*-sharp as well, which are touched most frequently.[5]

Two characteristic examples are "Grape Vine Twist" (see Musical Example 55)[6] and "The Boatman's Dance" (see Musical Example 56).[7] The beginning of the first tune is related to the Irish hornpipe "The Devil's Dream" (see Musical Example 57), whereas the second is a variant of a minstrel song of the same name (see Musical Example 58).[8] In both banjo versions there prevail melodic patterns dominated by *e'* and *b:* the tones appear either as part of implied six-chords and triads or as a recurrent figure which divides the melodic line into an upper and a lower region (see Musical Example 55, second part). The use of the recurrent figure, which consists of the interval of a fourth, sometimes leads to dissonant harmonic implications that have no parallel in European music of that time, such as *c sharp-b-e'; d-b-e'; and f sharp-b-e'* (see Musical Example 59).[9] The principle of repetition is also applied to *e'* alone, the tone of the so-called "thumb-string."

As far as the rhythm of the first melodic type is concerned, it is in the main traditional. In fact, the short, equal notes, the dotted notes, and the intermingling of duplets and triplets were taken over from the folk dance music of the British Isles; triadic and ostinato figurations too have precedents there, but the latter are more persistently employed in the American tunes.

[5] The tuning in the forties and early fifties was slightly lower. The highest string, the "fifth," was added to the banjo as late as the mid-forties (see Chap. 9, Note 4), though the banjoist Sweeney is reported to have made use of it earlier. It was always played unstopped.

[6] "Grape Vine Twist," in *Rice's Correct Method.*

[7] "The Boatman's Dance," in Frank B. Converse, *Frank B. Converse's Banjo Instructor* (New York, 1865).

[8] "The Devil's Dream," in O'Neill, *Music of Ireland. De Boatman's Dance* (Boston, 1843).

[9] "Whoop Jamboree Jig," in *Rice's Correct Method.*

(sounding an octave lower)

Musical Example 54

Tuning of the banjo.

Musical Example 55
"Grape Vine Twist"

Musical Example 56
"The Boatman's Dance"

Musical Example 57
"The Devil's Dream" (Irish) [transposed]

Musical Example 58
"De Boatman's Dance" [transposed]

193

Musical Example 59
"Whoop Jamboree Jig"

The next two types of banjo music do not rely on the physical properties of the instrument for which they were written: instead they depend on Irish and Scottish dance tunes. This is most conspicuous in the second type. For example, "Clem Titus' Jig" (see Musical Example 60) is almost identical with the Irish reel "Young Arthur Daly" (see Musical Example 61).[10] "Hell on the Wabash Jig" (see

---

[10] "Clem Titus' Jig," in Emmett's manuscript. "Young Arthur Daly," in O'Neill, *Music of Ireland*.

Musical Example 62) is a variant of "The Night We Made the Match," an Irish hornpipe (see Musical Example 63).[11] As for the "Quaker's Jig," (see Musical Example 64), its main motive derives from some such tune as "The Mourne Mountains" (see Musical Example 65), while its middle section is related to "The Devil's Dream" (see Musical Example 57).[12]

The originality of the second and third types lies in their rhythm. It is exactly this aspect of their style which, within the context of American and European art and folk music of the nineteenth century, is most unusual and intriguing. Moreover, it is of historical significance because it provided elements from which, later on, rags, blues, and finally jazz developed their idiom. The motion of the two types is animated by many irregular stresses: hectic offbeat accentuations projected against the relentless, metrical background of the accompanying taps, which change 2/4 into 4/8. A large number of accentuations result from brief, sudden rests on one of the four beats in the measure.

The omission of a tone and the subsequent continuation of the melodic line may merely cause the weakening of a metrically accented beat (see Musical Example 66). However, if the device is accumulated, as it often is, the re-entries of the melody, regardless of their place in the measure, will produce noticeable accentuations (see Musical Example 67 and 68).[13] An omitted first beat preceded by an upbeat serves to eliminate a bar line. In Musical Example 62, and in Musical Example 69,[14] the phrase (defined by melodic analogy, by the identity of its first two tones, or else by both) begins prematurely, that is, before the previous measure ends. In this way it creates new and uneven metrical units.

[11] D. Emmett, "Hell on the Wabash Jig," in Emmett's manuscript. "The Night We Made the Match," in O'Neill, *Music of Ireland*.

[12] R. Myers, "Quaker's Jig," in Emmett's manuscript. "The Mourne Mountains," an Irish reel, in O'Neill, *Music of Ireland*.

[13] D. Emmett, "Negro Jig," and "Nigger on de Wood Pile," in *Kendall's Clarinet Instruction Book*.

[14] "Gantz's Jig," in Emmett's manuscript.

Musical Example 60
"Clem Titus' Jig"

Musical Example 61
"Young Arthur Daly" (Irish)

Musical Example 62
"Hell on the Wabash Jig"

Musical Example 63
"The Night We Made the Match" (Irish)

Musical Example 64
"Quaker's Jig"

Musical Example 65
"The Mourne Mountains" (Irish) [transposed]

Musical Example 66
"Clem Titus' Jig"

Musical Example 67
"Negro Jig"

Musical Example 68
"Nigger on de Wood Pile"

Musical Example 69
"Gantz's Jig"

The excerpt from "Gantz's Jig" reveals an additional feature. Note that not only the last tone in measure one is accented but the penultimate also: because of the void caused by the subsequent rest, it is suspended in mid-air, so to speak, and thus stressed (see also Musical Example 70).[15] There are then two accentuations (one after *3 and*, the other on *4 and*) which follow each other at an unexpected time interval.

[15] "Joe Sweeney's Jig," in Emmett's manuscript.

The successive repetition of a motive, or of several kindred ones, is another means of upsetting the meter (see Musical Examples 59 and 71).[16] But the process is also reversed: while the meter remains intact, or almost so, it is the motive (in such cases usually consisting of two tones) which changes its accentuations (see Musical Examples 72 and 73).[17] In "Tom Brigg's Jig" the motive appears three times within a measure, each time with different stresses, followed by the restoration of its initial pattern. One cannot always speak of an actual motive; sometimes it is merely a case of adjacent tones which are bandied about (see Musical Example 74),[18] or even of single tones (see Musical Example 62).

There are four other devices which, in addition to strengthening already existing accentuations, also create new ones which contradict the meter: offbeat phrasing (see Musical Example 75); The sudden use of harmony within a monophonic style—usually only two tones appear simultaneously and never in parallel motion (see Musical Example 76); ornaments: ♪♪ (or ♪♪) and ∾ (or ⊕) on the note —the turn was probably performed as in Musical Example 77;[19] and accent marks which however were employed rarely (see Musical Example 78).[20]

In summary, accentuations occur in the following places: on *1 and, 2 and, 3 and,* and *4 and;* right after *2 and* (see Musical Example 70); right after *3 and* (see Musical Example 69); and right before *1 and* (see Musical Example 78). All of these offbeat devices, made more complex by accumulation, irregular appearance, and new metrical units, contribute to an intensification of the rhythm; but the opposite, as a means of contrast, is achieved also. In "Dr. Hekok Jig" (see Musical Example 79),[21] the first tone of the motive, which had

---

[16] R. Myers, "Sliding Jenny Jig," in Emmett's manuscript.

[17] "Tom Brigg's Jig" and "Dick Myers' Jig," in Emmett's manuscript.

[18] D. Emmett, "Pea-Patch Jig," in *Kendall's Clarinet Instruction Book.*

[19] Information according to Emmett, "Rudiments of Music," *Fife Instructor;* this work includes a number of tunes in the style of banjo music. Here, too, the first ornament is described as being executed like an appoggiatura with two equal note values, but this is unlikely to apply to banjo tunes.

[20] "Pea-Patch Jig," in Emmett's manuscript (not the published version).

[21] Z. Bacchus, "Dr. Hekok Jig," in Emmett's manuscript.

Musical Example 70
"Joe Sweeney's Jig"

Musical Example 71
"Sliding Jenny Jig"

Musical Example 72
"Tom Brigg's Jig"

Musical Example 73
"Dick Myers' Jig"

Musical Example 74
"Pea-Patch Jig"

Musical Example 75
"Genuine Negro Jig"

Musical Example 76
"Pea-Patch Jig"

Musical Example 77
An ornament in banjo music.

Musical Example 78
"Pea-Patch Jig"

Musical Example 79
"Dr. Hekok Jig"

been very brief before, is suddenly lengthened with the result that the forward drive of the melody is temporarily suspended.

The formal layout of types two and three, with its melodically differentiated sections (often two, each of which is usually repeated), derives from British folk dance music. Inside each section there reigns periodicity: a two-measure phrase, or one equivalent to it in beats, is complemented or simply followed by a somewhat different phrase of the same length; the whole is occasionally restated with a few changes. This structure, frequently strengthened by the repetition of the initial section, has what we would call balance, but any restfulness that might result from it is effectively counteracted by a system of unexpected accentuations and by the division of the melodic line into very brief and rapid particles. It is also disturbed by two principles—repetition and variation by contrast.

Within each section of a tune there is often nothing but a single motive which recurs literally or slightly altered. This is illustrated by the "Genuine Negro Jig" (see Musical Example 80), where one motive appears four times in the first section and another motive, only one measure long, appears eight times in the second section.[22] In "Dr. Hekok Jig," a unique tune because it consists of a single, extended section, the initial motive is repeated as often as twenty-six times. Moreover, it is constantly kept in a state of intensity through irregular accentuations, changes in length, changes in pitch, and other such devices. In the ordinary banjo tunes, there is also variation, but instead of being cumulative, it achieves its effect by contrast; that

[22] "Genuine Negro Jig," in Emmett's manuscript.

Musical Example 80
"Genuine Negro Jig"

Musical Example 81
"Marty Inglehart Jig"

is, complexity is set against simplicity and irregularity against regularity. Thus in "Nigger on de Wood Pile" (see Musical Example 68), the difference between measures nine to ten and measures five to six is deliberate. This contract is even more noticeable when a motive and its variant alternate several times in quick succession (see Musical Example 81).[23]

We are now able to characterize the banjo tunes which belong to type three. Although their melodic material is related to British dance music, they are more independent than type two. They have many offbeat accentuations and many brief, animated phrases whose narrow range is emphasized through their direction: as in the minstrel songs of the forties, they either turn back to their initial tone or to a tone near it, or else they end as if no continuation were needed. Finally, and this is a prominent feature, various phrases have a predominantly downward trend.

The style of the banjo tunes is so unusual in many respects that one must ask for its origin. It can be shown at the outset that the device of weakening a beat in a measure through the insertion of a rest is not as untraditional as it seems to be. It comes indeed from the very tunes which form the basis of a great part of American banjo music. A good example is "The Reel of Tulloch" which appears in a mid-eighteenth-century publication entitled *A Curious Collection of Scots Tunes*.[24] This reel contains the passage in Musical Example 82. A similar example, collected at a later time, is in Musical Example 83.[25] The device was no doubt known in the back country of America, though its first appearance in print did not occur until 1841 in the minstrel song "Massa Is a Stingy Man" (see Musical Example 84).[26]

Here is the starting point of American banjo music. But from it banjo music proceeded to an idiom infinitely more complex in rhythm than could have originated within a predominantly white cultural

[23] D. Emmett, "Marty Inglehart Jig," in *Kendall's Clarinet Instruction Book*.

[24] Edinburgh, printed and sold by R. Bremner, n.d., but according to *Grove's Dictionary of Music and Musicians*, the date is 1759. The accompanying bass has been omitted in Musical Example 82.

[25] No. 883 in Petrie and Stanford, *Irish Music*.

[26] New York, 1841.

Musical Example 82
"The Reel of Tulloch" (Scottish)

Musical Example 83
"Long Dance" (Irish)

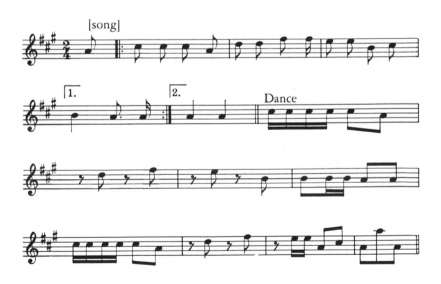

Musical Example 84
"Massa Is a Stingy Man"

milieu and its nineteenth-century concepts. May we assume Negro influences?

Let us for a moment consider the musical activities and interests of the antebellum slave of the southern plantation. His African musical heritage was discouraged. The folk tunes he heard from his master's lips were of Irish and Scottish origin. He sang them himself, no doubt usually with his own words adapted to them.[27] In addition, he played strains on his favorite instruments, the banjo and the fiddle. These strains are no longer known to us,[28] but it is most likely that many of them were those of the frontier—namely, the folk dance tunes of the British Isles. We are acquainted with at least one example, "Sugar in a Gourd," a tune in the style of an Irish reel which in the thirties was played on the banjo by Negroes in Virginia and elsewhere.[29] And we can safely take it as part of a tradition of long standing, when, in the "ball-rooms" of Sausage Row and Bucktown in Cincinnati as late as the eighteen-seventies, Negroes danced "the old slave dances" to the sound of white tunes, played by fiddle, banjo, and string-bass, some "old Virginia reel" and even "Devil's Dream" among them.[30]

When playing the banjo, the plantation Negro would tap his feet to the music. He would also enliven his songs with regular beats, produced by hand and foot.[31] Georgia oarsmen in the thirties are reported to have sung "with the rhythm of the row locks for accompaniment,"[32]

[27] Kemble, *Journal*, 127–28.

[28] The first comprehensive publication of Negro music was Allen, *Slave Songs*, a collection of hymns mainly. The editors regretted that they had found only a very small number of secular tunes, especially because they suspected them to be more typically Negroid (more "barbaric," as they put it on page vii) than the rest.

[29] See John Pendleton Kennedy, *Swallow Barn* (first edition of 1832), Chap. 11. This is a realistic novel on Virginia in which the slave Carey, an expert on the banjo, is credited with the knowledge of "Sugar in a Gourd" and "Jim Crow," two popular dances well known in this region. He also sings the minstrel song "Long Time Ago" with words improvised by him on the spur of the moment. There are additional references in two minstrel songs: "Jim Brown" (1835), facsimile in Damon, *Old American Songs*, "I practis on de Banjo sugar in de gourd"; and "Charleston Gals" (Boston, 1844), "De niggers dance upon de board / De fiddle play'd up Sugar in de Gourd." "The Sugar in the Gourd, Jig" is in Emmett's manuscript, and another version of the tune appears in his *Fife Instructor*.

[30] Hearn, *Levee Life*.

[31] Northup, *Twelve Years a Slave*.

[32] Kemble, *Journal*, 218.

just as, later, colored railroad workers sang to the sound of their hammers and picks.

The preference for offbeats is of African origin,[33] and undoubtedly existed on the southern plantation; it still survives in former slave settlements of the New World. We know, for example, that Negro oarsmen in the eighteen-thirties sang their song "just a trifle behind time . . . ,"[34] which can mean only one thing: they started sections of it on offbeats and thus created irregular accentuations. Furthermore, early Negro hymns contain various passages where a short tone, on an accented beat in the measure, is followed by a long one. In cases where this pattern appears repeatedly or where it contradicts the natural accentuation of the words, a noticeable offbeat effect is produced (see Musical Example 85).[35]

If, finally, we consider that the relentless repetition of brief motives and the downward direction of melodies are characteristics of primitive music, we can safely conclude that the minstrel banjo style is very similar to what the slaves played on their banjos and fiddles. Some of the tunes—such as "Genuine Negro Jig," "Negro Jig," and above all "Dr. Hekok Jig"—may very well be the originals or close imitations of them. This would be a most significant fact because no other record of early instrumental plantation music is left to us.

Minstrel banjo music toward the end of the past century was su-

You'd bet-ter lef' your sis-ter door, Go keep your own door clean.

Musical Example 85
"1 Saw the Beam in My Sister's Eye"

[33] Richard A. Waterman, " 'Hot' Rhythm in Negro Music," *Journal of the American Musicological Society,* Vol. I, No. 1 (Spring, 1948).

[34] In Allen, *Slave Songs,* xvi, there is a reference to a song which makes the remark unambiguous. See also hymn No. 38, end of measure 6, in the same collection.

[35] Allen, *Slave Songs,* No. 23.

perseded by other styles, but various of its elements survived.[36] For example, the principle of pitting highly irregular accentuations in the melody, chiefly produced by melodic rather than dynamic means, against a precise metrical accompaniment, which characterizes all American dance music up to the present, is anticipated by early banjo tunes and undoubtedly derives from them. The following rhythmic features of banjo music were utilized in the late nineteenth and the early twentieth centuries and were finally absorbed into jazz:

1. Omission of a tone on one of the four beats in the measure with the subsequent re-entry of the melody (see Musical Examples 86 and 87).[37]

2. Repetition of two adjacent tones in quick succession and with changing accentuations (compare Musical Example 88 to Musical Examples 72, 73, and 74).[38]

3. Repetition of more than two tones, adjacent or further apart, with changing accentuations (compare Musical Examples 86 and 89 to Musical Example 70).[39] When the accentuations remain constant, it is the meter that is affected (compare Musical Example 90 to Musical Example 71).[40] Note that the melody in Musical Example 89 should be accented as written (according to the dictates of the meter), but not, as we would do today in order to obtain polyrhythm, with a stress on each recurring *e*-flat.[41] This interpretation is confirmed by

[36] Winthrop Sargeant, *Jazz: Hot and Hybrid* (New York, 1938, republished, 1946), Chap. 8, was the first to see a connection between ragtime and Negro minstrel music, but his proofs were faulty. He believed he had discovered polyrhythm (in this particular case, groups of three eighth notes played against a quarter note accompaniment in common time) in rags as well as in the early minstrel song "Zip Coon" (his version is not of 1834, as he seems to imply, but of a later date) and the banjo-fiddle tune "Arkansas Traveler." However, this phrasing, as has already been pointed out by Aaron Copland, *Our New Music* (New York, 1941), 93, was not made audible before the advent of jazz or thereabouts. Previously it was at most a suggestion (and not even that in "Arkansas Traveler")—an unused possibility (see Musical Examples 89 and 91).

[37] Scott Joplin, "Maple Leaf Rag," in *The Ragtime Folio* (New York, 1950). W. C. Handy, "St. Louis Blues," *A Treasury of the Blues* (New York, 1926, reissued 1949). According to Ben Harney, *Ragtime Instructor* (1897), as quoted in Sargeant, *Jazz*, 132, the omission of the tone on the first beat was a landmark of ragtime.

[38] James Scott, "Hilarity Rag," in *The Ragtime Folio*.

[39] Euday L. Bowman, "12th Street Rag" (Fort Worth, Texas, 1914).

[40] Scott Joplin, "The Cascades (Rag)," in *The Ragtime Folio*.

[41] This, however, is the suggestion of Sargeant, *Jazz*, 135 (see his example 101).

Musical Example 86
"Maple Leaf Rag" (1899)

Hate to see ____ de eve-nin' sun go down.

Musical Example 87
"St. Louis Blues" (1914)

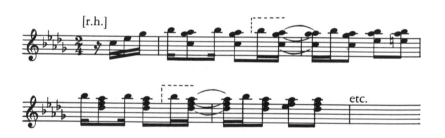

Musical Example 88
"Hilarity Rag" (1910)

Musical Example 89
"12th St. Rag" (1914)

Musical Example 90
"The Cascades" (Rag; 1904)

Musical Example 91
"The Memphis Blues" (1912)

Musical Example 92
"Maple Leaf Rag"

Musical Example 93
From a "Buck or Wing Dance" (early 1890's).

Musical Example 94
From a "Buck or Wing Dance" (early 1890's).

Musical Example 95
"12th St. Rag"

a passage from "The Memphis Blues" of 1912 (see Musical Example 91).[42]

4. Successive repetition of identical tones on offbeats (compare measure 5 of Musical Example 86 to Musical Example 62).

5. A measure is clipped through the premature entry of a phrase (compare Musical Examples 88 and 92 to Musical Examples 62 and 69).

6. Chords and (simultaneous) intervals in the melody in contrast to nonharmonic passages create offbeats (compare Musical Example 86 to Musical Example 76).

7. Dotted notes and (in jazz) triplets surrounded by duplets (compare Musical Example 95 to Musical Examples 55 and 64).

8. A pattern frequent in ragtime and the "buck and wing dances" of the nineties is ♪♪♪♪ (see Musical Examples 93 and 88).[43] It derives from banjo tunes (see Musical Examples 72 and 73) and turns

[42] W. C. Handy, "The Memphis Blues," *Blues.*
[43] "Buck or Wing Dance 'Ebenezer's Boy,'" in *Harding's Collection of 200 Jigs Reels and Country Dances* (1891, republished New York, 1905). See Sargeant, *Jazz,* 131.

up in early Negro hymns, though usually without the third note (see Musical Example 85); but to judge from printed versions, it is not frequent in early minstrel songs.[44]

The dance music at the turn of the century not only perpetuated many rhythmic elements of early banjo tunes but some of their melodic aspects as well (see Musical Examples 88 and 90).[45] Though it borrowed mainly from types two and three, it did not neglect type one, the traces of which appear in "buck and wing dances" (see Musical Example 94),[46] in rags (see Musical Examples 95 and 86), and, slightly varied, in the blues (see Musical Examples 91).

The history of jazz has now been extended backward. It does not begin with ragtime, Negro spirituals, or the songs of the early popular theater, but with a few dozen banjo tunes which have the flavor of the plantation. Although originating about one hundred years ago, they furnished the basic elements of an idiom of striking contemporaneity.

[44] It appears, for example, in one edition of "Ole Dan Tucker," *The Celebrated Negro Melodies, as sung by the Virginia Minstrels* (Boston, 1843), in the refrain.

[45] After this was published in *The Musical Quarterly* (October, 1956), the following early observation in Rupert Hughes, "A Eulogy of Ragtime," *Musical Record* (Boston, April, 1899), as quoted in Chase, *America's Music,* came to the author's attention: "Banjo figuration is very noticeable in ragtime music . . . ."

[46] "Buck or Wing Dance . . . 'Creole Blondes,' " in *Harding's Collection.*

Chapter 14

EMMETT'S ACTIVITIES DURING
THE FORTIES AND FIFTIES

EMMETT AND BROWER, ON THEIR ARRIVAL IN NEW YORK on October 7, 1844,[1] found Negro minstrelsy, now identical with the "minstrel show," thriving more vigorously than ever. In order to find themselves a place in it, they had to breach a phalanx of competitors who were busily exploiting a type of entertainment created by the Virginia Minstrels two years earlier. Without waiting for an engagement, the two comedians relied on their own initiative. They engaged two additional musicians and, avoiding the big city, proceeded to Salem, Massachusetts, where at the Lyceum Hall they gave an "Ethiopean [*sic*] Concert" on October 23. Their playbill[2] introduced the members of the band in the customary hyperbolic style:

Banjo, by the African Apollo . . . . Mr. D. Emmit
Castinetts [*sic*] by the Virginia Orpheus . . . . F. M. Brower
Violin by the Paganini of the South . . . . A. Evans
Tamborine [*sic*] by the fine Old North Carolinian . W. Donaldson

[1] Odell, *Annals*, V, 140.

[2] A remark on the playbill reads: "Old Dan Emmit and F. M. Brower respectfully announce . . . that their celebrated Ethiopian Band have returned from Europe and will give their First Concert . . . ." This reference to the Virginia Minstrels was only half true, but it was advantageous.

214

The last epithet was derived from the song "The Fine Old Colored Gemman" which Emmett, as a member of the Virginia Minstrels, had made popular and which he now performed again with his own "words and symphonies [banjo interludes]." The program, presented no doubt in the authentic manner of the pioneer troupe, included various tunes and texts that were published before the year was over in the second series of Emmett's *Original Banjo Melodies*.[3]

The next stop of the four musicians was Boston. Here they began to appear toward the end of the month at the Melodeon and stayed for almost two weeks, performing nearly every night as the "Legitimate Ethiopian Band."[4] It is not known how long they traveled as a group after their Boston engagement, but its two main members continued their activities for a while. A manuscript sketch of one of their acts dates from about 1846,[5] although Emmett was involved in enterprises of his own before that time.

There is no doubt that Emmett had quickly regained the position in American Negro minstrelsy that he had held before his European tour. From then until the late fifties he had many engagements—during the winter with urban theaters and in the warmer season with traveling circuses.[6] In the spring of 1845, or perhaps somewhat earlier, he is reported to have opened a "Hall of Novelty" in New York at Broadway and Chambers Streets.[7] A few months later he was in the Elysian Fields in Hoboken—Hoboken at that time being the "most

[3] "Old Joe," "The Jolly Raftsman," "Walk Jawbone," "My Old Dad," "Yellow Corn" (probably "Cornfield Green"), and "Dar He Goes."

[4] One of their playbills, republished in *The New York Clipper* (July 25, 1874), speaks of the "Last week of the Ethiopian Concerts" and mentions that from November 4 on, five more performances will be given.

[5] There is in the Longfellow House, Cambridge, a broadside (n.d. [early forties]), of "Gwine ober de Mountain" (New York, "Sold at 18 Division and 98 Nassau Streets"), to which this description is added: "An original Duetto for the banjo and bone castinetts [*sic*] composed by Old Dan Emmit and sung by him and the inimitable Frank Brower at all the principal Theatres and Circuses in the Union . . . ." Concerning the manuscript of the two comedians, see Chapter 9.

[6] Emmett's letter to the editor, *The New York Clipper* (May 19, 1877) reads: "I afterwards [after 1843] traveled . . . for two years with Spaulding's Circus . . . ." *The Daily Banner* (Mount Vernon, Ohio, June 29, 1904), reporting on Emmett's tour abroad, stated that he "returned to New York, playing the theatres in the winter and joining circuses and caravans in the summer."

[7] Odell, *Annals*, V, 144, after mentioning theatrical events in March, 1845, says that Emmett "had started a Hall of Novelty . . . ."

fashionable and favorite excursion in the summer," easily reached from New York by ferryboat.[8] At this genteel park one could enjoy drinks and "Vaudeville theatre."[9] It was here that Emmett, starting July 28 and continuing for a week, participated every afternoon in minstrelsy presented outdoors. He had assembled a new group which included his old friend, the banjoist Whitlock, Charles White with his accordion, and Jerry Bryant handling the tambourine.[10] As in the days of the Virginia Minstrels, Emmett performed on the fiddle. The group, seated "on a stage . . . in front of the Colonade [*sic*]," called itself "Operatic Brothers and Sisters," a name that recommended itself "to the families of New York." It was reminiscent of the then popular vocal ensemble, the Hutchinsons,[11] and the adjective "operatic," not infrequently used in this context, implied respectability. Since the four musicians were listed as the "male members" of the band, the female contingent was represented by the "wench" dancer Dan Gardner. They offered "their Original Songs, Glees, Choruses and Dances, in which they bid defiance to all competition."

In October, Emmett had a job with Tryon's Circus at the Bowery Amphitheatre in New York, billed as a banjoist and, with exaggeration, as the "author of all the popular and fashionable Negro Songs of the Day."[12] On the twenty-third, on the occasion of his "benefit," he directed a minstrel band consisting of Whitlock, Gardner, Charles White, Donaldson, and others. During the course of the evening he passed around his "Habana Fiddle," described on the playbill (probably in his own words) as having been "'made by a niggar at sea,'" an ambiguous reference to his trip across the Atlantic: "De top, back an sides am a segar Box, de neck is made ob a piece ob a boat oar. De bow is frum de side ob de boat," and for strings there is a "rope which

[8] *The New York Herald* (June 8, 1842).

[9] *Spirit of the Times* (July 19, 1845), as quoted in Odell, *Annals*, V, 162.

[10] Playbill (July 28, 1845), as republished in *The New York Clipper* (January 29, 1876).

[11] See Chapter 11.

[12] Playbill (October 17, 1845), as published in Charles C. Moreau, *A Collection of Playbills etc. relating to The Circus in New York City* (New York, 1894, Harvard Theatre Collection), and playbills (October 18 and 23, 1845), as published in Moreau, *Negro Minstrelsy*.

makes 'um soun de same like hoss harr." Whitlock, too, had something special to offer to his audience: a miniature locomotive, constructed by himself, which ran on "a track . . . across the Ring," while he narrated "the particulars of his adventures and dark doings."[13] It was on this evening that Emmett sang "his original Machine Poetry and walk Gerusalesum." The last song, which is not preserved, was perhaps an imitation of a real Negro "shout," a spiritual to which the believers moved around with slow, shuffling steps.[14] "Machine Poetry," on the other hand, must have been his "Oh, Ladies All!" a sample of a novel type of minstrel music whose humor belongs to the Dadaist variety. Its sparse, monotonous melody—a babble on a single tone, fizzling out into prose—lends a touch of idiocy to the story, already nonsensical by itself.[15] The name of the genre can be traced back to one of Emmett's English song sheets of about 1844, entitled "History ob de World." On its cover is pictured "Mr. D. D. Emmit, as The Machine Poet." Seated at his writing desk, he appears, with wide open eyes staring into the void and a long quill tensely held between his thick Negro lips, as the very image of inspiration. Around him are books with such facetious titles as *On Colour, The Dark Ages,* and *Blackstone,* and a jar labelled "Nigger Health"; in the background loom the busts of Byron, Shakespeare, and Scott. In view of the machine as the contemporaneous symbol of inventiveness and progress, "machine poet" might mean "poet and genius of the age." "Machine poetry" is his product: the finest and latest to be had, the most "advanced" artifact of literary fashion.

Up to the middle of the fifties Emmett was frequently associated with Charles White, who pursued a career as a minstrel manager,

---

[13] Playbill (October 23, 1845); an article on Whitlock, based on his manuscript autobiography in *The New York Clipper.*

[14] Allen, *Slave Songs,* hymn No. 58 and the accompanying footnote. Barton, *Old Plantation Hymns,* contains a hymn with the recurrent words "Walk Jerusalem."

[15] *Rice's Correct Method,* contains not only Emmett's piece but another example of "Machine Poetry," beginning: "De way dey bake de hoe cake, Virginny neber tire . . . ." Another very similar one, "Nigger stole a turkey," appears in Frank B. Converse, *Charley Fox's Minstrel's Companion* (Philadelphia, 1863). An announcement on a playbill of the Melodeon (Boston or New York, October 24, 1850), concerning a "New Comic Song and Extemporaneous Machine Poetry" proves that this type of song lent itself to improvisation.

though with varying success.[16] Nevertheless the circumstances were favorable. How important a place Negro minstrelsy held in the city of New York in those days can be gathered from an article in *Putman's Monthly,* which reads in part: "The only places of Amusement where the entertainments are indigenous are the African Opera Houses, where native American vocalists, with blackened faces, sing national songs, and utter none but native witticisms. These native theatricals . . . are among the best frequented and most profitable places of amusement in New York. While even [the] attempt to establish an Italian Opera here, though originating with the wealthiest and best educated classes, has resulted in bankruptcy, the Ethiopian Opera has flourished like a green bay tree . . . ."[17]

We hear now more frequently of Emmett's activities as an actor. Some time in 1847 he appeared in Charles White's "Going for The Cup; or Old Mrs. Williams' Dance," "an Ethiopian Interlude in one scene," at the Melodeon, 53 Bowery, playing "Knowall (a consequential Darkey)" in "fancy shirt and high hat."[18] During the winter of 1849–50, he was again a member of White's company at the same place.[19] For a while there is no record of his activities, but in late 1852 he opened at "White's Theatre of Varieties," 17 and 19 Bowery, to which its proprietor with his "Serenaders" had just moved. In spite of initial success, the shows came to an end, as usually happened with White's ventures, after a few months—February, 1853, to be exact.[20] During this time, Emmett performed not only his banjo act and played the accompaniment for a dancer, but participated in ensemble scenes as well. For example, he performed with White in the parody of "Old Uncle Ned or Effusions from Lord Byron."[21] In April,

[16] There must also have been tours, but very little is known of them. For example, an item in the *Sun* (New York[?], February 2, 1896), entitled "Billy Birch's Lost Art" (clipping in the Allen A. Brown Collection of the Boston Public Library), mentions that Emmett after 1848 appeared in Philadelphia. A playbill (Providence, R. I., August 30, 1852, with a reference to a performance on August 31), of "Well's Late the Original Fellow's Minstrels," lists Emmett as a performer.

[17] February, 1854.

[18] See the printed edition (New York, 1874).

[19] Odell, *Annals,* V, 581.

[20] *Ibid.,* VI, 244–46. "Charley White's Bowery Speculation in 1853," *The New York Clipper* (April 6, 1872).

[21] Playbill, (February 12, 1853). There exist also a playbill of October 18, 1852, and three that are undated, one of which was published in *The New York Clipper* (April 6, 1872).

he had an engagement with a circus at the Amphitheatre, 37 Bowery,[22] but in June he turned up again at 53 Bowery, to which the ever restless White and his troupe had returned; this time Emmett was both a performer and coproprietor.[23] The two announced themselves as "Inventors of cheap Amusements and originators of minstrelsy." Their playbills prove that they had responsive audiences because "gentlemen" had to be requested "not to keep time with their feet as it is annoying to the visitors generally, and also confuses the business of the stage." The company performed during the fall and probably through the winter. When it moved in April, 1854, to St. Nicholas Exhibition Room, 495 Broadway, Emmett went along but no longer took part in the management.[24]

Some time during the latter part of 1854, he was at Lea's Franklin Museum (at the site of White's Melodeon) the musical director and performing member of an ensemble that called itself "Lea's Female Opera Troupe."[25] It presented young ladies in dances and tableaux and in a minstrel band, though in white face. They were assisted by two blackface end men, a bone player and a tambourinist. Shows of this kind were, historically speaking, ushering in a trend in Negro minstrelsy towards prettiness and the erotic appeal—qualities foreign to the genre.[26]

Afterward, Emmett found his way back to White's company, which again occupied new quarters at 49 Bowery, proudly named "White's New Ethiopian Opera House." There he appeared on October 12, 1855, as the "showman" armed with "a peep show . . . and an old Organ [a hurdy-gurdy]" in the première of his own play *Hard Times* and probably at other times as well.[27] There is also evidence of an engagement at the Bowery Theatre in June.[28]

[22] Odell, *Annals*, VI, 259.

[23] *Ibid.*, 257. Playbills (October 1, 1853, and December 6, 1853).

[24] Odell, *Annals*, VI, 328. Playbill (April 10, 1853), the first day of their engagement, and playbill (April 12 and 22, 1853).

[25] Odell, *Annals*, VI, 329, 410. The troupe opened at the Melodeon in late April and continued until November. There are several undated playbills in existence, one with a picture of the band.

[26] Participation of women in Negro minstrelsy was rare, but instances of it occurred as early as 1844; see Odell, *Annals*, V, 142, 163.

[27] See the edition of the play (New York, 1874). On an undated ticket of "White's New Ethiopian Opera House," a "Banjo Song and Solo" by Emmett is listed.

Emmett wrote several minstrel plays in the fifties: *The Rappers,
German Farmer or The Barber Shop in an Uproar* (both "Ethiopian
Burlettas"), and *Hard Times.*[29] The first two are mere skits that offer
broad comical situations without pretense to literary standards. However, in the "Negro Extravaganza" *Hard Times,* Emmett proved that
a simple farce in dialect could have artistic qualities, if only he resorted to folklore both in action and verse. Such ideas as the pact with
"Belzebub, the Prince of Darkness" and its material rewards, the
taboo, the devil's threat when it is violated:

> Your time has come—prepare to go
> To regions of eternal woe!
> I've neither bridle, horse or saddle,
> Upon my tail you'll ride a-straddle

and his defeat through native wit are borrowed from mythological
tradition and given an American locale. At the end of the play, the
devil is compelled by virtue of the magic of music to dance around
with a chair sticking to the seat of his pants, while the other characters gleefully sing a song to banjo accompaniment that in crude
lines tells of previous tribulations and final victory.

What Emmett looked like as a solo performer in the fifties is suggested by a picture of his colleague Charles H. Fox who was said to
have imitated him.[30] Entering the stage he must have at once divested
himself of his tall minstrel hat by placing it, in accord with nineteenth-
century deportment, upside down on the floor. After that he settled
on a chair, with his legs crossed and one of his oversized feet standing
up at a right angle. In Illustration 50 he is seen in the act of greeting
his audience or acknowledging its applause with a broad smile and
one hand raised lazily with the palm open. Having grown up with the

[28] Playbill (June 13 [1855]).

[29] Concerning performances of *The Barber Shop* in the fifties, see Odell, *Annals,*
VI. *The Rappers* is undated but is probably of this time. There are three additional
plays in Emmett's handwriting. The title page of one of them is missing. The titles of
the others are *Returned Volunteer* and *Black Statue;* they are without Emmett's customary signature. For performances of the latter play in the fifties, see Odell, *Annals* VI.

[30] Mentioned in an open letter by J. Unsworth in *The New York Clipper* (July
31, 1858), where it is stated that "Dan Emmett . . . preceded him [Fox] in everything
pertaining to his original style of business."

Illustration 50. The banjoist Charley Fox. From the cover of the song by C. H. Fox, "Johnny's Equal Is Not Here" (New York, 1858).

Illustration 51. Photograph of Dan Emmett by Feldricks & Company of New York, undated but probably of the early sixties. Courtesy The University of Virginia.

primitive style of early minstrelsy, however, Emmett often appeared considerably less well-groomed than that. In a photo of the sixties, for example, he is caught in the process of delivering a stump speech (see Illustration 51). As he stands in coat and pants that seem to have been borrowed from a pawn shop, he rises to the occasion by putting as much seriousness into his face and intensity into his gestures as he can muster.

Emmett's reputation as a solo performer was enhanced by the popularity of his tunes and texts. It was during the late forties and the fifties that he composed his "jig songs" and banjo jigs, several of which are among the best and the best known of their kind. In 1861, *The New York Clipper* reports: "Old Dan Emmett's 'Root Hog or Die,' is, we hear, likely to become as popular in England as it has long been on this side . . . ."[31] The paper should also have mentioned "Jordan Is a Hard Road to Travel," which, since 1852 and 1853 when it appeared in print, was constantly heard on minstrel stages. The vigor of its melody was quickly recognized by the abolitionist Hutchinson Family who used it extensively, with appropriate words of their own, in their crusades for the freedom of the slave.[32] It is said that "its rendering to thousands of audiences did much to disgust the American people with the 'peculiar institution.' "[33] What distinguishes Emmett's "Jordan" from most of the minstrel songs of the forties and fifties is its relation to the religious music of the Negro. There is the reference to the river Jordan and to getting to "de odder side": traveling across means reaching Canaan, the promised land. This thought, however, is concealed by a wholly topical context. More relevant are the musical aspects. Both the predominant motive of the first section of the tune and that of the refrain are strongly reminiscent of early Negro spirituals (see Musical Examples 96, 97, and 98).[34]

[31] October 5, 1861.

[32] Published in sheet music form as "Slavery Is a Hard Foe to Battle" (New York, Horace Waters, 1855). A broadside of its text exists in the Baker Library of Dartmouth College.

[33] Joshua Hutchinson, *A Brief Narrative of the Hutchinson Family* (Boston, 1874), 38.

[34] Allen, *Slave Songs,* hymns No. 114 and 70.

Musical Example 96
"Jordan Is a Hard Road to Travel"

Musical Example 97
"O Daniel" (Negro spiritual)

(transposed)

Hal-le-lu-jah! Lin-ger no long-er Hal-le-lu-jah!

Musical Example 98
"Good-Bye" (Negro spiritual) [transposed]

In late 1855, Emmett decided to leave the East and try his luck in the Middle West. In early September it was announced in the Chicago press that he would direct minstrel performances at 104 Randolph Street, and a little later he opened what he called "Emmit's Burlesque Ethiopian Varieties" at the same place.[35] The earliest play-

[35] A. T. Andreas, *History of Chicago* (Chicago, 1884), I, 493: "September 5 [1854; actually 1855], a notice appeared in the Democratic Press that Phelps' Ethiopian Opera House (Warner's Hall), 104 Randolph Street, would be opened on the 8th of the month for the production of minstrel concerts, under the direction of Daniel D. Emmett; L. Phelps, proprietor." Playbills of "Emmit's Burlesque Ethiopian Varieties" (March 13 and April 24, 1856), the latter published in *The New York Clipper* (November 18, 1876). According to Robert L. Sherman, *Chicago Stage* (Chicago, 1947), I, 307, Emmett "was given a benefit . . . [on January 4, 1856] at the Metropolitan Hall," at which no doubt he appeared himself.

bills extant inform us that he was both proprietor and manager (and occasional performer), and that his company consisted of about ten members. They performed for more than three-quarters of a year. In July, 1856, they appeared at the Metropolitan Hall, but soon returned to their former abode.[36] In spite of apparent prosperity, something must have finally gone wrong, because on September 19, Emmett publicly offered for sale both the equipment of his theater and his lease. He even announced that he would "quit the profession."[37]

This, however, was mere rhetoric. Though we know nothing definite of his activities during 1857,[38] the year after he was still in the Middle West, this time in St. Paul, Minnesota, where on April 26, he began to present "Negro Minstrelsy, in all its various branches" with a newly organized company; Frank Lumbard, as in Chicago, was its musical director.[39] Headquarters was Irvine's Hall and later the Melodeon. In early May, Emmett was reported to be "doing a fine business."[40] He continued until July 26, when his farewell benefit took place. In between, the company must have played in neighboring towns, because on July 8, it appeared in Minneapolis. Here a typical frontier incident occurred. According to *The New York Clipper*[41] which ran reports on the company, "a large number of the 'townspeople,' or 'country roughs,' undertook to force their way into the hall without paying . . . . The doors were pushed against by the rowdy lumbermen, and guarded on the inside by some half a dozen resolute men, with clubs, some of whom had left their ladies to protect the hall. Dan Emmett, Frank Lumbard, Max Irwin and Johnny Ritter

[36] The playbill (July 19, 1856), republished in *The New York Clipper* (November, 7, 1874), carries this remark: "In order to make room for the extensive improvements which are about to be added to this hall [Metropolitan Hall], this company will perform at their old hall, No. 104 Randolph Street, commencing on Monday evening, July 21."
[37] Andreas, *History of Chicago*, I, 495, publishes the exact wording of Emmett's announcement: "I have entered into an agreement to quit the profession, whereby I can realize more than if I were to remain in the minstrel profession all my life, with all the success I could desire."
[38] Frank Moore, *Reminiscences of Pioneer Days in St. Paul* (St. Paul, 1908), 68, reports that Emmett and his company visited St. Paul "during the years 1857 and 1858," but gives no details.
[39] *The New York Clipper* (May 22, 1858). Advertisements in the *St. Paul Daily Minnesotian* (July 12 and 26, 1858).
[40] *The New York Clipper* (May 22, 1858).
[41] July 17, 1858.

[members of the company] came to the rescue and pitched in. Dan whaled three of them, and the last that was seen of Frank, he was 'putting in his left' on 'the nob' of a stalwart six foot lumberman . . . . The mob finally gave up the attempt, and the performance went on uninterrupted."

On leaving St. Paul, the company dissolved, but a new one styled "Emmett's Varieties" appeared in early November in Selma, Alabama.[42]

[42] *The New York Clipper* (November 20, 1858). Moore, *Reminiscences*, 69, writes: "When Emmett's company left St. Paul, they got stranded and many of them found engagements in other organizations."

Chapter 15

EMMETT ON THE STAGE
OF THE BRYANT'S MINSTRELS
AND HIS WALK-AROUNDS

———◆———

THE BRYANT'S MINSTRELS IN NEW YORK, whom Emmett joined in 1858, were one of the most energetic and resourceful troupes of their time. Directed by three young comedians—Dan, Jerry, and Neil— and consisting of about a dozen performers, they began their shows on February 23, 1857, at Mechanics' Hall, 472 Broadway,[1] a place made famous previously by E. P. Christy. They aroused immediate attention, and after a few months were so obviously ahead of their competitors that *The New York Clipper* observed: "The different bands of Minstrels, in this city, have experienced a wonderful falling off in patronage since the advent among us of the 'Bryants.'"[2] Soon the Clipper spoke of them as "a combination of comical talent . . . never before witnessed in Ethiopian Minstrelsy . . . ."[3]

During the fall of 1858, a financial crisis swept the country and was bound to affect public entertainment. But it was soon evident that minstrelsy did not suffer at all.[4] On the contrary, it was "increasing in popularity" to the point that it began "to become a formidable rival to the more legitimate branches of the profession."[5] The situation

[1] *The New York Herald* (February 23, 1857).
[2] *Ibid.* (June 20, 1857, and August 15, 1857).
[3] *Ibid.* (September 12, 1857).
[4] *Ibid.* (October 24, 1857).
[5] *Ibid.* (August 28, 1858, and May 22, 1858).

worked entirely to the advantage of the Bryants. Because of their high standards of performance, they drew enormous crowds and continued to do so even during the ensuing years when various reorganizations within the company and the death of Jerry[6] threatened to weaken them. There was a slight slackening of public interest in June, 1861,[7] at the outbreak of the Civil War, but prosperity returned shortly thereafter. Excelling in the "delineations of the plantation negro of the South, as well as of the uncommon darkey of the 'high latitudes' . . . ,"[8] the Bryants stayed at Mechanics' Hall with undiminished acclaim up to May of 1866.[9] This, for all practical purposes, was the end of their prominence as Negro impersonators, although they continued to appear at different places until the late seventies. The fault lay with minstrelsy itself, which no longer encouraged them. It had become more and more an efficient variety show, featuring "snatches of opera, songs abounding in high-flown sentiment and considerable orchestral crash" instead of the vigorous, crude old-time songs. No wonder that under these circumstances appearance in blackface was like "playing under false pretences . . ." and that minstrels seemed less Negroes than a "pack of Signor Maccaronis in disguise."[10]

What animated the Bryant's Minstrels was the musical and theatrical skill and imagination of the three brothers. Dan was a banjoist and, like Jerry, a tambourine and bone player; both were expert dancers, while Neil excelled on the accordion and the flutina.[11] Dan's and Jerry's abilities as comedians with a complete command of the Negro dialect[12] must have been impressive. The distinguished actor

[6] *Ibid.* (July 20, 1861).

[7] *Ibid.* (June 8, 1861).

[8] *Ibid.* (December 26, 1857).

[9] J. S. G. Hagan, *Records of the New York Stage 1860–1870*, XI, 181, in the Harvard Theatre Collection.

[10] *The New York Clipper* (November 14, 1868).

[11] Prefaces in the songsters *Bryant's Essence of Old Virginny* (New York, 1857), and *Bryant's Cane Brake Refrains* (New York, 1863). Jerry Bryant is listed as a tambourine player on the playbill of the Operatic Brothers and Sisters, a minstrel ensemble (July 28, 1845), as reprinted in *The New York Clipper* (January 29, 1876), and as a bone player and dancer on playbills of the Ethiopian Minstrels (American Museum, New York, January 18, 1847) and Ordway's Aeolians (Boston, 1851).

[12] *The New York Clipper* (August 21, 1858).

Edwin Forrest never became "weary of seeing Dan Bryant play the part of the hungry negro in 'Old Times Rocks,' " fully convinced "that there was not a finer bit of tragic acting to be seen in America at that time than . . . in this broadly funny" skit. Particularly memorable was the "pathos of . . . [Dan's] voice when, on being questioned as to when he had eaten a square meal, he answered humbly 'I had a peanut last week.' "[13]

When the Bryants began their activities in New York, they found that the realistic portrayal of the plantation was fading in favor of entertainment per se. They reversed this trend by displaying "the comicalities and eccentricities of negro life to a nicety";[14] and since they succeeded in reviving "the old and original style"[15] of the genre, they were justly recognized as the "connecting link between the days of minstrelsy of old, and those of the present time . . . ."[16] Fortunately they were at once imitated by their colleagues. Judged by its vitality, it seems then that the forties represent the first period of the minstrel show, the early fifties its partial decline, and the time from 1857 to the late sixties its grand conclusion. Negro impersonation continued up to the beginning of the twentieth century, but it was kept alive only through a few gifted individual performers. As a co-operative venture it was no more than a pale reflection of the past.

The performances of the Bryants revealed meticulous planning, though mainly in details of stage business.[17] Much of the acting itself, and certainly its finer points, was wisely left to improvisation.[18] Like minstrels before them, the Bryant's always blended Negro impersonation, which was both faithful and imaginatively slanted, with comment on the latest contemporary events. They possessed the "happy faculty of seizing upon prominent public matters . . ."[19] and

[13] Olive Logan, "The Ancestry of Brudder Bones," *Harper's New Monthly Magazine* (April, 1879).

[14] *The New York Clipper* (November 14, 1857).

[15] *Ibid.* (June 20, 1857).

[16] *Ibid.* (December 26, 1857).

[17] *Ibid.* (October 16, 1858).

[18] *Ibid.* (August 24, 1861).

[19] *The Programme* (August 7, 1858), and *The New York Clipper* (September 25, 1858). See also Chapter 16 and the discussion of Emmett's "Greenbacks" in Hans Nathan, "Two Inflation Songs of the Civil War," *The Musical Quarterly* (April, 1943).

upon prominent personages—white as well as black—and lampooning what seemed ludicrous or objectionable about them.

The setup of their programs was not unusual. It was divided into three parts customary in the fifties: the first consisted mainly of white songs, choruses, and instrumental pieces; the second, of a more noticeable Negro flavor, offered musical and choreographic virtuoso acts, often followed by an operatic burlesque or some such scene; and the third was almost entirely devoted to the southern plantation. The Negro element may not have appeared more frequently at the Bryants than elsewhere, but it was worked out in greater and more genuine detail. There were no women in the cast; in keeping with the earlier tradition, all female roles were played by men.

Emmett stayed with the Bryants from October or November of 1858 to July of 1866, except for his absence from New York during one season. When the outbreak of the Civil War in the summer of 1861 threatened the theatrical life of the city, or so it seemed, he again struck out for himself and went to Chicago where he knew he would be welcome, organizing minstrel shows from early September on.[20] But when he saw that New York was gayer than ever, he returned to Mechanics' Hall in the spring of 1862.[21]

His work for the Bryants called for all of his talents at once. His main task was to write the tune and the words for walk-arounds, the finale and high point of their shows. He also appeared as a musical performer, singing and playing on the banjo, probably the fiddle, and the fife and the drum as well.[22] These activities involved participation in many comical skits, some of which may have been penned by himself:[23] as an enthusiastic warbler in parodies of the popular

[20] Notices on Emmett's "Varieties," which included several female performers, in *The New York Clipper* (September 14, October 12, and November 2, 1861).

[21] According to Col. T. Allston Brown, "Early History of Negro Minstrelsy," *The New York Clipper* (June 29, 1912), he returned in March, 1862, but his name does not appear in the advertisements of the Bryants at that time. Odell, *Annals*, VII, 430, finds Emmett's name in advertisements of the Bryants in June.

[22] For example, he often took part in a scene entitled "Fife and Drum Major" and in a burlesque of *Un Ballo in Maschera* as the "orchestra," playing either the banjo or the fiddle.

[23] Moreau, *Negro Minstrelsy*, II: "Besides playing in the orchestra and upon the stage, Uncle Dan was employed as a composer of songs, sketches and walk-arounds, for the troupe."

singing families, Tyrolean or American; as the officer "Sig. Sardinero" in the burlesque of Italian opera; as the "Ghost of Hamlet" in a play called *Used Up, or the hop of fashion;* and as other characters in many take-offs on political events and current dramatic productions, and in straight plantation scenes as well. During his long association with the Bryants, his name was constantly before the public and his songs were not only known in New York but were circulated widely elsewhere by traveling minstrel companies who adopted them freely. In 1861 *The New York Clipper* referred to him as "one of the pioneers of minstrelsy, and even at this day one of the most useful men in the profession,"[24] and in a songster of 1863,[25] he is mentioned among the main representatives of his field. With a great deal of work on his hands as a member of the Bryants, he nevertheless found time to publish his *Fife Instructor* in 1862, a manual and collection of tunes used in the United States Army. The seven years he spent in New York were evidently the busiest and most productive of his career.

At the conclusion of his engagement with the Bryants, he went on tour with them in the summer of 1866.[26] Afterward, from late August on, he and other members of the troupe were with the Budworth's Minstrels at the Fifth Avenue Opera House, where he performed probably for a few weeks.[27] But his contact with the Bryants was not entirely broken, for in April, 1868, though once more residing in Chicago, he wrote for them a walk-around which was presented at the opening of their new theater at Tammany Hall on Fourteenth Street.[28]

Emmett saw most of his successful walk-arounds appear as sheet music. But he also entertained the hope of publishing a comprehensive collection of walk-arounds, for he assembled them in neat copies in one book and wrote this introduction for it:

[24] August 10, 1861.

[25] Converse, *Fox's Minstrel's Companion,* referred to Emmett as a "Utility Comedian."

[26] *The New York Clipper* (June 9 and 16, 1866).

[27] Odell, *Annals,* VIII, 218.

[28] The title of the walk-around was "The Wigwam." See *The New York Clipper* (April 25, 1868).

These 'Walk 'Rounds' were composed during the period from 1859 [1858]–1868. Most of them were first put upon the stage of the celebrated "Bryant Minstrels" in New York, and for whom, in fact most of them were composed, while the author was a member of that organization; and the immense popularity they attained (the W.R.) was in a great measure due to the effective manner in which the "Bryants" produced them.

In the composition of a 'Walk 'Round' (by this I mean the style of music and character of the words), I have always strictly confined myself to the habits and crude ideas of the slaves of the South. Their knowledge of the world at large was very limited, often not extending beyond the bounds of the next plantation; they could sing of nothing but everyday life or occurrences, and the scenes by which they were surrounded. This being the undeniable fact, to be true to the negro peculiarities of song, I have written in accordance.

Daniel Decatur Emmett[29]

To the title page he added the following notice, presumably as a protection against plagiarism:

In parting with the 'Walk 'Rounds' contained in this book, I reserve to myself the right of publication; as they are to be used only in a professional way: (in other words: for stage purposes;) and nothing shall be so construed, as to imply a contrary meaning.

Daniel D. Emmett—author
purchaser
witness[30]

Since these walk-arounds were originally incidental music, though they have value in their own right, it is useful to mention their manner of presentation. Names such as "Plantation Song and Dance," as a subtitle for the music, and "Plantation Festival," applied to the entire

[29] Galbreath, *Daniel Decatur Emmett,* 47. According to the author, this volume of walk-arounds still existed in 1904, but it was broken up in later years and some of its content disappeared.

[30] The title page which reads: "Complete sett [sic] of Walk 'Rounds. Composed by Daniel D. Emmett," is in the possession of Ogden Wintermute, Mount Vernon, Ohio.

scene, clearly suggest the type of stage décor. The "whole minstrel company attired in varied costumes, such as one might have seen on a southern levee, assembled on the stage . . . [standing] in a semi-circle."[31] Near the footlights were a few comedians who became active during the first part of the walk-around. They alternately stepped forth and sang a stanza, interrupted by brief, pithy passages of the entire group (see Illustration 52). Then everyone on the stage sounded the final chorus which followed immediately, and to the concluding instrumental music, the solo performers began to dance in a circle with boisterous and grotesque steps and rowdy gestures (see Illustration 53). They were probably joined by the rest of the company in the background, who had previously furnished the percussive accompaniment by clapping their hands—sometimes together over their heads, sometimes against "an elbow . . . as a diversity,"[32] or sometimes on their knees "with the outspread palms"[33]—and stamping the floor. In addition to this manner of performance,[34] in

Illustration 52. The first part of a walk-around. From a playbill of the Bryant's Minstrels (December 19, 1859).

[31] W. J. Henderson, *Negro Minstrel Melodies* (New York, 1910).
[32] Logan, "Brudder Bones."
[33] Sherlock, "Breakdown to Rag-Time."
[34] Our description has been gained from the markings and the structure of Emmett's music, choreographically confirmed by two illustrations and the occasional references in announcements of the Bryants to the appearance of both the entire troupe and solo performers in walk-arounds.

Illustration 53. The concluding dance of a walk-around. From a playbill of the Bryant's Minstrels (December 19, 1859).

which "Dixie" was presented, the Bryants no doubt knew a slightly different one which was customary with other troupes. Instead of a fixed group in the foreground, each member of the company took part in turn as a soloist, who "would advance to the center," walk "around the inside of the gathering three of four times," and "stopping in the center," begin to dance.[35] The final ensemble dance itself often included a considerable number of actors, so that a variety of comical characters were seen cavorting on the stage: "the lean, the fat, the tall, the short, the hunchbacked and the wooden legged, all mixed in, and hard at it . . .";[36] there were also dwarfs, children, and "wench dancers," who indulged in "saltatory exercises . . . with various hi's! hey's! and Oh Law's! . . . ."[37] One of their favorite dance steps "was little more than a jerky elevation of the legs below the knee, much like the 'buck and wing dances'" of later years.[38]

Performances like this closely approximated southern scenes, not only in detail but in the entire organization of the dance.[39] For exam-

[35] Henderson, *Minstrel Melodies;* Logan, "Brudder Bones."
[36] "Negro Minstrels and their Dances."
[37] Logan, "Brudder Bones."
[38] Sherlock, "Breakdown to Rag-Time."
[39] This was soon recognized. See "Negro Minstrels and their Dances," which speaks of the "true darky style . . . ." Henderson, *Minstrel Melodies:* "The walk-around . . . was a genuine form of slave song . . . ." Henry Edward Krehbiel, *Afro-*

234

ple, the Negro "shout" involved men and women who moved around in a circle; sometimes they sang themselves and sometimes they were accompanied by a group of onlookers who chanted the spiritual and clapped "their hands together or on the knees."[40] And even on secular occasions a ring was formed by the men and its center taken by a dancer, while the crowd provided for the usual percussive background.[41]

The early walk-around was a dance. When it appeared on the minstrel stage in the late forties, it was executed by a soloist.[42] A few years later, in the early fifties, it had grown into an ensemble act in which either a small number of dancers or the entire company participated.[43] Only from 1858 on, or slightly earlier, was it both danced and sung; in this form it was established by the Bryants as a regular feature in minstrel shows.[44]

No walk-arounds were published before that date, although three appeared then that probably date back to an earlier time.[45] These are purely instrumental tunes, and two of them differ slightly from the ordinary banjo jig in having a less ornate melodic style and a

American Folk Songs (New York, 1914), 33, calls the walk-around a "secular parody" of the Negro "shout."

[40] Allen, *Slave Songs*, pp. xiii–xv.

[41] Charles L. Edwards, *Bahama Songs and Stories* (Boston and New York, 1895), 17. See also Talley, *Negro Folk Rhymes*, 232.

[42] Playbill of the Dumbolton's Ethiopian Serenaders (1849), as published in *The New York Clipper* (March 24, 1877). In *The New York Clipper* (July 14, 1877), Fred Wilson reports that he danced walk-arounds as early as 1849. Charles White's minstrel play *Going for the Cup; Or Old Mrs. William's Dance* (New York, 1874, first performance 1847), includes solo walk-arounds.

[43] Playbill of "Well's Late the orginal Fellow's Minstrels" (New York, August 30 and 31, 1852), lists "The Alabama Festival Dance, introducing the Trial Walk Around." "Arkansas Walk-Around" with three performers was mentioned in a playbill of the Wood's Minstrels (1853), as published in *The New York Clipper* (March 25, 1876). A "Walk-Around Dance," presented by the entire company is listed on a playbill of Yankee Hill's Ethiopian Opera Troupe (December 25, 1854), as published in *The New York Clipper* (January 3, 1874).

[44] In 1857 the Bryants concluded their shows with the "Plantation Song and Dance, or Southern Life, Down in Alabama." See the playbill (May 27, 1857); *The New York Clipper* (April 25, 1857), commented on its "musical and . . . saltatory . . ." aspects as if they were something new. If the subtitle, "an original Ethiopian Walk Around in 1 act," of Emmett's play *Hard Times* referred mainly to the concluding scene, the walk-around combined vocal and choreographic elements as early as 1855.

[45] *Rice's Correct Method* includes a great deal of early material.

greater degree of metrical stability appropriate to the strutting character of the dance.

Emmett's walk-around is not the traditional one. Though including instrumental music, it is, aside from its theatrical function, essentially a vocal composition. In formal layout it owes to earlier minstrel songs only the final chorus; the division of its first part into alternating snatches for solo and ensemble was practically a novelty,[46] and definitely so in its consistent application.

The details of Emmett's walk-arounds were familiar, but they were welded together into an idiom that has a flavor all its own: one detects it in the heartiness of the final choruses and in the conciseness of the phrases (in the ensemble sections often paralleling the slangy character of the words) that animate the first part and, despite their brevity, lend it coherence. The style was limited but Emmett knew how to handle it with considerable variety. After several years, however, it turned into a formula and he finally abandoned it. Other minstrel composers continued to find it attractive, and it thus survived until the early eighties.[47]

Emmett maintained that he had composed his walk-arounds, as he put it, "true to the negro peculiarities of song." As far as the music was concerned, he was only partially right, for he utilized the most diverse elements, and not all of them were by any means the property of the black man.

The most tangible Negro element in his walk-arounds is the solo-ensemble alternation in their first part and the repetitiousness of its melodic and textual phrases. Another one is the interval of the minor third, upward and downward, which, as in Negro spirituals, often appears in a pentatonic formula (that is, with a preceding major second), while its larger context is regulated by a major or minor tonality. A few more specific relations to Negro music exist, but they are rather tenuous. A contemporary newspaper report on a Negro prayer meeting in New York City found a hymn "somewhat resem-

[46] This alternation appeared in only one song: W. L. Hargrave, "Old Bob Ridley" (Baltimore, J. E. Boswell, 1853).

[47] See "Good Bye, Liza Jane" (1871), as republished in *Minstrel Songs Old and New* (Boston, Oliver Ditson, 1882); Sam Lucas, "Hannah Boil Dat Cabbage Down" (Boston and Chicago, 1878); and Ned Straight, "Old Times Roxy" (New York, 1880).

bling" "Old K.Y. Ky." (see Musical Example 99).[48] The reference may have been to some such tune as "O'er the Crossing" (see Musical Example 100). One might also see similarities between "The Black Brigade" (see Musical Example 101) on the one hand, and on the other, "I'm Gwine to Albany" (see Musical Example 102), sung by colored deck hands on the "western steamboats," and "I'm in Trouble" (see Musical Example 103).[49] Whereas the tone repetitions of Emmett's opening and recurrent phrases, as in "Old K. Y. Ky.," "The Black Brigade," "Road to Richmond" (see Musical Example 104), and "I'm Going Home to Dixie" (see Musical Example 105), appear both in white and black hymns, the short-long note pattern at its end, especially in conjunction with a third, is a Negro characteristic (see also Musical Example 106).[50] "What O' Dat" (see Musical Examples 107 and 108) and "Sandy Gibson's" (see Musical Examples 109 and 110), however, are indebted to white sources.[51]

In keeping with the traditional style of performance of the Bryants, Emmett borrowed various melodic turns and rhythmic patterns from the minstrel songs of the forties, quite openly in "Turkey in de Straw," where he used "Zip Coon," and also in "Jonny Roach," "Sandy Gibson's," "What O' Dat," and other walk-arounds. From the same source he derived his pungent, ejaculatory phrases, such as "Don't y'e tell me" in "Billy Patterson," as well as such instrumental interludes as in "Jonny Roach." On a few occasions he also resorted to banjo tunes.[52] Other elements of his music came from British folk music; they show clearly in the concluding reels and in Scottish patterns that he employed in several walk-arounds.[53] And even a slight influence of early American marches is noticeable.[54]

Emmett's texts deal with typical Negro scenes in both the South

---

[48] *The New York Clipper* (October 12, 1861). "O'er the Crossing," hymn No. 93 in Allen, *Slave Songs*. It may be of interest to mention that the chorus of James Bland, "De Angels Am a Coming," a song in the style of a Negro spiritual (New York, 1880), is very similar to that of Emmett's "Old K.Y.Ky."

[49] Hymns No. 111 and 113 in Allen, *Slave Songs*.

[50] Hymn No. 7 in Allen, *Slave Songs*.

[51] George Pullen Jackson, *White and Negro Spirituals* (New York, 1943), 170, 148.

[52] "What O' Dat" ("ah ah"), and one passage in "Dixie" (see Chapter 16).

[53] See Musical Examples 118 and 119.

[54] "Ten to one, nebber done, jis begun" in "Road to Richmond" is related to passages in Nos. 72 and 73 in Emmett's *Fife Instructor*.

Musical Example 99
"Old K. Y. Ky." (Emmett)

(transposed)

Musical Example 100
"O'er the Crossing" (Negro spiritual) [transposed]

Musical Example 101
"The Black Brigade" (Emmett)

Musical Example 102
"I'm Gwine to Alabamy"
(sung by colored deckhands on "the Western steamboats")

Musical Example 103
"I'm in Trouble" (Negro spiritual)

Musical Example 104
"Road to Richmond" (Emmett)

Musical Example 105
"I'm Going Home to Dixie" (Emmett)

Musical Example 106
"The Lonesome Valley" (Negro spiritual)

Musical Example 107
"What O' Dat" (Emmett)

(transposed)

Musical Example 108
"Lay This Body Down" (white hymn) [transposed]

Musical Example 109
"Sandy Gibson's" (Emmett)

(transposed)

etc.

Musical Example 110
"Old Ship Zion" (white hymn) [transposed]

and the North, not merely with the plantation as their author claimed. And all of them, combining the slave's statements with commentaries about him, have topical allusions. In "Dixie" and "I'm Going Home to Dixie," the colored man is a political artifact rather than a copy from life. "The Black Brigade" and "Road to Richmond" are satires of the black regiments of the Union Army during the Civil War. "Sandy Gibson's" contains an episode that any New Yorker could have experienced, and "Billy Patterson" is the Negro version of an Irish-American story.[55]

Though the versification reveals Emmett's hand, numerous lines and images were nevertheless lifted, according to professional cus-

[55] The Boston *Daily Evening Transcript* (March 25, 1840), gives a racy report on "Billy Patterson: A Story Of The Broad Street Riot." It tells of Patrick Mahonie, an Irishman, who "talked loud and large," but whose "courage . . . was chiefly at his tongue's end." Convinced of his strength and importance, he considered himself responsible for the welfare of his friend Billy Patterson. When Billy one day "fell into the hands of a tall fireman . . ." and was badly roughed up, his protector sallied forth in search of the offender, shouting "Och, by my eyes, who struck Billy Patterson!" But when he finally found him, he was wise enough to offer him his compliments.

241

tom, from earlier minstrel songs. Appearing alongside passages from English folk texts[56] and such urban colloquialisms as "o.k."[57] are many bits from the workaday reality of the slave, as well as such expressions as "going home," "traveling a rocky road," and "joining the union," which, though stripped of their religious meaning, derive from Negro spirituals. The following song, which was sung in the early forties by colored plantation hands in South Carolina as they shucked corn, is a good example:

> Johnny come down de hollow. Oh, hollow!
> Johnny come down de hollow. Oh, hollow!
> De nigger-trader got me. Oh hollow!
> De speculator bought me. Oh hollow!
> I'm sold for silver dollars. Oh hollow!
> Boys, go catch de pony. Oh hollow!
> Bring him round de corner. Oh hollow!
> I'm goin' away to Georgia. Oh hollow!
> Boys, good-bye forever. Oh hollow![58]

Emmett remembered almost all of these lines when he composed his walk-arounds. The opening he borrowed literally for his "John Come down de Hollow," and the rest he paralleled, in practically the same sequence, in his "Road to Georgia" and its alternate text version "Road to Richmond" as follows: "De niggar trader tink me nice" ("De speculator tink me nice"), "De white folks sell me for half price" (later: "We'll fotch a thousand dollars down"), and "Under way, under way Ho! we are on de way to Georgia."

---

[56] "They say, old man, your horse will die," in W. B. Whall, *Sea Songs and Shanties* (Glasgow, 1927), 135; see "Billy Patterson"; "When I was young and in my prime . . . ," from "Poor Old Horse," in Cecil J. Sharp, *One Hundred English Folksongs* (Boston, 1916); see "Road to Richmond."

[57] In "High Daddy." See Boston *Daily Evening Transcript* (October 1, November 11 and 28, 1840).

[58] Quoted in Norris Yates, "Four Plantation Songs Noted by William Cullen Bryant," *Southern Folklore Quarterly* (December, 1951).

Chapter 16

"DIXIE"

EMMETT'S FIRST SONG for the Bryant's Minstrels in New York, performed at the end of November, 1858, was entitled "The Land of Freedom" or "I Ain't Got Time to Tarry." Catering to public sentiment, which was deeply involved in the question of southern slavery, he chose as the protagonist of his song a Negro who longs for his southern home. Home to the Negro is not only his girl Dinah, for in the refrain he and the chorus emphasize: "Yes, I am gwine home. Den I ain't got time to tarry, I ain't got time to dwell, I'm bound to de land of freedom, oh, niggars! fare you well."[1] The Negro character pining for the southern plantation was well known in minstrel music since the early fifties, but in Emmett's song his political implications were considerably more outspoken than before. In Emmett's second and third songs written for the Bryants, parody of Negro characteristics became more and more tinged with political overtones. In "Wide Awake" or "Dar's a Darkey in de Tent," performed in early February, 1859, the Negro is described as a worthless, troublesome item which the white man could dispose of at his leisure. An example of how annoyance was cloaked in humor is the beginning of the song:

[1] From the songster *Bryant's Power of Music* (New York, 1859).

Dar's a niggar in de tent, keep 'im in, keep 'im in, keep 'im in.
Dar's a niggar in de tent, kick 'im out, kick 'im out, kick 'im out.
Dar's a niggar in de tent, keep 'im in, keep 'im in, keep 'im in.
But he hasn't paid de rent, kick 'im out, kick 'im out, kick 'im out.[2]

In the last two lines of the song "Jonny Roach," performed by the middle of March, "Jonny" admits that as a contraband he cannot get along very well in the North:

To Canada old John was bound
All by de railroad underground;
He's got no clothes—he's got no "tin"
He wishes he was back agin.

And he makes clear what "back agin" means:

Gib me de place called "Dixie's Land,"
Wid hoe and shubble in my hand;
Whar fiddles ring an' banjos play,
I'll dance all night an' work all day.[3]

Here is the very first occurrence in print of the words *Dixie's Land* as another name for the South—the black one, to be exact.

The political situation worsened rapidly. It was analyzed with great insight in an editorial of the *New York Herald* (March 29, 1859), which ended on this ominous and prophetic note: "When we find the African slave traders in the South securely protected by public opinion against the federal authorities, and Southern public meetings deliberately resolving that 'all laws of the federal government interdicting the right of the Southern people to bring and import slaves from Africa are unconstitutional, null, and void,' there is every reason to fear that there is mischief in this thing, which, in 1860, will shake the Union to its foundations."

[2] *Ibid.*
[3] *Ibid.*

A few days later, on April 4, the song "Dixie's Land" appeared on the stage of the Bryants. Coming at the height of public concern over the Negro issue, its text and tune sharply focused the main cause of the political turmoil while affording relief in laughter from its tensions. The Negro protagonist of the song states with much greater emphasis than in any of the afore-mentioned songs that the South is the only place where he belongs and where he feels happy. Instead of the South, he speaks of Dixie's Land. Since he declares himself utterly contented with his social status, he is the embodiment of the daydreams of many white Americans shortly before the outbreak of the Civil War.

The date of the performance of "Dixie's Land" or "Dixie," as it was soon called, is usually given incorrectly. A copy of the playbill of the first night exists in the Harvard Theatre Collection (see Illustration 54). It is a typical minstrel playbill of the late fifties. The show started out with sentimental "white" ballads and, as it proceeded, took on increasingly comic and "Negro" features. Unlike earlier "plantation songs and dances" by Emmett, "Dixie" did not, at first, conclude the show, possibly because the Bryants did not consider it effective enough. Being a "walk 'round" (to use Emmett's own spelling), it was presented as a colorful spectacle illustrating the gay side of southern slave life, or more specifically, a "Cornshucking Dance." The first part of the song was acted out by a few comedians while the rest was performed by the entire company (see Chapter 15). The original cast, which consisted of about a dozen members, is no longer known, but the main actors in a performance given a little more than one-half year after the première were R. D. Sands, W. and T. Norton, J. Carrol, G. W. Charles, and Jerry and Dan Bryant, all of them not only comedians but skilled dancers.[4]

When Emmett was in his eighties, about forty years after the first performance of "Dixie," he made a number of picturesque but unreliable and even conflicting statements about how he came to write the song. Two remarks, however, are believable: one that he com-

---

[4] See *Bryant's Songs and Programmes* (1859–60), II, Program No. 38, now in the Harvard College Library. The song was then announced as "Way Down Souf in Dixie," a "Cornshucking Dance."

Illustration 54. Playbill of a performance of Bryant's Minstrels (New York, April 4, 1859), at which "Dixie" was presented for the first time. Courtesy Harvard Theatre Collection.

posed the tune first and the words afterwards; the other that he composed the song in New York "on one rainy Sunday in Elm Street, between Broome and Spring Streets, No. 197, Room No. 1."[5]

The style of the song connects it closely with the productions for the Bryants and with no songs of a previous period. Except for a single wholly uncorroborated statement by Emmett shortly before his death to the effect that "Dixie" had been written years before he came to New York, there is no evidence whatsoever for the persistent rumor of the song's origin in Minnesota.[6]

Like many walk-arounds by Emmett, "Dixie" consisted of thirty-two measures—a number still sacrosanct in Tin-Pan Alley. The song was divided into two equal sections: the first in its original version (see Illustration 55) showed an alternation of a soloist with a small group, whereas the second was performed by the entire company. The first part of a walk-around was by no means of introductory character. It was, in its way, just as distinctive as the chorus. Added to "Dixie," according to custom, was an instrumental section, a fiddle tune consisting of eight measures with a half-close in the middle.

The longevity of "Dixie" is due chiefly to its inherent qualities as a work of art, modest and unpretentious though it may be. The responses to the tune are unequivocal and, on the average, unchanging, if evoked by the piece played at its original tempo, which was considerably slower than the one now preferred by military bands. The tune is characterized by a heavy, nonchalant, inelegant strut—elements still alive in such recent dances as the Big Apple. If music, lyrics, and dance style are taken as an entity, there emerges a special kind of humor that mixes grotesqueness with lustiness and down-to-earth contentment—comparable, to overstate the case, to a blend of

---

[5] The first appears attached to his manuscript copy for DeWitt Miller; the second is in *The New York Clipper* (April 6, 1872). Late (unreliable) statements by Emmett are reported in interviews: Rev. L. W. Mulhane, "The Writer of 'Dixie,'" *Donahoe's Magazine* (June, 1900); Sheerin, "Dixie"; Hall, "Does It Pay"; White, "Negro Minstrelsy's Origin"; and M. B. Leavitt, *Fifty Years in Theatrical Managements* (New York, 1912).

[6] Hall, "Does It Pay." According to a claim advanced by Judge Dixon in a letter (April 1, 1937), to Judge Kenneth G. Brill, President of the Minnesota Historical Society, St. Paul, Dan Emmett composed "Dixie" at the home of his brother Lafayette during his stay in St. Paul during the winter of 1858–59. The story, based on hearsay, is without foundation, for Emmett lived in New York at this particular time.

Musical Example 111
The recurrent rhythmic motive of "Dixie."

Musical Example 112
A rhythmic jolt in "Dixie's Land," borrowed from "My First Jig."

Brueghel and Mickey Mouse. These specific qualities could have been developed nowhere but in the United States. And for this reason, "Dixie" may be called one of the most American musical products of the nineteenth century.

Like every popular tune, "Dixie" has one initial rhythmic motive which, literally or varied, recurs constantly (see Musical Example 111). But this motive is integrated into long melodic phrases. Note, for example, how the first two measures of the tune are naturally and compellingly developed up to the eighth measure, not counting here the introduction (see Illustration 55). The entrances of the small group, singing "Look away," are always on the crest of the melodic line that has been set in motion by the soloist. Another notable feature is the effective way in which the second part, starting with "Den I wish I was in Dixie," emerges from the first. It takes up the anapaestic motive of the preceding section (for example, "Look away"), stabilizes it, and spins it out into a new, more coherent phrase. In other words, the final chorus or "refrain" carries out, as it should, what is suggested previously. But the tune is of utmost simplicity: its line, describing

248

*Illustration 55. Facsimile of an early manuscript of "Dixie."
From* The Confederate Veteran *(Nashville, September, 1895).*

over and over the same triadic space, could hardly be of a more out-spoken major tonality than it is. The rhythm, too, holds no surprises except for a jolt in the middle of the song (see Musical Example 112), caused by a sudden shift of accents in two almost identical phrases —a device borrowed from early banjo tunes and, in particular, from a piece by Emmett entitled "My First Jig." Forward motion is vigorous, but it is deliberately qualified by an element of awkwardness by way of frequent halts and unpliable intervals that, as it were, hang at an angle. "Dixie" indeed is no polite, genteel tune. It has a considerable measure of toughness, and like most tunes that stir the millions, it sounds familiar. If this implies a tinge of triteness, it is made artistically palatable by various structural features, some of which have been mentioned. In addition, there is another quality that accounts for the popularity of the song: its melodic line, especially that of the second part, lends the text an inflection that approaches the naturalness of colloquial speech. No wonder, then, that text adaptations have not survived.

It is generally believed that the original manuscript of the song is lost. All the manuscript copies now extant were made by Emmett in the nineties and later, when he lived as a pauper in Mount Vernon, Ohio.[7] However, there is a facsimile of the song which is worthy of closer analysis (see Illustration 55). It appeared in the September, 1895, issue of the magazine *The Confederate Veteran,* published in Nashville, Tennessee. Along with it goes the facsimile of a letter written by Emmett and addressed to S. A. Cunningham, the editor of the magazine, who had visited him. It is dated July 31, 1895. Its last paragraph reads: "In compliment to you and the messages of good will you bring, I hand you to engrave for the Confederate Veterans the original copy of 'Dixie,' made on that rainy Sunday in New York

---

[7] Late autograph copies of the song are in the possession of the Harvard Theatre Collection; the National Symphony Orchestra Association, Washington, D. C.; and Cornell University Library. Thomas F. Madigan, New York, had for sale a copy made by Emmett for "DeWitt Miller, Dec. 20th, 1900"; a facsimile of the same manuscript and part of an attached autograph account of the origin of the song appear in the catalog of the American Art Association, Anderson Galleries (December 5 and 6, 1934). There are other facsimiles in Galbreath, *Daniel Decatur Emmett,* 16, 17; Madigan's Catalogue (June, 1928); Goodspeed's *The Month* (Boston, February, 1935); and Wintermute, *Emmett.*

City in 1859." Emmett's description of the manuscript as the original may be untrustworthy. We can rely better on a comparison with his manuscripts of the period when "Dixie" was composed. This comparison shows a practically complete agreement in handwriting, arrangement of the words, notes, text, title, and date on the page as well as the type of music paper used. Two more features which do not appear in the printed 1860 version of the song strengthen the impression that the manuscript of the facsimile is very early: the alternation between solo and ensemble in the first part of the song, which is characteristic of all of Emmett's walk-arounds, was most likely part of the original performance of "Dixie"; the text of the facsimile agrees far more with the one published in 1859 in the songster *Bryant's Power of Music* than with that of the sheet music edition of 1860.[8]

"Dixie" was considered public property, and many comedians and writers adapted their own verses to it. We will confine ourselves here to quoting those made by the composer himself. Assuming that the entire text version in *Bryant's Power of Music* is by Emmett, we will quote the sixth stanza, which, though related to a stanza of the original and the sheet music edition, offers a few new word images:

> Sugar in de gourd, an' stony batter
> De whites grow fat, an' de niggars fatter,

In 1866 Emmett wrote on the back of a photograph of himself the following stanza, calling it the first:

> I wish I was in de lann ob cotton,
> Ole time darr am not forgotten:

(Chorus)

---

[8] The original manuscript, from which the facsimile was made, has recently turned up as the property of George Bird Evans, Bruceton Mills, West Virginia, whose great-grandmother, Mrs. George Bird, née Mary Louise Brower, was Emmett's second wife. The stanzas of the manuscript are almost entirely identical to those of a manuscript which Galbreath, *Daniel Decatur Emmett*, 18, 19, having found it in Emmett's handwritten volume "Walk 'Rounds," called "the earliest manuscript of the song known to exist"; it is no longer extant.

In Dixie lann de darkies grow
If white foax only plant dar toe[9]

(Chorus)

In the seventies or eighties, at a time when Emmett's career was over, he occupied himself with writing comic Negro hymns. Here is one that he wrote to the tune of "Dixie":

1 I wish we was in Caanan's lann.
I wish we was dar eb'ry man;

Chorus We'se a gwine *(repeat)*
We'se a gwine, sho' as y'e bawn.

De sister dey will kum dar too.
And wear der high-heel rocker shoe.

Chorus. We'se a gwine *(3 times)*
Sho' as y'e bawn.

Chorus:

I wish I was in Caanan,
Oaber dar—Oaber dar,
In Caanan's lann de color'd man
Can lib an die in cloaber
Oaber dar—Oaber dar,
Oaber dar in de lann ob Caanan. *(repeat)*

2 Dar brackberries grow on de briar bush,
Dey grow so tick y'e got to push;
Yoa eat an eat till yoa git yoa fill,
Yoa belly soun's like a powder mill.

Chorus . . .

[9] In the possession of the Alderman Library, University of Virginia.

3   Dar de preacher man he aint no good,
     He hab to go to splittin wood;
     He loss de tex an he got no nickel,
     To sabe he soul he's put in pickle.

     Chorus . . .

4   De cawn stocks grow till y'e got to hoal 'em
     If dey don't stop den you got to scoal 'em;
     Den harness de mule and dribe 'im steady,
     Whoop—jamboree, we all am ready.

     Chorus . . .

In an undated text version which might easily be twenty years later than the previous one, Emmett wrote a partly new second stanza and entirely new third and fourth stanzas:

2   In Dixie Lann de darkies grow
     If white foax only plant dar toe;
     Dey wet de groun wid bakker smoke
     Den up de darkey's head will poke.

     Chorus . . .

3   Dey hoe an rake an dig de lann
     An plant de cotton seed by hann;
     When massas gone dey down will sit
     De young mokes dey git up an git!

     Chorus . . .

4   You court de galls right on de squarr
     An smoove de wool in dar curly harr,
     Dey am not drunk—dey am not sober,
     Dey try to faint but fall clarr ober!

     Chorus . . .[10]

[10] The manuscript, without music and with six stanzas altogether, is in the possession of the Library of Congress.

In another late autograph which was probably made around 1900, Emmett used many old stanzas but added a number of new lines:

1 Dis worl was made in jiss six days,
   An finish'd up in various ways;
   Look away etc.
   Dey den made Dixie trim an nice,
   But Adam call'd it "Paradise."

4 I used to hoe and dig de lann,
   But work dey say am contrabann;
   Driber he come poken 'bout,
   When massa sole me out-an-out.

5 Ole missus die—she took a decline,
   Her face was de color ob bacon rhine;
   To kingdom kum den let her go.
   For here on earth she stood no show.

6 De[n] hoe it down an scratch yoa grabble
   To Dixie Lann I'm boun to trabble;
   Whar de rake an hoe got double trigger
   An white man jiss as good as niggar![11]

Emmett asserted in 1900 that the above first stanza was the original first one, adding: "My first verse as I composed it I never published, although I sang it every night."[12] This statement, suddenly made almost half a century after the appearance of the song, can be discounted as mere fancy.

"Dixie's" melodic style is not unique among Emmett's songs composed for the Bryants. Before "Dixie" was written, a part of its chorus crops up, slightly varied, in "Jonny Roach," and afterwards reappears in "Billy Patterson" (see Musical Example 113). Even sev-

[11] There are seven stanzas altogether, according to Galbreath, *Daniel Decatur Emmett*, 16, 17.

[12] In the account of the song attached to the DeWitt Miller autograph, in which the same first stanza also appears.

"Dixie's Land"

"Jonny Roach" (transposed)

"Billy Patterson" (transposed)

Musical Example 113

Before "Dixie" was written, a part of its chorus was used in both "Jonny Roach" and "Billy Patterson."

eral years later, in "The Black Brigade," the rhythmic patterns of its opening and conclusion are still discernible.

Stylistic comparison, unaided by dates, clearly establishes Emmett as the composer of "Dixie." Nevertheless, a number of his contemporaries denied this. Only a little more than ten years after the appearance of the song, such a sentence as this was written: "his [Emmett's] claim to the authorship of 'Dixie' was and is still dis-

255

puted, both in and out of the minstrel profession."[13] For the South it was of course emotionally difficult, after the beginning of the Civil War, to acknowledge for "Dixie," by then a symbol of the Confederacy, anything but a southern origin and the anonymity of a folk song. A statement such as the following is typical, although it includes an extra bit of special pleading in the use of the world "noble": "The homely air of 'Dixie,' of extremely doubtful origin . . . [is] generally believed to have sprung from a noble stock of Southern stevedore melodies...."[14]

The tune of "Dixie" was also held identical with an old southern Negro air.[15] This air was indeed known in the first half of the past century. Its text appeared in full in *The Comic Forget-Me-Not Songster* (Philadelphia, probably middle forties), and *The Popular National Songster* (Philadelphia, 1845). It started with:

If I had a donkey wot wouldn't go
D'ye think I'd wollop him—no, no, no.

This was the American version of Henry R. Bishop's song "The Dashing White Sergeant," with words by General Sir John Burgoyne and published in New York in the late twenties as sheet music.[16] Its original text was printed in songsters up to the middle fifties, but the song soon acquired new words also, so that it circulated in at least two text versions among white and black folks alike.[17]

[13] "Cat and Dog Fight," *The New York Clipper* (September 7, 1872). Nevertheless, the same paper had spoken several years earlier (April 25, 1868), of "Dan Emmett . . . who composed the world renowned 'Dixie.'"

[14] In a postscript to the poem "War," by John Hill Hewitt (1862), as quoted in Richard B. Harwell, *Confederate Music* (Chapel Hill, 1950), 50.

[15] Statement of song writer Will S. Hays in the *Louisville Post*, as reprinted in *The New York Clipper* (March 6, 1886). A similar statement was made by Hays' publisher, D. P. Faulds (Louisville, Kentucky, 1907); along with additional material it was republished in the *Memphis Chamber of Commerce Journal* (June, 1924).

[16] Richard Northcott, *The Life of Sir Henry R. Bishop* (London, 1920). Bishop's song, inserted into an opera, was heard for the first time in Covent Garden (London, 1812).

[17] The original text of "The Dashing White Sergeant" appears in *The Universal Songster* (New York, 1829), *The American Songster* (Baltimore, 1836); and *Marsh's Selection or Singing for the Million* (New York, 1854), III. The tune is included in Elias Howe, comp., *Second Part of the Musician's Companion* (Boston, 1850).

"Dixie," it is true, does show affinities to the first measures of the tune "If I Had a Donkey [beau]" (see Musical Example 114). They are so slight, however, and in the face of other possible stimulation that Emmett might have received, so irrelevant that he cannot possibly be accused of plagiarism.

According to another story, Emmett admitted in a conversation to have "based the first part of Dixieland" on the "song of his childhood days," "Come Philander Let's Be Marchin, Every One for His True Love Searchin."[18] However, the facts do not bear him out. It is also well to remember his naïveté and goodheartedness which would have prompted him to admit almost anything if pressed hard. Of two published versions of "Come Philander," the first has absolutely no connection with "Dixie."[19] Parts of the second suggest merely the melodic outline, though not the rhythmic organization, of the opening of the chorus, "I wish I was in Dixie" (see Musical Example 115).[20] Again, on the basis of these relations, Emmett's authorship cannot be contested.[21] And when we proceed now to point out the true elements that did go into the making of "Dixie," we cannot fail to recognize that they have been integrated into a tune that the composer had every right to call his own.

In 1844, Emmett published a song entitled "De Wild Goose-Nation." Its tune was a variant of the minstrel song "Gumbo Chaff" of the thirties,[22] which in its turn traces back to an English eighteenth-

[18] T. C. De Leon, *Belles, Beaux, and Brains of the Sixties* (New York, 1909), 359–60.

[19] Fletcher Collins, Jr., *Alamance Play Party Songs and Singing Games* (Elon College, North Carolina, 1940).

[20] Lucien L. and Flora Lassiter McDowell, *Folk Dances of Tennessee* (Ann Arbor, Michigan, 1938).

[21] In the *Baltimore Sun* (July 11, 1904), only a few days after Emmett's death, someone mentioned the Arkansas comedian and song writer Harry Macarthy as the originator of "Dixie." This claim, based on very flimsy arguments, was refuted in the same paper by Charles B. Galbreath. To clinch his point, he could have mentioned that the style of Macarthy's own songs (see for example his "Bonnie Blue Flag," a Confederate song) rules out any connection with "Dixie." Both communications to the *Baltimore Sun* were reprinted in Galbreath, *Daniel Decatur Emmett*, 31–33. It was finally Will S. Hays who maintained to have written the words of "Dixie" "as a Confederate war ballad during the early part of the war," and not in "1857 to 1858" as the publisher Faulds claimed for him. This is obviously false, since "Dixie's" text was well known before the Civil War.

[22] Baltimore, G. Willig, Jr., n.d.

(transposed)

If   I   had   a   beau   for   a   sol - dier who'd go
(If   I   had   a   don - key wot would'   -   nt   go

Do   you   think   I'd   say   no?   No,   no   no   no
D'ye   think   I'd   wol - lop   him?   no   no   no

Musical Example 114

"Dixie" shows slight affinities to the first measures of the tune "If I Had a Donkey."

(transposed)

x   x   x   x   x   x   x

Musical Example 115

Parts of "Come Philander" suggest merely the melodic outline, though not the rhythmic organization, of the opening of the chorus, "I wish I was in Dixie."

Musical Example 116

The opening of "Gumbo Chaff."

A -   way down south   in   de   wild goose-nat- ion

Musical Example 117

The opening of "De Wild Goose-Nation."

Musical Example 118
Opening patterns of hornpipes and kindred tunes related to "Dixie."

century source (see Chapter 12). For the opening of "Gumbo Chaff,"
see Musical Example 116. Emmett changed it but slightly (see Musical Example 117); yet the result interests us particularly, because
rhythmically and, to some extent, melodically, it anticipates the initial measures of "Dixie." While "De Wild Goose-Nation" may have
been one source of "Dixie," there remains the possibility that Emmett
merely varied the opening patterns of hornpipes and kindred tunes
(see Musical Example 118).[23]

The second part of "Dixie" can probably be traced back to older
material, since the section of "Billy Patterson" to which it is related
is marked in the sheet music edition as "Old Melody." This melody,
if it exists at all, could not be found, but it is obvious that several

---

[23] "Vinton's Hornpipe," from Emmett, *Fife Instructor;* "Spirits of France," from
Howe, *Musician's Companion;* "Apollo Club-Hornpipe," from *Ryan's Mammoth Collection;* and "The Maid of Sweet Gurteen," from Petrie and Stanford, *Irish Music.*

passages in the second part of "Dixie" are variants of Scottish folk tunes (see Musical Example 119).[24]

The instrumental postludes of walk-arounds were frequently well-known fiddle tunes. As for "Dixie"'s dance, there is the testimony of the musician Oscar Coon, who knew the Bryants and who, many years later, remembered that they "tacked on the jig 'Beans of Albany' for the dance at the end [of 'Dixie']."[25] Since names in folk music are highly variable, it is not surprising to find the tune in Emmett's own *Fife Instructor* under the title of "Albany Beef." It is of Irish-Scottish ancestry,[26] and Emmett used its second part as the "dance" in his "Dixie." In his *Fife Instructor* he published a military version of "Dixie" and replaced the former "dance" with a new tune to which he added the name of "Walch"; the tune can be identified as part of the "Waterman Quickstep" by J. H. Walch, published in Boston in 1837.

The words of "Dixie," like the lyrics of almost all of his songs, were by Emmett himself. But like all minstrels and other folk musicians, he relied on a stock of well-known phrases and word pictures. "I wish I was in . . ." appears as early as the thirties in the minstrel song "Clare De Kitchen," in the form "I wish I was back in old Kentuck," and remains popular, though referring to various localities in the forties and fifties.[27] "Away down south in . . ." was firmly established in the minstrel songs of the fifties. Emmett himself had written as early as 1843, "Away down south in de Kentuck brake," in "I'm Gwine ober de Mountain."[28] The line "away down souf whar I was born" from the minstrel song "Picayune Butler" (Baltimore, 1847) is another early example which also anticipates "Dixie"'s "whar I was born in." The beginning of the second stanza of "Dixie" was fashioned after "Den Missus she did marry Big Bill de weaver / Soon she found out he

---

[24] The four fragments of Scottish tunes—"O, my love is like a red, red rose"; "O, Willie's fair and Willie's rare"; "O, Waly, Waly, up the bank"; and "See afar yon hill Ardmore"—are from Moffat, *Minstrelsy of Scotland*.

[25] "How Emmett Came to Write 'Dixie,'" *Musical America* (September 9, 1911).

[26] See tune No. 74 in Richard Henebry, *Handbook of Irish Music* (London, 1928), and "Buckley's Fancy," in O'Neill, *Music of Ireland*. These two sources have been pointed out to the author by Professor Samuel P. Bayard.

[27] "I wish I was in ole Varginny," in *The Ethiopian Glee Book*. Other examples are in *White's New Ethiopian Songbook* (Philadelphia, 1854).

[28] Stephen Foster, "Away Down South" (1848). Other examples are in *Christy's and White's Ethiopian Songster* (Philadelphia, 1854).

"Dixie"

Musical Example 119

Several passages in the second part of "Dixie" are variants of Scottish folk tunes.

was a gay deceiver" in "Gumbo Chaff" of the thirties. And at the end of the fifth stanza, Emmett merely rephrased lines of his own song "De Wild Goose-Nation," which read "De tarapin he thot it was time for to trabble / He screw aron his tail an begin to scratch grabble."[29] However, the history of "To Dixie's land I'm bound to trabble" requires additional commentary. What is here called "Dixie's land," for which an etymological explanation will be offered later, figures as "home" in the slightly earlier walk-around by Emmett "I Ain't Got Time to Tarry." In this song, as pointed out at the beginning of this chapter, the Negro protagonist, as in "Dixie," longs for a distant place, emphasizing "For I'se gwine home to Dinah . . ." and concluding "I'm bound to de land of freedom . . . ." The key words "going home" came originally from white and black camp meeting hymns in which "home" meant "the promised land" or paradise.[30] From these hymns the phrase "I am going home" strayed into the comical context of the minstrel songs of the fifties, where it soon acquired a geographical meaning and eventually, in Emmett, a political one.

For a long time people have been musing about the origin of the word Dixie, which, ever since the Civil War, has been a part of American speech. When the word was heard for the first time in New York in the spring of 1859, its meaning was clear from the literary and theatrical context in which it appeared. But one considered it novel and wondered about its derivation.[31] In 1861 two explanations were given out by New York publishers.[32] One reads as follows:

> In the popular mythology of New York City, Dixie was the negro's paradise on earth in times when slavery and the slave trade were

[29] Of additional derivations, only an extensive one will be mentioned: "In Souf Carolina de niggas grow / If de white man will only plant his toe / Den dey water de ground wid 'bacca smoke / And out ob dirt dar heels will poke"; from "The Old Pee Dee," in *Christy's Negro Songster* (New York, 1855).

[30] "Farewell, vain world, I'm going home" and "I'm on my journey home to the new Jerusalem. So fare you well, I am going home," from *The Sacred Harp* (Georgia, 1844), as reprinted in George Pullen Jackson, *White Spirituals in the Southern Uplands* (Chapel Hill, 1933), 221–24. There are more examples in the same volume as well as in Jackson, *White and Negro Spirituals*.

[31] A remark on the inside of Emmett, "I'm Going Home to Dixie": ". . . many inquiries have been made in regard to its meaning and location . . . ."

[32] One is in the songster *Bryant's Songs from Dixie's Land* (New York); the other is in "I'm Going Home to Dixie."

flourishing institutions in that quarter. Dixie owned a tract of land on Manhattan Island and also a large number of slaves; and his slaves increasing faster than his land, an emigration ensued such as has taken place in Virginia and other states. Naturally, the negroes who left it for distant parts, looked to it as a place of unalloyed happiness, and it was the "Old Virginny" of the negroes of that day. Hence Dixie became synonymous with an ideal locality, combining ineffable happiness and every imaginable requisite of earthly beatitude.

This is a fantastic story, and there is absolutely nothing in New York folklore that would corroborate it. The second explanation of Dixie briefly elaborates in prose what the song itself says in rhyme, namely that "with the southern negroes, Dixie's Land is but another name for Home. Hence it is but fair to conclude that all south of Mason's and Dixon's Line is the true 'Dixies Land.' " It is of course true that by 1861 the Negroes, like everyone else, used the expression "Dixie's Land," but the question is whether they did earlier. And for this there is no evidence.

One would expect the English correspondent William Howard Russell, when visiting the South in June, 1861, to have found the definitive local meaning of "Dixie's Land."[33] Instead he heard essentially the same explanations as quoted above. He reported:

> There are two explanations of the word Dixie—one is that it is the general term for the Slave-States, which are, of course, South of Mason and Dixon's Line; another that a planter named Dixie died long ago, to the intense grief of his animated property. Whether they were ill-treated after he died, and thus had reason to regret his loss; or that they had merely a longing in the abstract after Heaven, no fact known to me can determine; but certain it is that they long much after Dixie, in the land to which his spirit was supposed by them to have departed, and console themselves in their sorrow by clamorous wishes to follow their master . . . .

Another interpretation of Dixie, given sanction by Webster's Dictionary and the Encyclopaedia Britannica, associates the term with

[33] *My Diary,* Chapter 38.

bank notes. Before the Civil War there existed in Louisiana ten-dollar bills with the French imprint "Dix," which supposedly were nicknamed "Dixies" by the "ignorant Americans living along the upper Mississippi River."[34] After some time, so the story goes, the name was extended to Louisiana and later to the entire South. Again, all this is mere fiction. "Dix" notes did exist, even as early as the thirties, but there seems to be nothing in Louisiana folklore that would prove that they were called Dixies and that this term then came into general use. Moreover, "all other denominations likewise had the French names, and it is probable that most people . . . saw a $10 note only on rare occasions. As a matter of record, lower denominations had a much wider circulation . . . ."[35]

In previous quotations we have found references to Mason and Dixon's Line as a possible source for Dixie. Another more explicit one is a Philadelphia sheet music edition of 1860 of Emmett's song bearing the following title on its cover: "The Original Dixon's Line or Dixey Land with original words, arranged for the piano by Edgar Porter." The implied derivation is etymologically unsound, though not impossible. However, like other explanations, it presupposes the general use of the word in the South long before the Civil War. For this not the slightest evidence has been found.

A fourth, little-known theory was presented by *The New York Weekly* of December 30, 1872: "['Dixie's'] origin has been described as southern, but such is not the case. During any time within the last eighty years the term 'Dixie's Land' has been in use with the New York boys while engaged in the game of 'tag.' "[36] The statement about the time element has yet to be proved. However, the phrase "Dixie's Land" does appear in the early New York children's game "Tom Tidler's Ground," and it is reported that the phrase "antedates the war."[37] In another version of this game there is a literal quotation from the

[34] Quoted from an undated article of *The London Financial Times* in the pamphlet "The History of Dixie," issued by the Citizen's Bank & Trust Co. of Louisiana (New Orleans, [*c.*1915]).

[35] Quoted from an informative letter sent to the author by Professor Lewis M. Reagan of the University of Wichita, Kansas, an expert on numismatics.

[36] Quoted by Joseph Jones in *American Speech* (October, 1945), 238.

[37] Games No. 156 and 157 in William Wells Newell, *Games and Songs of American Children* (New York, 1883).

chorus of Emmett's song. From these facts, one could not possibly conclude that the expression "Dixie's Land" was known to New York children before Emmett had published it.

It seems to be significant that the name turns up for the first time on the northern minstrel stage in 1850, in a play entitled *United States Mail and Dixie in Difficulties*.[38] The only character in it who was a real stage Negro in speech and action, regardless of whether the other actors had blackened faces or not, was the "post-boy" named "Dixie." He was stupid, anxious for tips and silver spoons, and crazy about music. In other words, he was a Negro character that a prejudiced white audience of that time considered most realistic and typical. It is possible, then, that "Dixie" was a nickname with which the white man referred to the Negro, a nickname either originally coined by the author of the above play (no real Negro was named "Dixie") or merely borrowed by him from tradition. The word could not have been widely known. Limited to a small group of people, it may have been part of a professional jargon. That this was the jargon of northern show people is suggested by the appearance of the word in a northern minstrel play and two minstrel songs—Emmett's "Jonny Roach" and "Dixie's Land"—in the fifties, by its relation in sound to such earlier stage Negro names as "Pompey" and "Cuffee," and above all by a reference of Emmett. In his statement of 1872 (see Documents), he commented on what would seem to be an extension of the word: "In my traveling days [the time before 1859] amongst showmen, when we would start for a winter's season south, while speaking of the change, they would invariably ejaculate [*sic*] the stereotyped saying—'I Wish I Was in Dixie's Land' . . . ."[39] Since "Dixie" meant the Negro, "Dixie's Land" was obviously the land of

[38] It appears on a playbill of the Sabine Minstrels of Portsmouth (N. H.?), in the possession of the American Antiquarian Society (Worcester, Massachusetts). The play-bill is mutilated, but the following characters can be made out: Doctor Highirsell-backemspokem, Dixie (post-boy), and Lucy [?]. There is no printed copy of the play extant, except what is undoubtedly another version of it (New York, Ch. White, 1856), under the name of *United States Mail*. The post-boy has now become "postoffice Sam, a negro letter carrier," while the cast is completed by "Mr. Wagner, Mrs. Nipper, and Lucy."

[39] Emmett repeated this explanation in interviews published in Sheerin, "Dixie," and Hall, "Does It Pay."

the Negro—that is, according to the consensus of the mid-nineteenth century, the black South. When Emmett in his famous song abbreviated the phrase to "Dixie Land" and finally to "Dixie," the original name appeared again, though not referring to a person but to a locale. Thus "Dixie" had five connotations: it was first a synonym for the Negro; as a simplified version of "Dixie's Land" and "Dixie Land," it became a synonym for the Negro's South; next it became the South pure and simple; and finally it became a synonym for the South as seen by the Confederates. Parallel to this, "Dixie" was the popular title by which Emmett's song was known.

All these philological data concerning a single word would interest us but moderately had not Emmett circulated it widely and thus persuaded all Americans to include it in their vocabulary.

Emmett was devoid of any business instinct. Instead of publishing and immediately copyrighting "Dixie," which was on everyone's lips, he waited more than a year before giving it to Firth, Pond & Co. They deposited it with the District Court of the United States for the Southern District of New York on June 21, 1860 (see Illustration 56). Other publishers, considering the tune public property, were hard at their heels. For example, on June 26, John Church, Jr., in Cincinnati "filed" a piano arrangement of the song,[40] but acknowledged in a later edition, no doubt under pressure, the permission of the original publishers. A number of other editions of the song or variants of it apparently got away with mentioning neither the composer nor its original publishers and even with substituting other names for Emmett's.[41] However, P. P. Werlein of New Orleans became involved in difficulties with Firth, Pond & Co. This was undoubtedly due to the fact that he not only credited a J. C. Viereck as the composer of the tune and a J. Newcomb as the author of a text which differed but slightly from the original but preceded the New York firm with

[40] "Get Out of the Wilderness and Dixie's Land, two popular airs as played by Capt. A. Menter and his American Cornet Band." Inside was written, "arr. for the piano by Paul Jones."
[41] For example, one edition, published in Philadelphia in 1860 by Sep. Winner, reads on the inside: "Dixy's Land by John Cahr, arr. by Sep. Winner"; another edition is titled "Away Down in Dixie's Land as sung by Hooley & Campbell's Minstrels, Song and Chorus by 'Jerry Blossom,' Music by 'Dixie, Jr.'" (Louisville, Ky., D. P. Faulds & Co., 1860).

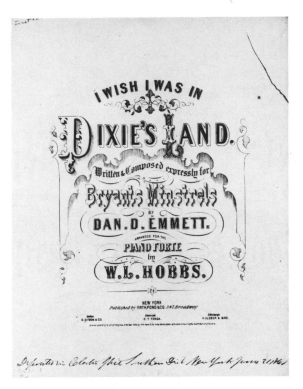

Illustration 56. Cover of the first authorized edition of "Dixie" (New York, 1860). Courtesy The Library of Congress.

the publication of two editions of the song by a few months (see Illustration 57).[42] The conflict was brought out into the open at a public hearing in New York, apparently at a convention of music dealers.[43]

[42] P. P. Werlein brought out two editions in 1860: the first was "I Wish I Was In Dixie, song by W. H. Peters, music by J. C. Viereck"; the second was "I Wish I Was In Dixie, words by J. Newcomb, music by J. C. Viereck, sung by Mrs. John Wood." This order, superseding the one given in *The Musical Quarterly* (January, 1949), 78, follows from the plate numbers: No. 547 for the first song and No. 549 for the second, which were conveyed to the author by James J. Fuld, New York. Emmett stated in *The New York Clipper* (April 6, 1872): "I did not publish it ['Dixie'] until it was . . . issued by a Mr. P. P. Werling [Werlein] of New Orleans . . . he wrote me a letter offering me $5.—for the copyright." *The Daily Picayune* (New Orleans, May 5, 1860), announced the receipt of "New Music," listing the Viereck-Newcomb edition published by Werlein.

[43] Emmett in his statement of 1872 merely speaks of a public "dispute" that took place in New York. White, "Negro Minstrelsy's Origin," states more specifically: "Mr. Pond brought the matter before a music publishers' convention and settled the question of authorship. But Dan reaped no benefit from this tardy justice."

Illustration 57. Cover of the first edition of "Dixie" (New Orleans, 1860).
Courtesy James J. Fuld, New York.

There, Firth, Pond & Co. proved Emmett's authorship of "Dixie" and
their own rights to the song. Werlein must have acknowledged them,
because in a new edition he mentioned the names of Emmett and the
original publishers, calling Viereck merely the arranger.[44] Werlein's
own imprint appeared on the cover of the second Firth & Pond edition. That the conflict between the two publishers was resolved to

[44] "Sung by Mrs. John Wood, I Wish I Was In Dixie's Land. [Left] Words by
Mr. J. Newcomb, Music by Dan¹. D. Emmett, Esq. [Right] Words by Mr. W. H. Peters,
Music by Dan¹. D. Emmett, Esq. [Bottom] Arranged by J. C. Viereck" (New Orleans,
P. P. Werlein, New York, Firth, Pond & Co., 1860).

Emmett's satisfaction, as well, is proved by his dedication to Werlein of his song "I'm Going Home to Dixie" in 1861.

On February 11, 1861, at the time when the outbreak of the Civil War was imminent, Firth, Pond & Co. paid Emmett three hundred dollars for relinquishing all his rights to the song (see Illustration 58 and Documents).[45] This action may have been prompted by the desire of the publishers to have a clean slate, fearing complications in the sale of "Dixie" in the North (because of its "traitorous sounding" chorus) and in the protection of their copyright in the South.

Indeed, a little later in utterly bad faith, Werlein ignored his legal obligations. He published a war edition of the song in which neither Emmett nor his publishers were referred to and Viereck again was named as the composer.[46] Other southern publishers followed suit in disregarding the northern copyright.

"Dixie" became one of the greatest song successes of the nineteenth century, not only in America but abroad as well.[47] Had Bryant's Minstrels been able to exploit "Dixie" all by themselves, it might have remained among the songs that become the vogue for a few months and then disappear forever. But other companies eagerly picked it up, as was their custom with Emmett's tunes, without ever giving him credit on their playbills. We may believe the publisher's claim of 1861 that the sale of the song, then available only one year, had been "altogether unprecedented."[48] *The New York Clipper* called it "one of the most popular compositions ever produced" and added that it "has been sung, whistled, and played in every quarter of the globe."[49] It circulated not only in the original text version but in dozens of adaptations which appeared on broadsides, in news-

[45] This contract is in the possession of the Library of Congress.

[46] "The War Song of Dixie. Words by Albert Pike. Music by J. C. Vierick [*sic*]" (New Orleans, P. P. Werlein & Halsey, 1861).

[47] At the end of 1860, "Dixie" was performed in London; see a playbill of the Buckley's Serenaders, as published in Harry Reynolds, *Minstrel Memories* (London, 1928), 253. Soon it was sung by British sailors on the high seas; see Whall, *Sea Songs*, 14: "the chief favorite with the sailor, as a shanty, was 'Dixie' [in the sixties] . . . the wild savagery of the melody was stirring."

[48] Remark inside "I'm Going Home to Dixie."

[49] August 10, 1861.

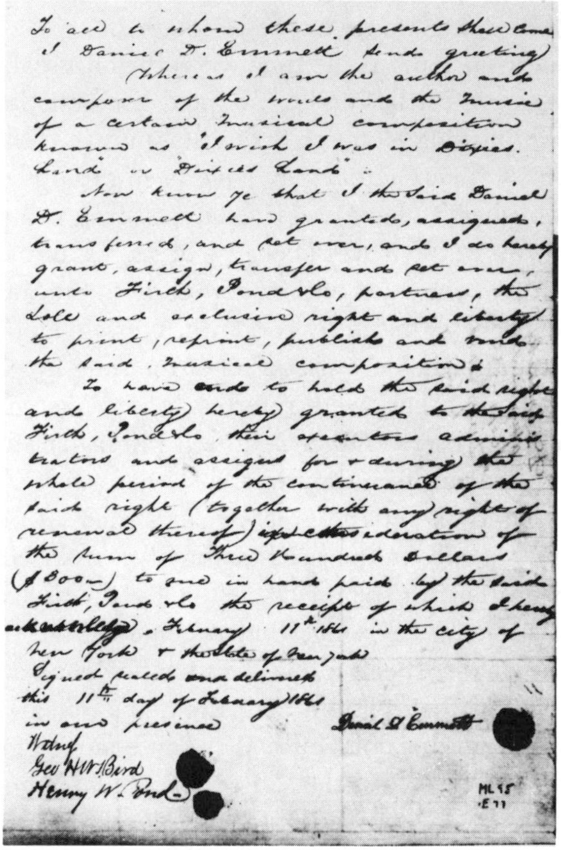
To all to whom these presents shall come
I Daniel D. Emmett send greeting
Whereas I am the author and
composer of the words and the music
of a certain musical composition
known as "I wish I was in Dixie's
Land" or "Dixie's Land".
Now know ye that I the said Daniel
D. Emmett have granted, assigned,
transferred, and set over, and I do hereby
grant, assign, transfer and set over,
unto Firth, Pond & Co, partners, the
sole and exclusive right and liberty
to print, reprint, publish and vend
the said musical composition.
To have and to hold the said right
and liberty hereby granted to the said
Firth, Pond & Co their executors administrators and assigns for & during the
whole period of the continuance of the
said right (together with any right of
renewal thereof) in consideration of
the sum of Three Hundred Dollars
($300) to me in hand paid by the said
Firth, Pond & Co the receipt of which I hereby
acknowledge. February 11th 1861 in the city of
New York & the State of New York
Signed sealed and delivered
this 11th day of February 1861
in our presence
Witness
Geo. W. W. Bird
Henry W. Pond
Daniel D. Emmett

Illustration 58. Emmett's contract with the New York publisher Firth, Pond & Co., dated February 11, 1861. Courtesy The Library of Congress.

papers, and in songsters. Moreover, many editions, arrangements, and variations flooded the market from 1860 to 1863.

At the outbreak of the Civil War, the song retained its popularity in the North. Only by stages did it become a "Southern Air." As a matter of fact, it was in 1861 that it reached the peak of its popularity in New York. A newspaperman wrote then: "this lively tune has in our city [doubtless New York] become as popular as the most ravishing airs of any of the operatic compositions." And another one spoke in even more enthusiastic terms:

"Dixie" has become an institution, an irrepressible institution in this section of the country. The itinerant musicians . . . have learned the fact and, by the insertion of a new barrel in their organs, have succeeded in producing the new melody in all its sweet shrillness. As a consequence, whenever "Dixie" is produced, the pen drops from the fingers of the plodding clerk, spectacles from the nose and the paper from the hands of the merchant, the needle from the nimble digits of the maid or matron, and all hands go hobbling, bobbling in time with the magical music of "Dixie." Won't somebody localize "Dixie," give it a habitation, a place where it may be hailed from? Set words of Union sentiment to its "ta la, ta la" and "rum di di di do" etc.[50]

The question was answered by Emmett's publisher who issued "Dixie for the Union," with words by Frances J. Crosby. He also published another version of "Dixie" under the title of "Dixie Unionized," with a new text dedicated to the "Washington Guards" which had been organized to defend the capital against the Confederate armies.[51] From then on many other war versions made their appearance. It should be noted that "Dixie" was played by bands of the Union Army at least until 1862; and as late as 1863, it was sung by Union soldiers, though not with the original words.[52]

The song soon enjoyed an even greater popularity in the South. "It is marvellous," reported a Confederate in May, 1861, "with what wild-fire rapidity this tune 'Dixie' has spread over the whole South.

[50] The two quotations are from a clipping in the scrap book of R. G. Shaw in the Harvard Theatre Collection. The first quotes the second, but they have been separated here. The second article, from the *New York Commercial Advertiser*, appeared in 1861 or slightly earlier, because it was reprinted in "Dixie Unionized, words by A. W. Muzzy, melody by D. D. Emmett" (New York, Firth, Pond & Co., 1861).

[51] Both songs have 1861 on their front cover, though "Dixie for the Union" has 1860 on the inside.

[52] On January 11, 1862, the *New York Herald*, as quoted in Harwell, *Confederate Music*, 4, could still proclaim: "Good martial, national music is one of the great advantages we have over the rebels . . . . They have not even one good national theme, if we except the 'Rogue's March,' for 'Dixie' belongs exclusively to our own Dan Bryant . . . ." "Dixie" does not appear in the Union songsters *The Flag of Our Union* (New York, 1861), and *Camp Songs* (Boston, 1862), but it turns up, with new words, in *John Brown and the Union Right or Wrong Songster* (San Francisco, 1863). Its tune is included in William Nevins, *Army Regulations for Drum, Fife, and Bugle* (Chicago, 1861), and in Emmett, *Fife Instructor*.

Considered as an intolerable nuisance when first the streets re-echoed it from the repertoire of wandering minstrels, it now bids fair to become the musical symbol of a new nationality, and we shall be fortunate if it does not impose its very name on our country."[53] Indeed, "Dixie" was about to become to southerners something considerably more serious than a lively piece of music. This was perforce recognized by northerners, for when they spoke of "Dixie," they carefully designated it as a northern version and treated the word *Dixie* as something debatable or something not their own. For example, a broadside was headed "The New Dixie, the True 'Dixie' for Northern Singers," and another was titled "The Union 'Dixie.' "[54] The early meaning of the word *Dixie* as held out by the white man, which suggested the Negro's never-never land, appeared for the last time in 1861 in Emmett's song "I'm Going Home to Dixie," although doubt about the feasibility of this vision creeps up in the lines "I will proclaim it loud and long, I love old Dixie right or wrong."

In the same year, the Confederates established as the symbol of a South insisting on its tradition and independence the meaning of the word "Dixie" in such verses as the following:

Southrons, hear your Country call you.
Up! less worse than death befall you!
To arms! to arms! to arms! in Dixie!
Lo! all the beacon fires are lighted,
Let all hearts be now united!

To arms! to arms! to arms! in Dixie!

(*Chorus*)

Advance the flag of Dixie!
Hurrah! Hurrah!
For Dixie's land we'll take our stand,
And live and die for Dixie!

[53] Henry Hotze, "Three Months in the Confederate Army: The Tune of Dixie" (Norfolk, May 5, 1861), *The Index* (London, June 26, 1862), as quoted in Harwell, *Confederate Music*, 43.

[54] The first is in the possession of Brown University Library; the second, printed by Peter Doyle in Philadelphia, is in the possession of the Newberry Library.

"Dixie"

To arms! to arms! And conquer peace for Dixie.
To arms! to arms! And conquer peace for Dixie.

Hear ye not the sounds of battle,
Sabres' clash and muskets' rattle?
To arms! to arms! to arms in Dixie!
Hostile footsteps on our border,
Hostile columns tread in order;
To Arms! to Arms! to Arms in Dixie!

(Chorus)

Oh, fly to arms in Dixie!
To Arms! to Arms!
From Dixie's land we'll rout the band,
That comes to conquer Dixie,
To Arms! To Arms! and rout the foe from Dixie!
To Arms! To Arms! and rout the foe from Dixie.[55]

Confederate soldiers occasionally sang the original words of the song but more often sang versions expressing war sentiment.[56] The original form of the chorus, however, containing the lines "In Dixie Land I'll took my stand, To lib an die in Dixie," meant so harmlessly by its author, was sometimes retained or only slightly modified.

Repeatedly writers have tried to determine when "Dixie" was sung in the South for the first time and when it was used for the first time by the Confederate armies. These are fruitless attempts because the song was well known in the South from 1859 on, and war texts were adapted to it at exactly the same time they were in the North —that is, at the opening of hostilities. A kind of official sanction was

[55] First stanzas of "The War Song of Dixie," as well as of "Dixie War Song, written by H. S. Stanton, Esq., arranged by A. Noir" (Augusta, Georgia, Blackmar & Bro., 1861).

[56] The Dixie Land Songster (Augusta, Georgia, Blackmar & Bro., 1863), contains the original words as well as two war versions. The New Confederate Flag Song Book, No. 1 (Mobile, 1864), includes only war versions, whereas the original text appears in The Army Songster (Richmond, Virginia, 1864).

given the song when it was played at the inauguration of President Jefferson Davis in Montgomery, Alabama, on February 18, 1861.[57]

It was not the words of the chorus alone that so inspired the Confederate soldiers. When the tune was performed like a military quickstep with hurried metallic accents and its "angular" intervals sounding like bugle calls, it quickened their pulse, obscured their reasoning, and made them insensitive to the strain and pain of battle. "Dixie" became the battle hymn of the Confederate armies. And still in our own time, when "Dixie" is played in the South, hats and rebel yells rise into the air.

The South has always been ashamed of the comedy style of the original text of the song but has never been able to eradicate this text from the memory of the people or to replace it with a more dignified one.[58]

Since Emmett's song had become a symbol of the southern cause, it is usually assumed that the composer had wished it to be so. This, like most opinions concerning "Dixie," is the result of wishful thinking. It is true that old Dan Emmett, when interviewed in 1895 by the editor of *The Confederate Veteran*, voiced his gratification about "the friendship of the Southern people" and mentioned the southern descent of his parents. But these were noncommittal words which proved nothing about his attitude toward the Confederacy. The following story is more significant. It is based on hearsay but has about it the ring of Emmett's own words. One day in 1861 Emmett and a number of other minstrels, Dan Bryant among them, were sitting in Tom Kingsland's on Broome Street in New York, "a famous bar and

[57] Bandmaster Herman Frank Arnold claimed to have made a band arrangement of "Dixie" and to have played it at the inauguration. His claim is quoted in De Leon, *Belles, Beaux, and Brains*. L. E. Fisher, of the Asheville Chapter, United Daughters of the Confederacy, in the pamphlet "The Story of How 'Dixie' Was Set to Music," published a photograph of this band arrangement. A memorial in honor of H. F. Arnold was unveiled in Fletcher, North Carolina on October 6, 1929.

[58] In 1905, committees of the United Daughters of the Confederacy, the United Confederate Veterans, and the United Sons of Confederate Veterans tried to start a movement that would finally select an official new southern version of "Dixie"; in the end they were unsuccessful. Generals John B. Gordon and Stephen D. Lee, when asked for their opinions, agreed on the necessity of "more appropriate words" but insisted that the original text of the chorus be left intact. See the pamphlet "Joint Committee Appointed to Consider and Report on a Selection of New Words for 'Dixie'" (Opelika, Alabama, 1905), which includes twenty-two text versions of the song; and *The Confederate Veteran* (Nashville, Tennessee, 1903–1904).

lunchroom," and hangout of the profession. A minstrel who had just returned from the front dropped in. He "told Emmett that, at night, he could hear the Confederate bands playing Dixie; and that they seemed to have adopted it down South, as their national air. Emmett replied warmly 'Yes: and if I had known to what use they were going to put my song, I will be damned if I'd have written it.' "[59] Like most minstrels he did not endorse southern separatism, nor, on the other hand, was he pro-Negro.

The political history of "Dixie" came to an end, to all intents and purposes, at the moment the Civil War was over. General Lee surrendered his army on April 9, 1865. With it, it seemed, he surrendered the song also, or at least allowed the North to share in it again. This seems a trifle to us but not so to Lincoln, who had an extremely acute feeling for the worth of ideas and events of his own period. He acted accordingly. On the morning of April 10, he was serenaded. Appearing before the crowd that had assembled in front of the White House, he declared that he would not make a real speech. After a few preliminary sentences he, therefore, cut himself short by saying: "I propose now closing up by requesting you to play a certain piece of music or a tune. I thought 'Dixie' one of the best tunes I ever heard . . . ." And with mock seriousness he added: "I had heard that our adversaries over the way had attempted to appropriate it. I insisted yesterday that we had fairly captured it . . . . I presented the question to the Attorney-General, and he gave his opinion that it is our lawful prize. . . . I ask the Band to give us a good turn upon it."[60] It did, but that "Dixie" thus actually became a trophy of the North, the South has never admitted.

[59] From a letter of Col. T. Allston Brown to T. C. De Leon, as published in De Leon, *Belles, Beaux, and Brains*, 359.
[60] Carl Sandburg, *Abraham Lincoln, The War Years* (New York, 1939), IV, 207–208.

Chapter 17

EMMETT'S LATER LIFE

———————◈———————

Emmett's work for the Bryant's Minstrels turned out to be the finale of his career. When he left New York he was only in his early fifties, and yet the profession he had served for almost a generation showed but little need for his talents. Negro minstrelsy was fast becoming an efficient, large-scale variety show which favored less and less the dry, tough humor of Emmett's texts and tunes and the primitive style of his performances.

He made his home in Chicago and stayed there, with few interruptions, from 1867 to the late eighties.[1] When he arrived he had an engagement with Haverly's minstrels,[2] but it must have been shortly afterward that he lost his voice[3] and was forced to make his living as a fiddler. He appeared at Peter Kerwin's Jupiter Concert Saloon on Dearborn Street and at similar places, and seems to have continued

[1] His address is listed in Chicago Directories from 1867 to 1886, except for the years 1870-71.

[2] S. A. Cunningham, "Uncle Dan' Emmett—'Dixie's Land,'" *The Confederate Veteran* (Nashville, September, 1895): "In 1867, he was with Haverly's minstrels in Illinois." According to a newspaper clipping (January 24, 1880), as quoted in Moreau, *Negro Minstrelsy*, II, "Uncle Dan was with Haverly's Minstrels at Wood's old Museum, in this city [Chicago], before the fire [1871] . . . ."

[3] In an open letter (May 1, 1877), as published in *The New York Clipper* (May 19, 1877), Emmett mentioned that he was "forced to relinquish the minstrel profession through the loss of my voice by bronchitis."

in this capacity until the late seventies.[4] Among the several hundred tunes that made up his repertoire[5] was his own version of the old minstrel ditty "Zip Coon," titled "Turkeys in de Straw," which was still remembered many years later. It was published in a collection of Irish folk music of 1907[6] with the remark: "played by Dan Emmett, a Celebrated Irish-American minstrel of the last generation."

Emmett's activities came abruptly to an end when the great fire of October 8 and 9, 1871, destroyed a large part of the city. How he fared this winter can be ascertained from an open letter in *The New York Clipper,* written August 1, 1872, and published August 17. Defending himself against the charge of plagiarism (such charges occurred not infrequently in the minstrel profession) he wrote: "I will merely say that I hope he [his accuser] will not (as he threatens) 'fix my mouth so that it won't hold soup,' as I have had it filled quite often this winter by our *Relief and Aid Society* and may yet have occasion for the same process. I am now an old man; my fighting qualities have been sadly neglected . . . ." In a preceding statement he pulled himself up by reminding his adversary, who had failed to recognize him, of his reputation: "I am a composer of several popular songs, in times past, that had quite a run, amongst which were 'High Daddy,' 'Jack On The Green,' etc., and, I am proud to say, of 'Dixie.' " The sequence of charges and counter-charges lasted several months,[7] and, if it did nothing more, it at least helped to keep Emmett's name before the public. Earlier, in 1871–72, he had published some lyrics in the *Clipper,* as he did again in 1873–74, but these being in plain English and in the Irish brogue were quite undistinguished. On April 6, 1872, at the request of the editor of the same paper, he

[4] Horace Herbert, "Dan Emmett and his famous song 'Dixie,' " an open letter in *The Morning Telegraph* (New York [?], May 25, 1908), clipping in the Harvard Theatre Collection. Peter Kerwin's establishment is also mentioned in "That Cat and Dog Fight," *The New York Clipper* (September 28, 1872).

[5] A manuscript of "Clog Hornpipes" bears the notation "property of D. Emmett, Chicago, Ill., 1868." There is also a large, bound volume that contains several hundred tunes, Emmett's name, and his address—620 Butterfield Street: according to the Chicago Directory, he lived at this address between 1872 and 1874.

[6] O'Neill, *Music of Ireland.*

[7] *The New York Clipper* (New York, July 13, August 3 and 17, and September 7 and 28, 1872).

made a statement on "Dixie" (see Documents), which to those interested in a piece of Americana is of some historical significance.

In spite of his misfortunes, Emmett did not give up the hope of doing something that would be congenial to his talents. He thus began to write comical Negro sermons for the *Clipper*, though it seems that only one, entitled "Bressed am dem dat 'spect nuttin', kase dey aint a gwine to git nuttin'," was accepted.[8] The Negro character of the piece offered him various opportunities for felicitous word pictures and situations; nevertheless, he was unable to sustain the tone throughout an entire piece, since it was quite extensive as compared with the brief text of a minstrel song. From the sixties on, the *Clipper* had published such sermons, which were more or less literal transcriptions of the exhortations of Brother Allen, a colored preacher in New York, and the exclamations of his excitable listeners.[9] And similar sermons existed as stump speeches on the minstrel stage. A specimen of Brother Allen's style that in its down-to-earth description of religious symbolism may have guided Emmett, is the following passage:

> Why, my preshus lams, de colored Christian is like de old warrior goose—he sees de black squall a comin' and a rarin' and a pitchin', threatenin' to swaller de whole barnyard; but dat old warrior goose is too knowin'; he sarkum wents de storm; he gits his fedders all smooved slick to his back, den he puts down his tail, and says—'Let de storm come—what do I keer?' So it is wid de rightyus man; he's always smoovin' his fedders, and when de storm hits 'em it glides off like dat coon brudder Simpson was arter last Sunday. ([Congregation:] Talk to 'em, honey; talk to 'em. Hail to de warrior goose.) Amen, and amen."[10]

In 1872, Emmett went into business as the owner or manager of

---

[8] August 9, 1873. There are several dozen of these sermons in manuscript. One called "The Hard-Shell Missionary" bears the remark "Written for the N. Y. Clipper by D. D. Emmett" and the note "rejected."

[9] For example, see issues of August 31, and October 5, 1867, and February 8, 1868.

[10] *The New York Clipper* (August 31, 1867).

278

a saloon and continued for about two years.[11] On June 3, 1876, the *Clipper* ran the laconic notice: "Dan Emmett is residing in Chicago, Ill., and performing occasionally." About a year later he plaintively reported: "After many adversities, I find myself all alone in the world ... humbly trying in my old age to eke out a living as a musician ...."[12] He was indeed alone because his wife, Katherine, to whom he had been married for more than twenty years, had died in 1875.[13] But the future seemed to look brighter when he remarried in 1879;[14] in the same year he also held a respectable job, though of short duration, as the "Leader" of the orchestra in a variety show in Toledo, Ohio.[15] His financial situation, however, was basically as desperate as ever. By 1880 the minstrel profession became alarmed and made public appeals to help him.[16] The response proved that he was by no means forgotten. There were at least two benefit variety performances in Chicago, one in 1880,[17] and the other, two years later. The first was at the Academy of Music on Halstead Street, the second at the Grand Opera House on October 5, 1882;[18] the proceeds of the two events netted him the substantial sum of more than one thousand dollars.[19] At the Opera House he himself appeared with his fiddle," and before

[11] In 1872–73 the Chicago directories list the saloon as "Emmett & Sawtelle" and "Emmette & Co.," respectively, both at 2 South Canal Street.

[12] Open letter (May 1, 1877), as published in *The New York Clipper* (May 19, 1877).

[13] William E. Hull, as quoted in Albert B. Williams, *Past and Present*, I: "The name of his first wife was Katherine Rives, born in New York City April 15, 1829, and died in Chicago May 3, 1875, and buried in Mound View Cemetery at Mount Vernon. The marriage occurred about 1852." According to Galbreath, *Daniel Decatur Emmett*, 8, she died on May 31, 1875.

[14] Hull, "D. D. Emmett": "On October 16, 1879, at Chicago, he married . . . Mrs. Mary Louise Bird . . . ."

[15] Playbill of the Coliseum Theatre (Toledo, Ohio, January 9, 1879), in the possession of H. Ogden Wintermute (Mount Vernon, Ohio). According to Edw. Le Roy Rice, *Monarchs of Minstrelsy* (New York, 1911), Emmett had a position as a "leader" [of the orchestra] in the Star Varieties in Chicago after 1875, but this is uncertain.

[16] *The New York Clipper* (March 13, 1880 and earlier issues).

[17] Mentioned in a draft of an undated letter from Emmett to Tony Pastor (Emmett's Manuscript Collection), in which Emmett refers to himself as "an old man of 65."

[18] Playbill of "Grand Testimonial Benefit to Uncle Dan Emmett" at the Grand Opera House (Chicago), in the possession of H. Ogden Wintermute.

[19] Letter to Tony Pastor; review of the performance of 1882 in the *Chicago Tribune* (October 6, 1882).

he came out on the stage the applause broke out and was continued until he struck up an old-fashioned reel. The time was tapped by feet all over the house, and when the old man struck up 'Dixie' the audience yelled and he smiled with pleasure and conscious pride."[20]

The publicity which Emmett had received led to an engagement in 1881–82 with Leavitt's Gigantean Minstrels for a weekly salary of thirty dollars plus expenses.[21] It was the manager's idea to combine modern and early minstrelsy by including in the show old-time songs performed by a band that consisted of a fiddle (played by Emmett), a tambourine, bones, a jawbone, and a banjo.[22] The company began its tour in Boston in late August, and after a stay of a week, traveled through Connecticut, New York, Canada, the South, the Middle West, and finished up in Pennsylvania in the spring of 1882.[23] There was enthusiastic response everywhere, and one Boston review was probably indicative of the general attitude when it said that "[the company] has achieved something long regarded as impossible—it presents something really novel and entertaining in minstrelsy."[24] Without question the success was, to a considerable extent, due to the partial revival of early minstrel acts, though, in the South, more so to Emmett's reputation as the composer of "Dixie." He was indeed "received with a tumult of cheers as a great hero and an exponent of Southern sentiment . . . ."[25]

After the tour, Emmett returned to Chicago[26] and remained there until 1888; he then decided to retire to his birthplace, Mount Vernon where he bought some land and a simple cottage.[27] His wife joined him a little later but, probably not finding enough comfort, left him

[20] *Chicago Tribune* (October 6, 1882).
[21] Contract of Leavitt's Amusement Enterprises (New York City, July 1, 1881), in the possession of H. Ogden Wintermute.
[22] Leavitt, *Fifty Years*, 414–15; playbills of Leavitt's Gigantean Minstrels (Boston, August 27 to September 3, 1881). According to Leavitt, the triangle and accordion were also used.
[23] Dates of all engagements are from *The New York Clipper*.
[24] *Boston Herald* (August 30, 1881), as quoted in *The New York Clipper* (September 10, 1881).
[25] Leavitt, *Fifty Years*, 415.
[26] He is listed in Chicago Directories for the last time in 1886.
[27] Galbreath, *Daniel Decatur Emmett*, 21; Hull, "D. D. Emmett." Documents concerning land owned by Emmett, between the early eighties and the late nineties, are in the Knox County Courthouse, Mount Vernon, Ohio.

soon; she was with him again during the last years of his life, and perhaps earlier as well.[28]

Emmett's cabin consisted of two rooms sparsely furnished. He had a vegetable garden and a few chickens.[29] Whereas he could live modestly in summertime, he was forced during the winter to chop and saw wood for neighboring farmers in order to have a little extra money and a few extra chips to heat his stove.[30] Though very poor, he was "independent and self-respecting," "thrust himself on no man's notice," and determinately refused financial assistance.[31] Occasionally people requested his photograph or an autographed copy of "Dixie,"[32] but the income from these sources did not go very far. In February, 1893, his misery was brought to the attention of the Actor's Fund of America in New York City, which responded without a moment's hesitation and with great tact. Overriding his suggestion "to give him three or four dollars a week . . . ," which, as he put it, would make him feel "quite an autocrat,"[33] he was granted a regular weekly stipend of five dollars up to the time of his death.[34] This apparently was sufficient to keep him alive and happy.

"Uncle Dan," as he was called, was often visited by people who were eager to meet the man who had composed "Dixie" and to hear him tell the story of how he composed it.[35] And sometimes he was asked to sing it in public.[36]

In the summer of 1895, he received a letter from a manager in

---

[28] Hull, "D. D. Emmett"; *The Daily Banner* (Mount Vernon, June 29, 1904).

[29] Cunningham, " 'Uncle Dan' Emmett"; Milton Nobles, "Shop Talk," *The New York Dramatic Mirror* (July 30, 1904).

[30] Nobles, "Shop Talk" (July 30, 1904); Vaughan Kester, "About the late Dan Emmett," *The New York Dramatic Mirror* (September 3, 1904).

[31] Kester, "About the late Dan Emmett."

[32] *Ibid.;* Cunningham, "Uncle Dan' Emmett."

[33] Nobles, "Shop Talk" (July 30, 1904).

[34] *Ibid.;* Kester, "About the late Dan Emmett." The Actor's Fund first offered to place Emmett in a home for the aged, but he declined because he did not wish to leave his wife alone; see Nobles, "Shop Talk" (August 27, 1904).

[35] Sheerin, "Dixie"; Cunningham, " *'Uncle Dan' Emmett,*" visit in 1895; Frederick E. Mortimer, a newspaper clipping (April 12, 1902), in the Allen A. Brown Collection, Boston Public Library, visit in 1898; *The Daily Banner* (Mount Vernon, June 29, 1904), visit in 1903; and Galbreath, *Daniel Decatur Emmett*, 26, visit in 1903.

[36] Mulhane, "The Writer of 'Dixie' "; and *The New York Dramatic Mirror* (July 9, 1904). Emmett's letter of thanks for a banquet to which he had been invited in 1895 is reprinted in *The Confederate Veteran* (March, 1905).

Tennessee, which said: "Having seen your address in the Newspapers, and the announcement that you are the author of 'Dixie,' the song that has been adopted as the National Air of the southland, and one that has electrified so many people North and South, I have a desire to help you with a benefit if it can be arranged at some proper place after the 1st of October."[37] Nothing came of this proposal, because in the meantime Emmett's old friend Al. G. Field had visited him in Mount Vernon and agreed to take him on a "farewell tour" with his minstrel company.[38]

The tour began in Newark, Ohio, on August 21, and ended the next year on April 11, in Ironton, Ohio.[39] Much time was spent in the southern states, and it was especially here that the company had its greatest success. Emmett had a decisive share in it, for whenever he sang or fiddled "Dixie" or led the orchestra in its performance, the response was phenomenal: old memories were awakened and the audience applauded with a fervor reminiscent of Confederate days.[40] The trip was taxing, but Emmett, who celebrated his eightieth birthday en route, showed no signs of fatigue and was reported being "as frisky as a colt."[41] He returned to Mount Vernon in April[42] with the knowledge that at least one of his songs had indelibly inscribed itself on the imagination of his countrymen. He was proud of it; when he signed his name he usually added "author of Dixie."

Living to the venerable age of eighty-eight, he was a "genial, simple, hale old fellow" whose handshake was something to reckon with.[43] From his cottage he regularly walked a mile to town in order to pick up his weekly allowance, even in adverse winter weather, turning up at the post office like "a formidable object in his large black overcoat belted with a heavy rope, improvised puttees of burlap and a fur cap on his unusually large head."[44]

[37] Letter of C. L. Ridley (July 14, 1895), in Emmett's Manuscript Collection.
[38] Al. G. Field, *Watch Yourself Go By* (Columbus, Ohio, 1912), 484.
[39] All engagements are listed in *The New York Clipper* (August, 1895 to April, 1896).
[40] Mulhane, "The Writer of 'Dixie' "; Paskman and Spaeth, *Gentlemen Be Seated*, 185–86; and *The New York Clipper* (September 28, October 12, 19, and 26, 1895, etc.).
[41] *The New York Clipper* (November 9, 1895 and March 21, 1896).
[42] *The New York Clipper* (April 18, 1896).
[43] Mulhane, "The Writer of 'Dixie.' "
[44] From a private letter (August 16, 1943), of Chas. V. Critchfield, who at Emmett's time was assistant postmaster in Mount Vernon.

He had long ceased to write music or verse except for a few prayers for his own satisfaction.[45] One of his last statements was of a practical sort. On a spring day he pulled a book from his shelves and wrote on it "Set black hen March 23d/04."[46] He lived until the evening of June 28. After having lain in state at the home of the Elks' Lodge, where he had performed at times, and after a service at St. Paul's Episcopal Church, he was buried in Mound View Cemetery.[47]

Almost immediately a local committee was organized with the purpose "to erect a monument to the memory of Daniel Decatur Emmett, in the public square of Mount Vernon . . . ."[48] Nothing came of it, however, and by 1912 not even the exact location of his grave was remembered.[49] It was the South and those involved in its history that paid him tribute. In 1927 in Fletcher, North Carolina, a memorial tablet was unveiled, and in 1931 an inscribed boulder was placed by the United Daughters of the Confederacy on the lawn in front of the Knox County Memorial Building in Mount Vernon.[50]

The ovations which Emmett received in his old age must have touched him to the core, but they were offered for a single song only and for its political overtones which he had not intended. Whatever else he had written and composed, though it had once echoed in minstrel theaters throughout the land, was forgotten, even though its vitality had not faded. As products of early minstrelsy which had brought the spirit of the back country to the urban stage—its heartiness, straightforwardness, and its sense of the grotesque—Emmett's tunes and texts no longer appealed to the genteel taste of the second half of the nineteenth century. After many years, the situation has finally improved. A new interest in the primitive elements of American culture may in time open our minds to the charm of the early popular theater and its music.

Emmett was a robust, simple, unassuming man who would never

[45] A few prayers, the dates of which can only be surmised, are published in Galbreath, *Daniel Decatur Emmett,* 59.
[46] Emmett's Manuscript Collection.
[47] *The Daily Banner* (June 29 and 30, and July 1, 1904). A letter of June 29, written at the request of Emmett's widow to the Actor's Fund, in which she expressed the hope for continued support, is published in Nobles, "Shop Talk" (July 30, 1904).
[48] *The New York Dramatic Mirror* (July 23, 1904).
[49] *Ibid.* (July 30, and August 13 and 27, 1904); Hull, "D. D. Emmett."
[50] *Musical Courier* (July 7, 1927).

have deemed himself worthy of a book on his life and work. He was not educated in the ordinary sense. While the Negro dialect came natural to him, he became self-conscious and awkward when he had to express himself in standard English. Even his musical skills were limited, for he could write only tunes, and always needed others to arrange his piano accompaniments. And though his memory was good, "he was a slow study and a very indifferent reader . . . ."[51]

Essentially a folk artist, he wrote and composed to make a living, and it is unlikely that he ever gave a thought to what we call originality. But since he was firmly rooted in a living tradition and in the local scene, he was more genuine and more genuinely American than the professional composers of his time and his country. There was a naïve, sinewy quality in what he did, and he preserved it as long as popular demand encouraged him.

[51] Field, *Watch Yourself Go By,* 485.

DOCUMENTS

Statement of Dan Emmett on the First Negro Minstrel Band
Published in *The New York Clipper,* May 19, 1877

Chicago, Illinois, May 1, 1877

Editor, New York Clipper: My attention has been drawn to a letter written
by Mr. Lance Durand (as we used to call him) and published in The
Clipper [March 10, 1877] in which he claims that E. P. Christy originated
the first minstrel troupe in the United States. I should not now take any
notice of Mr. Durand's communication, were it not for the claims of my
dead companions of the original troupe.

This is what I know of the claims of E. P. Christy. After the Virginia
Minstrels had left for England there were organizations of a kindred character springing up in and around New York City. The performances of
some of these were witnessed, if not participated in, by Mr. Enam Dickinson, and what I am now about to quote was repeatedly told me by him:
"I happened to be in Buffalo, and chance led me to Christy's dance-house.
Ned Christy asked me if I had seen any of 'these new-fashioned nigger
shows.' I told him that I had, and he then proposed that I should train
his dancers and fiddlers so that they could give a performance similar to
those I had witnessed. I accepted his offer, and perfected them."

Now, Mr. Editor, if this was prior to 1843, would not Mr. Dickinson
have told me so? He had ample opportunity to do so, as I afterwards traveled with him for two years with Spaulding's Circus.

As regards Mr. Durand, I was with him for nearly a year in Spaulding and Rogers' Circus, and he did not once allude to E. P. Christy's having organized a band prior to 1843, although he spoke of having traveled with him with a room-show and dancing-party. Mr. Cool White was with Spaulding and Rogers' Circus at the same time that I was; and if Mr. Durand had disputed my claims, Mr. White (who is now, I believe, in New York) would be very apt to recollect that circumstance.

What Mr. Christy really claimed on his bills was simply this and no more: "The first to harmonize and originate the Present Style of minstrelsy" —meaning thereby the singing in harmony and introducing the various acts, together with wench-dancing and solo-playing. If he had ever claimed to have started the first minstrel troupe that could give a whole perform- ance, without the aid of any other attraction, Mr. J. B. Donniker, who was his leader for years, would most certainly have heard him mention it. I respectfully refer this point to Mr. Donniker.

Allow me, in conclusion, to state most emphatically that I write this not on my own account but to vindicate the claims of those who have gone to another world.

> Your respectfully,
> DANIEL D. EMMETT
> Leader of the Virginia Minstrels

Statement of Dan Emmett on "Dixie"
Written for *The New York Clipper* and published in its issue of April 6, 1872

"AWAY DOWN SOUTH IN DIXIE"
The Story of Its Origin, as Told by its Author, Dan. Emmett.

There having appeared at various times during the widespread popu- larity of the song of "Dixie" different versions of the origin of the work, we requested its author, Daniel D. Emmett, now and for several years past residing in Chicago, to give us his statement concerning it, and this he has done in the following communication:—

Chicago, March 13th, '72

Frank Queen.—Dear Sir.—Having received your request for me to forward to you for publication in the *Clipper* a correct statement of the origin of

Documents

the song known as "Dixie," I will now endeavor to do so in as brief a manner
as possible. I have seen several erroneous statements at different times
since the close of the war, all of which are wide of the mark; and I never,
until now, have taken the trouble to contradict them. One principal reason
for my silence was, that I had no further interest in the song, and that its
popularity north was among the "things that were." To proceed then, it
is necessary for me to state that I have been south of New York but *once
since* 1851, and that was on a short trip to Washington with the Bryants'
Minstrels some 6 years since, all other statements to the contrary notwithstanding. [However, in early November 1858, Emmett played with his own
company "Emmett's Varieties" in Selma, Alabama.]

In the spring of 1858 [1859], I was playing in New York with the
"Bryants"; my particular business was to compose new walkrounds for
them as fast as required. Some time in the spring of that year (1858)
[1859], amongst others, I composed the words and music of a song that
I afterwards published by the title of "*I wish I was in Dixie's Land,*" which
was afterwards, by universal custom, called "Dixie." It was composed on
one rainy Sunday in Elm Street, between Broome and Spring Streets, No.
197, Room No. 1. Previous to that time neither I nor any other person had
ever heard anything like it, although "Dixie's Land" is an old phrase applied
to the Southern States, at least to that part of it lying south of Mason and
Dixon's line. [The implied derivation is based on legend rather than fact.]
In my traveling days amongst showmen, when we would start for a winter's
season south, while speaking of the change, they would invariably ejaculate [*sic*] the stereotyped saying:—"I Wish I was in Dixie's Land," meaning the southern country; though others have attempted, in vain, to locate
it on Staten Island. The song of "Dixie" was never heard south until it was
taken there first by the "Buckleys" and the "Newcombs," each of whom
purchased a copy of me while they were in New York. [This purchase
does not prove that it was these companies that introduced Dixie to the
South. To judge at least by a number of northern playbills, minstrel companies simply picked up the song by ear as soon as it appeared and performed it.] It took amazingly south *as some-thing new!* Show people generally, if not always, have a chance to hear every local song as they pass
through the different sections of [the] country, and particularly so with
minstrel companies, who are always on the look out for songs and sayings
that will answer for their business; but none had ever heard anything like
my song of "Dixie." I did not publish it until it had become common property and then not until it was issued by Mr. P. P. Werling [Werlein], of

287

New Orleans. He published it in Mr. Peters' name, at the same time he wrote me a letter offering me *five dollars for the copyright!* (His letter is now in the possession of Mr. Wm. Pond, of New York, who published my copy.) Mr. Pond compelled all those who had published my words and music to disfigure their plates of Dixie and discontinue its further publication. Every showman and minstrel that was in New York at the time of the dispute about the authorship signed a paper to the effect that they had never heard anything like my song of "Dixie," either north, south, east or west, until they heard it sung at the Bryants' Minstrels in New York. And now to conclude this short, but correct statement, I will merely say that it [*Dixie*] is nothing but a plain, simple melody, with plantation words, the purport of which is that a negro in the north feels himself out of place and, thinking of his old home in the south, is made to exclaim, in the words of the song:—"I wish I was in Dixie's Land!" This is the first and only statement I ever made. With great respect, I am yours,

DANIEL DECATUR EMMETT

EMMETT'S CONTRACT WITH FIRTH, POND & CO. OF 1861
[in the possession of the Library of Congress]

To all to whom these presents shall come I Daniel D. Emmett send greeting

Whereas I am the author and composer of the words and the music of a certain musical composition known as "I wish I was in Dixies Land" or "Dixies Land."

Now know ye that I the said Daniel D. Emmett have granted, assigned, transferred, and set over, and I do hereby grant, assign, transfer and set over, unto Firth, Pond & Co., partners, the sole and exclusive right and liberty to print, reprint, publish and vend the said, musical composition.

To have and to hold the said right and liberty hereby granted to the said Firth, Pond & Co., their executors, administrators, and assigned for and during the whole period of the continuance of the said right (together with any right of renewal thereof) in consideration of the sum of Three Hundred Dollars ($300.00—) to me in hand paid by the said Firth, Pond & Co., the receipt of which I hereby acknowledge, February 11th 1861 in the city of New York and the State of New York

Signed sealed and delivered
this 11th day of February 1861
in our presence

DANIEL D. EMMETT

Witness
GEO. H. W. BIRD
HENRY W. POND

BIBLIOGRAPHY OF THE WORKS
OF D. D. EMMETT

EMMETT'S MANUSCRIPTS ARE PRESERVED in the State Library, Columbus, Ohio. They contain songs and tunes, variants and sketches, minstrel lyrics, several dozen hymns, more than forty sermons (both types in Negro dialect), and a number of minstrel plays, including several of doubtful origin in Emmett's handwriting.

This bibliography chiefly lists Emmett's songs and tunes. It mentions only those of his numerous lyrics for which an original tune of his exists or can be assumed to have existed. In all cases, the tune as well as the words are by Emmett, unless stated otherwise. Piano accompaniments, however, are always by someone else.

The origin of a number of tunes and texts is not entirely certain. For some of them it may never be convincingly established because of the custom among minstrels of freely borrowing from each other. Under the circumstances, the following rough method has been adopted: whenever Emmett made specific claims concerning text or tune, and whenever he signed his name to a manuscript, his claim has been recognized; in all other instances the attempt has been made to clarify the question of attribution by additional evidence. It should be noted that the designation "composed by" on sheet covers, broadsides, and songsters, sometimes also used by Emmett, was found to be obscure (in contrast to the unambiguous English eighteenth-century designation "written and composed"), and that this obscurity was even deliberate. One can rarely be certain whether the designation "composed by," before the 1860's, refers to the tune only

or to the text or to both. This doubt disappears with the manuscripts of
Emmett's walk-arounds.

Charles Burleigh Galbreath in his *Daniel Decatur Emmett / Author
of "Dixie"* (Columbus, Ohio, 1904), published a list of most of Emmett's
walk-arounds written between 1859 and 1881. This list was based on
Emmett's manuscripts as they existed when he examined them. Some of
these manuscripts, however, have disappeared since, and the rest are
no longer bound together in the volume to which Galbreath makes reference (see page 46). Of Emmett's unpublished lyrics, Galbreath reprinted a few in Irish dialect and several prayers in plain English (see
pages 51–56 and 59 in Galbreath).

1. Songs and Tunes

De Boatman's Dance [inside: "De Boatmen's Dance"] ("High row, de
boatmen row"). "An original Banjo Melody, by Old Dan. D. Emmit"
(Boston, C. H. Keith, 1843). The words are by Emmett (see the Collection of Lyrics below) except for the chorus which was known in
the twenties or thirties to Ohio boatmen (see W. P. Strickland, *The
Pioneers of the West* [New York, 1856], 198). This fact suggests also
that the tune contains earlier material. A facsimile edition of the song
appears in S. Foster Damon, *Series of Old American Songs* (Providence, Rhode Island, 1936).

I'm Gwine ober de Mountains ("Away down in de Kentuck brake"). "Music
and Words by Old Dan Emmit" (Boston, C. H. Keith, 1843).

'Twill Nebber Do to Gib It up So ("De old Jim River I float down"). "Music
and Words by Old Dan D. Emmit" (Boston, C. H. Keith, 1843).

Dar He Goes! Dats Him! ("When first I come to dis here place"). "Words
and Music by Old Dan Emmit" (Boston, C. H. Keith, 1844).

Dandy Jim from Caroline ("I've heard it often said ob late"). "Composed
by D. D. Emmit" (London, D'Almaine & Co., n.d. [*c.*1844]). The
words are probably by Emmett and perhaps even the tune. *The
New York Clipper* (May 19, 1877), reported in a story based on information furnished by Emmett himself that "Emmett's song 'Dandy
Jim'" was played by the Virginia Minstrels on their trip to England
in the spring of 1843. A playbill of Emmett and Brower (Salem,
Massachusetts, October 23, 1844) reads: "Dandy Jim from de Caro-
lines . . . . This song, which has been claimed by others, was composed
by Old Dan Emmit on board the Packet Ship New York while on her

passage to England." The words, extant in manuscript, differ from the printed ones only in a few details. Emmett's American publisher, C. H. Keith, instead of including the song in the composer's Boston collections of 1843–44, issued a version of it as "written by S. S. Steel . . . Music by Dan Myers" in 1844. However, the very first edition of the song appeared a year earlier as "a Popular Negro Melody" without the mention of either composer or author (see the facsimile in Damon, *Old American Songs*).

Come Back Steben. A playbill of Emmett and Brower (Salem, Massachusetts, October 23, 1844) reads: "Come Back Steben—a genuine specimen of the real negro song—words and music by Emmit." Only a manuscript text entitled "Steben" is extant ("I went to ball last saturday ebenin"); the tune may possibly be identical with that of "Don't Mind Steven" in *Phil. Rice's Correct Method for the Banjo* (Boston, 1858).

Marty Inglehart Jig, Moze Haymar Jig, Negro Jig, Nigger on de Wood Pile, and *Pea-Patch Jig* are attributed to Emmett in *Kendall's Clarinet Instruction Book* (Boston, 1845). Signed by the composer and slightly varied, in manuscript they are under the following titles: "Peter Story Jig," "Moze Haymer Jig," "Camp-Meeting-Jig," "Negro on the Wood-Pile-Jig," and "Pea-Patch Jig."

Blister Plaster. Jig, Brown-Jug. Jig, Eelam Moore. Jig, Hell on the Wabash Jig, My First Jig, None-Such Jig, Root Hog or Die. Jig, and *Seely Simpkins. Jig* appear in the same manuscript, signed by Emmett. "Eelam [Elam] Moore" and "Root Hog or Die" were also used as songs in the early fifties (see below). This is no doubt also true of "Blister Plaster"; there is a manuscript text entitled "Plister Plaster." "Hell on the Wabash," slightly varied, and "Seely Simpkins" were published in Emmett's *Fife Instructor* of 1862. Another banjo tune, unsigned in the same manuscript, is "Tycoon Jig"; in James Buckley, *Buckley's New Banjo Book* (New York, 1860), it is marked "Arranged by Dan Emmett."

Machine Poetry—Oh, Ladies All! ("I went from here to Baltimore"). The words are in manuscript. The song with a banjo accompaniment is in *Rice's Correct Method*, with the remark "Composed by Dan Emmit"; here the first stanza of the manuscript version is used, only slightly changed. A playbill of Tryon's Circus, Bowery Amphitheatre (New York, October 23, [1845]), as republished in Charles C. Moreau, *Negro Minstrelsy in New York* (New York, 1891), II, reads: "Mr.

Emmit will sing his original Machine Poetry . . . ." This must be assumed to refer to "Oh, Ladies All," which is not merely in the style of the forties but the only one of its kind among the composer's songs.

Peter Story ("Wake up, Jake"). The words appear in *White's New Ethiopian Song Book* (Philadelphia, 1854), with the remark "Composed and sung by Old Dan Emmett at White's Melodeon . . . ." Two versions of the text are in manuscript, one with the remark "An original negro jig song. Composed by Old Dan Emmit." The tune is no doubt identical with Emmett's "Peter Story Jig" ["Marty Inglehart Jig"].

Jordan Is a Hard Road to Travel ("I just arrived in town"). The tune is by Emmett and possibly the words as well. Oliver Ditson (Boston) published it in 1853 with the inside remark "Composed by Old Dan Emmet." The front cover of the David A. Truax edition (Cincinnati, 1853) reads: "Authorized Edition / 'Jordan Is a Hard Road to Travel' / The Celebrated Banjo Song / As sung by / Young Dan Emmett. At Well's Opera House / Music Composed by / Old Dan Emmett." On the inside both editions have the name of the Ohio publisher Dunton & Thurston. The tune had been picked up as early as 1852 by the New York publisher C. G. Christman and issued in a version and arrangement of his own and with a new text, though without mentioning either a composer or an author. The composer's name appears on the cover of another 1853 edition, the "Jordan Polka Introducing the Favorite Melody Jordon [*sic*] Is a Hard Road to Travel Composed by Old Dan Emmett" (Philadelphia, J. E. Gould), "By Permission of the Proprietor of the Copyright."

Elam Moore-Jig ("Ole Dandy Cox on de big hoss"). The words are in manuscript and published in *White's New Ethiopian Song Book,* with the remark "Composed and sung by the Prince of Jig-players, Old Dan Emmett, at the Melodeon, No. 53 Bowery, N. Y." The tune is no doubt identical with Emmett's jig "Eelam Moore." It is listed as a song on a minstrel program as early as 1851 (see Ralph Keeler, *Vagabond Adventures* [Boston, 1870], opposite 120).

Root, Hog or Die ("Mule is in stable a bitin ob de trough"). The tune is no doubt identical with Emmett's jig "Root Hog or Die." The manuscript of the words carries at the top the remark "original by Old Dan Emmit" and at the bottom "N. Y. Apl [April] 1st, 1853." *The New York Clipper* (October 5, 1861) reported: "Old Dan Emmett's 'Root Hog or Die' is, we hear, likely to become as popular in England as it has been on this side . . . ." Two 1856 sheet editions of the song

(Boston, Oliver Ditson; and New York, Horace Waters) make no mention of the composer. In the fifties and sixties variants of the tune appeared as "Essence of Old Virginia Dance" in *Rice's Correct Method* and as "Essence of Old Virginny" and "Original Essence" in *Buckley's New Banjo Book.*

Tuckey-Hoe ("White folks an brack folks I'm gwine to de apple cuttin"). The tune is no longer extant. The words are in manuscript with the remark "At de Apple cuttin—original banjo solo song composed by Old Dan Emmit."

I Ain't Got Time to Tarry ["The Land of Freedom"] ("I put dat sheep skin in de ground"). The words appear in *Bryant's Power of Music* (New York, 1859), with the remark "Ethiopian Walk 'Round, composed by D. D. Emmett and sung only at Bryant's Minstrels." The first performance was in November, 1858. The tune is no doubt identical with "I'm Going Home to Dixie" of 1861 (see below). The opening lines of the chorus of the two songs are practically alike, and the remaining parts of their text are interchangeable.

Wide Awake ["Dar's a Darkey in de Tent"] ("Dar's a darkey in de tent, keep 'im in, keep 'im in, keep 'im in"). "Words and Music by D. D. Emmett" (Boston, Firth, Pond and Co., 1860). The words, slightly varied, appear in *Bryant's Power of Music.* The manuscript, dated 1859, contains the tune and the first stanza but different additional stanzas; it carries the remark " 'Walk 'Round,' Composed by Daniel D. Emmett, for Bryant's Minstrels." The first performance was in February, 1859.

Jonny Roach ("In old Kentuck in de arter noon"). The tune and words are in manuscript with the remark " 'Walk 'Round,' Composed by Daniel D. Emmett, for Bryant's Minstrels." The first performance was in March, 1859. The words, under the title of "Johnny Roach," are on a program of 1859 in a bound volume of Bryant's programs of 1859–60, now in the Harvard College Library.

I Wish I Was in Dixie's Land [inside: "Dixie's Land"] ("I wish I was in de land ob cotton"). "Written & Composed expressly for Bryants Minstrels by Dan D. Emmett" (New York, Firth, Pond & Co., 1860), first authorized edition. The words are in *Bryant's Power of Music.* The first performance was on April 4, 1859. A manuscript dated 1859, in the possession of George Bird Evans of Bruceton Mills, West Virginia (a facsimile is in the magazine *The Confederate Veteran* [Nashville, September, 1895], recently issued separately by the United

Daughters of the Confederacy), calls the song a "'Walk 'Round.'" A version for the fife is in Emmett's *Fife Instructor*.

Sandy Gibson's [Chaw Roast Beef or Water Soak at Sandy Gibson's] ("In eighteen-hundred and forty-four"). The words are in *Bryant's Power of Music,* with the remark "Ethiopian 'Walk 'Round' composed by D. D. Emmett and sung only at Bryant's Minstrels." The tune and parts of the first stanza are in manuscript. The first performance took place in late April, 1859.

Road to Georgia ["White Wash Army"] ("When I was young and in my prime"). The tune and words are in manuscript, dated 1859, with the remark "'Walk 'Round,' Composed by Daniel D. Emmett for Bryants Minstrels." The first performance was in May, 1859. "White Wash Army" and "Road to Georgia" are listed as separate "Plantation Songs" in an advertisement of the Bryants in *The New York Clipper* (April 20, 1861), but they are identical: in *Billy Birch's Ethiopian Melodist* (New York, 1862), the text of "Road to Georgia" has the heading "White Wash Army." The tune is practically identical with the one of "Road to Richmond" (see below).

Johnny Gouler ["Johnny Goulder"]. Listed by Galbreath among Emmett's walk-arounds of 1859; it is no longer extant. The first performance was by the Bryants in August, 1859.

High, Low, Jack ("Old Massa was de best ob men"). The words are in *Birch's Ethiopian Melodist*. The tune is in manuscript. The song is listed as one of Emmett's "Plantation Songs" in an advertisement of the Bryant's Minstrels in *The New York Clipper* (April 20, 1861), and as one of his walk-arounds in a newspaper clipping (August 11, 1895), entitled "Negro Minstrels and their Dances" (now in the Harvard Theatre Collection and the New York Public Library). The first performance was by the Bryants in September, 1859.

Billy Patterson ("Dar was an old nigg dat got hit wid a brick"). "Words and Music by D. D. Emmett" (New York, Firth, Pond & Co., 1860), "Composed for Bryant's Minstrels." It is listed by Galbreath among the walk-arounds of 1859. The first performance was given by the Bryants in October, 1859.

Loozyanna Low Grounds ("Dar is a place call'd Loozyann"). The tune and words are in manuscript with the remark "Composed by Daniel D. Emmett." It is listed by Galbreath among the walk-arounds of 1859, and the first performance was by the Bryants in November, 1859.

Flat Foot Jake. Listed by Galbreath among the walk-arounds of 1859, the song is no longer extant, unless it is identical with a manuscript sketch of a song (and a few additional manuscript stanzas) which begins with "Flat foot Joe he was my name sake."

Go 'Way Boys ("Come ebry jolly niggar"). The tune and words are in manuscript, dated 1859, with the remark " 'Walk 'Round' Composed by Daniel D. Emmett, for Bryant's Minstrels." The sheet music edition, published by Firth, Pond & Co. (New York, 1860), could not be located.

John Come down de Hollow ("I've heard de white folks say"). The tune and words are in manuscript, dated 1859, with the remark " 'Walk 'Round.' Composed by Daniel D. Emmett for Bryant's Minstrels." In another manuscript, an incomplete one, the song is dated 1860. The sheet music edition, published by Firth, Pond & Co. (New York, 1860), could not be located.

What O' Dat ("Old Pompey cotch a crow"). The tune and words are in manuscript, dated 1859, with the remark " 'Walk 'Round,' Composed by Daniel D. Emmett for Bryant's Minstrels." The words are in *Bryant's Power of Music.*

Turkey in de Straw ("De color'd man is berry good"). The H. B. Dodworth edition (New York, 1861) contains the remark "Composed by Dan Bryant." The tune and words are nevertheless by Emmett. The tune and parts of the first stanza are in manuscript. The song is listed by Galbreath among Emmett's walk-arounds of 1859, and it is mentioned among Emmett's walk-arounds in "Negro Minstrels and their Dances."

Old K. Y. Ky. ["Who's Foot Dat Burnin';" "Who's Heel Dat a Burnin'"] ("De snow am in de cloud"). "Words & Music by D. D. Emmett" (New York, Firth, Pond & Co., 1860), "Composed for Bryant's Minstrels." It is listed by Galbreath among Emmett's walk-arounds of 1860. The same tune, with Confederate words by Eugene Raymond (John Hill Hewitt), was published under the title "Three Cheers for Our Jack Morgan" (Augusta, Georgia, Blackmar & Bro., 1864).

Massa Greely, O ("De 'Conflict' rages at my expence"). The tune and words are in manuscript, dated 1860, with the remark " 'Walk Round' Composed expressly for W. W. Newcomb, Esq., by D. D. Emmett."

Darrow Arrow ("In Darrow Arrow Stormy grew"). Published by H. B. Dodworth (New York, 1861), with the remark "Composed by Niel [*sic*] Bryant," the tune and words are nevertheless by Emmett. The melodic style reveals Emmett as the composer. Galbreath lists the song among Emmett's walk-arounds of 1860.

De Contrack or Down on de Beach-Low Farm ("Old hoss an me went partnership, we did as sure's your born"). Published by H. B. Dodworth (New York, 1861), with the remark "Composed by Jerry Bryant," the tune and words are nevertheless by Emmett. The melodic style reveals Emmett as the composer. Galbreath lists the song among Emmett's walk-arounds of 1860.

I'm Going Home to Dixie ("There is a land where cotton grows"). "Words and Music by D. D. Emmett" (New York, Firth, Pond & Co., 1861). (See *"I Ain't Got Time to Tarry"*). The first performance was by Bryant's Minstrels.

Heenan and Sayers. In an advertisement of the Bryant's Minstrels in *The New York Clipper* (April 20, 1861), the song is listed as one of Emmett's "Plantation Songs"; this, however, is the only evidence of its existence. It is not impossible that "Heenan and Sayers" was merely another title for the walk-around "Billy Patterson" which in stanza four contains references to these two names.

De Back-Log. Listed by Galbreath among Emmett's walk-arounds of 1862, it is no longer extant.

Bress Old Gen. Jackson ("Den bress old Ginral Jackson"). The tune and first stanza are in manuscript. It is listed by Galbreath among Emmett's walk-arounds of 1862, under the title of "Bress Old Andy Jackson."

Mr. Per Coon ("Come darkies evry one"). The tune and words are in manuscript, dated 1862, with the remark " 'Walk Round' Composed by Daniel D. Emmett and Dedicated to Bryant's Minstrels." The words are in *Hooley's Opera House Songster* (New York, 1863).

The Black Brigade ("Dar's someting rong a brewin' "). "Words and Music by Dan. D. Emmett" (New York, Wm. A. Pond & Co., 1863), "Plantation Song & Dance Sung . . . At Bryant's Minstrels." The tune and words are in manuscript, dated 1862.

Ober in Jarsey ("Gib me de wing to fly wid away ober in Jarsey"). Listed by Galbreath among Emmett's walk-arounds of 1863, the tune and first stanza are in manuscript. The words are in *Hooley's "High Daddy" Songster* (New York, 1865), with the remark "Written by Dan. Emmett."

High Daddy ("The sun's gone down to take a little sleep"). "Words and Music by D. D. Emmett" (New York, Wm. A. Pond & Co., 1863), "Written & Composed Expressly for Bryant's Minstrels . . . ." It is listed by Galbreath among Emmett's walk-arounds of 1863.

Here We Are! Here We Are! or "Cross Ober Jordan" ["Who Can Find Us Now"] ("Oh don't you hear de Capting say"). "Walk around by Daniel

D. Emmett" (New York, William Hall & Son, 1863); it is also dated 1863 by Galbreath. The first performance was by Bryant's Minstrels.

Greenbacks ("How are you Greenbacks ten or twenty"). "Words and Music by Dan. D. Emmett" (New York, Wm. A. Pond & Co., 1863). The tune and words are in manuscript with the remark " 'Walk 'Round.' Composed by Daniel D. Emmett and Dedicated to Bryant's Minstrels, New York, 1863." A facsimile of the song is in Philip D. Jordan and Lillian Kessler, *Songs of Yesterday* (New York, 1941).

Jack on the Green (" 'Tis ober de hills so high, an down in de valleys low"). Published as a "Walk-Round" by Wm. A. Pond & Co. (New York, 1864), Galbreath dates the manuscript 1863.

Goose and Gander. Listed by Galbreath among Emmett's walk-arounds of 1863, it is no longer extant.

Road To Richmond ("When I was young and in my prime"). "Walk 'Round Sung By the Bryant's Minstrels Composed by Dan D. Emmett" (New York, Wm. Hall & Son, 1864). It is identical with "Road to Georgia" of 1859, except for a few changes in the tune and the text and for the instrumental ending which was borrowed from "Sandy Gibson's."

U. S. G. ("I suppose you have heard of the great commander"). A "National Walk 'Round" with "Words and Music by Dan D. Emmett" (New York, Wm. A. Pond & Co., 1864), it is also dated 1864 by Galbreath.

Foot-Falls on de Carpet. Listed by Galbreath among Emmett's walk-arounds of 1864, there is nothing but a brief passage of the tune extant in a medley in manuscript.

Reel o'er de Mountain ("De valleys dey am low de mountains dey am high"). The tune and words in manuscript are marked "Walk Round."

Mac Will Win the Union Back ("Mid cheers that rend the air"). The tune is by Emmett, with "Words Arranged to the Music by A. Oakey Hall. Composed by Dan Emmett" (New York, Wm. Hall & Son, 1864). The melody of the refrain is identical with the refrain of "Reel o'er de Mountain."

Little Mac Is on de Track ("De cannons roar; we beat de drum"). The tune and words are in manuscript, dated 1864. Published as a broadside by Wm. A. Pond & Co. (New York, 1864) in McClellan Songs, No. 4, it is preserved among Emmett's manuscripts. The tune is in the style of Emmett's walk-arounds.

Whar Y'e Been So Long. The tune in manuscript and the words no longer extant, it is listed by Galbreath among Emmett's walk-arounds of 1865.

298

Striking Ile ("The world it revolves on its own axle tree"). "Written expressly for Dan Bryant, Esq., by Dan D. Emmett ..." (New York, Wm. Pond & Co., 1865), the tune and some of the words are in manuscript as well.

Whar's De Army Gone ("I'll sing dis song but dat wont harm me"). The tune and words are in manuscript; the style of the tune as well as the words point to the mid-sixties.

Old Times Rocks ("Dar was two gemmelmen dey'er [deyre] clothes look'd rather seedy"). The tune and words are in manuscript with the remark "Walk Round by D. D. Emmett." It was performed by the Bryant's Minstrels in 1865.

Barr-Grass ["Burr Grass," according to Galbreath] ("De poor mans labor is nebber done"). The tune and words are in manuscript with the remark " 'Walk Round' ... by D. D. Emmett, 1868."

Pancake-Joe ("O here I am as you diskiber"). The tune and words are in manuscript with the remark "Walk Round by D. D. Emmett 1868."

Want Any Shad. Listed by Galbreath among Emmett's walk-arounds of 1868, it is no longer extant.

Sugar In De Gourd ("Twas on a cold an frosty night"). The tune and words are in manuscript with the remark "Walk Round ... by D. D. Emmett, 1868."

Whoa! Bally! ("When I was but a colt kept in a stable"). The tune is no longer extant. The words are in Galbreath, 58, and the song is listed by him among Emmett's walk-arounds of 1868.

Yes or No ("My lubs a brack an tan, jis like a cake ob taller"). The tune and words are in manuscript with the remark "Walk round ... By D. D. Emmett 1868."

Abner Isham Still. Listed by Galbreath among Emmett's walk-arounds of 1868, it is no longer extant.

I Am Free! ("I used to chuck de corn an put it in de crib"). The tune and words are in manuscript with the remark "Walk round by D. D. Emmett 1868."

The Wigwam. The New York Clipper (April 25, 1868), announced: "Dan Emmett ... has just completed a new walk around song and dance for that troupe [the Bryants] called 'The Wigwam.' " Being no longer extant, a manuscript of a part of a song with such words as "the new wigwam" may be a sketch of the walk-around.

Walk Sheep ("I went to de market to buy some lamb"). The tune and words are in manuscript with the remark "A patting song and Dance by Dan D. Emmett. Written expressly for Mr. Holley." Its date is possibly in the sixties.

Dutchman's Corner (" 'Twas old Yoecup Snider come to town"). The tune and words are in manuscript with the remark " 'Walk 'Round by D. D. Emmett." It was probably written in the late sixties.

The Beaux-Knot ("Myself an me togedder, we took a promenade"). The tune and words are probably by Emmett. Both are in manuscript; they were written during the late sixties or later.

Count Andy Cojay ("O, I am de swell ob all de colord men"). The tune and words are in manuscript with the remark "Song and Dance, Words and music D. D. Emmett." It was written in the late sixties or later.

Poor Old Gabe ("This life is but a span that lotted unto man"). The tune and words are in manuscript with the remark "Old Man Song Written & Composed by Dan Emmit." In spite of the early spelling of the name, the song is approximately of the late sixties because of the reference of the words to Lincoln's death and the Reconstruction.

I Will Go Back to Dixie (" 'Twas in the month of May"). The tune and words, probably by Emmett, are both in manuscript, and date from the late sixties or later.

Turkeys in de Straw. Emmett's fiddle version of the early minstrel tune "Zip Coon," published in Francis O'Neill, *The Dance Music of Ireland* (Chicago, 1907), who says in the preface: "Our setting is a very superior one, being the version played by Dan Emmett, a celebrated Irish American minstrel of the last generation." It was probably written in the seventies, when Emmett lived in Chicago.

15th Amendment ("In the year of our Lord eighteen hundred-sixty-three"). A sketch of the tune is in manuscript. The words are in manuscript with the remark "Words & Music by D. D. Emmett." It is listed by Galbreath as a walk-around of 1881.

2. Addenda to Songs and Tunes

Emmett's manuscript collection includes various sketches of tunes and songs, such as "Brudder Chip," "Fish Kill Landin" (a "walk 'round"), and "Fadder Abram Fadder Abram's Got So Thin." The words of "Hot Corn" ("Yaller Gal stood on de walk") appear in *San Francisco Theatre Research* (San Francisco, n.d. [series starting in 1938]), Monograph XXV, Vol. XIII,

240, with this comment: "The words are those recalled by Jake Wallace. 'Hot Corn' . . . was purchased by Wallace from Dan Emmett in 1855. He also bought a banjo duet from Emmett."

3. Collections

Old Dan Emmit's Original Banjo Melodies (Boston, Chas. H. Keith, 1843).
   The series includes the following sheets:
   a. "De Boatman's Dance."
   b. " 'Twill Nebber Do to Gib It up So."
   c. "Old Dan Tucker" ("I come to town de udder night"). With "Words by Old Dan D. Emmit," the tune is not by him even though he claimed it in later years. An early manuscript copy of the text (Galbreath, 49) merely carries the remark "Composed by Old Dan Emmit," which proves nothing about the tune. On a late manuscript copy of the song, dated 1840, now in the possession of the Harvard Theatre Collection, Emmett asserted to have "composed [it], as a 'Banjo Song.' " In a late interview (Galbreath, 9), he said "I composed Old Dan Tucker in 1830 or 1831 . . . ." It should be noted, however, that the origin of the tune was already uncertain when it was published in 1843. (See two 1843 editions—one in Damon, *Old American Songs,* and the other published under the heading of *The Celebrated Negro Melodies as sung by the Virginia Minstrels* [Boston, Geo. P. Reed, 1843].) None of the editions of 1843 mentions the name of a composer. The song is reported to have appeared, no doubt in performance, about 1841 (see "Negro Minstrelsy—Ancient and Modern," *Putnam's Monthly* [January, 1855]).
   d. "I'm Gwine ober de Mountains."
   e. "The Fine Old Colored Gentleman" ("In Tenn'see as I've heard say dare once did use to dwell"). "Music: Old English Gent. Words by D. D. Emmit."
   f. "My Old Aunt Sally" ("Agwine down to New Orleans I got upon de landin"). "Composed by Old Dan D. Emmit" (see the Collection of Lyrics below). The tune is a variant of "Peggy Perkins" by Charles Dibdin; the latter appeared in an English edition of 1790 and in an American edition between 1795 and 1797. A facsimile of "My Old Aunt Sally" is in Damon, *Old American Songs.*
   g. "O Lud Gals Gib Me" ("Its up de rope an down de cable"). With

"Words by Old Dan. Emmit," the tune is attributed to Charles White in the preface to *White's New Ethiopian Song Book* (Philadelphia, 1854).

Second Series / Old Dan Emmit's Original Banjo Melodies (Boston, Keith's Publishing House, 1844). The series includes the following sheets:
a. "Dar He Goes! Dats Him!
b. "My Old Dad" ["Ole Dad"] ("Ibe sung so much ob Dandy Jim"). Neither composer nor author is mentioned.
c. "Corn Field Green" ("On a night in de fall ob de year"). "A Parody on 'A Summer's Day' Music by J. Freidheim [Friedheim] words by Old Dan Emmit."
d. "School Master Abroad." The sheet could not be located. If its tune was identical with that of "The Schoolmaster" (Boston, 1834), it was "Ah, voux dirai-je maman," well known to Europeans and Americans, including the Negroes on the southern plantations (see Frances Anne Kemble, *Journal of a Residence on a Georgian Plantation in 1838–1839* [New York, 1863], 127).
e. "De Old Banjo." The sheet could not be located, but it is available in an English edition (see below).
f. "De Blue Tail Fly" ("O when you come in summer time"). Neither composer nor author is mentioned. The edition is dated 1844 on the title page and, by mistake, 1846 on the inside.
g. "Rock Susander." The sheet could not be located, but what was probably its text appeared under the title "Rock Susanna Banjo Solo" in *George Christy and Wood's Melodies* (Philadelphia, 1854). The first line began: "Old Simon Buckheart." A tune called "Rock Susana" was published in S. S. Stewart, *The Complete American Banjo School* (Philadelphia, 1887). The text and tune, however, do not match.
h. "Pompy O'Smash" ("One Pompy O'Smash courted Dinar Coal"). "An original Parody by Old Dan Emmit." The words are by Emmett; the tune is the Irish "Rory O'More" (see Alfred Moffat, *Minstrelsy of Ireland* [London, 1897]).
i. "Ledder Breeches" ("Near Richmond town, dat place ob renown"). "A Parody On Brother Jonathan by Old Dan Emmit And Dedicated with due respect to Alexander Elliott Esq. of Mount Vernon, Ohio." The words are by Emmett; the tune is the Irish "Saint Patrick Was a Gentleman" (see George Petrie and Charles Villiers Stanford,

The Complete Collection of Irish Music [London, 1902], I). An Irish version of Emmett's text ("The old Leather Breeches") appears on broadside No. 105, printed by Horace Partridge (see *Ballads of the Street* [Boston], II, in the Rare Book Room of the Boston Public Library).

j. "De Banjo Nigger." The sheet could not be located.

k. "De Wild Goose-Nation" ("Away down south in de wild goose nation"). "Composed by Old Dan Emmit and Dedicated by permission to Thomas Rice Esq. The original Jim Crow." The words are by Emmett; the tune is that of "Gumbo Chaff," a minstrel song of the thirties.

l. "The Back Action Spring." The sheet could not be located; it is available in an English edition entitled "The Double Action Spring" (see below).

m. "Walk Jaw Bone." The sheet could not be located, but the song is available in an English edition (see below). The words are attributed to Emmett in *The Negro Singer's Own Book,* (Philadelphia and New York, n.d. [forties]). The tune was published with different words and without the name of a composer as "De Ole Jaw Bone" (Boston, 1840).

n. "The Jolly Raftsman" ("Oh I was born in ole Virginny"). "Words by Andrew Evans." The tune is called an "Italian Air" in M. Carcassi, *New Instructions for the Guitar* (Philadelphia, Klemm & Brother, n.d. [probably fifties]).

o. "Gwine 'Long Down" ("De turkey buzzard's a berry fine bird, much larger dan de crow"). "An original song sung by . . . Frank M. Brower." Neither composer nor author is mentioned.

p. "Old Joe" ("'Twas Old Jo stood at de garden gate"). "A Plantation Refrain. Composed and sung by . . . F. M. Brower." The words are probably by Brower, but the origin of the tune is uncertain.

Emmit's Celebrated Negro Melodies or Songs of the Virginny Banjoist composed & sung . . . By D. D. Emmit (London, D'Almaine & Co., n.d. [c.1844]). The series includes the following sheets:

a. "Dandy Jim from Caroline."

b. "Old Dan Tucker."

c. "The Boatman's Dance."

d. "Gwine ober de Mountains" (see above "I'm Gwine ober de Mountains").

e. "Nebber Do to Gib It up So" (see above " 'Twill Nebber Do . . .").
f. "My Old Aunt Sally."
g. "Walk Along John" ("Johnny come from Chickasaw"). The tune appeared in an 1843 edition (Boston, C. H. Keith) with the remark "Written and Composed by J. P. Carter." All of the six stanzas by Carter also appear in a manuscript by Emmett ("Go Along John") and several of them in the present English edition of the song.
h. "Walk-Jaw-Bone" ("De jawbone hung agin de wall").
i. "De Old Banjo" ("I am a niggar from de south"). Most of the words are in manuscript under the title "Charleston Galls." Seven of the stanzas also appear in a song of the same title (Boston, C. H. Keith, 1844) without mention of the composer or the author. And the words, under the original title, are ascribed to D. W. Lull in *The Negro Singer's Own Book*.
j. "Fine Old Color'd Gemman."
k. "De Double Action Spring" ("I'm old saucy Jack, an I come from old Kentuck"). The tune is a variant of "Jumbo Jum" (Boston, 1840).
l. "De Blue Tail Fly."
m. "History ob de World" ("I come from old Virginny, wid my head chuck full ob knowledge"). The text, possibly by Emmett, appears along with a few additional stanzas in J. W. Sharp (ed.), *The Vauxhall Comic Song-Book* (London, n.d. [forties]), with the remark "Sung by Dan Emmit, at Boston, United States." The origin of the tune is uncertain.

4. Manuals

Fife Instructor: Being A Thorough and Progressive Method, Embracing The Rudiments Of Music And a complete collection of All the Calls and Tunes as used in the Regular Army of the United States, published as a part of George B. Bruce, *The Drummer's And Fifer's Guide* (New York, Firth, Pond & Co., 1862). A modern photostatic reprint has been produced by Photopress Publishing Co. (Chicago, n.d.).

Emmett's Standard Drummer. The manuscript of this manual is no longer extant. According to Galbreath, 47–48, the title page and preface read: "EMMETT'S STANDARD DRUMMER. Being the regular School for the U. S. Army containing all the beats and routine duty for the *Drum and Fife.* According to the 'Ashworth Mode.' The whole rendered plain and concise by DANIEL D. EMMETT." Probably this was incorporated into the *Fife Instructor.* Only a similarly worded title page with a few musical examples is extant among Emmett's manuscripts.

5. Collection of Lyrics

Songs Of The Virginia Minstrels A Correct Edition Of The Celebrated Songs Of The Virginia Minstrels, originally composed and sung by them at their Concerts (Boston, Charles H. Keith, 1843). Included in the collection are words of " 'Twill Nebber Do to Gib It up So, Mr. Brown"; "Old Dan Tucker"; "Gwine ober de Mountain"; "Boatman's Dance"; "My Old Aunt Sally"; "The Fine Old Colored Gentleman"; "O Lawd, Gals, Gib Me a Chaw Terbackur"; and "Miss Lucy Long and Her Answer." The first seven lyrics are credited to Emmett with the words "Composed by . . . ." "O Lawd, Gals" also refers to Emmett with "Words by . . . ." The eighth is not annotated.

6. Plays

Hard Times / A Negro Extravaganza (New York, Robert M. De Witt, 1855), mounted and arranged by Charles White. According to a note in this edition, the first performance took place at White's Opera House (New York, October 12, 1855). Written in 1854 (according to Galbreath, 46), the manuscript is no longer extant. The original title page ("HARD TIMES / an original / ETHIOPIAN WALK-'ROUND . . . .") and the opening lines are in Galbreath, 57–58.

German Farmer or The Barber Shop in an Uproar, "an original Ethiopian Burletta in 1 act [top] Dan Emmit." Extant in manuscript, it was performed in the 1850's.

The Rappers. "An original Ethiopian Burletta in 1 act by Daniel D. Emmit." Extant in manuscript, it was written possibly in the 1850's.

7. Contributions to *The New York Clipper*

> *Away down South in Dixie,* "The Story of its Origin, as Told by its Author Dan. Emmett" (April 6, 1872).
>
> *Bressed Am Dem Dat 'Spects Nuttin', Kase Dey Aint a Gwine to Git Nuttin',* "a Negro Sermon" (August 9, 1873), and republished in part in Galbreath, 44–45.
>
> A letter to the editor, written May 1, 1877, concerning the first minstrel band (May 19, 1877).
>
> Emmett's story of the Virginia Minstrels, as retold by the editor (May 19, 1877). A "complete history of the band" by Emmett was "lost during the great fire in Chicago."
>
> Lyrics in plain English (September 30, 1871; July 13, 1872; and February 15, 1873); lyrics in Irish dialect (December 26, 1874).
>
> Letters to the editor about "Cat-Doggerell," one of the published lyrics (July 13, August 17, and September 28, 1872); the September 28 letter is republished in part in Galbreath, 44.

Anthology

The music and text of this anthology appear in their original versions. Two technical changes, however, have been made: the vocal line has been included in the top part of the piano accompaniment and various repeat signs (to be strictly observed in performance) have been added to the scores.

CONTENTS

PART I. A Selection from Dan Emmett's Works

A. *Songs and Banjo Tunes of the Forties and Fifties*

" 'Twill Nebber Do to Gib It Up So"   313
"I'm Gwine ober de Mountains"   316
"De Boatman's Dance"   320
"Dandy Jim from Caroline"   324
"Dar He Goes! Dats Him!"   328
"Oh, Ladies All!"   332
"Hop Light, Loo"   334
"Jordan Is a Hard Road to Travel"   335
"Nigger on de Wood Pile"   340
"Moze Haymar Jig"   340
"Marty Inglehart Jig"   341
"Peter Story Jig"   341
"Peter Story"   342
"Negro Jig"   343
"Pea-Patch Jig"   344
"Eelam Moore. Jig"   345
"Elam Moore—Jig"   345
"Root Hog or Die. Jig"   347
"My First Jig"   348

B. *Walk-Arounds*

"I'm Going Home to Dixie"   351
"I Ain't Got Time to Tarry"   354
"Jonny Roach"   355
"Dixie's Land (early manuscript)"   359
"I Wish I Was in Dixie's Land" (first authorized edition)   362
"Sandy Gibson's"   366
"Road to Richmond"   370
"Billy Patterson"   374
"Loozyanna Low Grounds"   379
"What O' Dat"   381
"Old K. Y. Ky."   385
"The Black Brigade"   390
"High Daddy"   395

C. *Miscellaneous*

" 'Twill Nebber Do to Gib It Up So"
    (score for an early minstrel band)   403
"Bressed Am Dem Dat 'Spects Nuttin' " (Negro sermon)   410
"Dey Hab a Camp Meetin" (Negro hymn)   413
"I See de Clouds a Risin" (Negro hymn)   414
Hard Times (Negro extravaganza)   415

PART II. A Selection from Minstrel Songs of the Forties
and from Banjo Tunes

"De Blue Tail Fly"   429
"Gwine to de Mill"   432
"Jim Along Josey"   435
"Jonny Boker"   439
"Juba"   443
"My Old Dad"   447
"Oh, Come Along John"   450
"Walk Along, John"   452
"Old Dan Tucker"   454
"Old Joe"   457
"The Ole Grey Goose"   461
"De Ole Jaw Bone"   464
"Ole Joe Golden"   467
"Ole Pee Dee"   469
"Ole Tare River"   471
"O Lud Gals Gib Me"   475
"Who's Dat Nigga Dar a Peepin?"   479
"Briggs' Breakdown"   483
"Bull upon the Battery—Jig"   483
"Dick Myers' Jig"   484
"Division Street Jig"   485
"Dr. Hekok Jig"   486
"Gantz's Jig"   487
"The Newton Jig"   488
"Peel's Jig"   489
"Rise Old Napper"   489
"Rock Susana"   490
"Sliding Jenny Jig"   490
"Van Bramer's Jig"   491

PART ONE

A Selection from Dan Emmett's Works

A. SONGS AND BANJO TUNES OF THE FORTIES AND FIFTIES

'Twill Nebber Do to Gib It Up So *(Boston, 1843)*

De old Jim riv - er   I   float down   I   run   my   bac - ker

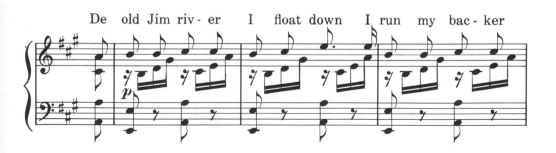

boat up - on   de   groun,   De   drift   log   come   wid   a

rush- in din An stove both ends ob de ole boat in. It will

neb - ber do to gib it up so! It will

neb - ber do to gib it up so! It will

neb- ber do to gib it up Old Mis - ter Brown, It will

314

neb - ber do to gib it up so!!

2   De old log rake me aft and fore.
     An leff my cook-house on de shore;
     I tho't it would'nt do to gib it up so,
     So I scull mysef ashore wid de ole banjo.
     It will nebber do . . . .

3   I lite on de sand an feel sorter glad,
     I looks at de banjo an feels bery mad;
     I walks up de bank dat slick as glass,
     Up went my heels an I lite upon de grass.
     It will nebber do . . . .

4   It will nebber do to gib it up so Mr. Brown,
     I jump up agin an stood upon de groun;
     I haul de boat out high an dry up de bank,
     Den float down de ribber wid de backer on a plank.
     It will nebber do . . . .

5   Nigger on de wood-pile barkin like a dog,
     Toad in de mill-pond sittin on a log,
     Possum up a gum tree, sarcy, fat an dirty;
     Come kiss me gals or I'll run like turky.
     It will nebber do . . . .

I'm Gwine ober de Mountains *(Boston, 1843)*

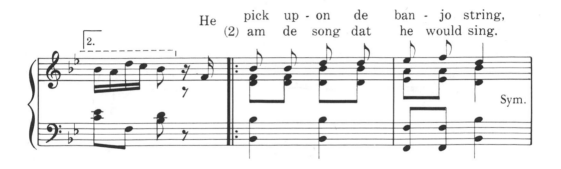

He pick up-on de ban - jo string,
(2) am de song dat he would sing.

Banjo and Bone Castanets

Reε - ro my true lub, O come a - long my

dar - lin, So fare you well, my Di - nah gal,

I'm gwine o - ber de moun - tains.

repeat from 𝄋

2   Come my lub an go wid me,
I'm gwine away to Tennessee;
A hoss an cart shall put you roun,
Walk up hill an foot it down.
Ree ro . . . .

3   One kind kiss before we part,
One more kiss would break my heart;
Hitch your hoss up to a rail,
Make him fast both head an tail.
Ree ro . . . .

4   I fed my hoss in a poplar trough,
De old hoss catch de hoopin cough,
I lick him wid a hick'ry stick
He paw de groun an begin to kick.
Ree ro . . . .

5   I hitch him to a swingin limb
De ole hoss cut a pidgeon-wing;
Den I rote de tanner a letter
I thought de hoss was gettin no better.
Ree ro . . . .

6   De tanner made me dis reply
"I want de hoss-hide when he die,"
De tanner he was well enuff,
De hoss-hide was ole an tuff.
Ree ro . . . .

7 De ole hoss die, I dig a hole,
  I cover him up both body an soul,
  De tanner come but soon he found,
  De hoss was too deep under ground.
  Ree ro . . . .

De Boatman's Dance

(Boston, 1843)

Chorus

High   row,   de

boat-men row, float-in down de ri - ver de   O - hi - o.

[1st time]

Moderato

[Solo] De boat-men dance, de boat-men sing, de boat-men up to

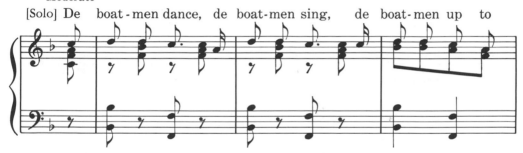

eb - ry ting, An when de boat men gets on shore, he

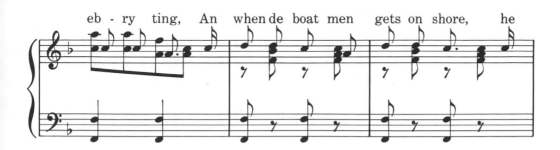

spends his cash an works for more, Den dance de boat-men

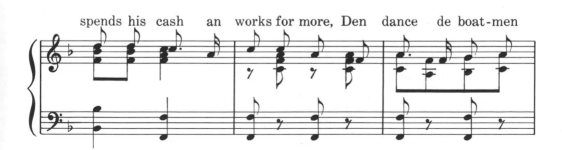

dance, O dance de boat - men dance, O

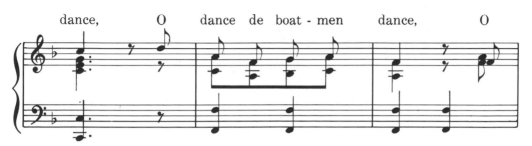

dance all night till broad day - light, an go

home wid de gals in de mor - ning.

2   De oyster boat should keep to de shore,
     De fishin smack should venture more,
     De schooner sails before de wind,
     De steamboat leaves a streak behind.
     O dance . . . .

3   I went on board de odder day
     To see what de boatmen had to say;
     Dar I let my passion loose
     An dey cram me in de callaboose.
     O dance . . . .

4   I've come dis time, I'll come no more,
     Let me loose I'll go on shore;
     For dey whole hoss, an dey a bully crew
     Wid a hoosier mate an a captin too.
     O dance . . . .

5   When you go to de boatmen's ball,
    Dance wid my wife, or dont dance at all;
    Sky blue jacket an tarpaulin hat,
    Look out my boys for de nine tail cat.
    O dance . . . .

6   De boatman is a thrifty man,
    Dars none can do as de boatman can;
    I neber see a putty gal in my life
    But dat she was a boatman's wife.
    O dance . . . .

7   When de boatman blows his horn,
    Look out old man your hog is gone;
    He cotch my sheep, he cotch my shoat,
    Den put em in a bag an toat em to de boat.
    O dance . . . .

Dandy Jim from Caroline   *(London, [c.1844])*

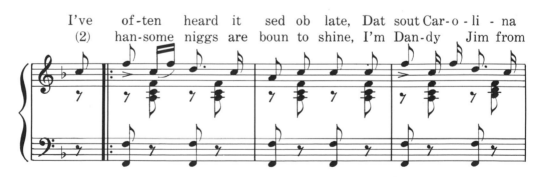

I've   of-ten   heard it   sed ob late, Dat sout Car-o-li - na
(2)   han-some niggs are boun to shine, I'm Dan-dy Jim from

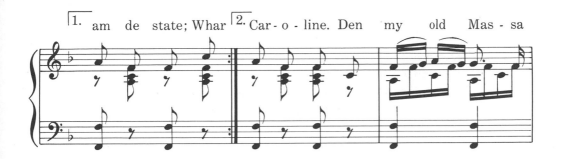
1. am de state; Whar 2. Car - o - line. Den my old Mas - sa

told me, O, I'm de best look - in nigg in de

coun - ty O; I look - ed in de glass an

foun it so Jis what mas - sa told me O.

repeat from 𝄋

2   Den beauty dat is but skin deep,
    But thro' my skin 'tis hard to peep;
    Dar's none can suit a brack gall's mine,
    Like Dandy Jim from Caroline.
    Den my old Massa . . . .

3   I dress myseff from top to toe,
    To see Miss Dinar I did goe;
    Wid trowselloon strap't down so fine,
    Went Dandy Jim from Caroline.
    My old Massa . . . .

4   De bull dog keep me out de yard,
    I tho't I'de better leff my card;
    I tied it fast wid a piece ob twine,
    Sign'd Dandy Jim from Caroline.
    My old Massa . . . .

5   She read my card den wrote me a letter,
    De more she wrote she felt de better;
    An ebery word in ebery line,
    Was—Dandy Jim from Caroline.
    My old Massa . . . .

6   To read her letter I begun,
    O, Moses! how de sweat did run;
    She went de hog wid a perfec swine,
    For Dandy Jim from Caroline.
    My old Massa . . . .

7   Sez she I lub you well enuff,
    Bekaze I noe you're up to snuff;
    Iff you'll be hers, she will be thine,
    Sweet Dandy Jim from Caroline.
    My old Massa . . . .

8   De hottest lub is soonest cold,
    De shortest story soonest told;

She change her name from lubly Dine,
To Miss Dandy Jim from Caroline.
My old Massa . . . .

9 Now ebery little nig she's had,
Is jis de image ob his dad;
His heel sticks out three feet behine,
Like Dandy Jim's from Caroline.
My old Massa . . . .

10 To church I went widout delay,
To christen dem all right away;
Dey christen all, 'sept eight or nine,
Young Dandy Jim's from Caroline.
My old Massa . . . .

Dar He Goes! Dats Him!

(Boston, 1844)

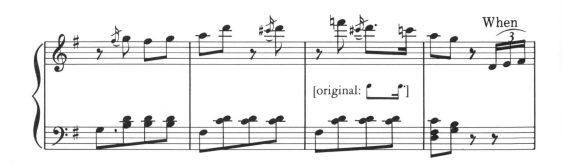

[original: ♪ ♩.]

When

first   I   come to   dis here place,   Dey   took   me   for   a

hard-end case, De   white folks sed when dey seen my face,   O

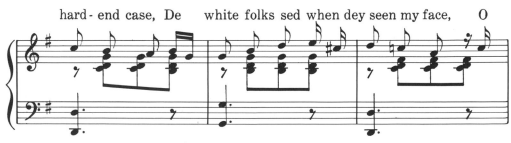

Dar he goes! O Dat's him! O Dar he goes! O

Dat's him! O Dar he goes! O

Dat's him! Dat's him plays De OLD BAN-JO.

2   Dey raise blinds when I pass by,
    An from behind dey peep so sly,
    It's den I heard de brack galls sigh,
    O Dar . . . .

3   Into de kitchen den I ran,
    An dodge behin de fryin pan,
    To sing dis song I den began,
    O Dar . . . .

4   De galls come in to hab some fun,
    De old man sez Fotch me de gun!
    My sweet heart holler'd as I run,
    O Dar . . . .

5   I run till I got out ob sight,
    Which did put me into a fright,
    De white folks yell wid all dar might,
    O Dar . . . .

6   I trabbled till de broke ob day,
    De Rasslejack begin to bray,
    An eb'ry word he seem to say,
    Was Dar he goes . . . .

Illustrations of songs of the Virginia Minstrels inspired by the gestures and grimaces of the troupe. The alligator recalls George W. Cable's statement, "Cocodrie...was the nickname for the unmixed black man" ("Creole Slave Songs," *The Century Magazine*, April, 1886). From the cover of *Old Dan Emmit's Original Banjo Melodies* (Boston, 1843).

Oh, Ladies All!

(*Boston, 1858*)[1]

[1] Published in Boston, 1858, but probably written in the forties.

332

Ah, ah!　　　my dear ho-ney!

2　Eighteen pounds in de corner ob de fence,
　　Lynchburg gals hant got no larning,
　　I danc'd all night wid Fanny on de fence,
　　Until I run my head against a post.
　　Oh . . . .

3　Wid Fanny B. I fell in lub.
　　But darn my skin she gib me de sack,
　　When Fanny me began to snub,
　　Dis nigger felt as tho' he'd been struck wid a hot tater.
　　Oh . . . .

4　My heart was broke, I like to died,
　　I stuck me head into a pint of water,
　　To drown myself it was my pride,
　　When Fan step'd up and ask'd me in to take a chowder
　　Oh . . . .

Hop Light, Loo[1]

1   My ole missus she's a widder,
Only waitin' for a bidder;
Him dat's lucky 'nuff to get her,
Takes her all for worse or better.
Hop light, Loo! de debbil's in de bee gum,
A-hoop, hop light, Loo!
Don't take it all, kase you must leabe me some.
I am Bo-num-bo.—who dar!

2   Missus on de hen-coop smokin',
Rain come down, she got a soakin'.
No one cares, I've money plenty,
Dressed to deff—her ole trunk empty.
Hop . . . .

3   Missus didn't look well dancin',
Kase her legs was most too slantin',
Wash dem well wid gin an' water,
Soon come straight, so says de doctor.
Hop . . . .

4   In idea pop in her head quicker,
What's de use of wasting licker;
Wid de gin I'll wet my throt'le,
Den I'll rub my leg wid de bottle.
Hop . . . .

---

[1] The lyrics are printed in *White's New Ethiopian Song Book* (Philadelphia, 1854), "Composed by Old Dan Emmett . . . ." The last three stanzas appear in "Old Dan Tucker" (London, D'Almaine & Co., n.d. [c.1844]). The tune is no longer extant.

Jordan Is a Hard Road to Travel *(Cincinnati, 1853)*

I just ar-rived in town For to pass de time a-

way   And   I   set - tled   all   my   bis' - ness   ac-

cor - din   But   I   found   it   so   cold   When   I

went   up   de   street   Dat   I   wish'd   I   was   on   de

o - der   side   ob   Jor - dan.   So   take   off   your coat boys, And roll up your sleeves, For Jor- dan is a

hard road to tra - bel So take off your

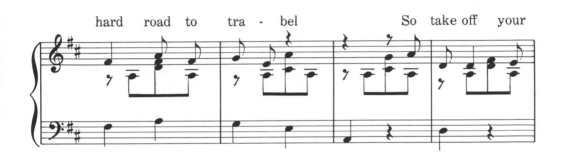

coat boys And roll up your sleeves, For Jor- dan is a

hard road to tra - bel I be - lieve.

2   I look to the East, I look to the West
    And I see ole Kossuth a comin
    With four bay horses hitch'd up in front,
    To tote his money to de oder side ob Jordan.
    So take off . . . .

3   David and Goliath both had a fight
    A cullud man come up behind 'em
    He hit Goliath on de head, wid a bar of soft soap
    And it sounded to de oder side o Jordan.
    So take off . . . .

338

4   If I was de legislator ob dese United States
    I'd settle de fish question accordin
    I'd give de British all de bones and de Yankees all de meat
    And stretch de boundary line to de oder side o Jordan.
    So take off . . . .

5   Der's been excitin times for de last month or two
    About de great Presidential election
    Frank Pierce got elected and sent a hasty plate ob soup
    To his opponent on de oder side ob Jordan.
    So take off . . . .

6   Louis Napoleon after all is emperor of France
    And all Europe begins to tremble accordin
    But the Yankees dont care for if with us he wants to fight
    He'll wish he'd staid on de oder side ob Jordan.
    So take off . . . .

Nigger on de Wood Pile

(Boston, 1845)

Moderato[1]

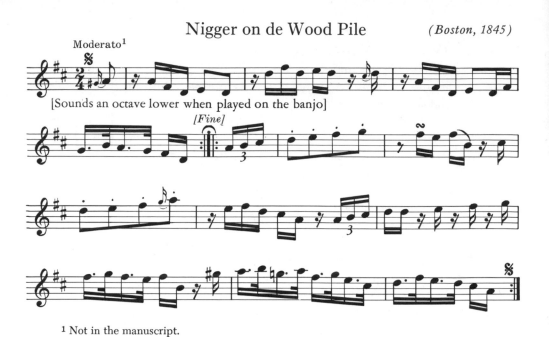

[Sounds an octave lower when played on the banjo]

[Fine]

[1] Not in the manuscript.

Moze Haymar Jig

(Boston, 1845)

Moderato[1]

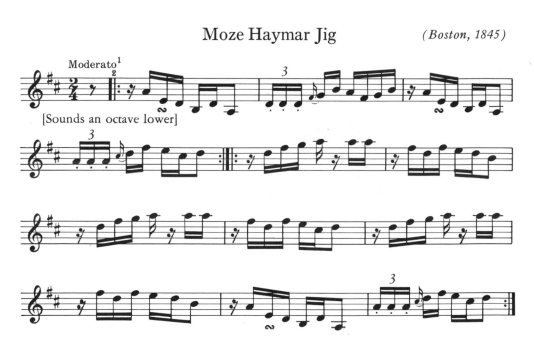

[Sounds an octave lower]

[1] Not in the manuscript.
[2] Repeat sign is from the manuscript.

Marty Inglehart Jig

(Boston, 1845)

[Sounds an octave lower]

[Fine]

1 Not in the manuscript.
2 Repeat sign is from the manuscript.

Peter Story Jig

(manuscript)

[Sounds an octave lower]

[Fine]

Peter Story[1]

1   Wake up, Jake, [banjo solo]
    Ole massa being sick, an' missy got de gripes—
    Wake up, Jake
    Go fotch ole Doctor Graggum,
    In come Peter Story, captain ob de patroller.
    Good bye, ole Peter Story, [banjo solo]
    Stone dead an' gone to glory, [banjo solo]
    Look out I'se dar before you. [banjo solo]

2   Black dog bite, [banjo solo]
    He cotch you by de heel-tap, an' bite you on de shinbone—
    Black dog bite,
    De white dog smell de lamp-post,
    He bark up de wrong tree, den back out an' said nuffin.
    Call de dog, I'm gwine a gunnin', [banjo solo]
    Katy cotch'd me I was runnin', [banjo solo]
    Lay low, de coon is comin'. [banjo solo]

3   Ole Massa Gabe, [banjo solo]
    Full-breasted in de back, an' shouldered Bunker's Hill,
    Ole Massa Gabe.
    What for you look so slemencholly,
    Go way nigger don't come nigh me, for I am de gassty Kutus.
    Take care, Uncle Gabriel, [banjo solo]
    Leab de matter on de table, [banjo solo]
    Put de nigger in de stable. [banjo solo]

4   Do little Liz, [banjo solo]
    De cold chills run down de back ob de chair,
    Do little Lizzy do.
    Slap on de linsy-woolsy,
    De colored gemmen ob de town am gettin' berry tickelar about you.
    Look out for little Lizzy, [banjo solo]
    By-an-by she like her missy, [banjo solo]
    Dat's all so come an' kiss me. [banjo solo]

[1] Philadelphia, 1854. The tune, which is no longer extant, was no doubt a variant of the "Peter Story Jig." The references to banjo interludes appear in two of Emmett's manuscripts.

Negro Jig

(Boston, 1845)

[Sounds an octave lower]

---

¹ Not in the manuscript.
² Repeat sign is from the manuscript.
³ Following the manuscript, the repeat sign, which appears only at this place, has been omitted.

Pea-Patch Jig

(Boston, 1845)

---

[1] Not in the manuscript.

Eelam Moore. Jig

(manuscript)[1]

[Sounds an octave lower]

[Fine]

¹ Written in the forties or early fifties.
² Originally a repeat sign is here, but none appears at the end of the section.

Elam Moore—Jig[1]

1   Ole Dandy Cox on de big hoss,
    Ole Dandy Cox on de big hoss,
    All three four shoes on one foot.
    All three four shoes on one foot.
    Ruffle shirt wid standin' collar,
    Fit so tight he couldn't swaller,
    All de time de nigger holler,

¹ Philadelphia, 1854. The tune, which is no longer extant, was no doubt a variant of "Eelam Moore. Jig."

Go way wid your pewter dollar,
Ah! ah! de google gollar.
Walk, Elam Moore,
Walk, Elam Moore,
Walk, Elam Moore, an I'll be your friend,
Got long ways to go, an' I hasn't got a red cent.

2   Sheep meat is too good for niggers,
Sheep meat is too good for niggers,
Hog meat I gets a plenty.
Hog meat I gets a plenty.
Ole massa kill de barrow,
Crack de bones—git de marrow,
Gib de nigger tail an' bristle,
Good to make de nigger whistle,
High up upon de tribble.
Walk . . . .

3   Who likes gravy on dar taters,
Who likes gravy on dar taters,
Say dem greasy words ober agin,
Say dem greasy words ober agin,
Ole Guinea nigger glutton,
Eat a whole leg ob mutton,
Eye shine like pewter button,
Gwin de hog neck or nottin,
Nebber stop to pay de footin.
Walk . . . .

4   Ole hen flew ober de garden,
Ole hen flew ober de garden,
Tail too short for to fly high,
Tail too short for to fly high.
Set sick a week a hatchin',
Wasn't dat a half a patchin',
Little chicken 'gin to fedder,
All three both togedder,
Like a piece ob upper leadder.
Walk . . . .

346

Root Hog or Die. Jig

(manuscript)[1]

[Sounds an octave lower]

[Fine]

[1] Written in the forties or early fifties.

My First Jig

(manuscript)[1]

[Sounds an octave lower]

[1] Probably written in the forties.
[2] Like a short baroque trill from above (four notes); see Emmett's *Fife Instructor*, 21.

PART ONE

A Selection from Dan Emmett's Works

B. WALK-AROUNDS

I'm Going Home to Dixie (New York, 1861)[1]

[1] Tune composed in 1858.

tar-ry,   I've   got no time to   stay.   'Tis a

rock- y   road   to   trav- el,   to Dix-ie   far a-

1. way.   I've   2. way.   Symphony

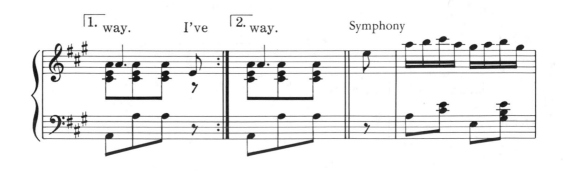

2 I will climb up the highest hill,
  And sing your praise with right good will
  I'm going home . . . .

3 I've wander'd far both to and fro'
  But Dixie's heaven here below
  I'm going home . . . .

4 O list to what I've got to say
  Freedom to me will never pay!
  I'm going home . . . .

5 A shadow and a phantom frail,
  The mighty truth it must prevail!
  I'm going home . . . .

6 In Dixie Land the fields do bloom
  And color'd men have welcome room
  I'm going home . . . .

7 I will proclaim it loud and long
  I love old Dixie right or wrong
  I'm going home . . . .

I Ain't Got Time to Tarry[1]

1   I put dat sheep skin in de ground,
    I buried so deep it couldn't be found;
    For I'se gwine home to Dinah,
    Yes, I am gwine home.
    Den I ain't got time to tarry, I ain't got time to dwell,
    I'm bound to de land of freedom, oh, niggars! fare you well.

2   Oh! come down-stairs and took some wine,
    Open de windows, say you're mine;
    For . . . .

3   Not for a day, nor two or three,
    But so long as we can agree;
    For . . . .

4   I'm nine feet ten, an' tall an' straight,
    De best man in dis 'nited State,
    For . . . .

5   De nicest gall dats in dis town,
    She wears a new shin-plaster gown;
    For . . . .

6   Come out my lub, come out to me,
    I'll leff dis world an' clime a tree;
    For . . . .

[1] Sung to the tune of "I'm Going Home to Dixie" (New York, 1859).

Jonny Roach

(manuscript, 1859)[1]

[1] Arranged by Hans Nathan.
[2] In all walk-arounds, the introduction is played at the beginning only.

must - 'nt wear y'er gal - lus - ses a - cross - ways

Chorus

Den I does - 'nt know de nig - gar dat can beat us,

work all day,

1. work for de pay, an I dun for my dol - lar an a

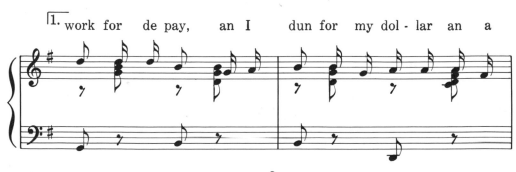

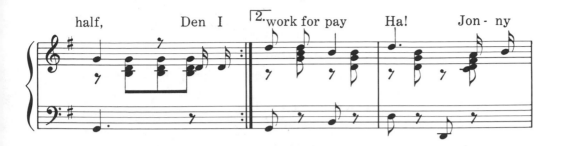

half,   Den I [2.] work for pay   Ha!   Jon - ny

Roach.   Dance   [1.]

[2.]   [2.] [for last stanza]

2   Jonny fell in a tanners vat,
    He look jis like a drown-ded rat;
    Dey pulled him out an alter'd man,
    He turn'd from brack to de color ob tan.
    Den . . . .

3   Den John jump up an crack his heel,
    He dance about like a half skin'd eel;

357

He open'd his mouth like my old hat,
Say white folks what y'e tink ob dat.
Den . . . .

4   Jonny sailed from Kalamazoo,
De Michiganders put him thro';
He raked de bottom ob de lake,
His heel stick out like a young earthquake.
Den . . . .

5   To Canada old John was bound,
All by de rail-road under ground;
He's got no clothes—he's got no tin,
He wishes he was back agin.
Den . . . .

6   Gib me de place called Dixie Land,
Wid hoe an shubble in my hand;
Whar fiddles ring an banjos play,
I'de dance all night an work all day.
Den . . . .

Dixie's Land

(manuscript, 1859)

Song [Solo]

I wish I was in de land ob cot-ton, Cim-mon seed an san-dy bot-tom, Look a-way look 'way, a-way, Dix-ie Land,

Song

In Dix-ie land whar I was born in, Ear-ly on one fros-ty mor-nin, Look a-way look 'way, a-way Dix-ie Land,

Song

Den I wish I was in Dix-ie, Hoo-ray, Hoo-ray, In Dix-ie's land, we'll took our stand, To lib an die in Dix-ie, a-way, a-way, a-way down south in

Dix - ie,   a - way,   a - way,   a - way down south in   Dix - ie.

[for last stanza]

2   Old missus marry Will de Weaber,
      William was a gay deceaber;
      Look away . . .
      When he put his arm around'er,
      He look as fierce as a forty pound'er.
      Look away . . . .

3   His face was sharp like a butchers cleaber,
      But dat did not seem to greab 'er;
      Look away . . .
      Will run away missus took a decline, O'
      Her face was de color ob bacon rhine, O'
      Look away . . . .

4   While missus libbed she libbed in clover,
      When she died she died all ober;
      Look away . . .
      How could she act such a foolish part, O'
      An marry a man to break her heart, O'
      Look away . . . .

5   Buck-wheat cakes an stony batter,
      Makes you fat or a little fatter;
      Look away . . .
      Here's a health to de next old missus,

An all de galls dat wants to kiss us.
Look away . . . .

6   Now if you want to drive 'way sorrow,
Come an hear dis song to-morrow;
Look away . . .
Den hoe it down an scratch y'er grabble,
To Dixies land I'm bound to trabble
Look away . . . .

I Wish I Was in Dixie's Land   *(New York, 1860)*[1]

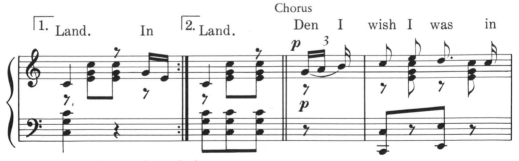

[1] First authorized edition.

Dix - ie, Hoo - ray! Hoo - ray! In Dix - ie Land, I'll

took my stand, To lib an die in Dix - ie, A -

way, A - way, A -way down south in Dix - ie, A -

way, A - way, A - way down south in Dix - ie.

Fine

2 Old Missus marry "Will-de-weaber,"
   Willium was a gay deceaber;
   Look away . . .
   But when he put his arm around'er,
   He smilled [*sic*] as fierce as a forty-pound'er.
   Look away . . . .

3 His face was sharp as a butchers cleaber,
   But dat did not seem to greab'er;
   Look away . . .
   Old Missus acted de foolish part,
   And died for a man dat broke her heart.
   Look away . . . .

4 Now here's a health to the next old Missus,
   An all de galls dat want to kiss us;
   Look away . . .
   But if you want to drive 'way sorrow,
   Come an hear dis song to-morrow.
   Look away . . . .

364

5   Dar's buck-wheat cakes an 'Ingen' batter,
    Makes you fat or a little fatter;
    Look away . . .
    Den hoe it down an scratch your grabble,
    To Dixie land I'm bound to trabble.
    Look away . . . .

Sandy Gibson's[1]   *(manuscript, 1859)*[2]

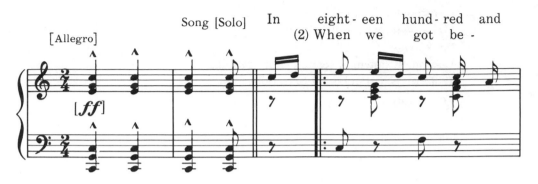

Song [Solo] In eight-een hund-red and
(2) When we got be-

for-ty-four,   Chorus   Oh,   hur-ry up,   Song We
yond the reef,   Oh,   hur-ry up,   (2)The

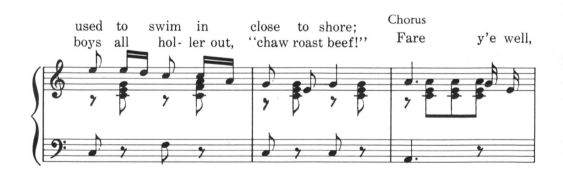

used to swim in close to shore;   Chorus Fare y'e well,
boys all hol-ler out, "chaw roast beef!"   Fare y'e well,

[1] The complete text appears in *Bryant's Power of Music* (New York, 1859), in which the words "chaw roast beef!" appear in the refrain after "day" and "away," respectively. However, there is no room for them in the extant manuscript version of the song. Since the melody of the instrumental ending is identical to that of the dance in "Road to Richmond," the latter's accompaniment has been borrowed.

[2] Arranged by Hans Nathan.

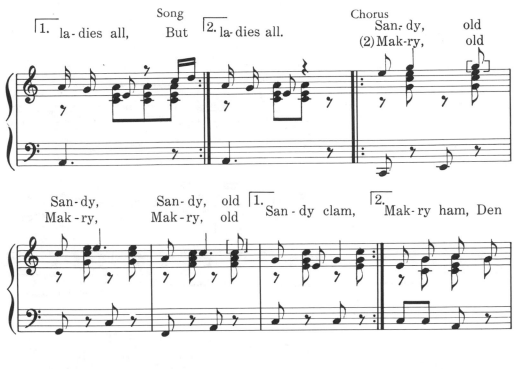

Song   Chorus

1. la-dies all,   But   2. la-dies all.

San-dy,   old
(2) Mak-ry,   old

San-dy,   San-dy, old 1. San-dy clam,   2. Mak-ry ham, Den
Mak-ry,   Mak-ry, old

jis be-fore de broke ob day, Dem boys dey stole our

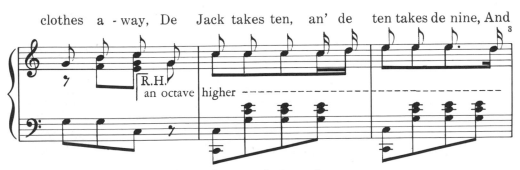

clothes a-way, De Jack takes ten, an' de ten takes de nine, And

R.H. an octave higher -------------------------

³ Alternate version: the two last notes, high *g* and *e*.

367

we "chaw roast beef" for de rail - road line.

2 I dressed myself both neat an' trim,
   Oh . . .
   Den off to Gibson's to took a swim;
   Fare y'e well . . .
   De shark he cotch me in his teef,
   Oh . . .
   But found it tough to "chaw roast beef."
   Fare y'e well . . . .

3 He bite an' bite till he drawed de blood,
   Oh . . .

He took me for an eel in de mud;
Fare y'e well . . .
Old Sandy come to my relief,
Oh . . .
We had no time to "chaw roast beef."
Fare y'e well . . . .

4 Den Sandy Gibson make some punch,
   Oh . . .
   Bekaze he know I'm death on lunch;
   Fare y'e well . . .
   I den sail'd in to make it brief,
   Oh . . .
   I've nebber since dat "chawed roast beef."
   Fare y'e well . . . .

5 Now "water soak" am berry good,
   Oh . . .
   If baked in de stove or boil'd wid wood;
   Fare y'e well . . .
   But de best ob all to my belief,
   Oh . . .
   Is Sandy Gibson's "chaw roast beef."
   Fare y'e well . . . .

Road to Richmond[1]

(New York, 1864)

[1] Almost identical in tune and text to "Road to Georgia" of 1859.

hail! All hail! for we are un-der way.

Chorus
Un - der way, un - der way, Yah! we be-long to de
(2) way, un - der way, 'Ho! we are on de

Un - ion Ar - my. Say! did y'e
road to Rich - mond, Say! did y'e

say: we leab old Belch-er
say: we'll "doo" old Jeff up 1. town? Un - der 2. brown!

2   De trader rode upon a mule.
      Labor . . .
      The "hog-eye" kept his temper cool;
      Ten . . .
      He gib de word to go ahead!
      Labor . . .
      Den crack his whip an say "nuff sed."
      All . . . .

3   Up de hill an down de dale,
      Labor . . .
      We followed up de Union trail
      Ten . . .
      No time to rest nor time to stop,
      Labor . . .
      One foot raise den tudder drop.
      All . . . .

4   When night come on we pitch our tent,
      Labor . . .

Den sing dis song an "let 'er went";
Ten . . .
We all got hot: de door keep shet,
Labor . . .
Which put de trader in a sweat.
All . . . .

5 We stirred him up—'twas wid a pole,
Labor . . .
For fear dat he might cotch a cole;
Ten . . .
When he come too—Jee-hossey-fat!
Labor . . .
Didn't we cotch de nine tail'd catt.
All . . . .

6 Now from dat time we mind our eye,
Labor . . .
De trader blow us up sky high!
Ten . . .
But when we get to Richmond town,
Labor . . .
We'll fotch a thousand dollars down.
All . . . .

Billy Patterson

(*New York, 1860*)

Allegro

Song [Solo]

Dar was an old nigg dat got

hit wid a brick,   Oh!   Bil - ly Pat -ter- son,   He

Chorus

Song

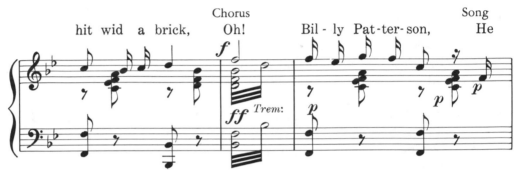

was'nt knock'd down kaze his   head   too   thick;   Don't y'e

Chorus

tell   me,   Don't y'e tell   me.   De first word he said when he

Song

was come too,

Chorus
Oh!   Bil - ly Pat - ter - son,   Song
"O,

don't hit a - gin for   dat will doo!" Don't y'e tell me, Don't y'e

Chorus

tell me.   Bill Pat - ter - son   rode bye,   Old

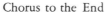

Chorus to the End

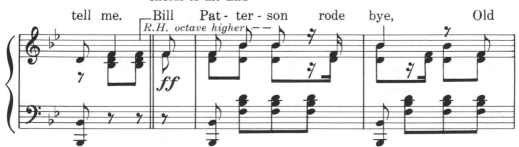

Bill your horse will die,   "He dies—I'll tan his

skin;   He lives--I'll ride a   gin!''   Old I'll

Melody
gib ten dol - lars down,   an leab dem in my

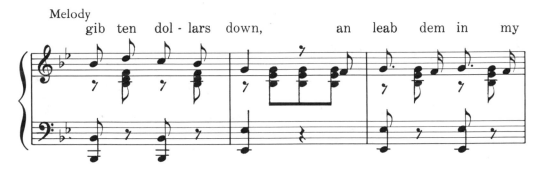

will,   If an - y   one can show   de man dat

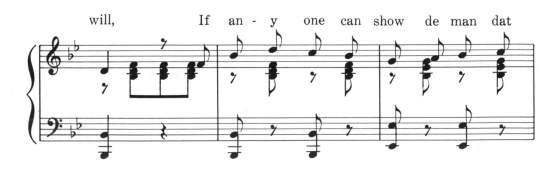

eb - ber struck old Bill.

ff

376

2   I eat up de goose dat rais'd de quill,
     Dat wrote de question: "Who struck Bill?"
     I work'd at de kiln whar de brick was burnt,
     But who throw'd de brick was nebber learn't.
     Bill Patterson . . . .

3   I knows ob a chap dat's up to de fun,
     He knows who struck Bill Patterson;
     But take my word he will nebber tell,
     Unless somebody pays him well.
     Bill Patterson . . . .

4   Dar's one ting sartin an plain for to see,
     'Twas neider "Sayres" [Sayers] nor "Morrisey";
     Dey both told me (or I is a liar),
     'Twas eider "Heenan" or "Old Tom Hyer."
     Bill Patterson . . . .

5   Money in de pocket shines so bright,
     Old Bill got struck on Saturday night;
     De lightnin flash—he seen de 'seben stars!
     He tink he was struck wid de bullgine cars!
     Bill Patterson . . . .

6　If ebber you get to de "Fiddler's Green,"
　　A labelled niggar can be seen,
　　Wid a sign on his back dat weighs a ton,
　　"I'm de darkie struck Bill Patterson!"
　　Bill Patterson . . . .

Loozyanna Low Grounds *(manuscript, 1859)*

Dar is a place call'd Loo-zy-ann,
(2) nig-gars fat an sas-sy grow,

ah, my love, I'm gwine a-way,
(2) In de Loo-zy-an-na

col-ord man,
low-grounds low, I'm bound to de Loo-zy-ann, Whar

Loo-zy-ann. Loo-zy-ann, Loo-zy-ann, whar de

cane brakes grow and de cot-ton blos-som,
(2) rac-coons howl at de roar ob de pos-sum, Ann, Loo-zy-

ann, I wish I was down dar now; Loo-zy-ann, Loo-zy-

an-na, low grounds, low.

379

2 I drove a hoss when I was young,
  Across his neck de reins I flung;
  Dar's hosses fast, and hosses slow,
  In Loozyanna low grounds, low.
  Loozyann . . . .

3 Now my old missus hab two "sins"
  One was a boy—de udder was twins;
  She call'd one Pete—de udder one Joe,
  From Loozyanna low grounds, low.
  Loozyann . . . .

4 Gin'ral Jackson fought a fight,
  Below New Orleans—out ob sight;
  He was de boy to face de foe,
  On Loozyanna low grounds, low.
  Loozyann . . . .

5 Dar's dat old war hoss—Gin'ral Scott,
  Dey sent him to de 'sputed spot;
  When he got dar he let dem know,
  He's from Loozyanna low grounds, low.
  Loozyann . . . .

6 If I could hab my choice to day,
  O places in dis world to stay;
  Ide pack my "kitt" an off I'de go,
  To Loozyanna low grounds, low.
  Loozyann . . . .

What O' Dat[1]

(manuscript, 1859)

Song [Solo]

Old Pom - pey cotch a

crow, An den he let 'im go, He

pick 'im clean, As a cas - tor bean, What o' dat?

Chorus
Whar, whar's old Pom - pey gone.

[1] Arranged by Hans Nathan.

Chorus

Ah, ah!   ah, ah!

[*sf*]   [*sf*]

Walk   in   Joe,   raise   up   de   door   latch,
(2) Stop   dat   noise,   stop   dat   rack - et,

Dont   stan   dar   out   in   de   pea   patch,
Mas - sa   come, He'll   warm   your   jack - et.

[for repeat]

repeat from 𝄋 (section "Ah.."
with repeat); then Dance.

Dance

f   *[for repeat]*

3
[for last stanza]

382

2   Old Pompey cotch a cold,
       'Twas berry hard to hold;
       He took a spree,
       On bone-set tea,
       What o' dat?

       Chorus

3   His head begin to swell,
       De size no one can tell;
       He sold de wool,
       By de bushel full,
       What o' dat?

       Chorus

4   He's on his journey home,
       He rode de old bey roan;
       Get up—gee whoa!
       An away we go,
       What o' dat?

       Chorus

5   He met Melehazedick,
       An told him he was sick;
       Den beat his hoss,
       Till he gib him goss,
       What o' dat!

       Chorus

6   But now ole Pompey's dead,
    Wid de wool all off his head;
    His ghost come back,
    By de rail road track,
    What o' dat?

    Chorus

7   His ghost it plays and sings,
    De "harp ob a thousand strings";
    An beats de gong,
    While I sing dis song,
    What o' dat?

    Chorus

Old K. Y. Ky.

(New York, 1860)

Solo

De snow am in de

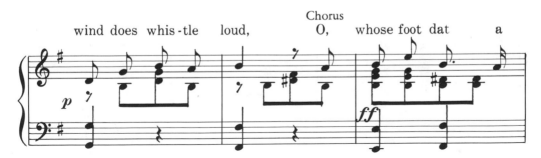

cloud,   Chorus   O,   whose foot dat   a   burn-in?   Solo   De

wind does whis-tle   loud,   Chorus   O,   whose foot dat   a

burn-in?   Solo   We'll 'round de   fire   crowd.   Chorus   O,

whose foot dat a burn-in? Dat foot did come, it

told me so: A - way from old K. Y. Ky.

Chorus to the End

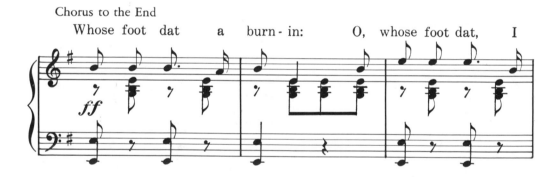

Whose foot dat a burn- in: O, whose foot dat, I

say! O, whose foot dat a - burn- in: O,

take dat foot a - way. O, whose foot dat a

burn-in: O, whose foot dat I say! Dat

foot did come, (it told me so.) A - way from old K. Y. Ky.

[Dance]

2　O course I took my seat,
　　O, whose foot . . .
　　An den stuck out my feet;
　　O, whose foot . . .
　　To cotch in all de heat.
　　Whose foot . . . .

3　De fire got too hot,
　　O, whose foot . . .
　　While fore it I did sot;
　　O, whose foot . . .
　　I fast asleep did got.
　　Whose foot . . . .

4　De shoe begin to pinch,
　　O, whose foot . . .
　　Dis darkie nebber flinch;
　　O, whose foot . . .
　　I could'nt move an inch.
　　Whose foot . . . .

5   Somebody's foot must roast,
      O, whose foot . . .
      Some foot as hot as toast;
      O, whose foot . . .
      It crack like hickory post.
      Whose foot . . . .

6   De hide begin to peel,
      O, whose foot . . .
      'Tis mine! I 'gin to feel,
      O, whose foot . . .
      De fire! at my heel!
      Whose foot . . . .

The Black Brigade

(New York, 1863)

Song [Solo]

390

Un - ion, Ah, ah, ah, ah! de

boys from Link - um Land. Grand Chorus Den har - ness up de

mule, Be care - ful how ye whip, An'

mind your eye, Sam John - son am de

[lower notes: alternate version]

nig - ga Gin'- ral, We're de Brack Bri - gade, Why

don't ye let her rip? Jeemeses

[altern. v.]

Rib - ber Mas - sa Gree - ly, O!

Dance

ff

2   We am de snolly-gosters,
        Gwine . . .
    We am de snolly-gosters,
        Hyro! . . .
    An' lubs Jim Ribber oysters.
        Gwine . . . .

3   We're gwine to fight de South, O,
        Gwine . . .
    We're gwine to fight de South, O,
        Hyro! . . .
    All by de 'word ob mouth,' O.
        Gwine . . . .

4   To fight for death an' glory,
        Gwine . . .
    To fight for death an' glory,
        Hyro! . . .
    Am quite annudder story.
        Gwine . . . .

5   Old John Brown dey strung 'im,
Gwine . . .
Old John Brown dey strung 'im,
Hyro! . . .
As high as Haman hung 'im.
Gwine . . . .

6   I'll take my boat an' paddle,
Gwine . . .
I'll take my boat an' paddle,
Hyro! . . .
For freedom will skydaddle.
Gwine . . . .

High Daddy

(New York, 1863)

Song [Solo]

The sun's gone down to take a litle sleep,

Chorus

I met High Dad-dy in the

Song

morn - ing; The moon's come out to take an-o-ther peep,

Chorus

I met High Dad-dy and I

wont go home a - ny more, a - ny more; Then

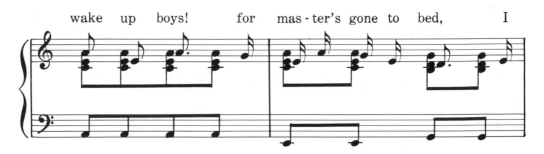

wake up boys! for mas - ter's gone to bed, I

met High Dad - dy in the morn - ing; We'll

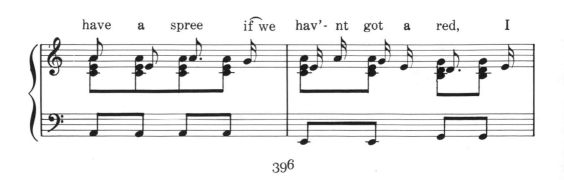

have a spree if we hav' - nt got a red, I

met High Dad - dy and I wont go home a - ny

more, a - ny more! Then dar - ky, ne - ver

Chorus

die, Black face and chi - na eye; Go

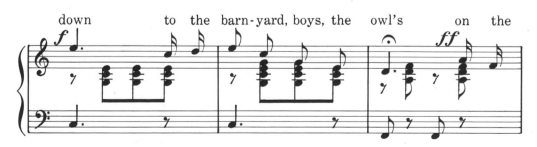

down to the barn - yard, boys, the owl's on the

roos', High Dad-dy wont come nigh, He's

chok'd on chick-en pie; 'Tis all "O

K," I say and right up-on the goose.

Dance

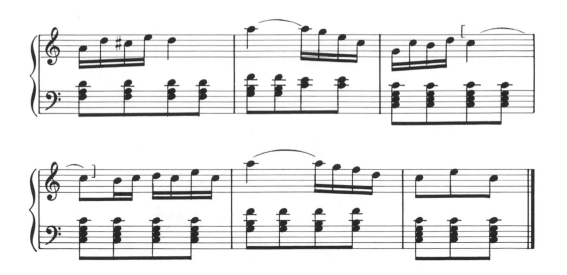

2 I know a darkie and his name it was Joe,
  I met . . .
  I know it was, for he once told me so;
  I met . . .
  He used to hoe and dig up all the land,
  I met . . .
  But now he says that work is contraband.
  I met . . . .

3 He drank skimm'd milk from morn 'till night,
  I met . . .
  Sombody said that it would make him white;
  I met . . .
  But let him drink untill he gets his fill,
  I met . . .
  He's always bound to be a darkie still!
  I met . . . .

4 His color will stick, but that's not a sin,
  I met . . .
  To wash it off, you're compell'd to rub it in;
  I met . . .

For darkie will be darkie as I've said before,
I met . . .
To the end of the world, and for two days more!
I met . . . .

5 The black man is a very curious thing,
I met . . .
His jay-bird heel can shuffle cut and wing;
I met . . .
But fill him up with gin and lay him in the shade,
I met . . .
He'll work very well, especially if he's made!
I met . . . .

PART ONE

A Selection from Dan Emmett's Works

C. MISCELLANEOUS

'TWILL NEBBER DO TO GIB IT UP SO
A Score for an Early Minstrel Band

THIS SCORE IS AN OUTLINE of an ensemble version of Emmett's song
" 'Twill Nebber Do to Gib It up So" that approximates the manner
of performance of minstrel bands in the early forties. The score is
based on the sheet music edition of the song, published by the composer in 1843.

The fiddle part follows the melody of the arrangement. The banjo
part has been reconstructed in the style of accompaniments as published in banjo methods, such as *Phil. Rice's Correct Method for the
Banjo* (Boston, 1858). Measures nine through fourteen have been
borrowed from a version of the tune in Frank B. Converse, *Banjo
Instructor* (New York, 1865). Both books represent an earlier practice.

Contrary to the sheet music arrangement, which was simplified
for popular usage, groups consisting of two notes of equal duration
have been intensified to ♩♫.♫ or ♩♫. The first pattern, as well as
the syncopated one in measure fifteen of the fiddle part, appearing also
in the sheet music edition, are typical of minstrel banjo pieces. The
second pattern was well known to the slaves (see William Francis
Allen, *et al.*, *Slave Songs of the United States* [New York, 1867]) and
was also utilized on the minstrel stage. The parts of the tambourine
and the bones are mere skeletons; they allow any number of shakes
and syncopations, though mainly those resulting from the omission
of accentuated beats as exemplified by banjo jigs. Finally, the banjoist
should tap his foot to the music—four times within a measure.

403

'Twill Nebber Do to Gib It Up So[1]

[1] Arranged by Hans Nathan.

404

405

boat up-on de groun. De drift log come wid a rush-in din An stove both ends ob de ole boat in.

neb-ber do to gib it up Old Mis-ter Brown, It will

neb - ber do to gib it up so!²

² For additional stanzas, see page 315.

Bressed Am Dem Dat 'Spects Nuttin', Kaze Dey Aint a Gwine to Git Nuttin'!

A *Negro Sermon*
(New York, 1873)

BREDREN AN' SISTAHS—I'm gwine to preach, I is: an' spose dis am de fust time, tho' I come berry nigh it once 'afoa when I swept out de chuch. I'ze gwine to 'splain de troof to de nebberlastin' bressin' ob yoa poar souls. I doesn't mean de soles on yoa foot, de soles ob yoa boots, nor de corns on yoa heels; but, as de pote sez, "de soul dat lies widin de sarkumdicklar ob de human frame." Fust ob all, I'm a rale true beleaber; dat is to say, I lubs de wimmin an' hate snakes; an' I can't let dis 'casion slip widout spreadin myseff 'fore you like a coon-skin on de gable end ob a barn; an' if I was a big bladder blowed full of wind an' stretched wid a blacksmiff's bellus, I couldn't feel puffed up wid pride any moa dan I now duz to see myseff confruntin' so much speckability.

Bredren, de text am foun' in de inside ob Job, whar Paul draw'd him pistol on 'Feesians, lebenteenth chapter, an' no 'ticklar verse: *"Bressed am dem, dat 'spects nuttin', kase dey aint a gwine to git nuttin'!"* Dem's em!

Long time ago, my frens, 'foar de seben stars sung togedder an' all de niggas shouted for joy, dar was commoshum in de arr, an' white men was seen marchin' wid knap-sacks on, and dey wore white garmants made ob sack-cloff an' ashes, an' dar har was straight, same like a billy goat's; an' dar was an alumblaster face so brack, an' a hole head an' shoulders higher dan de udders, an' in him hann a lighted taller candle, lookin' for daylight, an' him head was jis like a brack 'rino sheep, an' he smile like a hoss-collar lined wid red 'rocker, an' he open he mouph like a clam-pot, sayin': "Hearr ye! hearr ye! de white man's a buckgoat; de niggar am de sheep! kase de whites ha straight harr an' de niggars wearr wool! den wharfoa culled man call 'im a ram. Hallylooyar to sheep, an' free cheers for de wool!"

My brudders, de firs time I got 'liggion it was down in ole War-ginny, whar I 'longed to de church foa weeks, an' bress de lam I habn't back'd out yet. It war jis afoa de chickens crow for daybreak; I war toatin' a tick ob wood to cook ole massa's breckfuss, an' I hear a loud voice sayin', Stebin Guess, drap dat tick ob wood an' don't wear yoa galluses crossways!" I run for de house so fass 'twould make yoa head swim to look at me! You'd dream about divin' for a hole munph arterwards. I takes down de banjo an I 'gins to play: but's no use— I felt no better fass: I gets down "old Uncle Tom" an I reads de fust chapter to "Topsy in Hebben," an when I kum to de verse dat says: "I 'speck I growed," my sins 'gin to flow like de seeds of de squash. Warfoa, bredren, *"Bressed am dem dat 'spects nuttin, kaze dey aint a gwine to git nuttin!"*

Bredren: You all noes Judge Hawkins (an a mighty nice man he am); he goes to de market, an axes de butcher: "How much for dat mutton?" He pays de price an toats it home; he nebber axes whedder it was a brack or a white sheep; all he wanted was good mutton—jes so wid our Marster. A soul comes along, an if it am good, he don't ax: "Whar did ye kum frum?" he don't carr whedder de body war brack or white, nor whedder he head war kiverd wid wool or wid harr; all he wants am a clean soul, same as de judge wanted good mutton; den oo'oh! come along wid me an ride on de same carrs wid de white folks. Sin, my frens, am a compack, same like a niggar an he massa gwine snucks: de niggar hoes all de corn an gits all de lickins, an he massa sells de corn an keeps all de proffits. It am jis so wid de debble an de sinner: de sinner steals all de chickens an does all de swearin, but de debble gets de soul an den roasts him in de bargain. Den *"Bressed am dem dat 'spects nuttin, kaze dey aint a gwine to git nuttin."*

Agin: We am told dat Adam was de firs man an Ebe was de tudder; dey was boaf brack men, an so was Cain an Abel. Dar am a mistake in de printer, for some udder man made ole Missus Adam, an set her up agin de barn to dry; an now, my frens, who built dat barn? (Ha! ha! ha!). Bredren, de debble am now in Baltimoa—he ha a notion ob comin to Fillamadelfy—now he on de carrs—now he in Jarsy City —now he in New Yawk—he in hear! dat's him—dat dar white man settin in de corner laffin!

Once again: Who talks soft sodder an gibs de wimmin allama-goosalem? Who makes de chickens leab darr roos, an hide under de barn when dey see dem comein? Who eats you out ob house an home an gibs you no tanks for it, but comes foolin roun yoa wife and darters when yoa back am turned? Now, who does all dis, an moa too? It aint de culled preacher-man, not by a gourd full! Who am it den? It am de straight harr'd fraternity, but bress de lam, I done stick fass to my integrity, an no culled gall can make a secon Joseph ob dis child. *You hear me!* Den *"Bressed am dem dat 'spects nuttin, kaze dey aint a gwine to git nuttin!"*

Now, we'be got to lassly: I sees a great many heah dis ebenin dat cares no moa what 'comes ob darr souls dan I does myseff. Suppose, 'frinstance, dat yoa eat yoa full ob possam fat an hominy; you go to bed, an in de mornin you woke up an find youseff dead! Whar you speck yoa gwine to? You keep gwine down, down, down, till de bottam falls out! What 'comes ob ye den? You see de debble comein down de hill on a rasslejack, wid a ear like a backer leaf an a tail like a corn-stalk; out ob he mouff comes pitchforks an lightnin, an him tail smoke like a tar kill! Whar is you now? No time for 'pentin; de debble kotch ye, shoa! but bress de lam, he han't kotch dis child yet! What's gwine to come ob ye on de great gittin-up-day? Maby yoa tink you hold on to my coat-tail; but I'm gwine to fool yoa bad on dat 'casion, kaze I'm gwine to wear my coon-skin jacket! Yoa crawl up de hill on yoa hans an nees, you fall down agin, wallup! den yoa's call'd a backslider. Dar's de brimstone, de grindstone, de millstone, de blue stone, an eb'ry udder kind o' stone de debble's got to tie 'roun yoa neck, to sink ye in de nebberlastin gulf ob bottomless ruin. Yoa call for a cup ob cold water an de debble say: "No! I sees yoa d—n fust!" Den yoa weep an wail an smash out yoa teef out. Den wake up, sinners, an let de daybroke in on ye!

My frens, I neider preach for de lub ob de lam, de good ob yoa souls, nor de fear ob de debble; but, if you got any ole shoe, ole coat, ole hat, jis pass em roun dis way, an I'll light upon 'em like a raccoon upon a green cornstalk. It's no use passin roun de plate, for *"Bressed am dem dat 'spects nuttin, kaze dey aint a gwine to git nuttin!"*

412

Dey Hab a Camp Meetin
A Negro Hymn

Dey hab a camp meetin down in de swamp—
De night was so dark dat dey burned de lamp;
Dey preach so long and dey preach so loud,
De alligator come an he skeered de crowd.

Chorus   I'm moanin an a groanin—dars shoutin round about,
            Hallymaloojar to de lamb! we've cleaned de debble out.

When I prays—I prays wid all my might,
When I squeeze, I squeezes berry tight;
For de papers say as I've heard tell
Whateber ye duz—you must duz it well!

Chorus . . .

[De bred]ren shout while de sisters sing.
[To praise de] lamb dis am de berry ting;
[Let's do it] louder for its my belief
[I'm gittin] old, an a gittin little deaf.

Chorus . . .

I See de Clouds a Risin
A Negro Hymn

I see de clouds a risin, de storm am comin [roun']
Hear de sinners moanin, dar fightin for de crown
Dey'l win de crown ob glory an wear it on dar head
Stan back satan! clar de track! I'll wear it foa I'm dead.

Chorus   But I aint gone yet—no—no!
            Yet a little while to tarry;
            My troubles here below
            Am a heaby load to carry.

When I'm dead an gone for shoa—de debble miss me moas
I'm chock full ob religion—and de shoutin make me hoa[s]
Gib me wings ob de buzzard—gib me wings ob de g[oose]
Brudders dont you hoal me—some niggar cut me loose!

Chorus . . .

I look 'way up to glory—I see sum curious tings,
I hear de angels flying by de russling o dar [wings]
Lawd bress fader Abramham, he was [a nice] ole Jew.
Bress Isaac an bress Jacob—dey [was] one too.

Chorus . . .

HARD TIMES
A Negro Extravaganza

"Mounted and Arranged by Charles White."
Published by Robert M. De Witt (New York, 1874).
Written in 1854 and Performed in 1855.

CAST OF CHARACTERS
White's Opera House, New York, Oct. 12, 1855.

Old Dan Tucker, a sufferer by the
    pressure of the times . . . . Mr. CHARLES WHITE
Belzebub, the Prince of Darkness . . . . Mr. J. CARROLL
Gabe Tucker, one of the Brack Boys . . . . Mr. J. NEIL
Chummie, companion to Gabe . . . . Mr. T. NORTON
Showman, a chap that won't work . . . . . Mr. D. EMMETT
Old Mrs. Tucker, one that sticks to her rights . . Mr. W. VINCENT

SCENERY

SCENE I.—*Kitchen in 2d or 3d grooves. Common table. Two chairs. Pail and broom. Working trap,* R. C. *Buck and saw. Barrel, with both heads out.*

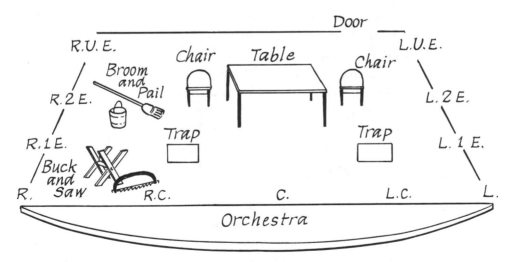

415

OLD TUCKER.—Very poorly dressed. Short grey wig. Old white hat. Second dress, rather fancy.

BELZEBUB.—Black tights. Black dress coat. Fright wig. Sugar-loaf hat. Thin red necktie, with long ends. Black slippers, with buckles on. Red pocket flaps on his tights.

GABE TUCKER.—Common juvenile make-up.

CHUMMIE.—Dress, most any style; low Negro characteristic.

SHOWMAN.—Make up similar to Jake Strop, or Hungry Jake.

OLD MRS. TUCKER.—Make up showy, in calico, quite extravagant.

PROPERTIES

A Stuffed Sack; Almanac; Barrel, both heads out; Cane; Banjo; Buck and Saw; Gong; Blue Fire; Red Fire; a Peep Show Box, with strap, and an old Organ; common Table; two Chairs; Pail and Broom; working Traps; Quill, for Pen, piece of Paper.

SCENE I. *Enter* OLD TUCKER, D. F. [front part of the stage], *advances to foot-lights.*

Tucker: Hard times! hard times! an' worse a comin';
Hard times thro' my old head keeps runnin';
I'll cotch de nigger make dat song,
To shake him well would not be 'rong;
I'd shake him up, and shake him down,
An' shake him 'till good times come roun';
As soap suds will a washboard trace,
Salt tears roll down my furrowed face.
If some, perchance, should ax de cause,
'Tis "tings ain't as dey used to was."
My banjo hangs against de wall,
My fiddle will not play at all.
Ob him dat's rich, I won't be jealous,
For don't de big book 'spressly tell us—
And tells us, too, widout much fussin',
Whedder we're white or color'd pusson—
"Bressed am dem dat's berry poor,
Dey'll nothing get, dats berry sure?"

Take ort from ort an naught remains;
But "you're a damn fool for your pains."
My wife an' children are most froze,
For want ob fire, food an' clothes.
I'd sell myself, both body an' soul,
For jist a peck ob fire coal!

Gong beats and BELZEBUB *appears through the trap,* R. C.

Belz.: That's very cheap, I own, 'tis true,
For one that's known so well as you;
But poverty and hunger pinches—
'Tis foolish, Dan, to die by inches.

Tucker: An' who is you? from whence ye come?
By all dis noise you must be "*some.*"

Belz.: My name is Bub; but do not quake!

Tucker: What, "Belzebub, for shortness sake?"

Belz.: Yes. Come from home (at your desire),
Where none do freeze for want of fire.
To go straight back, 'tis my intent,
When you have signed this document.

Tucker: I see—you want my "buck and saw"
On what you hold dar in your paw.

Belz: Yes, sign it quick! I've pencil got.

Tucker: Well, if I do may I be shot!

Belz.: Think on the coon on which you'll sup!

Tucker: I didn't t'ink you'd took me up!

Belz.: Think of the comforts you'll enjoy.
Sign quick! Do as I bid, my boy,
And you shall live—wife, son and daughter—
On fat o' the land and drink stump water.

Tucker: Well, hand it here; I'll quickly do it:
I hope to de Lord I'll nebber rue it. *(Signs)*
Dar's my buck *(signs)* an' dar's my saw,
De deed is done—now hold your jaw!

Belz.: You'll know no want, but with a wish,

417

I'll put good grub on every dish;
I'll money put in every pocket,
And in your chest—but mind you lock it.
Good clothes I'll put upon your back—
For those you wear fit like a sack;
But all the coal you'll get's a peck—
Be sure you burn it! every speck!
But longer here I can't remain.
Farewell—until we meet again.

Exit Belzebub *through the trap—(gong beats).*

Tucker: Good-bye, Belzebub,
I'm sorry at our partin';
I'm sure to lib until I die,
Dats one t'ing berry sartin.
I'll fool ye bad, my lubbin' friend—
An' you will quickly learn it—
Dat once I git de peck ob coal
I'll took my time to burn it!

Exit Tucker, r. 2 e.—*Enter* Gabe *and* Chummie, *quarrelling,* d. f.

Gabe: I say dey *was* a rock in dat snow ball!
Chum.:   No, dey wasn't!
Gabe: Yes, dey was; an' you frow stones at our wood pile.
Chum.:   You go to de debble—you wanted me to steal a dog, but I wouldn't tho'.
Gabe: I'll mark you *(Blows.)* I can whip any nigger on de hill! I struck at a nigger yesterday an' my fist glanced off an' killed a hoss.
Chum.:   Wonder you didn't kill a cow.
Gabe: Well, I would o'loosened your horns for ye if you'd been comin' dat way.
Chum.:   Does you call me a cow?
Gabe: Yes, an' a blame brack cow!

Chum.:	Jis come out ob doors an' I'll amuse you a little while!
Gabe:	Dat's me! I'm wid ye. I'll gib ye somet'ing ye can't buy at de 'pottecary's.
Chum.:	I'll gib you someting you must took dar to get mended!
Gabe:	Go out o' de house an' I'm wid you. I struck a nigger last night an' he jump up and axed if lightning hit any ob de udder niggers.

Both exit D. F. *quarrelling. Enter* 2 R. E. OLD TUCKER
and MRS. TUCKER, *both well dressed.*

Mrs. T.:	I say, Daniel, how well we hab got 'long in de world lately, heh?
Tucker:	Yes, dat's a fack; an' we'll get along first rate all de time— as long as you don't burn de coal in dat peck measure what's under de bed.
Mrs. T.:	Dar's no 'casion to burn it; habn't we got forty tons in de cellar? we've got all in dis world dat our hearts wish—good clothes, good fire, good eatin', good ebry t'ing; an jis' as we tought we should starve to death, we got rich all at once. "I've often heard de white folks say de darkest hour am jis' afore day."
Gabe:	*(Outside)* Dat ain't fair! you throw stones; I can lick you, tho', for all dat! I fights wid my fist—I does: dar! took dat! now "git up an' git!" an' if you don't git up you'll git it any how! *(Noise like fighting outside.)*
Tucker:	You, Gabe! come in here! *(Enter* GABE, D. F., *shying).* What's you doin' out dar, makin' such a hellaballoo?
Gabe:	I was fightin' Chummie—he keeps throwin' stones at me; but I lick 'im wid my fist.
Tucker:	Come here, sir *(Seizes Gabe.)* How often hab I told ye dat when dey fight wid a stone you fight wid a stone, an' when dey fight wid deyre fist, why, you fight wid your fist. Now, sir, I'm gwine to sarch ye. *(Beats Gabe with cane.)*
Mrs. T.:	Daniel Tucker! are you gwine to kill dat child?

Tucker:	Hold your tongue, old woman. T'ink I don't know how to correct my own childer? "Train up a child in de way he should walk" an' when he grows up—(*Gabe escapes, and exits* D. F.) away he goes!
Mrs. T.:	I 'spect you t'ink ye done it, don't ye.
Tucker:	I'll larn him. I was bad 'nuff—but not so bad as de boys am now days, or I'd o' been hung, dat's sartin.
Mrs. T.:	Did you ebber 'sperience a mudder's feelin's? Hab you got any children?
Tucker:	Yes!
Mrs. T.:	What 'come ob dem?
Tucker:	Dey leff as soon as dey seen deyre daddy.
Mrs. T.:	No wonder—you'd scare de debble any time!
Tucker:	Don't you 'buse my friend! don't you do it.
Mrs. T.:	What! is de debble your friend?
Tucker:	Em! I guess he is, honey—he gibs me ebry ting dat I wish for jis' soon as I ax 'im.
Mrs. T.:	An' what doos you gib him for doin' all dis?
Tucker:	Myseff, to be sure!
Mrs. T.:	What! you! bone ob my bone, an' sinner ob my sinner! sold yourseff to de debble! How much did ye fotch?
Tucker:	Coal 'nuff to last forebber, if you'll only keep it in de peck measure; if ebber you burn de coal in dat I'se a gone coon.
Mrs. T.:	Ha! ha! I understand. You sold yourself to de debble for a peck ob coal, when you orter bring a thousom dollar. Wher's de dockyments?
Tucker:	De debble's got 'em.
Mrs. T.:	Dey isn't good; for don't de law say what belongs to de woman belongs to herseff, an' what's her's am her own?
Tucker:	Why, old woman, you talk like a law book wid a red 'rocker kivver on it.
Mrs. T.:	Didn't my fadder kill a dog an' sell his hide to buy de license what I marry you wid?
Tucker:	Berry true—dat's a fack.
Mrs. T.:	Didn't I gib my yearling calf to pay for de marriage cere-

420

mony—an' didn't de calf run off when he found out de preacher man belong to de Millerumites?

Tucker: Yes. Smart calf dat.

Mrs. T.:   Den you is *mine!* De debble ain't got my pot-hooks to de paper.

Organ plays outside—enter SHOWMAN, D. F.

Showman: Does you want to hear de music?

Tucker: Yes. What ye got in dat box under your arm?

Showman: Dat's a show.

Mrs. T.:   Let me look in it? (*Showman fixes his box.*)

Showman: Now, old woman, I'll took a shillin'.

Tucker: Ain't our name on de free list?

Showman: No! owing to de immense expense of fitting up dis exumbition de free list am suspended, wid de exception ob de press.

Mrs. T.:   I'll took a peep any how.

Tucker: Yes, who cares for de expense while de coal lasts.

(MRS. T. *peeps in the box.*)

Mrs. T.:   I declare, old man, I nebber seen so many t'ings afore.

Showman: Yes, you can see de whole world.

Tucker: What! see de whole world? I say, old woman, can you see any t'ing ob dat calf what run away from de preacher man?

Showman: Get away from de box. Dar's no calf in dar, 'cept yourself.

Mrs. T.:   Be off wid yer show!

Showman: Pay me first.

Mrs. T.:   I won't do it! I didn't see nothin'.

Showman: I'm gwine (*Shoulders box.*) I hope de debble will get ye both. (*Exits* D. F.)

Tucker: Old woman, does ye hear dat 'jackulation?

Mrs. T.:   Yes. But I can tell you how to fool de debble, should he ebber hab de 'dacity to come arter ye.

421

Tucker: How? how?

Mrs. T.:   *(Pulling out book.)* Here's de almanac. De white folks say if you carry one in your pocket de debble won't come nigh you.

Tucker: I'll do so. *(Puts book in his pocket.)* Now, old woman, mind what I tell you 'bout de coal. De day you burns it up I'll hab hot work ob it. So come 'long wid me into de yard an' look at de chickens. *(Both exit 2 R. E.)*

Enter Gabe, d. *with a filled sack on his shoulder*
*—*Belzebub *enters behind him,*
whispering mischief in his ears
at appropriate points during the following speech from Gabe.

Gabe: *(Throws down sack.)* Dat's de heabbiest bag ob eatables I ebber lifted. I wonder whar I'll get some coal to make a fire to cook it wid? De cellar door am locked an' I can't get any dar: let me see. *(B. whispers.)* I hab it: dar's a peck ob coal under de bed in de kitchen; it's been dar some time—I guess it ain't worth much or dey'd burnt it up long ago. Arter I get de coal I hab nothin' to kindle it wid. *(B. whispers.)* I hab it: dar's de old almanac what dad toates in his pocket, 'twill be de berry t'ing to start de fire. *(Shoulders sack.)* Now for de chowder! *(Exits 2 L. E.)*

Belz.:   Thus far my schemes work well; conscious of his safety while the coal lasts, the old man adheres to his resolution firmly not to burn the same. I have stirred up his unruly son to rebellion; and in the dead hour of night, like the stealthy wolf seeking for his prey, have I urged him on to deeds of theft; when, with one full grab of his huge paw, has whole coops of chickens and litters of pigs disappeared. But some one comes; I'll retire to observe their movements. *(Exits anywhere.)*

Tucker: *(Outside.)* Come dis way, old woman; come along. *(Enter* Tucker *and* Mrs. Tucker.) Now took a seat 'long side ob

422

me an' rest yourself. (*Both sit down.*) I wonder whar dat child Gabe has gone to? he's too old for his age. Only t'ink, a boy sixteen years old up all night, frolickin' 'round de country.

Mrs. T.: You is a little mistaken in de child's age, he is eighteen years old next Mickalmas.

Tucker: He is sixteen years old de fourth of July, caze we've only been harnessed up in de state of wedlock fourteen years, deezackly.

Mrs. T.: We was harnessed up in de State ob old Warginny, eighteen years ago next Mickalmas, for I marked de place in de almanac.

Tucker: You did? what kind ob mark?

Mrs. T.: I smash a fly on de berry spot.

Tucker: I'll look an' see. (*Looks for the almanac.*) I tho't I put it in my coat pocket. What could I hab done wid it?

Mrs. T.: I smell brimstone!

Tucker: I smell de debble! (*Gong beats.*) Whar's de coal? de coal?

Gong beats—Blue Fire.
Belzebub *appears through the trap* R. C. *at the word "coal."*

Belz.: Burned! yes burnt to cinders black
With every leaf of your old almanac!
And ne'er in story nor in song
Was coal e'er known to burn so long.
Your time has come—prepare to go
To regions of eternal woe!
I've neither bridle, horse or saddle,
Upon my tail you'll ride a-straddle.

Mrs. T.: I have a word or two to say,
Before you took old Dan away.
De laws dey do thus spressnify,
"He libs wid me until I die."
An' by de kink in dis here wool
"I'm not dead yet by a jug full!"

423

	Your contrac is not worth a straw—
	"Possession's nine points ob de law!" *(Embraces.)*
Tucker:	I must hab been fast sound asleep
	To ebber sell myself so cheap;
	Considerin' I was bought so low,
	Grant me one wish before we go.
Belz.:	Well—seeing you're so very smart—
	That I will do with all my heart.
Tucker:	Den took a seat an' let me think. *(Sits in chair.)*

Mrs. T. *points to chair and winks at* Tucker.

Tucker:	*(To* Mrs. T.) Old gal, I understand your wink.
Tucker:	*(To* Belz.) Well since you're seated in dat cha'r,
	I wish you always may sit dar!

Belzebub *tries to separate himself from the chair but cannot.*
Gong—blue fire and general confusion.

Tucker:	Old woman, fotch my banjo; I'll make him dance to
	annudder kind ob music. (Mrs. T. *gets banjo.*)
Belz.:	My good old friend, great Daniel Tucker.
Tucker:	De man dat come too late to supper?
Belz.:	Yes. Let me loose and I'll agree
	That you come rather soon for me.
Tucker:	My fortune I shall surely make
	Wid some ob dem new steps you take.
	De two best steps you hab forgot—
	De "long-jay-bow" an' "turkey trot."
	You practice dem before we go—
	Myself will play dis old banjo.

Tucker *plays and* Belz. *attempts to dance with the chair fast*
to him, when Gabe, Chummie *and* Showman *enter,*
D. F. *Congratulations between all the characters.*

Gabe:	I say, fadder, who is dat what's fast to de cha'r?

Tucker:	Dat's Mr. Belzebub.
All:	Ah!
Tucker:	Now, boys, I'm gwine to sing a song, an' I want you all to dance in chorus. Mr. Belzebub will took his turn along wid ye.

TUCKER's *song—Tune*, "Old Tar River." ["Ole Tare River"]

Up de hill an' down de lebble;
Chorus—Ah-oo-oo-oo-oo-ah-oo-ah.
Old Dan Tucker fool de debble;
Chorus—Jang-o-blang-o-joo-jang-o-lay.
He sold hisse'f, so it is said—rum;
Chorus—Ah-oo-ge.
An' hid de charcoal under de bed—rum
Chorus—Gango-ge.

When de debble come to cotch 'em
Daniel t'ink he'd better watch 'em:
De debble t'ink he got 'em safer
Kaze he saw-buck on de paper.

He made Gabe Tucker fight wid Chummie;
Gabe pound de nigger to a mummy;
He stole my goose, he stole my tayter
At ten o'clock, or a little later.

Ole Dan Tucker dress in buckrum
Bekaze he hab a streak of luckrum;
Mrs. Tucker's a law expounder,
She went in like a forty-pounder.

Dan ax him if he won't be seated,
Belzebub found out him cheated;
He kick an' pull, but 'twas no use—rum,
Tucker wouldn't let him loose—rum.

Old Belzebub draw in your horn—rum,
Look out! de niggers smash your corn—rum;
Hoe it down an' scratch de grabble,
Jordan is a hard road for to trabble.

BELZEBUB *dances.*

De debble cut such funny capers
'Kaze old Tucker sign de papers;
He's got de almanac in his pocket,
De fourth ob July marked on de docket.

Get a barrel an' put him in it,
Fotch the handsaw in a minit;
If he should lib to grow any bigger
He'll nebber fool anudder nigger.

They force BELZEBUB *into the barrel head foremost.*
MRS. TUCKER *pulls his tail*
*—*GABE *saws on the barrel—Gong*
—Blue Fire—confusion, and close in.

END

PART TWO

A Selection from Minstrel Songs
of the Forties and from Banjo Tunes

De Blúe Tail Fly[1]

O   when you   come in   sum - mer time,
(2)   in   de   shade you   chance to lie,

[Fine]

p

[2nd time]

f

To   South Car - li - nar's
You'll   soon   find out   de

p

[2nd time]

[1] Inside the date is 1846, outside it is 1844 (Boston, Keith's Publishing House, 1844).

429

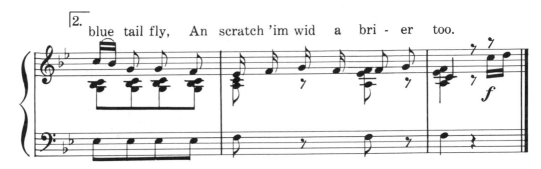

repeat from 𝄋

2   Dar's many kind ob dese here tings,
     From diff'rent sort ob insects springs;
     Some hatch in June, an some July,
     But August fotches de blue tail fly,
     An scratch 'im . . . .

3   When I was young, I used to wait
     On Massa's table an hand de plate;
     I'de pass de bottle when he dry,
     An brush away de blue tail fly,
     An scratch 'im . . . .

4   Den arter dinner massa sleep,
     He bid me vigilance to keep;

An when he gwine to shut he eye,
He tell me watch de blue tail fly,
An scratch 'im . . . .

5   When he ride in de arternoon,
    I foller wid a hickory broom;
    De poney being berry shy,
    When bitten by de blue tail fly,
    An scratch 'im . . . .

6   One day he rode aroun de farm,
    De flies so numerous did swarm;
    One chance to bite 'im on de thigh,
    De debble take dat blue tail fly,
    An scratch 'im . . . .

7   De poney run, he jump, an pitch,
    An tumble massa in de ditch;
    He died, an de Jury wonder why,
    De verdict was de "blue tail fly,"
    An scratch 'im . . . .

8   Dey laid 'im under a simmon tree,
    His epitaph am dar to see;
    Beneath dis stone I'm forced to lie,
    All by de means ob de blue tail fly,
    An scratch 'im . . . .

9   Ole Massa's gone, now let him rest,
    Dey say all tings am for de best;
    I neber shall forget till de day I die,
    Ole Massa an de blue tail fly,
    An scratch 'im . . . .

10 De hornet gets in your eyes an nose,
    De 'skeeter bites y'e through your close,
    De gallinipper sweeten high,
    But wusser yet de blue tail fly,
    An scratch 'im . . . .

Gwine to de Mill[1]

I drove my cart to de mill one day, An I

met Jule Glo - ver gwine dat way; She spressed a wish dat

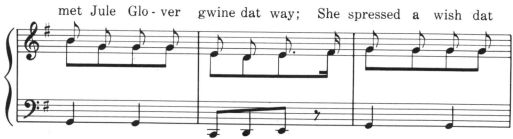

she mout ride, Yes dat you may Jule by my side.

Set down dar my Ju - lia Glo - ver, Ban - jo I - sam

[1] Composed and written by Jay R. Jenkins (Boston, C. Bradlee & Co., 1846).
[2] Originally: d f-sharp.

am your lo - ver; Gwine to de mill wid Ju - lia Glo - ver,

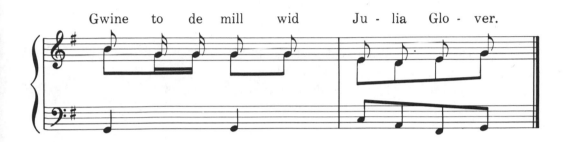

Gwine to de mill wid Ju - lia Glo - ver.

2 I kissed at Julia on de road,
   But de fool she screamed and squalled so loud,
   De oxens run, an de cart turned over,
   An spilt out I an Julia Glover.
   Set down . . . .

3 O Jule was a chick ob de ole blue hen,
   An she gin me jaw wid a vengeance den;
   She cuffed my ears and set 'em a ringing,
   But I said nothing an kep on singing
   Set down . . . .

4 Jule den called me a banjo fool,
   She clawed my face, and pulled my wool;
   I gin her a lick dat tipped her over,
   An dar I lef my Julia Glover.
   Set down . . . .

433

5   De miller's a man wid a mealy hat,
    An he keeps his hogs an his chickens fat;
    He thinks he's great singing "Hey git along,"
    But he jes gin it up when I sing dis song,
    Set down . . . .

6   O Jule got lazy an she came to me
    To cure an ache in her misery;
    I gin her a hickory mesmerising,
    An de way I cured her was surprising.
    Set down . . . .

7   De bread am baked an de coffee's biling,
    Meat in de smoke-house all a spiling;
    Jule cotch a cold in de chrismas freezes,
    Now I sings, an Jule she sneezes,
    Set down . . . .

Jim Along Josey[1]

Oh! I'se from Lu - ci - an-na as you all know,

Ad lib:

Dar whare Jim a - long Jo - sey's all de go, Dem

Tempo [a tempo]

nig - gars all rise when de bell does ring, And

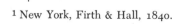

[1] New York, Firth & Hall, 1840.

Ad lib: dis is de song dat dey do sing. Allegro Hey get a - long,

get a-long Jo - sey Hey get a - long Jim a - long Joe!

Hey get a - long, get a - long Jo - sey

Hey get a - long, Jim a - long Joe!

2 Oh! when I gets dat new coat which I expects to hab soon,
   Likewise a new pair tight-knee'd trousaloon,
   Den I walks up and down Broadway wid my Susanna,
   And de white folks will take me to be Santa Anna,
   Hey . . . .

3 My sister Rose de oder night did dream,
   Dat she was floating up and down de stream,
   And when she woke she began to cry,
   And de white cat picked out de black cat's eye.
   Hey . . . .

4 Now way down south not very far off,
   A Bullfrog died with de hooping cough,
   And de oder side of Mississippi as you must know,
   Dare's when I was christen'd Jim along Joe.
   Hey . . . .

5 De new York niggers tink dey're fine,
   Because dey drink de genuine,
   De southern niggers dey lib on mush,
   And where de laugh dey say Oh Hush.
   Hey . . . .

6 I'me de nigger that dont mind my troubles,
   Because dey are noting more dan bubbles
   De ambition that dis nigger feels
   Is showing de science of his heels.
   Hey . . . .

7   De fust President we eber had was Gen'ral Washington,
      And de one we've got now is Martin Van Buren,
      But altho' Gen'ral Washington's dead
      As long as de country stands his name shall float ahead.
      Hey . . . .

Jonny Boker *or*
De Broken Yoke in de Coaling Ground[1]

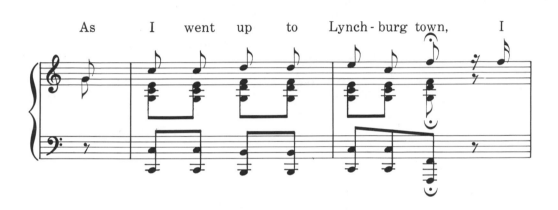

As I went up to Lynch-burg town, I

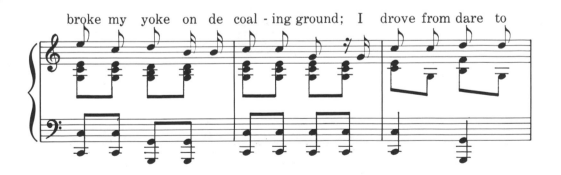

broke my yoke on de coal-ing ground; I drove from dare to

[1] Boston, Henry Prentiss, 1840.

bowl -ing spring, And tried for to mend my yoke and ring.

O Jon - ny Bo - ker help dat nig - ger

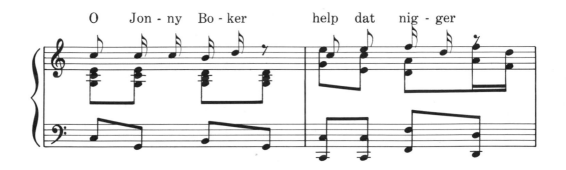

do Jon - ny Bo - ker do.

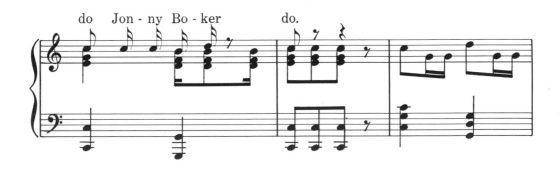

2 I drove from dare to Wright's ole shop
 Hollered to my driver and told him to stop
 Says I Mr Wright have you got a yoke
 He seized his bellows and blew up a smoke
 O Jonny Boker . . . .

3 Says I Mr Wright habnt long for to stay
 He cotched up his hammer knocked right away
 Soon as he mended my staple and ring
 Says I Mr Wright do you charge any thing
 O Jonny Boker . . . .

4 Says he to me I neber charge
 Unless de job is werry large
 For little jobs dat is so small
 I neber charge any ting at all
 O Jonny Boker . . . .
 [spoken:] (Save three cents dat time.)

5 I drove from dar to Anthony's Mill
 And tried to pull up dat are hill
 I whipped my steers and pushed my cart
 But all I could do I could'nt make a start
 O Jonny Boker . . . .
 [spoken:] (De ole nigger was fast stalled dat time.)

6 I put my shoulder to the wheel
 Upon de ground I placed my heel
 Den we make a mighty strain

441

But all out efforts prove in vain
O Jonny Boker . . . .

7 Dare cum a waggoner driving by
   I sat on de ground and 'gan for to cry
   Says me to him some pity take
   And help me up for conscience sake
   O Jonny Boker . . . .

8 Says he to me I will help thee
   He tuk out his horses No. 3
   I wiped from my eyes the falling tears
   He hitched his horses before my steers
   O Jonny Boker . . . .

9 Den to me he did much please
   He pulled me up wid so much ease
   His horses were so big and strong
   De way dey pulled dis nigger along
   O Jonny Boker . . . .

Juba[1]

1   Ruberii, de cimmon seed
     Seed de Billy hop in jist in time,
     Juba dis, Juba dat,
     Round de kittle ob possum fat;
     A-hoop a-hoy, a-hoop a-hoy,
     Double step for Juberii,
     Sandy crab, de macreli, ham,
     And half a pint ob Juba.

2   Want to borrow two or three eggs,
     A picayune a dozen,
     Stir about de hominy hot,
     De pig is in de cellar;
     Neighbor, neighbor, lend me your axe,
     Lend you mine tomorrow,
     I keeps de axe tu use myself,
     Who'll turn de grindstone.

3   Forty pound of candle grease,
     Sittin' on de mantlepiece,
     Don't you see ole Granny Grace,
     She look so ugly in de face;
     Yankle Doodle come to town,
     Claim Maria for his own,
     Git up dar, you little nigger,
     Can't you pat for Juba.

4   Up de wall, down de 'tition,
     Gib me a knife sharp as sickle,
     To cut dat nigger's wizen pipe,
     Dat eat up all de sassengers;
     Apple jack wid wenison sauce,
     Sittin' by de fire-place,
     One eye up de dinner-pot
     And t'other up de stove pipe.

[1] "Juba / The great Banjo Solo, as sung by George Christy and Wood's Minstrels," in *White's New Illustrated Melodeon Song Book* (New York, 1848). The original tune seems never to have been published. It was probably similar to versions one and two (especially the latter), to judge by their close relation to the banjo variant of 1858.

AMERICAN THEATRE BOWERY NEW YORK

iew of the Stage on the fifty seventh night of Mr T.D.RICE of Kentucky in his original and celebrated extravaganza of JIM CROW on which occasion every department of the house was thronged to an excess unprecedented in the records of theatrical attraction — New York 25th November 1833

Thomas D. Rice as "Jim Crow" on a New York stage in 1833. Courtesy Frederic R. Sanborn, New York.

444

5 Make de fire most too hot,
   Fotch along de waterin' pot,
   Bake de bread, gib me de crust,
   Shock de corn gib me de husk,
   Bile de beef, gib me de bone,
   Gib me a kick and send me home,
   Peel de tater, gib me de skin,
   And dats de way she suck me in.

6 Shadrack an' Abednego,
   Don't care whether I hit 'em or no,
   Eighteen pence an' a peck ob corn,
   Milk de cow wid de crumple horn,
   Gib me a quart, gib me some,
   I'm gettin' a pitcher full,
   Stay back, stay back,
   Bucket full ob Juba.

Two Versions of "Juba" as Sung by Southern Negroes

One [2]

Ju - ba dis an' Ju - ba dat   Ju - ba killed a yel - low cat.

Two [3]

[2] W. C. Handy, *A Treasury of the Blues* (New York, 1926), 44.
[3] Dorothy Scarborough, *On the Trail of Negro Folk-Songs* (Cambridge, 1925), 99. Juba is called "one of the best known of the 'jig,' or short-step, dance tunes of the old South."

445

Four Banjo Versions of "Juba"[4]

One [5]

Two [6]

Three [7]

Four [8]

[4] The actual sound is an octave lower.
[5] "Juba, A Jig Dance," in *Phil. Rice's Correct Method for the Banjo* (Boston, 1858).
[6] "Buckley's Juba," in James Buckley, *Buckley's New Banjo Book* (New York, 1860).
[7] "Juba," in Buckley, *Banjo Book*. There is yet another brief version of the tune.
[8] *Frank B. Converse's Banjo Instructor* (New York, 1865).

My Old Dad[1]

[Fine]

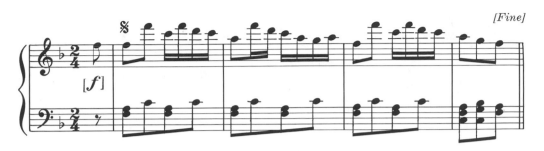

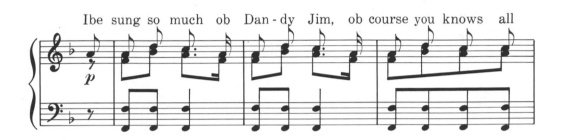

Ibe sung so much ob Dan - dy Jim, ob course you knows all

a - bout him; I'be heard it sed when I was a lad, Twas a

wise child knew his own old dad. Old Dad!

[1] On the inside the title is written "Ole Dad" (Boston, Keith's Publishing House, 1844).

Old Dad!   Old Dad he took a

swim all a - long, He Dive like a fed-der an he swim like a stone.

repeat from 𝄋

2 One day my daddy took a swim,
   Him hung he clothes on a hick'ry limb,
   He could not swim an dibe berry bad,
   So dat was de last ob my ole dad.
   Old Dad . . . .

3 My mudder once did 'spres a wish,
   Dat I should go an cotch some fish;
   I bate my hook to cotch a shad,
   But de first fish bit, was my ole dad.
   Old Dad . . . .

4 I puld away wid all my mought,
   All for to get de ole man out;
   My fish pole broke an I got mad,
   An down to de bottom went my ole dad.
   Old Dad . . . .

448

5   Way down below his ghost was bent,
    An to de debble he did went;
    But Satan he looked berry sad,
    He'd no place left for my old dad.
    Old Dad . . . .

6   He stirrd de sinners wid a pole
    All for to make a little hole
    He hit em on de head wid a big ox gad
    Make room! sez Satan for my ole dad.
    Old Dad . . . .

7   De debble told him to go back,
    De old man shoulderd his knapsack,
    But when dar's more room to be had,
    He's gwine to send for my ole dad.
    Old Dad . . . .

8   Den Satan on him put his mark,
    Kaze he might loss him in de dark;
    Wid ears like a backer leaf tail like a shad,
    De debble put a mark on my ole dad.
    Old Dad . . . .

9   One night while mudder laid asleep,
    A nigg into de house did creep;
    What dat? sed she but soon felt glad,
    When she found out 'twas my old Dad.
    Old Dad . . . .

Oh, Come Along John[1]

Banjo — Way down in old Car-li-na Went to see my old aunt Di-nah, Says I, old la-dy how's de goose, When de gan-der jumped from de old hen roost, Come a-long John, Come a-long John,

[Sounds an octave lower]

[1] *Rice's Correct Method.* The tune appeared first as "Walk Along John" (Boston, C. H. Keith, 1843).

Come a-long John, de fi-fer's son,

Ain't you migh-ty glad dat your day's work done.

2   Milk in de dairy nine days old,
    Rats and de mice are gettin mighty bold,
    Long tailed rat in de pail of souse
    Dat's just come down from de white folks house.
    Come along John . . . .

3   An alligator cum from Tuscaloo
    For to fight de Kangaroo,
    Dey fought till day dey swallowed each odder down,
    Den wid dere tails dey took anudder round.
    Come along John . . . .

451

Walk Along, John[1]

1   Johnny come from Chickasaw,
    De dardes fool I ebber saw;
    He put his shirt outside his coat,
    An tied his breeches roun his throat.
    So walk along John!
    Walk along John!
    Walk along John! high for de Sun,
    Aint you mighty glad your day's work done.

2   Johnny went to Tenessee,
    He grin de possum up a tree;
    He grin an fotch his body down,
    An leff de tail for anudder roun.
    So walk along . . . .

3   Behind de hen cook on my knees,
    I tink I hear old Johnny sneeze;
    Goose chew tobackur duck drink wine,
    De brack snake sleep wid de punkin vine.
    So walk along . . . .

4   Johnny's cheese was nine years old,
    De skippers gittin mighty bold;
    A long tail rat in a bucket of souse,
    Jist come from de white folks house.
    Walk along . . . .

5   Johnny's rooster had a fit,
    De niggs all thot he'd die of it;
    De fedders flew out his tail flew in,
    Den he jump up an crowed agin.
    Walk along . . . .

6   Walk 'long Johnny he got drunk,
    He fell in de fire an kick de chunk;
    De charcoal got inside his shoe,

[1] *Emmit's Celebrated Negro Melodies* (London, D'Almaine & Co., n.d. [c.1844]).

Lawd bress y'e how de ashes flew.
Walk along . . . .

7   Johnny lay on de rail road track,
He tied de engine on his back;
He pair'd his corn wid a rail road wheel,
It gib 'im de tooth ache in de heel.
Walk along . . . .

8   Way down south on beaver creek,
Old Johnny grew about ten feet;
He went to bed, but 'twas no use,
His leg hung out for de chicken roose.
Walk along . . . .

Old Dan Tucker[1]

I come to town de ud-der night, I hear de noise an

saw de fight, De watch-man was a run-nin roun, cry-in

[1] Words by Dan. D. Emmit (Boston, C. H. Keith, 1843).

Old Dan Tuck-er's come to town, So get out de way!

get out de way!   get out de way!

Old Dan Tuck-er your to late to come to sup-per.

repeat from 𝄋

2   Tucker is a nice old man,
     He use to ride our darby ram;
     He sent him whizzen down de hill,
     If he had'nt got up he'd lay dar still.
     Get out . . . .

3   Here's my razor in good order
     Magnum bonum—jis hab bought 'er;
     Sheep shell oats, Tucker shell de corn,
     I'll shabe you soon as de water get warm.
     Get out . . . .

4   Ole Dan Tucker an I got drunk,
     He fell in de fire an kick up a chunk,
     De charcoal got inside he shoe
     Lor bless you honey how de ashes flew.
     Get out . . . .

5   Down de road foremost de stump,
     Massa make me work de pump;
     I pump so hard I broke de sucker,
     Dar was work for ole Dan Tucker.
     Get out . . . .

6   I went to town to buy some goods
     I lost myself in a piece of woods,
     De night was dark I had to suffer,
     It froze de heel of Daniel Tucker.
     Get out . . . .

7   Tucker was a hardened sinner,
     He nebber said his grace at dinner;
     De ole sow squeel, de pigs did squall
     He 'hole hog wid de tail and all.
     Get out . . . .

Old Joe[1]

Twas Old Jo stood at de gar-den gate, But he couldn't get in he come to late; He pick up a stone an he knock at de doa, I

[1] Composed and written by F. M. Brower. (Boston, C. H. Keith, 1844).

457

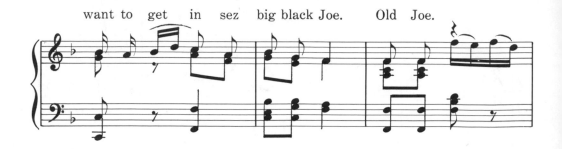

want to get in sez big black Joe. Old Joe.

Old Joe.

Old Jo kick-in up be-hind an be-foa, An de

young gall kick-en up be-hind ole Jo.

2 Out come Dinah, Joe what you doin dar?
   I want to get a gun to go shoot a barr;
   Sez he ole Joe dat game wont do,
   Joe got so mad he busted his shoe.
   Old Joe . . . .

3 Den old Joe started strait off home,
   He walk all de way by de light ob de moon;
   His old wife laff his children grin;
   To see old Joe come back again.
   Old Joe . . . .

4 Den berry early de next morn,
   He went to de field to hoe de corn;
   He work berry hard to get it done,
   An finish all by de set ob sun.
   Old Joe . . . .

5 He got done work an flung down he hoe,
   Sez he I'll play on de ole banjo;
   He started off for flat foot Sam,
   But on de way he took a dram.
   Old Joe . . . .

6 De whiskey flew into his head,
   Him reel an fall down in de shed;
   He's taken sick an put to bed;
   Bout tree weeks arter he is dead.
   Old Joe . . . .

7   Old Joe has gone an leff his place,
    We nebber more shall see his face;
    He's leff one behind dat am not slow,
    He plays like de debble on de ole banjo.
    Old Joe . . . .

The Ole Grey Goose[1]

Mon-day was my wed-ding day Tues-day I was mar-ried,

Wen's-dy night my wife took sick Sat'-day she was bur-ied.

Oh! look-y har,   Oh! look-y whar,   Look right o - ber

[1] Philadelphia, A. Fiot, 1844.

461

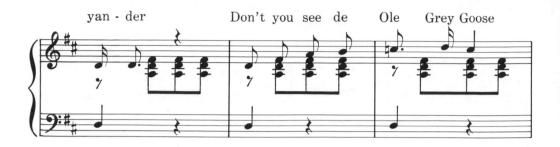

yan - der　　Don't you see de　Ole　Grey Goose

Smil - ing　at　de　Gan - der.

2　Wen'sdy night my wife took sick
　Despair ob death cum o'er her
　O! some did cry, but I did laff
　To see dat death go from her.
　Oh . . . .

3　I ask Miss Dinah Rose one day
　In de ole cart to ride
　She war by gosh so bery fat
　I couldn't sit beside her.
　Oh . . . .

4　When she was gittin out de cart
　Miss Dinah loose her shoe
　And den I spied a great big hole
　Right in her stocking through.
　Oh . . . .

462

5   Says I to her: you Dinah Gal
      Only looky dar
      Dem heels are sticking out too far
      As a niggar I declar.
      Oh . . . .

6   Says she to me you nigger Jo
      What are you about
      Dere's science in dem are heels
      And I want em to stick out.
      Oh . . . .

De Ole Jaw Bone[1]

[1] Boston, Henry Prentiss, 1840.

[2] Originally, the accompaniment has c-sharp instead of d throughout this measure and the first half of the next.

tur - key   too   Neb - er mind dat   bu - ger   bu.

2 De lute string blue it will not do
   I want a string to tie my shoe
   A cotton [string] it will not do
   A cotton string will break into
   Walk Jaw Bone . . . .

3 As I was cum from Tennessee
   My hoss got mired up to his knee
   I whipped him till I saw de blood
   Den he hauled me out ob de mud
   Walk Jaw Bone . . . .

4 There was a little man he had a little hoss
   Went to de riber couldnt get across
   I fed my hoss in de poplar troff
   Ole Cow died ob de hooppin coff
   Walk Jaw Bone . . . .

   3 The second g was originally with a natural sign (perhaps a misprint for a sharp).

5   De niggers at de south dont dress berry well
    Day walk about and try for to cut a swell
    In de night day meet for to play
    Dance all night until de next day
    Walk Jaw Bone . . . .

6   Jay Bird pon a swinging limb
    Winked at me I winked at him
    Cotched up a stone hit him on de shin
    And dats de way we sucked him in
    Walk Jaw Bone . . . .

Ole Joe Golden[1]

One Sun-day day when de sun was hot, I'd take a nap ob
(2) hung my coat on de fence to dry, An Ole Joe Gold-en

1. sleep I thought, I 2. come along by. D'ye see him den?

See him when? When he stole my knife and bas-ker too.

2 Ole Joel's cousin, yaller Sal,
   I used to court when she was a gal,
   But it am my real trew belief,
   Dat de whole biling am a thief.
   D'ye see him den?

1 Actually for three voices, in *The Ethiopian Glee Book* (Boston, 1849).

467

See him when?
When he stole my knife and basker too.

3   Ole Joel Golden went to plough,
And put his gear on de muley cow,
De cow gin a beller, and off she run,
And de mule died laughing to see de fun.
D'ye see him den?
See him when?
When he did'nt know de mule from de muley cow.

4   Ole Joel Golden libed on de coast,
Where de niggers lib on herrings most;
De herrin' bones choke him ten times a minute,
And dat's de way he got dat squint.
D'ye seem him den?
See him when?
When de herrin' bones choke him and make him squint.

5   Ole Joel's wife and my wife together,
Went to town to sell chicken fedder.
O buy my fedders, said Ole Yaller Sal,
O come buy fedders of dis yaller gal.
D'ye see em den?
Seen em when?
When dey bought deir fedders of Ole Yaller Sal.

6   A lizzard in de sun, a settin on a rail,
His head went a bobbin and wiggle went his tail;
"O come alang lang," de lizzard say,
"I'se hungry, bug, so don't stay away."
D'ye see him den?
See him when?
When his head went a bobbin and wiggle went his tail.

Ole Pee Dee[1]

In   Souf Car - li - na   I   was born   I   husk de wood an
(2) roast - in ear   to de house I bring, De nig - ger cotch me

1. chop de corn, De 2. an I sing; Ring de hoop! blow de horn!

Cotch de   nig - ger   a steal-in corn   Way down   in   de

[1] Written and composed by J. P. Carter (Boston, Keith's Publishing House, 1844).

low groun fiel 3,   4 mile from Pom-pey's heel.

repeat from 𝄋

2 Dey took me out on a tater hill
   Dey made me dance against my will,
   I dance all roun de tater hole
   De niggers punch me wid a pole.
   Ring . . . .

3 Down de riber I spied a ship,
   I slid down on my under lip,
   Hop on board an cross de drink,
   It make de niggers gizzard wink.
   Ring de hoop! an blow de horn,
   Nebber felt so glad since I was born;
   Way . . . .

4 To Boston port I den sail roun,
   Dey said de Dickens was in town;
   I ax dem who de Dickens was
   Dey sed 'twas massa Pickwick Boz.
   Ring de hoop! an blow de horn!
   Massa Dickens eat de corn,
   Way . . . .

5 Dey fed ole massa Boz so tall
   His trowsaloons dey grow too small;
   In Boston I couldnt get any pickins
   Caze all de victuals went to de Dickens.
   Ring de bell! and sown de gong!
   Massa Dickens' feedin strong,
   Way . . . .

Ole Tare River[1]

Way down in North Caro-li-na [Ah - -]

On de banks of Ole Tare Ri-ver [Ah - -]

[1] Boston, Henry Prentiss, 1840.

I go from dar to Al - a - ba - ma [Ah - -

- -] For to see my ole Aunt Han - nah.

[Ah - - - -]

8va

2 Raccoon and possum got in a fray
Ah . . .
Fought all night untill de next day
Ah . . .
When de day broke de Pos cut to de hollow
Ah . . .
Old Coon says I guess I better follow.
Ah . . . .

3 Da met next on de top ob de hill
Ah . . .
For to settle dis great diffikil
Ah . . .
Possum seized de Coon by de tail
Ah . . .
Make him wish he was on a rail.
Ah . . . .

4 Ole nigger cum along wid his dog
Ah . . .
Possum cut for de hollow log
Ah . . .
Coon he looked and saw dat nig
Ah . . .
So up de tree he den dig dig.
Ah . . . .

5 De ole dog watch, smelt all around
Ah . . .
He found the Coon jest lef de ground
Ah . . .
Den he bark rite up de tree
Ah . . .
De ole Coon says you cant ketch me.
Ah . . . .

6 De ole dog bark, de nigger blow his horn
Ah . . .

473

Ole Coon begin to tink he was gone
Ah . . .
Ole nigger cum he cast up his eye
Ah . . .
On a big limb dat coon did lie.
Ah . . . .

7   Nigger went to work and cut de tree down
Ah . . .
De ole Coon he could not be found
Ah . . .
De Coon cut stick he was afraid ob de dog
Ah . . .
He run slap in anoder hollow log.
Ah . . . .

8   De Pos says Coon get out ob dis log
Ah . . .
Lay rite still for I believe I hear de dog
Ah . . .
De nigger den cum and stopt up de hole
Ah . . .
And day couldnt get out to save dar souls.
Ah . . . .

9   Now Miss Dinah I'm going to leave you
Ah . . .
And when I'm gone dont let it grieve you
Ah . . .
First to the window den to de door
Ah . . .
Looking for to see de banjo.
Ah . . . .

O Lud Gals Gib Me[1]

Its   up   de rope an   down   de   ca - ble,   For - ty   hos - ses

in   de   sta - ble,   First an   in - jun   den   a   squaw

[1] Words by Dan Emmit (Boston, C. H. Keith, 1843).

Gwine a - way to de Ar - kan - saw. O lud gals,

gib me chaw te - bac - kur.

O lud gals, fotch a - long de whis - key,

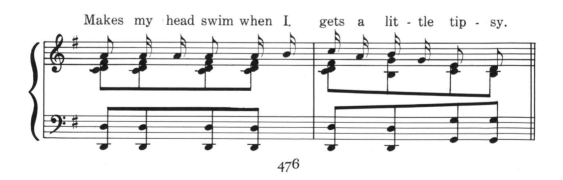

Makes my head swim when I gets a lit - tle tip - sy.

2 Vinegar shoes an paper stockins,
   Set to me Miss Polly Hopkins
   My wife's dead an I'm a widder,
   All de way from roarin ribber.
   O lud gals . . . .

3 If I had a wife an a little baby,
   I'd support her like a lady;
   God's of war an little fishes
   Yearthern plates an puter dishes.
   O lud gals . . . .

4 Cowhide shoes an buckskin breeches,
   Gib me de gal dat sewed de stitches:
   De prettiest ting in creation
   Is a little yaller gal in de wild goose nation.
   O lud gals . . . .

5 Pompey Smash an ole Pete Acre
   Two best men in human natur,

Hop in de creek, an roll in de ribber
Two oberseers to one little nigger.
O lud gals . . . .

6   All de way from de injun nation,
    Big corn crib on little plantation;
    My wife's dead an I'll get anudder
    Pretty little black gal jis like tudder.
    O lud gals . . . .

7   Blow away ye gentle breezes
    All among de cimmon treeses,
    Dar I set long wid de muses,
    Mendin my old boots an shuses.
    O lud gals . . . .

Who's Dat Nigga Dar a Peepin?[1]

O here I cum jist for to sing, Bout
dis and dat and de od - er ting; O
I am a gwine for to tell you all, How I

[1] The chorus is originally for three voices (Boston, Keith's Publishing House, 1844).

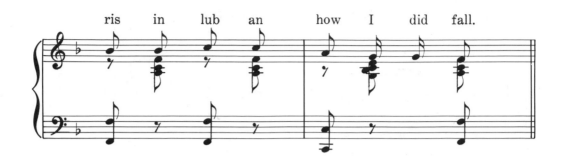

ris in lub an how I did fall.

Spoken   But first ob all, for I spress myself
on dis kashun, I should like to know

Chorus

Who's dat nig-ga   dar dat's peep-in,
(2) Who's dat nig-ga   dar a peep-in   Who's dat nig-ga

dat I see;   Go a-way nig-ga you

cant cum to tea.

Who's dat nigga . . . .

2 Oh I fell in lub wid Miss Dinah Crow
   And her teef was like de clar grit snow
   And her eyes like dem beams dat shine from de moon
   Sharper dan de teef of de Possum and de Koon

       Spoken Yes you see dis nigga first exprised herseff
               by seeing her promulgating herseff up and down
               Chesnut Street persipitating dat foot ob hers up
               so high dat when it dropt it was death to all
               creeping insects and den wid de poet I sclaimed

   Who's dat nigga . . . .

3 Oh I went dar one ebening kording to rule
   And I was exprised to see a nigga squattin on a stool
   Dar was Massa Zip Coon squatting down by de fire
   Singing dat song ob Ole Virginny neber tire

       Spoken Yes indeed dare de nigga was dares no sception in
               dat and as soon as dis nigga lit his eye pon him
               dare was quite a conservation mongst us niggas kase
               I axed Dinah if she would jist spress herself openly
               pon de raison and inform dis nigger

   Who's dat nigga . . . .

4 Oh den us niggers you ort for to see
   Dar was me hugging him and he was hugging me
   Oh he bit me pon my arm and tore my close
   I fotch him a lick and broke Miss Dinahs nose

481

Spoken Den says I jist look at here Miss Dinah dats
de fects ob your habbing more dan one nigga dressing
himseff to you at one time and now den Miss Dinah
I shall leave you for de present but next time I sees
any gemman ob color sept myself I shant be under de
discumgresable necessity of axing you

Who's dat nigga . . . .

5   Oh de next morning dey took dem fore de mare
Who taught dey had not acted fair
So he sent dem down jist for thirty days apiece
For kickin up a row and brakin de police

Spoken   Oh Lord lova lova ha ha hush honey hush. De fust ting
I knew in de morning dere Mass Zip was poking his ugly
mug out o Black Maria and den you ort to hear
dis child fling out to him and ax

Who's dat nigga . . . .

6   Now ladies and gemmen my song is sung
And I hope you all hab had some fun
If you want to hear a song dat will keep you from sleepin
Hear Who's dat nigga dar dats peepin

Spoken   Yes indeed dares so much percipation in it dat it
probitates de promulgation ob all oder sentimations and
de only spression dat you hear is

Who's dat nigga . . . .

Briggs' Breakdown[1]

[Sounds an octave lower when played on the banjo]

[1] Thomas F. Briggs, *Briggs' Banjo Instructor* (Boston, 1855).

Bull upon the Battery—Jig[1]

[Sounds an octave lower]

[Fine]

[1] Composed by Z. Bacchus; in the Manuscript Collection of D. D. Emmett, State Library, Columbus, Ohio.

Dick Myers' Jig[1]

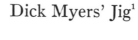
[Sounds an
octave lower]

[Fine]

[1] In the Manuscript Collection of D. D. Emmett; the tune is not by Emmett.

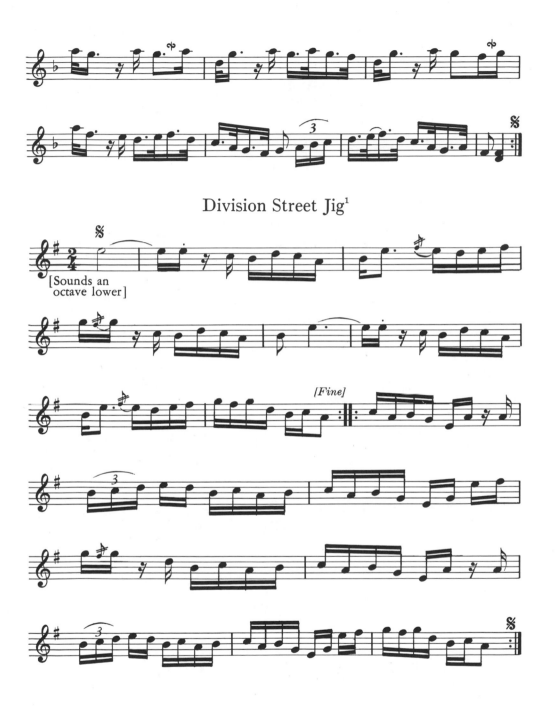

Division Street Jig[1]

[Sounds an octave lower]

[Fine]

[1] Composed by Z. Bacchus; in the Manuscript Collection of D. D. Emmett.

485

Dr. Hekok Jig[1]

[Sounds an octave lower]

[1] Composed by Z. Bacchus; in the Manuscript Collection of D. D. Emmett.

486

Gantz's Jig[1]

[Sounds an *p*
octave lower]

[Fine]

[1] In the Manuscript Collection of D. D. Emmett; the tune is not by Emmett.
[2] The lengthening of the measure seems to be deliberate.

487

[3] The lengthening of the measure seems to be deliberate.

The Newton Jig[1]

[Sounds an octave lower]

[1] James Buckley, *Buckley's New Banjo Book* (New York, 1860).

Peel's Jig[1]

[Sounds an octave lower]

p

[Fine]

[1] In the Manuscript Collection of D. D. Emmett; the tune is not by Emmett.

Rise Old Napper[1]

[Sounds an octave lower]

[1] Arranged by Phil. Rice, in *Rice's Correct Method.*
[2] Originally a quarter note.

Rock Susana[1]

[Sounds an octave lower]

[1] Composed by Horace Weston; in S. S. Stewart, *The Complete American Banjo School* (Philadelphia, 1887).

Sliding Jenny Jig[1]

[Sounds an octave lower]

[1] Composed by R. Myers; in the Manuscript Collection of D. D. Emmett.

Van Bramer's Jig[1]

[Sounds an octave lower]

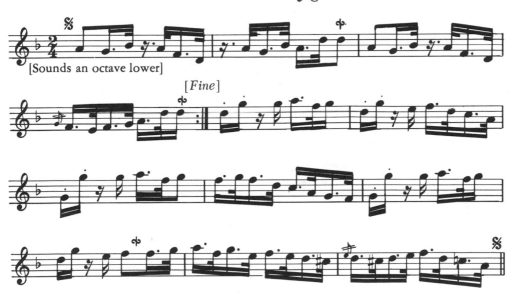

[1] In the Manuscript Collection of D. D. Emmett; the tune is not by Emmett.

491

GENERAL INDEX

Accordion: 147, 149, 149n., 150
Alpine singers: 94
Arlecchino: 3
Arnold, Samuel: 13

Banjo: 59, 126, 126n., 127, 128, 153, 154, 190, 191, 191n.; *see also* Negro minstrelsy (minstrel band)
Banjo tunes: 189ff., 250; performance of, 190
Ballad opera: 68
Barnum: 115
Barthélemon, F. H.: 7
Bate, Henry: 13
Beggar's Opera, The: 20
Bickerstaffe, Isaac: 13, 20, 23
Bishop, Henry R.: 14, 256
Blues: 195, 212, 213
Bones: 111, 127, 154
Bowles, W. L.: 7
Broadside in Negro dialect: 48–49
Brother Allen: sermon of, 278
Brower, Frank: 93, 111–13, 113n., 114, 214, 215; *see also* Virginia Minstrels
Bryant, Dan: 93, 227, 228, 245, 274
Bryant, Jerry: 216, 227, 228, 245
Bryant, Neil: 227, 228
Bryant's Minstrels: 227ff.
Buck or wing dances: 212, 213, 234
Burgoyne, J.: 34, 256
Byron: 217

Carr, Benjamin: 33, 175
Carrol, J.: 245
Cavendish, Georgiana (Duchess of Devonshire): 7, 33
Cervantes: 20
Charles, G. W.: 245
Christy, E. P.: 145
Christy, George: 131, 145
Christy Minstrels: 143–46
Clementi, Muzio: 4, 16; *"alla Negra,"* 5, 16, 16n.
Cobb, James: 13
"Cohea": 126
Collins, John: 5
Colman, George, the Younger: 13

Colman, S. S.: 7
Commedia dell'Arte: 3
Courteville, Raphael: 4n.
Cowper, William: 4, 5
Crabbe, George: 7
Crockett, David: 52, 56, 87
Cross, J. C.: 13

Dale, Joseph: 7
Dances: of early stage "Negroes," 33, 34; on the minstrel stage, 52, 62, 67, 69–97; of frontiersmen, 72, 83–85, 87, 91, 92; breakdown, 61, 62, 69, 86, 92, 93, 132, 154; tap, 72, 74, 75, 92; shuffle, 73, 82–84, 84n., 85, 96; clog, 75; essence, 93, 94; quintessence, 93n.
Daniels, John: 66, 113n.
Davis, Jefferson: 274
De Cleve, V.: 5
Dezède, N.: 16n.
Diamond, Frank: 113n., 115
Diamond, John: 61, 62, 64, 66, 73, 83, 95, 113n., 115
Dibdin, Charles: *The Padlock,* 13, 15, 20–23, 33, 34; songs of, 16, 27–30, 175; performance of, 24, 27; Negro anecdote, 28–30
Dibdin, Thomas: 33
Dickens, Charles: 78, 83, 154
"Dixie": performance, 245, 247; statements of Emmett on, 247, 275, 286–88; manuscripts, 250, 250n., 251, 251n., 253n.; versions of the text, 251–54, 272, 273; sources, 254–57, 259, 260, 262; meaning of the word, 262–66; editions, 266–73
Donaldson, W.: 214, 216
Dulcimer: 149

Emmett, D. D.: "Old shot gun," 31; songs of the forties, 88, 91, 132, 175, 179, 181–83, 186, 191, 217, 257, 259, 262; songs of the fifties: 93, 223; family of, 98, 99, 99n., 101, 102, 102n., 104n.; early life, 104ff., 107–12; "Bill Crowder," 109–10; in the forties and fifties, 113ff., 135ff., 214ff.; plays, 219, 220; with the

Bryants, 230–32; from the sixties on, 231, 276ff.; writings in plain English, 277, 283; "Turkeys in de Straw," 277; marriages, 279, 279n.; *see also* "Dixie," banjo tunes, Virginia Minstrels, *and* walk-arounds
"Ethiopian Opera": 67–69
Evans, A.: 214
Extravaganza: 62, 66

Fawcett, John: 13
Ferguson (banjo player): 110, 111
Ferrari, G. G.: 7
Fiddle: 126, 128, 155, 207
Field, A. G.: 282
Fink, Mike: 52
Firetongs: 149
Fisin, James: 5
Forrest, Edwin: 44
Fox, Charles, H.: 220

Gardner, Dan: 65, 66, 131, 216
Garrick, D.: 20
Grattan, H. P.: 144, 145
Graupner, G.: 34n.

Hamlet: 20, 46
Hawkins, Micah: 35
Haydn, J.: 10
Hoare, Prince: 13
Hook, James: 5
Howard, William: 5
Hutchinson family: 158, 216, 223

Irwin, Max: 226

J., R. W.: 5
Jawbone: 149, 150, 155
Jazz: rhythmic sources, 209, 212, 213; melodic sources, 213
"Jim Crow": 44, 50–52, 87; *see also* Negro minstrelsy (songs)
Juba: dancer, 61, 67, 71, 73, 74, 81, 83; dance, 89, 91–93; rhythmic pattern, 92

Kant, I.: 4
Kelly, Michael: 14
Kemble, Fanny: 71, 81
Kreutzer, Rodolphe: 16

Lee, R. E.: 275
Lesueur, J. F.: 16n.
Lincoln, A.: 275
Linley, Thomas, the Elder: 10n.
Long Island Negroes: 71, 83, 85
Lumbard, Frank: 225, 226

"Machine poetry": 217
Mallet, Frances: 33
Mathews, Charles: 44–48; Negro sermon, 45, 46
Mazzinghi, Joseph: 13
Miller, Edward, 6n.
Montgomery, James: 7
Moody (actor): 20
Moorehead, John: 7
Morton, Thomas: 14
Moulds, John: 6n.
Mozart: 22
Murdock, John: 33

Natchez under the Hill: 186
Nathan (dancer): 67
Negro dialect: 15, 16, 130
Negro minstrelsy: scenes, 34ff., 52, 59, 61ff., 87, 114, 118, 121, 130–33; types, 49n., 50–52, 54–57, 59; "wench" performances, 49n., 131, 131n., 216, 233; songs, 55–57, 59, 62, 65, 69, 72, 73, 75, 81, 83–92, 130–32, 155, 159–88, 205, 215, 217, 257, 259, 260, 262, 277; minstrel show, 119, 120, 129, 146, 150, 153, 219, 228–30; minstrel band, 127, 128, 147, 149, 150, 280; "sayings," 133; troupes, 71n., 146, 147; origin of the word (Ethiopian) "minstrel," 158
Negro songs: 7, 10, 186, 187, 242
Negro subjects: composers of music on, 4, 4n., 5, 6n., 7, 10n., 13, 14, 16, 16n., 33, 35; songs on, 4–16, 27–30, 32–35, 38, 46–48, 175, 186; stage works on, 4, 13–16, 33–35, 44; writers on, 4, 4n., 5, 7, 10n., 13, 14, 16n., 20, 24, 33, 34, 45
Norton, T.: 245
Norton, W.: 245

Padlock, The: 20
Park, Mungo: 7, 33
Parkman, Francis: 188
Pelham, Gilbert: 64, 65, 87, 115

Pelham, Richard W.: 64, 65, 113n., 115, 139, 139n.; *see also* Virginia Minstrels
Pelissier, Victor: 33
Phallophoroi: 3
Pierce (dancer): 114
Pitt, C. J.: 5
Plantation slaves: music of, 153–56, 207, 208
Pulcinella: 3

Ragtime: 195, 212, 213
Rainer family: 158
Rameau: 19
Reed, David: 75
Reeve, William: 5, 13
Rice, Thomas D.: 50, 52, 56, 59, 67, 70, 75, 87, 89
Ritter, Johnny: 226
Roberts, James: 35
Robinson, J.: 33
Ross, John: 5
Russell, William Howard: 263

Sanford, James: 113n.
Sands, R. D.; 245
Saunderson, James: 13
Sauvigny, L. E. Billardon de: 16n.
Scott, W.: 217
Shakers: 94
Shakespeare: 217
Sheeres, H.: 4n.
Simpkins, Seeley: 106
Smith, John: 62, 113n.

Southerne, Thomas: 4
Storace, Stephen: 13
"Sugar in a Gourd": 207
Sweeney, Joe: 115, 139, 140
Syncopation: 128, 187, 195ff.

Tambourine: 126, 127, 153
Triangle: 147, 154
"Tuckahoe": 126
Twain, Mark: 86; 92

Vaughn, T.: 145, 146
Virginia Minstrels: first rehearsal, 116, 117; performances, 118–22, 135ff.; style of performance, 123ff.; sources of their scenes, 147; program pattern, 151; origin of the band, 157, 158; statement of Emmett on the, 285, 286

Walch, J. H.: 260
Walk-arounds: Emmett's, 88, 229, 229n., 231, 237, 241, 242, 243ff., 254, 255, 259, 265, 277; elements of Emmett's, 236, 237, 241, 242; performance of, 233, 235, 245, 247; development of, 234–36; statements of Emmett on his, 232
White, Charles: 70, 216–19
Whitlock, William M.: 62, 65, 66, 71, 115, 216, 217; *see also* Virginia Minstrels
Wooldridge, G. B.: 116, 119, 138

INDEX OF TITLES
IN ANTHOLOGY

"Billy Paterson": 374
"Black Brigade, The": 390
"Blue Tail Fly, De": 429
"Boatman's Dance, De": 320
"Bressed Am Dem Dat 'Spects Nuttin' ":
  410
"Briggs' Breakdown": 483
"Bull Upon the Battery—Jig": 483

"Dandy Jim from Caroline": 324
"Dar He Goes! Dats Him!": 328
"Dey Hab a Camp Meetin": 413
"Dick Myers' Jig": 484
"Division Street Jig": 485
"Dixie's Land": 359; see also "I Wish I
  Was in Dixie's Land"
"Dr. Hekok Jig": 486

"Eelam Moore. Jig": 345
"Elam Moore—Jig": 345

"Gantz's Jig": 487
"Gwine to de Mill": 432

Hard Times: 415
"High Daddy": 395
"Hop Light, Loo": 334

"I Ain't Got Time to Tarry": 354
"I'm Going Home to Dixie": 351
"I'm Gwine ober de Mountains": 316
"I See de Clouds a Risin": 414
"I Wish I Was in Dixie's Land": 362; see
  also "Dixie's Land"

"Jim Along Josey": 435
"Jonny Boker": 439
"Jonny Roach": 355
"Jordan Is a Hard Road to Travel": 335
"Juba": 443

"Loozyanna Low Grounds": 379

"Marty Inglehart Jig": 341
"Moze Haymar Jig": 340
"My First Jig": 348
"My Old Dad": 447

"Negro Jig": 343
"Newton Jig, The": 488
"Nigger on de Wood Pile": 340

"Oh, Come Along John": 450
"Oh, Ladies All!": 332
"Old Dan Tucker": 454
"Old Joe": 457
"Old K. Y. Ky.": 385
"Ole Grey Goose, The": 461
"Ole Jaw Bone, De": 464
"Ole Joe Golden": 467
"Ole Pee Dee": 469
"Ole Tare River": 471
"O Lud Gals Gib Me": 475

"Pea-Patch Jig": 344
"Peel's Jig": 489
"Peter Story": 342
"Peter Story Jig": 341

"Rise Old Napper": 489
"Road to Richmond": 370
"Rock Susana": 490
"Root Hog or Die. Jig": 347

"Sandy Gibson's": 366
"Sliding Jenny Jig": 490

" 'Twill Nebber Do to Gib It Up So": 313,
  403

"Van Bramer's Jig": 491

"Walk Along, John": 452
"Who's Dat Nigga Dar a Peepin?": 479
"What O' Dat": 381

SELECTIVE LIST OF SOURCES

Allen, William Francis et al. *Slave Songs of the United States.* 1867 (republished, New York, 1951).

Cheney, John Vance, ed. *Travels of John Davis in the United States of America 1798–1802.* Boston, 1910.

Claiborne, J. F. H. *Life and Correspondence of John A. Quitman.* New York, 1860.

Damon, S. Foster. "The Negro in Early American Songsters." *The Papers of the Bibliographical Society of America* XXVIII (1934).

———. *Series of Old American Songs.* Providence, R.I., 1936.

Dickens, Charles. *American Notes.* London, 1907.

Chaff, Gumbo [Howe, Elias]. *The Ethiopian Gleebook.* Boston, 1849.

Galbreath, Charles Burleigh. *Daniel Decatur Emmett / Author of Dixie.* Columbus, Ohio, 1904.

Hall, William D. "Does It Pay To Be Famous?" *The Lamp,* January, 1905.

Jekyll, Walter. *Jamaican Song and Story.* London, 1907.

The Journal of Nicholas Creswell. 1774 (republished, New York, 1924).

Kemble, Frances Anne. *Journal of a Residence on a Georgian Plantation 1838–1839.* New York, 1863.

Longstreet, Augustus Baldwin. *Georgia Scenes.* New York, 1840.

Moreau, Charles C., ed. *Negro Minstrelsy in New York.* Vol. II. New York, 1891 (Harvard Theatre Collection).

Mulhane, L. W. "The Writer of 'Dixie.'" *Donahoe Magazine,* June, 1900.

"Negro Minstrels and Their Dances." Newspaper clipping of August 11, 1895 (Harvard Theatre Collection and New York Public Library).

"Negro Minstrelsy—Ancient and Modern." *Putnam's Monthly,* January, 1855.

Odell, George C. D. *Annals of the New York Stage.* II, New York, 1927; IV, 1928; V, 1931; VI, 1931; VIII, 1936.

O'Neill, Francis. *O'Neill's Music of Ireland.* Chicago, 1903.

Parrish, Lydia. *Slave Songs of the Georgia Sea Islands.* New York, 1942.

Phil. Rice's Correct Method for the Banjo. Boston, 1858.

Russell, William Howard. *My Diary North and South.* Boston, 1863.

Scarborough, Dorothy. *On the Trail of Negro Folk-Songs.* Cambridge, Mass., 1925.

Sheerin, Robert. "Dixie and Its Author." *The Century Magazine,* October, 1895.

Sketches and Eccentricities of Col. David Crockett of West Tennessee. New York, 1833.

Talley, Thomas. *Negro Folk Rhymes.* New York, 1922.

White, H. B. "The Origin of Ethiopian Minstrelsy." Newspaper clipping (Harvard Theatre Collection).

William, Albert B. *Past and Present of Knox County, Ohio.* Indianapolis, 1912.

Winter, Marian Hannah. "Juba and American Minstrelsy." *Chronicles of the American Dance.* Edited by Paul Magriel. New York, 1948.